The Soul of the North

Histories, Cultures, Contexts

Series editors: Anthony Grafton, Robert Nelson, Nancy Troy

Histories, Cultures, Contexts is a series that provides a home for highly innovative histories. The aim is to combine analysis of the political, social, economic and intellectual contexts within which, for example, painting, architecture, film and literature are created, with equally precise readings of the art itself. These histories will offer narratives which set the cultural dynamics of a period in their social and political contexts, often reinvigorating the problems of periodization by presenting unconventional timeframes of study.
They will also venture into little-explored geographies. This interdisciplinary series will recover lost moments of intensive creativity and create new views of past societies for a wide readership.

The Soul of the North

A Social, Architectural and Cultural History
of the Nordic Countries, 1700–1940

NEIL KENT

REAKTION BOOKS

Published by Reaktion Books Ltd
79 Farringdon Road
London EC1M 3JU, UK

www.reaktionbooks.co.uk

First published 2000

Designed by Andrew Barron & Collis Clements Associates
Printed in Hong Kong by C & C Offset Printing Co., Ltd

British Library Cataloguing in Publication Data
Kent, Neil
    The soul of the north: a social, architectural and
    cultural history of the Nordic countries, 1700–1940. –
    (Histories, cultures, contexts)
    1. Architecture – Scandinavia 2. Scandinavia – History
    3. Scandinavia – Social life and customs
    I. Title
    948

ISBN 1 86189 041 9

Back cover: Edvard Petersen,
Emigrants in Larsen's Square, 1890.
Århus Kunstmuseum. Photo: Thomas Pedersen
(Title page) Detail of illus. 82.

Contents

Detail of illus. 118.

Acknowledgements

In the first instance, I should like to thank the
Finnish Academy, which made possible a year-long
stay in Finland as a guest lecturer at the University
of Helsinki, and to acknowledge the sponsorship
provided for another year by FIBA Nordic
Securities. The Swedish and Finnish embassies in
London were also particularly supportive.
Considerable academic assistance was provided
by Professors Anders Aman of Uppsala University,
Matti Klinge of Helsinki University and Kalevi
Pöykkö of Jyväskylä University. I am also grateful to
Dr Ole Grell of the University of Cambridge and
Dr Henrik Stenius of Helsinki University for reading
my manuscript before publication, and to the Earl
of St Andrews for his assistance with bibliographical
information. Finally, but most importantly, I would
like to express my gratitude for years of support to
my mother, Mrs Arline Kent Stewart.

Introduction

Despite numerous books on Nordic political and diplomatic history in the English language, and even a few on Nordic art history, the broad interdisciplinary realm of Nordic social, architectural and cultural history has provided little literature. This book seeks to address this gap with respect to Scandinavia, here taken to signify the entire Nordic region.[1]

To begin to accomplish this task, albeit with many lacunae, I have rejected any attempt to write a comprehensive analysis of 'Nordic' culture or society and have chosen instead to focus upon a selection of different aspects of Nordic life since the Reformation, concentrating principally on the eighteenth and nineteenth centuries. Though based on a highly personal and therefore rather arbitrary selection, it could still provide a broad view of various aspects of the Nordic world, especially of those rarely considered even in native works. To this end I have used not only informative statistics, other types of demographic material and literary references, but also architectural and artistic forms and images to illustrate some of the material covered, though certain areas, like music and dance, have been largely excluded.

To attempt to understand the nature of Nordic life, it is necessary to have a wide overview of important historical events, whether political, cultural, social or scientific, and for this reason two chronologies have been provided: one focuses on the major political events and their dates, the other on significant cultural and scientific occurrences. But it is also necessary to consider certain broad, underlying themes in order to understand some of the rudiments of the complex social and cultural historical developments which have occurred in the region over the last five hundred years. At the advent of this period, the Reformation in the Nordic countries signalled a growing dislocation, not only with much of continental Europe, but with one another as well. The Kalmar Union of Denmark, Norway and Sweden, together with Finland, formed in 1397 under the Danish Queen Margrethe I, was already beginning to unravel. Indeed, it is against this background that the massacre in 1520 in Stockholm of many Swedish aristocrats by the Danish King Christian II, with the connivance of the Swedish Archbishop of Uppsala, Gustaf Trolle, can be seen as a brutal if vain attempt to crush opposition and to prevent the Union's dissolution. It failed and by 1523 the Nordic union was at an end. In its stead, a fault line was formed, on one side of which Denmark and Norway (to be reduced to a province in 1536) confronted Sweden and her province of Finland on the other. Political enmity

(Opposite) Detail of illus. 168.

between the two blocks would persist until well into the nineteenth century and, despite much political rhetoric, a new political union of the Nordic region was never again to become a reality.

In its place, two highly centralized kingdoms developed with autocratic monarchies strengthened by burgeoning bureaucracies largely paid for by a financially castrated church. In Sweden, Gustaf Vasa was able to establish his dynasty on a hereditary basis (it was to last almost three hundred years), discarding thereby the previous elective monarchical system which had applied. In Denmark, internal dynastic upheavals and civil war, with competing figures for the throne, ensued with a new king, Christian III, becoming monarch in 1536. Protestantism triumphed.

In all the Nordic countries, the Roman Catholic Church was disavowed and rooted out in such draconian fashion that by the seventeenth century recusancy for those who did not flee abroad was an impossibility. In its stead a reformed and intolerant Christianity based upon the teachings of Martin Luther became established, which looked with disapproval upon the Calvinists on its other flank. The former was episcopal in its organization; the latter, based upon the beliefs of the French reformer Jean Calvin, was presbyterial and, while both were Protestant, Calvinism, particularly in the later sixteenth and early seventeenth centuries, gave great emphasis to salvation by divine election.

The practical implications of the Reformation were great and affected many aspects of social and cultural life, though it took the good part of a century to consolidate. On the one hand, many cultural and social ties to the heartland of Europe and the Mediterranean countries were broken; on the other, close links were forged with those cities of northern Germany, like Wismar, Wittenberg and Greifswald, where Protestantism had taken firm and lasting root. While the Nordic region thus became marginalized in European terms within its own Lutheran corner, it became a bulwark and guarantor of its co-religionists to the south. This new alignment had immense political consequences, after the eruption of the Thirty Years War in Germany in 1618, when both Sweden and Denmark intervened against the Catholic Holy Roman Emperor on behalf of German Protestants. Yet the complicated military and political scenario produced major and unexpected repercussions. For one thing, the defeat of Denmark, under Christian IV, by German Imperial forces, left Sweden the leading political and military power in northern Europe. Not only did this lead to its victory in the containment of Catholicism and Imperial ambitions during the Thirty Years War, but it also enabled it to subdue a weakened Protestant Denmark, from whom Sweden seized Scania and other eastern territories in 1658, permanently incorporating them into Sweden itself.

Strange political bedfellows were also brought together as a result of this tumultuous period. Denmark, keen to encircle her arch-enemy Sweden, increasingly allied herself with Orthodox Russia, who first strengthened and then extended her position on the eastern Baltic at the expense of her western neighbour. Sweden, in turn, forged a lasting alliance with Catholic France which, under the influence of Cardinal Richelieu, sided with the Protestant powers against the Holy Roman Emperor. Thus, power politics, rather than religion, came to be the driving force on the level of diplomatic international relations.

On a cultural plane, the Reformation also inaugurated a new focus on art and architecture which elevated both to instruments of political expression. In the centres of monarchical power in both Sweden and Denmark, the Renaissance visions of Italian humanist princes were translated into works of art and palaces which would bolster monarchical authority through both the symbolism and function of their forms and decoration. Gustaf Vasa, for example, employed Henrik von Cölen at Gripsholm Castle, in 1537, to carry out major renovation and building work. However, Christian IV became the supreme example of the humanist prince with respect to the arts and architecture in early modern Nordic history. Churches, royal palaces, even a stock exchange, were amongst the numerous splendid buildings he had built, which, together with an assembly of magnificent works of art, make his reign a Golden Age in early seventeenth century Scandinavia.

After Sweden's victory against the Holy Roman Emperor in the Thirty Years War, the magnificent collection of the Emperor Rudolph, brought back from Prague as war booty, was briefly to adorn Sweden, but the conversion to Catholicism by the eccentric Queen Christina and her abdication and removal to Rome, led to its dispersal. As a result, Stockholm never became the triumphal royal capital which it might have been. Her nephew Karl XII initiated the building of a new and vast Baroque royal residence, after a fire had destroyed the old palace of Tre Kronor (Three Crowns, still a Swedish royal symbol) in 1697. But Karl XII was a warrior king and military disaster soon overwhelmed Sweden at the Battle of Poltava in 1709, where Sweden's disastrous defeat left Russia with the primacy in the Baltic region. Perhaps, if the Grand Vizier of the Ottoman Empire, Ali Pasha of Chorlu, fearful of war, had not held back Devlet-Girei II, Khan of the Crimea, from allying himself with Sweden and the Cossacks against Russia, Sweden might have maintained its Baltic hegemony. The reality was, however, that Sweden lost a considerable amount of territory and economic ruin threatened both the state and, indeed, monarchical authority itself, thereby precluding for an extended period of time any further great architectural endeavours.

Harsh geographical and climatic conditions had also taken their toll on the Swedish realm. While it is true that the coastal regions of Scandinavia are exceptionally mild (Vardø, in the extreme north of Norway, for example, has never suffered the low temperature extremes of Paris and Berlin), the interior is prone to intense cold, with frost even, in the worse years, during the summer months. Because of this grievous famines could occur, as in the late 1690s, wreaking immense havoc through starvation and disease, particularly in remote areas and poor communications and transport compounded the problem in a region where ports could be icebound until May. The Nordic region was stricken by epidemic diseases well into the modern era. Bubonic plague, leprosy, smallpox, malaria and cholera all took their periodic toll, and their spread was facilitated by ubiquitous poor hygiene. While those living relatively isolated lives in rural areas might be spared the worst ravages of diseases prevalent in urban environments, the lack of natural immunity to new diseases when they did strike could be disastrous. Thus, mortality rates were very high, especially by comparison to the Nordic region today, though compared with the rest of Europe at that time they were by no means unfavourable.[2] Furthermore, the measures taken to cope with those afflicted by disease in Scandinavia led to many humane innovations, not least the establishment of institutions where long-term care was provided for those unable to cope on their own or within their families. It also saw the early introduction of what we would call 'care in the community', albeit largely for financial rather than ideological reasons, in which the disabled or ill were lodged with families or provided with their own accommodation.

Despite the poverty and sparse population of most of the Nordic region, art and architecture sometimes came to be given a role, astonishing for the grandiloquence of its vision. Just as Rome was beautified by the popes with classical architecture and adornments, so Christian IV, Gustaf III and Alexander I beautified or endeavoured to beautify their own capitals. For theirs was an aesthetic vision in which symbolism was to be used to express both moral and political values, hand in hand with fashionable stylistic ones. In fact it can be said that architectural forms and features were frequently used to attempt to order both domestic and public life. To this end allusions and references to classical allegory, richly didactic, persisted well into the twentieth century. Such allegory could also be married to Gothic symbols, as literary inspiration might require. Thus, the fake Gothic epic *Ossian*, in reality by the Scot James McPherson, provided considerable inspiration in the Nordic world, just as it did in England and Germany. This led to a romanticized vision of Nordic antiquity with its artistic and literary focus upon the Norse and derivative Nordic concepts of ethnic identity, both spiritual and secular. But the Nordic in Norden was by no means the same as the Nordic in Germany. Scandinavians, unlike Germans, had long-established nation-states each with a strong identity and cherished historical associations and myths from which they could confidently take inspiration, whereas the Germans had to borrow and piece together an artificial national identity from their neighbours.

Endeavours of another sort were also to prosper and thrive especially in the eighteenth century. Colonial forays, tentatively begun in the seventeenth century, by both Sweden and Denmark, began to bring in not inconsiderable riches to the mother countries. Sweden's territorial expansion into Pomerania, in northern Germany, at the end of the Thirty Years War and into the Caribbean islands in the late eighteenth century gave her an economic and political interest in both regions, while Denmark's colonization of Greenland, the Danish Virgin Islands and a part of the Coromandel coast of India made her an important colonial power with which to be reckoned. Moreover, Denmark's not inconsequential involvement in the African slave trade and sugar cane plantations helped to make Copenhagen one of Europe's most important sugar-processing centres, bringing great riches to Denmark. Only after the Napoleonic Wars, when Swedish Pomerania was lost and the non-European colonies had become economic and social liabilities, were ties with the mother countries loosened and ultimately severed.

By that stage, however, other ties, political, economic and social, had formed in a new constellation of relationships which reflected the new nineteenth-century Europe. Finland had been taken away from Sweden in 1809, after centuries of political integration, only to be given to the Russian tsar, as a grand-duchy, albeit with a guarantee to preserve many traditional Finnish religious, political and social institutions, in particular the legal code. Norway was granted a constitution and transferred to Sweden as a dual kingdom under her new king Karl Johan Bernadotte, a French Napoleonic field marshal who had assumed the throne of Sweden in 1818 through adoption by the last Vasa monarch King Karl XIII.

At this time, Sweden and Denmark were both multi-ethnic states. In Europe, the relatively autonomous regions of the Swedish realm included Finland, Sweden proper and her German territories, so that several large ethnic groups, Swedes, Finns, Germans and Saami were encompassed. Similarly in the Danish realm, Danes, Norwegians, Germans and Icelanders and Saami, lived together in largely, though not by any means totally, separate administrative regions. In another political dimension, though, these countries were very different. In Denmark, an absolute monarch held sway, comparable with those in France or Spain, with the royal will dominating both nobility and church. In Sweden, on the other hand, a more democratic system prevailed after the death of Charles XII in 1718, in which the king and the nobility shared the bulk of power, making Sweden, along with the United Kingdom, one of Europe's most liberal states.

Occasionally, however, Sweden's political equilibrium was destroyed, when the monarch's attempt to assume a more autocratic stance led to confrontation. When Queen Lovisa Ulrika, a sister of Frederick the Great of Prussia, and her husband Adolf Fredrik, failed in an attempt to seize greater powers in 1756, their principal collaborators were executed and they themselves retired to their country palace, Drottningholm, in virtual political banishment. After their son Gustaf III assumed the throne in 1771, he succeeded in his coup d'état to re-establish autocratic rule, only to be assassinated by a disaffected aristocrat two decades later. In Denmark, at about the same time, somewhat the reverse can be said to have happened though the effects were similar: the liberal Court doctor and adul-terous lover of the queen, Johan Struensee, had succeeded in becoming virtual ruler of Denmark in place of the weak-minded Christian VII, only to be ousted by the Dowager Queen and her supporters and thereafter executed. Absolute monarchy was thereby preserved.

Yet such events belied profound economic and social changes within society, which soon found political expression. For example, serfdom was abolished in 1787–8 by the Danish minister Count A. P. Bernstorff, in accord with the enlight-ened economic and political outlook of the government of that time, rather than through pressures from an agitated populus; this emancipation became the first major step in a social progression which was to lead, in 1849, to the voluntary abrogation of absolute monarchy by the king, the establishment of a constitution and a bicameral national assembly. In Sweden, however, some final vestiges of serfdom remained well into the twentieth century, even if the political authority of the monarch was gradually eroded throughout the nineteenth century and into the twentieth. By then, however, the social democracy of the political agitator and later Social Democratic Prime Minister Hjalmar Branting had taken root, becoming the dominating, indeed, monolithic, political ideology in the country until our own day.

Meanwhile, a developing sense of national identity was taking form in Finland, Norway and Iceland, which would lead to their complete independence. In Finland, long cherished freedoms had become increasingly eroded in the late nineteenth century by a Russian tsar, Nicholas II, keen to centralize the reigns of administration in his empire. Therefore, the collapse of the imperial government in Russia in 1917 opened the way for a unilateral declaration of independence for Finland. Shortly thereafter, a vicious civil war ensued in which conservative forces proved rapidly victorious, though many years would elapse before the wounds it left healed. Indeed, it was, perhaps, more the Second World War (first a Winter War and then a Continuation War as it was experienced by Finns), in which Finland found itself in an uneasy alliance with Germany against Russia that the Finns, whatever their political or ethnic background, can be said to have really been forged together into a single nation. Yet these wars had not ended in victory. Much of Finnish Karelia was absorbed into the Soviet Union, including the important port city of Viipuri, and a Russian military base was established, if only temporarily, at Porkkala, on what remained Finnish soil. On the other hand, Finland never suffered a complete defeat and therefore remained the only Axis power neither occupied nor politically destroyed by the Allies. Indeed, it seems the western Allies realized that the Finnish wartime alliance with Nazi Germany had been dictated by realpolitik through a desperate need to find immediate support in her armed confrontation with Russia. This was a state of affairs even understood from within, for Finland remained the one Axis power in which racial laws were never instituted and in which Jews volunteered to fight in defence of their homeland. In any case, towards the close of the Second World War, Finland did turn against the Nazis and made a peaceful accommodation with the Soviet Union which survived in mutually beneficial ways until the latter's collapse. In Iceland, independence was achieved more gradually and without recourse to arms, and yet it, too, required the impetus and peculiar conditions of war, for its own unilateral declaration in 1944, while occupied by Allied troops. Only Norway achieved its unilateral declaration of independence in peacetime, in 1905, though it did so at the risk of a war with Sweden, while other European nations looked on with their own political agenda in mind. The German Kaiser Wilhelm II, for example, had originally promised Sweden military aid in the event of a violent confrontation with Norway over her independence. However, he was also keen to place a German prince upon the Norwegian throne and Germany became the first nation to recognize the new independent state even though a Danish prince was eventually chosen as king. The Kaiser had seen Sweden-Norway as a principal partner in the union of German peoples. He wrote to his brother Gustaf in 1895, 'all my political thoughts are concentrated upon uniting the Germanic peoples in the world especially in Europe – closer together, in order to secure ourselves against the Slavic-Czech invasion, which in the highest degree threatens us all. [...] Sweden-Norway is one of the principal partners in this union of German peoples.'[3] This point of view was to have an ominous significance for the Nordic region during the Second World War, in which Denmark and Norway were over-run by German troops, while Sweden remained a precarious neutrality with Finland, as we have seen, in reluctant alliance with Nazi Germany.

Christianity, Spirituality and the Church

Outbreak of the Reformation in Scandinavia

While theology may be the queen of all branches of knowledge, the Catholic Church as an ecclesiastical institution enjoyed a very masculine role as the most powerful social authority in the pre-Reformation Nordic region, a supranational power even vying with kings in the exercising of temporal and political authority. However, the advent of the Reformation and the changes which followed in its wake created a violent break with the Nordic Catholic past, itself only a few centuries old. The Church's power has been eroded slowly from a position around 1500 of immense and unassailable spiritual and temporal authority, to one which by our own century more resembles a charitable society for the liberally minded. The first serious fissures were apparent in the early years of the sixteenth century and may be seen as a beginning to a centuries-long process in which the rigid reign of one all-encompassing and autocratic church was thrown off for a more circumscribed ecclesiastical authority, held in tight rein by the monarch and his government. This, in turn, was itself to give way in more recent times to a pluralistic and tolerant church, living in peace and harmony (unthinkable in earlier years) with both heretics and non-believers, and with contemporary power politics playing only a very indirect role.

In the 1520s, however, such a pacific stance was certainly not in evidence. On the contrary, it was a period of militant confrontation with respect to both politics and religion; indeed, the two were inextricably linked. This state of affairs must, of course, be seen against the background of the Protestant Reformation in Germany and the views of Martin Luther, Philip Melanchthon and others who rejected many established Catholic beliefs and traditions. For it was at this time that itinerant German preachers began to spread the Protestant message, especially in coastal towns.[1] The German-educated King Christian III of Denmark (1503–1559) had met Martin Luther himself and had been considerably influenced by the latter's Protestant beliefs. Assuming the throne after a bloody civil war in 1536, this deeply religious king went on to establish Lutheranism as the one church of Denmark, an event commemorated in a sketch of 1780 for decoration in Christiansborg Palace by Nikolaj Abildgaard (illus. 1). Abildgaard's intention was undoubtedly to glorify the Oldenborg dynasty, which had ruled Denmark since the early Middle Ages, in one of the relatively rare history paintings commissioned there at that time. However, the key role played by the king in both re-establishing political order and severing Denmark's links to her

Catholic past has not been over-stressed. He ended Denmark's vicious civil war and helped to insure that Protestantism was bolstered by a major re-organization of the Church the following year in 1537, which he undertook with the aid of Johannes Bugenhagen, a Lutheran theologian from Wittenberg and had a translation of Luther's Bible into Danish published in 1550. Yet for some contemporary viewers of Abildgaard's painting, like the Danish nationalist Tyge Rothe, the work emphasized more Denmark's humiliation at the foot of a tyrannical monarch, rather than her spiritual uplifting. However, the fact remains that Christian III successfully secured Denmark within the Protestant fold. While cathedral chapters, monasteries and convents were at first tolerated, in spite of their general opposition to the Reformation, the Catholic bishops were dismissed, though some settled down quite happily to the life of rural noblemen and a few even became Lutherans.[2]

That the king could rely on popular support for the Protestant reformers greatly facilitated the implementation of his ecclesiastical policy. This was in large

measure due to the labours of preachers like Hans Tausen (1494–1561), a native of Birkende, on the island of Fyn, who had studied under Luther at Wittenberg. Furthermore, royal authority itself was strengthened by a return to a tradition from the reign of Frederik I, whereby episcopal sees were restricted to Danish subjects, thus bringing the Church under greater royal, rather than aristocratic or ecclesiastical, control. These circumstances enabled dissenting bishops and priests to be silenced through either imprisonment or exile, while the Protestant Tausen was made bishop of Ribe. The nineteenth-century Danish artist Jørgen Roed depicted his seat in Ribe Cathedral much as it looked in the days of the Reformation when he introduced a new Lutheran liturgy there (illus. 2). Important changes were occurring in the cathedral's interior arrangement. For example, Lutheran priests were now required to face the laity during the Eucharist, thereby requiring a new arrangement for the high altar, while side altars disappeared and epitaphs came increasingly to replace images of saints.

2 Jørgen Roed, *Ribe Cathedral*, c. 1836, paper laid down on canvas.

The Church also changed socially, in both Denmark and to a lesser degree Sweden. The clergy increasingly drew almost all its bishops from the middle and lower classes, a trend which had actually begun towards the end of the previous century.[3] Indeed, the new Bishop of Sjælland and most prominent theologian of these early years, Peder Palladius, who wrote the *Visitation Book*, an important work of Lutheran spirituality, was the son of a shoemaker.

There was also a break with the previous Catholic approach to religious art which took its cue from Wittenberg, where Luther had been a monk. There Augustinian friars destroyed many religious paintings in 1522. Luther's own views on religious images were ambiguous: although he recognized the need for both religious art and patronage, he felt that too great a dependency upon didactic art in churches was childish and failed to stress the primacy of God's grace over good works.[4] Moreover, the endowing of images as a form of acquiring indulgence particularly appalled him.[5] While thereby not justified, it is not surprising that iconoclastic disturbances broke out first in Stockholm and then in both Copenhagen and Malmö in the 1520s.[6] The destruction of a considerable number of churches and monasteries soon followed, though not for reasons of iconoclasm but rather from political and economic motivations, which created new problems. For example, the disappearance of church bells, which had divided up the activities of the day for country people by their ringing now obliged magistrates to provide a new system of bell-ringing in their place.[7]

The progress of the Reformation was not uniform in Copenhagen and Malmö. In the former, a significant evangelical movement only developed from 1529, while in the latter, it was by then well established.[8] Still, there was an important economic dimension to the Reformation common to both Denmark and Sweden, and one with considerable political implications. The confiscation of ecclesiastical property, monasteries, convents and other lands held in *morte main* (the Catholic Church had held about one-third of all arable land) meant that the Crown itself came into possession of increased wealth and concomitant political power.[9] The new and bountiful financial resources which now accrued to the king meant that he was able to extend his bureaucratic power far beyond that of his predecessors. Furthermore, aristocrats granted these confiscated estates could now be expected to be particularly loyal to a monarch to whom they owed their new-found wealth, even if it is true that the monasteries themselves had increasingly come under their administrative control in Catholic days. The only loser by the new arrangement was, of course, the Church, but since the higher echelons of the church hierarchy were now men of humbler origins who owed their newly won positions to the crown, their loyalty was ensured.

Not everywhere in the Nordic region embraced the Reformation with equal enthusiasm. By contrast with Denmark, the general population of Norway remained ardently Catholic and in Schleswig-Holstein popular support for the Reformation was minimal.[10] In Norway, Archbishop Olav Engelbriktsson did all he could during the reign of Frederik I to hinder the progress of the Reformation, but his political machinations merely served to strengthen the hand of the Protestants. The ascension of Christian III to the throne saw the acceleration of Lutheran innovations introduced in the 1520s, through the removal from office of the Catholic bishops, which led to the reorganization of the church in 1539. As the decades of the sixteenth century rolled by, the old local Catholic clergy found themselves increasingly marginalized, while new ecclesiastics, such as Jørgen Erikssøn, promoted the Lutheran teachings. This he did as bishop of Stavanger from 1571, not only through preaching, but in his popular collected sermons, published in 1592.[11] It is perhaps true to say that Catholicism in Norway was more starved to death than crushed, but there was another dimension which mirrored the state of ecclesiastical affairs, for, as the church became subject to the king in Copenhagen, so Norway itself lost its last vestiges of political independence from Denmark.[12]

The Reformation in Iceland took a similar if more violent path. Oddur Gottskálksson had translated the New Testament into Icelandic by 1540, based upon Martin Luther's German translation, but the Icelandic people by and large did not welcome the new doctrines and a period of violent upheaval ensued. Jón Arason (1484–1550), Bishop of Hólar, in the north, who had introduced the first printing press to Iceland, led the Catholic resistance, but after his capture in 1550 and subsequent beheading, Catholicism was crushed in Iceland. The episcopal see of Skálholt had been filled by a Lutheran in 1541 and now the vacated see of Hólar was rapidly filled by another. When, in 1584, the then incumbent, Gudbrandur Thorláksson, published the first complete translation of the Bible in Icelandic, Lutheranism was firmly established. In architectural terms, though, the Reformation made little impact. Icelandic churches continued to be humble rectangular affairs built of turf in the old medieval fashion, though one unhappy attempt in stone was made, a failure not repeated until the eighteenth century.[13] That said, the late sixteenth and seventeenth centuries in Iceland was a period rich in literary, if not architectural terms. For example, Arngrímur Jónsson (1568–1648), director of the Latin school at Hólar where many of the Icelandic clergy were educated, produced a number of works based upon his study of Icelandic sagas and other aspects of cultural history, while the renowned Lutheran priest and poet Hallgrímur Pétursson (1614–1674) published his *Hymns on the Passion*, a collection which achieved immense popularity over centuries. Pétursson was also a noted preacher and instrumental in the re-conversion in 1636 of an unfortunate group of Icelanders, lately ransomed by the Danish king, who had been kidnapped and held captive for nine years by Moslem Barbary pirates. One of the prodigal victims, Gudridur Símonardóttir, went on to bear Pétursson a child, before they eventually married, a state of affairs not unusual amongst the clergy in Iceland, then or now. Also popular, if part of a more oral literary tradition, were the so-called 'lying sagas', generally recited at home during the long winters, which derived inspiration, not only from the ancient Icelandic saga tradition but eclectically, from Continental European and Middle Eastern themes, as well.

By contrast with the arrival of the Reformation in Denmark, that in Sweden was more temporally motivated. Indeed, King Gustaf Vasa (1496?–1560) (illus. 3) was notorious for his lack of theological interest. However, he was not unaware of the implications of the theological debates then raging about him, though he only took full control of the Swedish Church at the end of the 1530s.[14] While he knew that Protestantism held little appeal in the Swedish and Finnish provinces, the eruption of pro-Catholic civil strife in 1542 convinced him of the need to establish the Lutheran church in order to bolster his own authority and help in his consolidation of political power. He coveted the rich and vast estates of the church which, when confiscated, provided him with financial resources and concomitant power making both his and his family's political position unassailable.

This dominant position had further been bolstered, albeit unintentionally, by

Christian II's so-called Stockholm's blood-bath on 8 November 1520, when approximately 80 noblemen, including two bishops, opposed to the union with Denmark, were slaughtered attending a festive assembly of the nobility. Ostensibly, the Danish king, in alliance with Gustaf Trolle, Archbishop of Uppsala, had ordered these executions on the grounds of heresy. In reality, however, this justification masked Christian II's wish to eliminate opposition to his rule. It, also, inadvertently, served to rid Gustaf Vasa of any rivals for the throne, after the death of the Swedish regent, Sten Sture the Younger, as well as discrediting some members of the church hierarchy. This cleared the way for Gustaf Vasa to secure his throne in 1523 which he made hereditary, as well as to oust, once and for all, Christian II and the Danes from Sweden. The Kalmar Union was thereby destroyed and with its demise ended the political unity of the Nordic countries forever.

3 Jacob Binck, *Portrait of Gustaf Vasa*, 1542, oil on canvas.

Politically and economically, the Catholic Church in Sweden was now castrated by the enactments of the assembly of the estates which Gustaf Vasa summoned at Västerås in 1527. This was achieved not only through the 'realpolitik' of Gustaf Vasa and his son, greedy for its wealth, but also by the passionate exhortations of preachers like Olaus Petri, a former student at Wittenberg in the second decade of the sixteenth century, whose uncompromising zeal and hostility to the mendicant orders carried many into the Protestant fold, though sometimes leading Petri himself into violent opposition to the king whose dubious religious motives were obvious.

None the less, an accommodation of sorts was accomplished and the benefits of the Reformation proved enormous for the king, in economic if not spiritual terms: the Crown, which before the Reformation had owned only six per cent of landed property had, by 1560, increased its share to 28 per cent, all at the expense of the Church.[15] This wealth meant that both national independence and a hereditary monarchy could be lastingly secured.

Not only the economics, but, of course, the practice of religion was also deeply affected and ultimately altered. At the great convocation of clergy in Västerås in 1544, the saying of requiem masses, adoration of saints and use of incense were all prohibited.[16] As a result of the ecclesiastical laws of 1571 and later, many of the old Catholic holy days were removed from the calendar.

Despite the success of the Reformation in Sweden not all adhered to orthodox Lutheranism. Various Reformed sects, especially Calvinism, vied to set their imprint upon the Swedish Church. Indeed, Gustaf Vasa's tolerant son, Erik XIV, though publicly a Lutheran, may have been a crypto-Calvinist, having been educated by two Calvinist tutors, Dionysius Beurreus and Jan van Hervoville. He showed considerable tolerance of a wide spectrum of views, though his fear of alienating the predominately Lutheran clergy sometimes led him to appear less favourable to the Calvinists than was probably the case.

This situation changed, however, under his successor Johan III who was married to the Polish Catholic princess, Catherine Jagellonica. A Catholic chapel was opened at the Swedish court for her use, and the Jesuits were briefly allowed to re-establish an educational academy in Stockholm, under the direction of the priest Nicolai Laurentius Nicolai. Its institutional success aroused Protestant fears and the resulting riots forced its closure. (In Denmark, where Jesuits were forbidden, Laurentius attempted to resuscitate Catholicism by providing young Danes with a Jesuit education abroad. But this attempt proved futile when the Danish government forbade those educated by Jesuits to hold positions in churches or schools).[17]

Even more disturbing for Swedish Protestants was the fact that Crown Prince Sigismund, Queen Catherine's son, had been raised as a Catholic. His succession to the throne of Poland in 1587 created no problems in this regard, but when he ascended the Swedish throne as a Catholic matters became critical in a Sweden which, through the yearly visitations to parishioners by Lutheran priests, had come to accept the Protestant catechism. Confrontation was therefore imminent and, indeed, reached a head when, in 1593, the Lutheran Church became the official church of Sweden and Finland by declaration of a council of clergy at Uppsala and the practice of Roman Catholicism was forbidden. In 1598, Sigismund's deeply Protestant uncle, Duke Karl, followed a year later by the Estates themselves, therefore disavowed their allegiance to Sigismund and Karl was declared king in his place. With monarch and clergy now united in their support for orthodox Lutheranism (even if Karl frequently had call to quarrel with the clergy), the Church of Sweden became the unassailable established church which it has remained until today, though its function has altered beyond recognition, maintaining its principal significance in education and as the official registrar of births and deaths.

Finland, as a province of Sweden since the early Middle Ages, was also obliged with the rest of the kingdom to embrace Lutheranism, and to acquiesce in the dissolution of the monasteries, a process assisted by the Finnish prelate Mikael Agricola (c. 1510–57), a follower of Luther under whom he had studied at Wittenberg, as well as under Philip Melanchthon. He had devoted his considerable literary talents to translating the New Testament into Finnish, which he completed in 1548, eleven years after the Finnish vernacular had been introduced in Finland for religious services. While Agricola was elevated to the episcopal see of Turku in 1554, the new bishopric of Viipuri was also established, with Paavali Juusten, a student at Wittenberg from 1543–6, invested as bishop. From such seats of ecclesiastical authority these two staunch Lutherans were able to steer Finland, where popular hostility to Reformed beliefs had been considerable, firmly into the Protestant fold.

Agricola also helped to hinder any inroads of Orthodoxy from the East, which had, of course, already split with Catholicism in 1054. He did this not only

at home in Finland, but in Russia itself where he had been sent as a peace nego-
tiator in the mid-1550s (he died upon the return journey from Moscow).
Attempts to introduce Orthodoxy into Finland were encouraged by the Russian
tsar, Ivan the Terrible, who held a particular loathing for Protestantism, which he
frequently equated with Judaism. His massacre of followers of both religions at
Polotsk, in White Russia, in 1563, was singularly ecumenical in the lack of
distinctions he made between the two religions. None the less, his militant
Orthodoxy failed to achieve significant conversions in Finland, serving instead
merely to heighten antagonisms between the two northern powers.[18] That said,
Ericus Erici Sorolainen, invested as bishop in Turku in 1583, used numerous occasions over the almost 40 years of his episcopate to enter into dialogue with the
Orthodox church, supported by the Swedish Catholic king Johan III.[19]

Conflict between Lutherans and Members of the Reformed Church

In Denmark, the relationship between Lutherans and those of the Reformed
Church was less harmonious than in Sweden. Since the Lutheran Confession had
been embraced by the Danish church, its government was anti-Calvinist in
stance. This state of affairs contrasted with that in Sweden, an Erastian kingdom,
in which the state exerted much more control in religious matters than in
Denmark and where there was no sacrament of confession until the late seventeenth century. As a result, the Swedish government looked much more
favourably upon the immigration of Calvinist Protestants than did the Danish
government.

In 1553 Christian III prohibited Calvinists from taking refuge in Denmark,
while the unwanted arrival of 200 members of the Dutch Reformed Church only
exacerbated the situation, resulting in a renewed royal promulgation of the death
penalty for both heretics and those who sheltered them. However, in 1551 Calvin
had dedicated the first part of his religious commentary on the Acts of the
Apostles to Christian III; the second part was later dedicated to Crown Prince
Frederik.[20] That Denmark's leading theologian of the later Reformation, Niels
Hemmingsen (1513–1600), a professor at the University of Copenhagen, had a
Calvinistic view of the Eucharist further complicated matters, especially when the
King of Saxony, Frederik's brother-in-law who had been outraged by
Hemmingson's theological work, *Syntagma*, demanded its recanting; this
Hemmingsen was eventually to do, albeit under duress. While he was never re-
instated in his chair, his influence did continue and, indeed, he was involved in
the drawing up of the Marriage Act of 1582 which legalized divorce and re-
marriage in Denmark.

None the less, religious harmony between rival Protestant theologians had
not been achieved. Though the *Formula of Concord* establishing Lutheran orthodoxy
was published in 1580, celebrating the fiftieth anniversary of the Augsburg
Confession, its publication and import continued to be forbidden, even though
the king's sister had personally sent him two splendidly bound copies, both of
which he had burnt.[21] Catholics, of course, fared worse: not only were they

forbidden, in 1613, to hold office, but any person convicted of adherence to the old religion was disinherited, whilst Catholic immigration was prohibited.[22]

Though a somewhat deviant theology, based on a justification first by faith and then by works, was advocated by the Danish aristocrat and member of the Council of State, Holger Rosencrantz, Lutheran uniformity, accompanied by a Bible newly translated from the original languages, was finally achieved by the early seventeenth century.[23] But the political implications of Denmark's desire to provide Protestant solidarity for adherents of Lutheranism abroad was to have considerable negative consequences. Indeed, Christian IV's entry into the Thirty Years War in Germany, in 1625, in support of the Protestant powers, left him with the dire legacy of defeat in Jutland at the hands of Wallenstein's troops and a humiliating peace treaty in Lübeck with the Holy Roman Emperor. Nor was there a growth of religious toleration.

King Gustaf Adolf of Sweden, a devoted Lutheran, was aware of both the spiritual and temporal needs of a united Protestantism and so the religious climate in Sweden remained more tolerant than was the case in Denmark. In fact, during the reign of Gustaf Vasa, members of the Protestant Reformed Church, as well as Lutherans, were invited to settle in 1627, even though the king's coronation charter had required his adherence to the prohibitions on non-Lutheran immigration,[24] motivated by the practical needs of state as well as the interests of the

4 G. Theudon and L. Ottani, *Monument to Queen Christina of Sweden*, 1702, marble and bronze.

Lutheran powers. Among the Reformed refugees from the Low Countries was Louis de Geer, who established an important entrepreneurial dynasty in Sweden, by means of effectively supplying the king's troops during the Thirty Years War. Gustaf Adolf himself went on to become the leader of the Lutheran Protestant powers in the Thirty Years War, before falling in the Battle of Lützen in 1632. Yet despite his death, his military exertions helped to ensure that the Protestant states of Germany were able to survive the onslaught of the Holy Roman Emperor and his allies, thereby preserving the North of Europe as a bastion of Protestantism.

Gustaf Adolf's daughter and successor Queen Christina (1626–89) sought to undo this very achievement. Achieving her majority in 1644, she demonstrated a varied and vast range of intellectual interests, not least in religion. A very intelligent and astute girl (see illus. 47), she developed a keen interest in Catholicism which led to her conversion to the religion her father had spent his life opposing. Yet to remain a Catholic monarch in Lutheran Sweden was totally impossible at this time and she abdicated in 1654, before going into exile (though she did return to Sweden informally on visits). First, she travelled to Brussels, where she was formally received into the Church and from there she proceeded to Rome, where Pope Alexander VII received her with great pomp and ceremony in 1655, some 200 coaches turning out for her arrival.[25] Once there, she set herself up in the fifteenth-century Palazzo Riario in the Lungara,[26] and soon became

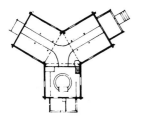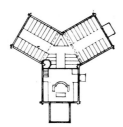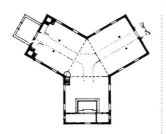

5 Plans of three Norwegian 'Y' churches: Rennebu, Nord-Trøndelag (1668); Horg, Sør-Trøndelag (1670); Holmestrand, Vestfold (1674).

embroiled in a variety of political machinations with respect to both international politics and that of the Vatican Curia, seriously tarnishing her religious reputation. The interest she took in certain nuns aroused attention (even scandalously so), as did her friendship with Cardinal Decio Azzolino. Yet her public good works were considerable and she did her best financially to help the military drive to push the Turks out of Europe, even voluntarily relinquishing her pension for the good of the Christian war efforts in the Balkans, while her general benevolence and financial largesse towards the Jews of Rome became legendary.

After her death from erysipelas, Christina was buried with enormous pomp and ceremony in the crypt of St Peter's and a suitable memorial was commissioned by Pope Innocent XII (illus. 4), which was erected just inside the entrance to the nave. Its enormous relief shows the queen who relinquished her throne for the sake of the true Religion. To the side, unobtrusively situated by a column, another smaller relief shows the embodiment of Religion driving out Heresy.[27] By such means, the personal foibles of the monarch were ignored in the interest of the great allegorical symbolism which her life afforded to the Church whose hopes of reclaiming Sweden to the Catholic fold had as yet by no means been extinguished.

In Norway, towards the end of the seventeenth century, the governor Hannibal Sehested opened the door to religious toleration for members of the Reformed Church, despite the intense resistance of the Norwegian bishops.[28] This was also a period of architectural innovation in Norway. The building of 'Y' plan churches permitted a good view of the altar to all in the congregation, positioning the choir in one arm of the church, women in another and men in a third, an architectural arrangement which became popular over the next century (illus. 5).

Witch-hunting and Witchcraft

Along with the consolidation of Protestantism in the Nordic region during the seventeenth century, there was also a vigorous revival of the persecution of alleged witches. It has for some years been suggested that the sudden and deadly explosion of syphilis, imported from the New World by Columbus's ships, led to a growing fear of the power of women, sometimes seen as diabolical in origin. Certainly, many scholars and men of law in the seventeenth century did place a greater emphasis than previously on diabolism, that is, devil worship, rather than merely on malevolent actions perceived to be perpetrated by witches on their neighbours,[29] and this had been growing since Peder Palladius himself had urged the prosecution of witches in the 1540s. Christian IV of Denmark was particularly disturbed by witchcraft and is known to have feared diabolical intervention when one of the ships in the entourage bearing his sister Anne of Denmark to James VI of Scotland (later James I of England) sank in 1590; thereafter, numerous witch-hunts had ensued.[30] Later in 1612–13, the Danish king took an active interest in the case of fifteen suspected witches in Køge, near Copenhagen, one of whom was later subjected to judicial torture in Christiansborg Palace before being executed. Within just over a dozen years, some 297 witch trials took place in Denmark, 60 per cent of all judicial trials held during that period.[31]

Thereafter, the frequency of witch trials declined in Denmark, though a woman convicted of witchcraft was burned as late as 1693. None the less, over two thousand people had been prosecuted since 1520, a thousand of whom were executed.[32] The flogging of witches continued well into the eighteenth century, since the drawing of a witch's blood even at that date was still considered to be an efficacious means of breaking her spells. Such popular belief in witches was to continue in some quarters well into the nineteenth century: in 1800, a woman accused of witchcraft was murdered in Denmark, while in 1897, a woman was severely beaten for the same offence.[33]

In Norway there were some 1,400 prosecutions for witchcraft, mostly of women from the poorer classes, of whom a quarter were ultimately convicted and executed. That said, Norway's most notorious witch-trial involved the widow of the country's most famous Humanist scholar, the Lutheran pastor Absalon Pedersen Beyer. She was burnt at the stake in 1590. It has been said that his iconoclasm and virulent assault on the vestiges of Catholicism had incurred the ire of many Norwegian notables who then took vengeance on his widow Anne.[34] Whatever the truth may be, her gruesome fate stirred the imagination of Norwegians for centuries and in 1908, the Norwegian playwright Hans Wiers Jenssen (1866–1925), wrote his acclaimed play *Anne Pedersdotter* about the witch-trial and execution, which, in turn, went on to inspire Carl Theodore Dreyer's film *Day of Wrath*.

Though most witch-trials took place in the second half of the seventeenth century, the fearful preoccupation with powerful women believed to have made pacts with Satan and his cohorts in return for material and social benefits had long-established roots. The cautionary image (illus. 6) from Tuse Church is Danish, but similar church paintings represented this theme throughout Scandinavia. A fear of diabolism and malevolent actions came to obsess many devout Christians as confrontations between Protestant and Catholic, Calvinist and Lutheran, old traditions and new forms reached their most virulent pitch and enemies were perceived in every corner, especially in the home where women had their place.

Witch-trials in Iceland were rather different. There, while twenty-five witches were burnt at the stake between 1625 and 1685, all but two were men, in sharp contrast to the predominantly female witches elsewhere in the Nordic coun-

6 *Woman with a Butter Churn, Surrounded by Devils*, wall painting. Tuse Church (Denmark).

tries.[35] In fact, out of the 120 trials which took place between 1604 and 1720, many of which were on the north-western corner of the island, women accounted for merely 8 per cent of the accused, and of these only one was burnt at the stake. None the suspects was accused of holding black sabbaths, but they were rather convicted for specific acts of perpetrating evil upon individuals.[36] The most notorious of these trials were held on the instigation of the Icelandic priest Jón Magnússon (c. 1610–96), who wrote his bizzare *Passion Story* (only published in 1914) to describe the physical and spiritual horrors he was obliged to endure in 1655 at the hands of those he perceived to be witches in his native village of Eyri.

In Sweden, accusations of witchcraft and the trials of witches followed the Danish pattern with a greater emphasis placed on pacts with the devil. The witches of Lapland were especially notorious in this regard and many saw these northern reaches of Scandinavia as a citadel of witchcraft.[37] The prominence of a case involving a Saami shaman, Anders Nilsson from Sädvajaur in the parish of Arjeplog, confirmed this prejudice, after he attacked a Lutheran priest who had confiscated the Saami drums of local shamans. Having forcibly repossessed them, he was later burnt at the stake as a witch, as well as for his audacity.[38] The little island of Blå Jungfrun in Kalmarsund, near the town of Kalmar in the south-east of Sweden, and the hill Blåkulla at Marstrand, in the south-west of the country, were most notorious for the alleged practice of magic, an identity in which their geographical reality was often blended into a mythical one (also known as Blåkulla), which lent its name to a series of trials (1668–75) of 856 people, many of whom were children. In a swathe in Sweden from Dalecarlia to Stockholm, they were accused and prosecuted for witchcraft, until the authorities uncovered a conspiracy of lies involving the witnesses who had made the accusations. Some two hundred people, however, had by then already been executed.[39] As a result of what was now perceived to have been a needless slaughter, a growing scepticism followed and the prosecution of witch-trials diminished suddenly in both Sweden and her dependent provinces.[40]

This change was, however, not merely a sceptical backlash, but also the result of new theological insights in which an individual's virtue and moral responsibly for the good and evil which befell him or her was of growing importance and witchcraft played a diminishing role. Though it is true that Luther had condoned judicial witch-trials, some later seventeenth-century theologians believed that suffering came from God as a chastisement for sinful man, and not from the malevolent magical conjurings of witches. Judicial trials of witchcraft soon ceased to occur in the Swedish dominions, even if Finland well into the 1680s witnessed numerous witch-hunts and trials, though with men, not women, making up half of the accused.[41] Nils Psilander, a judge in the civil court on the Åland Islands, was actively involved in the prosecution of witches for diabolism and though torture was used to extract confessions, the Court of Appeal in Turku confirmed the death penalty for only six 'witches'. Elsewhere in Finland, the other Swedish-speaking province of Ostrobothnia also had its share of witch-trials between 1665 and 1685, but of the 152 persons prosecuted, only 28 were actually put to death and these were not convicted of diabolism but of malevolent conduct. In Finnish-speaking areas, even fewer witch-trials appear to have taken place and only one execution seems to have occurred outside the Swedish-speaking areas.[42] Despite a rich folkloric tradition of epic poetry involving witches, Finnish-speaking Finns had avoided most of the excesses of the Continental witch-trials which afflicted the other Nordic lands.

In the Danish West Indies magic and witchcraft was considered a force to be reckoned with, especially amongst the African population, but there the judicial massacre of witches which took place in Europe during the seventeenth century did not occur at all. By the eighteenth century a belief in magic and employment of its ritual was largely confined to those of African descent. During the late eighteenth and early nineteenth centuries, continual African immigration through the slave trade invigorated the existing traditions of magic, healing and spiritual belief, relevant to all aspects and stages of life, as well as the day's routine.

Despite a diminishing faith in the power of witchcraft in all the Nordic countries, one aspect of religious practice relating to evil spirits has persisted into the twentieth century: exorcism. Christian IV and other members of the Danish royal family who shared a Philippist view towards exorcism,[43] rejected its use at christenings, but in more orthodox households, including the growing number of Catholic ones in the late nineteenth and twentieth centuries, exorcism has continued to play an integral feature in baptisms, and occasionally in the blessings of houses.

The Rise of Pietism

As belief in witchcraft abated, so the belief in the voluntary choice of the individual to lead a virtuous Christian life grew among all segments of the population, a new spiritual trend amongst certain Lutheran Christians which came to be known as Pietism. Although an early eighteenth-century phenomenon, the origins of Pietism in the Nordic countries, like those of the Protestant Reformation itself, are principally to be found in Germany. There, in such universities as Halle and Greifswald, the new spiritual movement was gaining ground by the first decade of the eighteenth century, focusing more upon the individual's experience of God, rather than the doctrinal implications of Lutheran Protestantism. August Hermann Francke, a German religious leader and schoolmaster wrote to the Swedish crown prince on the implications of the new movement and its implicit theology with respect to politics in 1711. Francke was convinced its social activism and greater Biblical focus would provide 'a sound foundation for the fear of God, from which the powers that be may expect loyal subjects and faithful servants among all the estates'.[44]

To this end Francke had established a variety of schools and seminaries in Halle, catering to both rich and poor, and encouraging universal literacy. Practical and scientific, as well as classical subjects, were taught, in an atmosphere which discouraged all forms of frivolity. After Francke's death in 1727, Julius Hecker who had come to Halle shortly before, continued to propagate Francke's Pietistic teachings and approach, and his views found followers who went to Scandinavia. Theologians and philosophers who adhered to Pietistic beliefs established themselves at the University of Greifswald, in Swedish Pomerania.

Pietism also reached Sweden through the many officers who had been made prisoners of war in the Battle of Perelovochna, during the Swedish-Russian war. They were incarcerated in Moscow and Tobolsk, where German Pietists had been permitted to preach. Even as far afield as Siberia, where some Swedish officers were deported, religious tracts had carried the Pietist spiritual message. When they returned home after the peace was concluded in 1721, many of these military converts, moved by their powerful, if stern, religious zeal, used their positions of privilege to translate Pietist values into practice on their own estates, and, through example, in neighbouring estates and villages as well, exerting a particularly powerful influence on religious education well into the nineteenth century.[45] More mystical and radical variations of Pietism, including speaking in tongues, also made headway in Sweden, but, through the proselytizing of German missionaries such as Johann Konrad Dippel (1673–1734), a more rational tradition came to dominate in which human reason was deemed to work hand in hand with an inner spiritual light.

A later variety of Lutheran Pietism came to Scandinavia, with roots in the Hussite heresy of the fifteenth century, but largely moulded by Francke's college, the 'Paedagogium', in Halle. Founded in 1722 in his native Saxony by the German Count Nikolaus Ludwig von Zinzendorf (1700–1760), this new Lutheran sect, the ecumenical 'Unitas Fratrum' (United Brethren) movement, or Moravians as they came to be known, developed its own ecclesiastical organization and provided at Herrnhut a new community where the persecuted 'Unitas Fratrum' refugees from the provinces of Moravia and Bohemia could seek refuge. There, a rigidly hierarchical but communitarian settlement took form, with sharp distinctions based upon age, sex and marital status. Accommodation, work and social life were all communally organized, with food and clothing provided as required.

In Saxony, Zinzendorf's religious activities led to his banishment in 1736, but his extensive foreign journeys spread the message of the Moravians from the Baltic states, including Sweden and Denmark, to the West Indies, where two mission stations were established in the Danish Virgin Islands. There, on a visit to far-flung St Thomas, he gave a sermon in improvised Creole to some three hundred slaves at the Mosquito Bay Plantation. The sermon was prepared by Johann Lorenz Carstens, the enlightened Danish planter who had himself become a Moravian Pietist, under the influence of Count Carl Adolf von Plessen, Lord Chamberlain of Denmark.[46]

Zinzendorf's inspiration to preach in the Caribbean can be traced back to a visit to Copenhagen in 1731, when he had met Anton, a slave of Count Danneskiold-Laurvig, who had been converted to Christianity. This meeting resulted in the first missionaries being sent to the Danish colony towards the end of 1733. This was followed in 1734 by a further eighteen Moravian Pietists of both sexes from Herrnhut itself, before he himself went out. Though the Moravian message may have been radical in theological terms, in secular ones it was deeply conservative, even condoning slavery. Exhorting the slaves to diligent labour and obedience to Carstens and his wife, as well as their overseer and bombas (African foremen), Zinzendorf exclaimed in his sermon, 'You shall know that Christ requires work of all his children, for the Lord Himself is the Creator of everything: Kings, lords, servants and slaves, each must willingly accept his allotted place, according to where God has placed him, and to be content with God's wise exhortations'.[47] Needless to say, such preaching found ready acceptance amongst the relatively small, but somewhat insecure, planters of St Thomas.

Soon considerable numbers of the inhabitants of the colony, both planters and slaves, had been won over. Furthermore, by 1736, fourteen missionaries had been sent from the Danish Virgin Islands directly to the Guinea coast in order to convert the slaves even before their departure for the Caribbean, but the death of eleven of the missionaries shortly after their arrival led to the abandonment of this missionary endeavour and the three survivors returned to the Virgin Islands.[48] There, the Moravians were thriving and, by 1762, a Moravian episcopal seat had been established. Although some missionaries were opposed to slavery, most, whether Moravian or orthodox Lutheran, considered it an unpleasant necessity for the preservation of the social order, like the beating of children, with whom it was felt slaves were most comparable in intellectual and moral terms. In fact, one missionary by the name of Oldentord even deemed the floggings a sign of God's wisdom and providence, explaining, 'Yes, the condition of these people is lamentable, but who can change it other than God? And as far as punishment is concerned, it really is not as bad as it seems, if one realizes how tough their skin is'.[49]

Slavery found considerable support even among the upper echelons of the orthodox Lutheran Church at home. Erik Pontoppidan (1698–1764), the Danish bishop of Bergen, in Norway, praised it in about 1760 as a means of improving the lot of black slaves, by placing them under the authority of Christians, by definition benign, rather than by leaving them subject to the brutality of African slave owners, untempered by Christian belief and morality. For the slave dealer Ludewig Ferdinand Rømer it was a moral endeavour, a means by which Christianity could be spread, with its virtues of faith, love, hope and, above all, patience.[50]

Slavery, therefore, was not incompatible with the beliefs of Zinzendorf, for whom the Gospel consisted of an emphasis upon Christ as Saviour and considered faith was 'not in thoughts nor in the head, but in the heart, a light illuminated in the heart'[51], and to the north, as well as to the south, missionaries arrived from Herrnhut. Their proselytizing carried them as far as Greenland which proved to be a particularly rich soil for their missionary activities, where the simple communities they established sought to embody their austere vision of the ideal Christian community.

Others Pietist missionaries journeyed eastwards to Scandinavia's Indian colonies. The German missionaries Bartholmaeus Ziegenbalg and Heinrich Plütschau went to the Danish Indian colony of Tranquebar, where they succeeded in winning many native converts. Whether it was their winsome preaching which brought about the conversions or the fact that a royal Danish proclamation required the manumission of slaves who had converted to Christianity there is not clear. In any case, local slave owners showed considerably less enthusiasm for the missionary activities of the Moravians in Tranquebar than their counterparts did in the Danish Virgin Islands, even if they could do little to hinder their activities.[52]

The Moravians arrived in Sweden in 1732 and they achieved such a large following that the orthodox Lutheran clergy sought measures to curb them. However, the aristocracy, where the Moravians had made considerable inroads, prevented the more conservative churchmen from restricting them further, even though they had prohibited their prayer assemblies in 1726. Concentrated as they were in Stockholm and Gothenburg, theirs was a largely urban profile and it was only in the mid-1780s that Gustaf III's promulgation of greater religious toleration gave them the freedom to congregate at all, even though more and more members of the aristocracy joined the sect.

Perhaps the most lasting legacy of Pietism was the support it gave to religious toleration and ecumenism at a time when few sought such *rapprochement* between the various Christian denominations and sects. The Moravians were, of course, not alone in the Nordic region in this respect. Already in 1744, the Danish playwright Ludwig Holberg had exhorted a man's right to evaluate his religion rationally in his philosophical work, *Moral Thoughts*. As the German statesman and chancellor of the University of Halle, Veit von Seckendorff (1626–1692), had already implied in his *History of Lutheranism* (1688), the true Christian was he who led a virtuous life, whatever his denomination. But few governmental or ecclesiastical figures heeded such ecumenism at the time and even in charitable institutions like hospitals it was largely absent. In the Seraphim Infirmary (1752) in Stockholm, Lutherans were well provided with care but only two beds for the accommodation of Roman Catholics were available (for foreign-born merchants and seamen, for example), and these only because private subscriptions provided the funds.[53]

Swedenborg and the Church of New Jerusalem

The cult of Swedenborg provided a spiritual alternative to that of the Pietists. Emanuel Svedberg (1688–1772), or Swedenborg, as he was renamed after the family was ennobled in 1719, evolved his own mystical interpretation of Christianity. The son of a theological professor at Uppsala University, he went on to become a specialist in mechanics and metallurgy, before turning his attention to theological matters, especially biblical studies, after a spiritual crisis in the early 1740s. His great eight-volume work *Heavenly Arcana* (1749–56) and later *On Heaven and Its Wonders and on Hell* (1758) encapsulate this theological system. For Swedenborg, the soul, body and mind of man form a unity which reflects that of the Trinity which permeates man and the rest of creation. Man, through his free will, has damaged the harmony of the natural world and only through the Redemption, which Jesus Christ has brought the world by virtue of his blameless life, has a path been created to bridge the gulf. Thus, the material world reflects the spiritual world in such a way that the division between the two ultimately disappears.

This arcane view, containing as it does both mystical and rational elements, inspired admirers of his writings in Sweden to establish societies to study his thoughts. By the 1780s this led to the establishment of a new sect, The Church of the New Jerusalem. Highly intellectual as well as spiritual, its members tended to be drawn, like the Moravians, from the aristocracy and literate sections of the population, especially in Stockholm. His influence was considerable in other spheres, as well. Indeed, his student, Carl Bernard Wadström, at one time a West African colonist, became the leading Swedish opponent to the continuation of the African slave trade. More than a century after his death, even such a towering literary figure as August Strindberg, though himself not a Christian, was deeply influenced by Swedenborg's writings. Not merely Strindberg's plays, but also his paintings, profoundly reflect aspects of Swedenborg's arcane spiritual world. Strindberg's largely abstract painting *Inferno* (see illus. 49) may ostensibly depict a violent storm on the Baltic Sea but on another level, it captures not only a period of deep turmoil in the playwright's emotional life, but it seems to explore a spiritual crisis, at a time when the playwright's experiments in alchemy brought him to the frontiers of the spiritual and scientific, leaving him in a mælström of the soul from which only an expressionistic form of painting seemed to offer him any relief.

As such it provided a catharsis, like his *roman à clef* of the same title through which he was able to expiate his own feelings of guilt and, perhaps, even of sinfulness.[54] Yet, at the same time, it is a hell from which new life can spring, one which looks back to that of Swedenborg's own literary dream vision of 1744 and even Dante beyond.[55] As Swedenborg himself wrote in his essay 'A Hieroglyphic Key to Natural and Spiritual Arcana by way of Representations and Correspondences' (1742), visual images necessarily expressed the spiritual world of which all nature was a reflection. Strindberg was aware of this belief and shared it. He was subject to other spiritual influences including Hinduism and by the mid-1890s, the metaphysical concept of Maya – nature's seductive creative force, as expounded by Schopenauer in his *World as Will* – had come to play a key role in Strindberg's spritual framework, one in which time and space are illusory, yet able to reflect a deeper spiritual reality.

Pietism in Denmark in the Eighteenth Century

As in Sweden, so in Denmark, Pietism and Swedenborgianism were to exert long lasting effects. King Frederik IV of Denmark (1671–1730), despite his bigamous marriages to Louise of Mecklenburg-Güstrow and Elisabeth Vieregg (as well as a later marriage to Anna Sophie Reventlow, after the latter's death), also became a devoted adherent of Pietism towards the end of his life, while afflicted by the tuberculosis which eventually killed him. Taking to heart the Pietist admonitions to lead a strict life, devoid of worldly frivolities, he banned entertainments on Sundays and feast days, frowned upon dancing and closed the theatres. Indeed, the destruction of the Royal Theatre by fire in 1728 was seen by some as a divine judgement upon the immorality which many believed made its seat there and the theatre did not open again until after the reign of his son. Failure to attend church, previously decriminalized, was once again made a misdemeanour.

When Christian VI (1699–1746) assumed the throne with his consort Sofie Magdalene, the Pietist values propagated by his father were reinforced and, indeed, strengthened. Pontoppidan and Jeremias Friedrich Reuss (1700–1777), Professor of Theology at Copenhagen University, chose to fortify the cause of Pietism within the established church while Court Chaplains, and kept the Moravians at bay. Not only were Pontoppidan's writings to have immense influence over Danish spirituality but they were to be of considerable importance throughout the other Nordic dominions as well. His catechism of 1737, *Truth which is unto Godliness*, remained popular until well into the 1930s, whilst his *Marvelous Mirror of Belief* took its place next to the Bible in countless households in Denmark and Sweden even after it was published in its tenth edition in 1899.[56]

The practical expression of Pontoppidan's theology was the encouragement of private austerity and a rejection of such social pleasures as dancing and the playing of cards, while the reading of worldly literature was also eschewed. These were views to which Christian VI was especially sympathetic, especially Pontoppidan's support for patriotism and civic morality. Pontoppidan's personal austere morality was reflected in the king's own life, both public and private. Unlike his father, Christian avoided the military embroilments of his father and he was faithful to his spouse throughout their married life. Perhaps, it was more through the assistance and control of his wife, than through his own strength of character, that his virtue was maintained. Indeed, the French ambassador was reputed to have said that the Queen chose only those for ladies-in-waiting who were 'long-legged, lean, sallow, big-nosed and blinking'.

Not only the provinces, but Copenhagen itself was affected by this austere Pietism. As the playwright Ludwig Holberg bemoaned, the citizens of Copenhagen who had previously been 'as merry as calves' were now 'as demure and earnest as old cats.' Presiding over this dour regime, the King and Queen remained piously ensconced in their new royal palace of Christiansborg, dutifully fulfilling their royal obligations. Only hunting, one of the few recreations the king permitted himself to enjoy, alleviated the austerity of public court life. Public virtue may have been the result, but it failed to compensate grand visitors for the Spartan qualities of the regime and the private ennui of daily life at court. As Frederick the Great's sister caustically remarked, the royal pair did nothing but 'pray to God and be bored'.[57]

By contrast to his parents, Crown Prince Frederik and his English wife Princess Louise, daughter of King George II of England, were more worldly in their outlook. Fond of cards and amusing entertainments, they increasingly softened the austerity of court, to the passive consternation of the ageing King and Queen. As the reign of the old king ebbed, Copenhagen gradually lightened its tone, but in the provinces, Pietism continued to make significant inroads, especially in Jutland. There such clergymen as Hans Adolf Brorson, Bishop of Ribe, wrote poems and hymns, which became immensely popular, focusing upon the paltriness of man when confronted with divine power and might. For Brorson, divine consolation offered the only sanctuary from the constant onslaught of terrestrial afflictions. These views set the tone for much spiritual life on the west coast of Jutland, reflected in such stories as *Babette's Feast* by the twentieth-century Danish author Karen Blixen (later turned into a film released in 1987 by the Danish film director Gabriel Axel (1918–). In the work an austere Pietist community is thrown into spiritual and emotional disarray by the arrival of a hedonistic Frenchwoman and her plans to hold a great culinary celebration. Perhaps, though, it is a painting by the Danish artist Niels Bjerre (1864–1942), a native of nearby Lemvig, which best illustrates the sense of community and Spartan devotion among many Jutlanders from the North Sea coastal areas, whose deep inner spirituality and hostility to materialism is so alien to the dominant secularism in the Nordic region today (illus. 7).

Geographical Expansion of the Swedish Lutheran Church

In Denmark, there had been little room for any geographical expansion of the established church since the early Middle Ages, but this was not the case in Sweden and Finland where the slow spread of the population northwards and westwards demanded the creation of new parishes and the need for new churches. Whereas medieval churches had been built largely of stone, these later churches, especially in Norrland, were constructed almost exclusively of wood well into the eighteenth century. Karl IX of Sweden had ordered the construction of five such new churches in Swedish and Finnish Lapland by 1605, sending out his emissary Daniel Hjort to select suitable locations. Four of these new churches were built in the heart of Saami territory at Lycksele, Arvidsjaur, Jokkmokk and Kukkasjärvi, on the Swedish side of the Torneå River, and one at Enontekiö, on the Finnish side. These churches adequately served not only their religious function, but also the king's keen wish to integrate all of Lapland, including adjacent Norwegian Finnmark, into the Swedish kingdom.

With the Treaty of Käred in 1613, however, all claims to Norwegian Lapland

7 Niels Bjerre, *The Children of God's Prayer Meeting at Harboøre*, 1897, oil on canvas.

were permanently abandoned; but, in Finnish Lapland, the power of the Swedish crown was strengthened. Not only did Lutheran pastors preach the Word of God there and elsewhere in Sweden, they also used their pulpits after 1766 to promulgate royal proclamations, which had previously been read out in parish halls or other public buildings. The pulpit, thus, became the voice of the Crown, as well as that of God. That said, such a practice in no way hindered a considerable organizational independence for the new ecclesiastical regions. For example, Härnösand, elevated to a superintendancy in 1647, became an independent diocese with its own bishop in 1772. This had practical disadvantages, however, for a loosening of the bonds to the archepiscopal seat at Uppsala, with its relatively bountiful economic resources, forced greater local reliance upon the diocese's own much more limited means.[58]

In the Swedish provinces of the south, the Church continued to function much as it had done since the eruption of the Reformation, each parish dominated by its local priest, usually the most educated man in the parish. A good if exceptionally enlightened example of this type was the early eighteenth-century vicar of Släps Church in Halland. *The Portrait of Gustaf Fredrik Hjortberg with his Family* (c. 1780; see illus. 48) by the German Jonas Dürchs (active as a church artist from the 1760s to the 1780s), shows this committed Lutheran priest, in the bosom of his vast family (including his deceased children) in a painting given to the church as his epitaph. Books from his large library are depicted along with a large variety of geographical instruments, an ape from Madagascar, a preserved tortoise and other creatures from his extensive journeys abroad. A well-educated humanist, he was a member of the Academy of Science in Stockholm, and kept himself informed of the latest scientific discoveries while maintaining a keen interest in foreign wildlife. As chaplain on board a vessel of the Swedish East India Company, he had made the voyage to China no less than three times before settling down in his quiet rural vicarage.[59] Hjortberg was an exceptionally well-travelled priest, but it was far from unusual for men of the cloth to travel overseas, whether to foreign climes or the far-off reaches of the Swedish dominions.

The Expansion of Lutheranism to the Nordic Colonies

After the establishment of the colony of New Sweden at Fort Christina by the Delaware River in 1638, it was natural for the Swedish Lutheran church to follow in its wake. Thus, a little church was built on Tinicum Island, in the Delaware, which became the seat of the colony's sole priest, Lars Lock, from 1648 to 1654.[60] However, the presence not only of the heathen Delaware Indians, but of Dutch colonists, members of the Calvinist Dutch Reformed Church who settled about twenty miles from Fort Christina, led to a considerable amount of confrontation between the two Protestant faiths, reflecting that which occasionally erupted in the mother country.[61] Johan Printz, governor of the colony from 1643 to 1653, was particularly noted for his religious intolerance towards the Dutch but even more towards the Indians. Indeed, he advocated the extermination of all of them who refused to accept 'the only true religion', a solution he was unable to

accomplish because of his chronic lack of Swedish military might.[62] After his departure, however, the situation improved for Dissenters and, by 1655, even a few Jews had come to the colony as traders where they were free to practice their religion as best they might.[63]

The Lutheran church extended itself even to Sweden's tropical colony of St Barthelemy, acquired from France in 1785, where the bulk of the population was Roman Catholic. A Lutheran church was completed there in 1787 and given the name of the Swedish queen, Sophia Magdalena, which became the principal house of worship on St Barthelemy. A further 149 Anglicans, 234 Methodists and 60 members of other Protestant denominations, including the Reformed Church, made for considerable religious diversity, sometimes, in the early days, sharing the Lutheran church. Demolished in the late 1850s, it was a half-timbered building, with boarding and unglazed windows, surmounted by a shingled roof and set on a height above Gustavia. Its crowning position can be seen in illustration 8, in which the little mercantile port spreads out around its sheltered harbour, a multi-ethnic entrepôt where the inhabitants enjoyed a freedom of religion not available in Sweden itself. Such toleration was, of course, a necessity in a colony where only 21 of the residents were Lutheran and 519 Catholics. Previously, during the French colonial period, there had been a small stone Catholic church at L'Orient, occasionally visited by a monk from St Martin's, but this had fallen into disuse. Therefore, the Lutheran church was given over, not only to the Lutheran priest, Sven Thunborg, but also to the Catholic one, the French Father Épiphane who said mass there twice a month. Later, in the nineteenth century, the Catholic priest was even recommended by the colony's governor Rosenstein to the Swedish crown for financial remuneration for his services.[64] Then, the Catholic Church of Our Lady of the Assumption was built

8 After Carl David Gyllenborg, *A View of the City of Gustavia on the Island of St Barthelemy*, 1793, ink, wash and water-colour.

in 1829 opposite the waterfront, only to be destroyed by a hurricane in 1837. Rebuilt in 1842, with massive stone walls, it found itself in 1855 adjacent to the Anglican church. Funds for its construction were provided by Sir Richard Dinzey, a native of the near-by Dutch island of Saba who had immigrated to St Barthelemy. He was later to be made a Knight of the Order of Vasa by the Swedish King Oscar I for his financial munificence to the colony.

During the latter days of the colony, religious toleration seems to have been less in evidence, especially amongst the Protestant sects. Since English was the predominant language on the island, sermons were given in that language, though this temporarily stopped when the new Swedish priest, F. A. Lönner, felt he was not being properly reimbursed for his efforts in a foreign language. More disturbingly, a prolonged feud broke out during the 1830s between the Lutheran priest Carl Adolf Carlsson and the Methodists, in which the former accused the latter of a persecuting fanaticism towards the established church.[65] Since each church had its own house of worship, close religious co-operation was no longer necessary.

On St Thomas in the Danish Virgin Islands, the first Lutheran Frederik Church had been built at Charlotte Amalie early in the colony's history, but it had burnt down twice, first in 1750 and then in 1789, leaving only its grand three-storeyed parsonage standing. However, it was again rebuilt in 1793, this time in a fairly elaborate neo-classical style, only to be destroyed once more in a fire in 1825. Reconstructed once more the following year in the Gothic Revival style, it needed major renovations after a disastrous hurricane in 1870. The second Lutheran church to be built was that of Our Lord God of Sabaoth, built in the colony's capital Christiansted on the island of St Croix, between 1750 and 1753. An elegant Baroque edifice, it has a simple hip-roof of rectangular shape with moulded gutters under the eaves-line. To this a tower and steeple were later added in the 1790s, crowned by an octagonal cupola. A Dutch Reform Church was also constructed in Charlotte Amalie in 1804, made of half-timber and masonry infill, though it too was rebuilt in 1844 in the grand Greek Revival style typical of Reform churches in Europe at the time.

Between 1849 and 1858, the Anglican Church of St John was built in stone in Christiansted, in the Gothic Revival style so popular in England. The erection of the Catholic Cathedral Saints Peter and Paul, in 1848, with its ribbed vault, and fortress-like exterior, and the Moravian Memorial Church, in 1882, built to commemorate the arrival of the Moravians in the colony, completed the principal ecclesiastical edifices of the century, along with the Jewish synagogue of 1833.[66]

Growth of Religious Toleration

While toleration in the Nordic Caribbean colonies was in advance of that in Scandinavia itself, religious toleration in the mother countries did grow by fits and starts. During the middle years of the eighteenth century the Swedish Count Nils Bielke had been obliged to settle in Rome, because of his conversion to Catholicism, a capital crime in Sweden at the time. Yet, once established there, and appointed papal courtier and Roman senator, he was able to serve his native country by facilitating commerce between the Papal States and Sweden, as well as acting as cicerone for visiting Swedes. The ridiculous anomaly of his situation, which made him a felon in Sweden because of his religious convictions but sought after by Swedish visitors to Italy, did not hinder the fact that vested interests of church and state in Sweden prevented any liberalizing of the law against conversion to Catholicism by natives. As a result, this legal prohibition on conversion to Catholicism continued to exist for more than a century. None the less, under the initiative of Gustaf III, an enlightened monarch of rational and sceptical bent whose travels to France and Italy had served to develop his liberal and tolerant approach to religion, the situation began to improve. He succeeded in granting religious toleration to Catholic immigrants to Sweden, despite much clerical opposition; their mercantile and other skills were too valuable to this worldly monarch to be foregone for mere reasons of religion. Such a clear-sighted economic perspective also applied to Jews. During Gustaf III's reign, in 1782, Jews, previously forbidden entry to the country, were granted leave to settle in Stockholm, Gothenburg and Norrköping, where they were encouraged to engage in trade and industry and even permitted to erect synagogues. But, the ownership of land in Sweden, as well as the membership of craft guilds, remained barred to them. Nor were Jews allowed to marry or employ Christians. Despite these impediments, many Jews came to prosper in Sweden. One, Aron Isack, became a leading religious and mercantile personage of the age and other immigrants followed in his wake where they assumed growing economic and cultural importance throughout the nineteenth century.

A significant number of these new immigrants were younger sons of prosperous Jewish families well established in Germany, especially in Wismar, in Mecklenburg, which for a time was under Swedish jurisdiction. For them, Sweden offered new horizons for both dynastic and economic expansion and, by 1815, there were more than 800 Jews living in Sweden.[67] One such family, the Josephsons, would go on over two centuries to make a very considerable mark on Sweden culturally, most importantly the artist Ernst Josephson (1851–1906), whose works often focused upon literary themes, sometimes drawn from the Old Testament. David and Saul (illus. 9) are portrayed with strong Semitic physiognomic characteristics. The king, staring morosely into a pictorial black hole, as it were, sits in sartorial splendour, whilst the young David delicately plays his harp, fixing his eyes above, as if receiving a heavenly vision. It is as if an allegory is being presented of the Jews in Sweden in the nineteenth century, leavening the loaf of the Swedish nation with their fresh talents and loyalty, attributes which were increasingly rewarded.

By 1838, Jews had received most of the rights of Swedish subjects, though, popular unrest at the time led to certain curtailments. However, by the 1870s, Jewish emancipation was firmly established in Sweden and images of Jewry began to change. Josephson's portrait of his cousin (see illus. 51) depicts this young society lady in an elegant outfit of Far Eastern inspiration, in which

9 Ernst Josephson, *David and Saul*, 1878, oil on canvas.

Swedish and oriental elements merge into a unified whole, just as Jews were assimilating into Swedish society.

In the Nordic dependencies of the Danish Caribbean, though, such toleration towards Jews had long been practised. As far back as the late seventeenth century a Jewish colonial governor was appointed. By 1796, after an influx of Jewish refugees from St Eustatius, the Danish king Christian VII granted the Jews of St Thomas permission to form their own congregation. This consisted of only nine families in 1801, growing to some 22 by 1803. The following year, however, the newly erected synagogue was destroyed in a major fire which also claimed some 1200 other buildings in Charlotte Amalie and it was replaced by a second one in 1812. This, in turn, was replace by a much larger wooden one, built eleven years later, to accommodate the now 64 Jewish families in the congregation. This, too, fell victim to a fire in 1831, which destroyed a further 800 buildings. Once again a new synagogue was erected, with a French architect imported for the purpose, partly financed by the non-Jewish governor, Peter von Scholten, who contributed $100. Constructed in 1833 in traditional fashion of native stone, with mortar mixed of sand and molasses, it can be seen in illustration 10. Formerly Orthodox, the Jewish Reformed liturgy was introduced there in 1841, though the size of the congregation soon rapidly declined, as many Jews emigrated to Panama, where they provided ancillary services for the construction of the canal there. As a result, by 1890, there were only 141 Jews remaining in the congregation, a number which fell to only about 50 by the beginning of the Second World War.[68]

10 Synagogue of Charlotte Amalie, St Thomas, Virgin Islands.

The Church in Iceland until the Mid-Nineteenth Century

By contrast with the Caribbean colonies, the Lutheran church continued to maintain its dominant position in Iceland, Greenland and the other Arctic dependencies, even if religious groups such as the Moravians did make inroads. To some degree, its continued strength owed much to the quality of its leadership. Jón Thorkelsson Vídalín, Bishop of Skáholt (1666–1720), a grandson of Arngrímur Jónsson, was immensely respected not only as a man of the church, but as a man of letters. In particular, his *Sermons for the Home* (1718–20) achieved great fame in Iceland throughout the eighteenth and nineteenth centuries, for their spiritual and literary qualities. His rhetorical zeal, moreover, in fighting to improve the material lot of his countrymen in a time of great hardship won him many admirers, even in Denmark where the reins of both political and ecclesiastical power were held.

The cathedral of Skáholt (built in 1056), in the south of the country, was the more important of Iceland's two episcopal seats and boasted of being the largest medieval church of wood in the Nordic region until it was destroyed by an earthquake in 1785. Until its destruction, its Romanesque forms exerted a powerful influence on church architecture, particularly on the cathedral church of Hólar, in the north (an episcopal seat from 1106–1798), whose large wooden church (replacing an earlier one) was completed in 1765. However, the majority of churches in Iceland during the seventeenth and eighteenth centuries were simple affairs of wood, earth, turf and bits of stone. Usually about 5 x 2.5 metres in size, the nave and choir formed a spatial entity, divided by a screen, containing a door and balusters.[69]

In 1700, there were still some 30 of these wooden churches.[70] These stood mainly on the sites of monasteries dissolved during the Reformation and sometimes became the focus of great spiritual significance. For example, after the eruption of the volcano Krafla in 1727, the resulting lava flow had reduced houses and farms in the vicinity of Mývatn to rubble. Yet the church of Reykjalið, surrounded by the flow, survived, an event deemed so miraculous that even the imaginations of many sceptics were stirred.[71] Other disasters, whether eruptions, epidemics or famines, led many Icelanders to seek solace in religion, but the eighteenth century was an age of increasing faith in the powers of reason in Iceland as on the Continent and the old orthodox Lutheran piety tended to decline even if, in administrative terms, the Church in Iceland was undergoing a period of consolidation and centralization. Stone churches were built at Vestmannaeyjar and Viðey, as well as Bessastaðir, near Reykjavik, the newly founded capital. Reykjavik soon became the ecclesiastical centre of the island and in the eighteenth century a new cathedral was constructed in the centre, situated by a pond. Major renovations were later carried out between 1847 and 1848 by L. A. Winstrup on the original stone church. From 1801, all of Iceland was placed under the ecclesiastical jurisdiction of one bishop there, in place of the two who formerly had seats at Skálholt and Hólar. Thus, both church and state came to be administered from Reykjavik, with the new city's Latin school (1844–6) by

Jørgen Hansen Koch serving the educational needs of many young men who would serve both church and state.

By contrast to elsewhere in the Nordic region, the numerous evangelical sects which flourished in the early nineteenth century did not take root in Iceland. On the contrary, all religious movements seemed to be on the wane, for, as the Icelandic historian Jón Espólín put it in 1829, the Icelanders were 'a cool-tempered people [...] generally not pious'; indeed, he continued, 'one can hardly find a religious fanatic in the whole country'.[72]

The Church in Lapland

The Saami people (traditionally known as Lapps among non-Saami peoples) resided within the interior of the far north of Scandinavia, that is, Lapland, including some parts of the coast of Norway, but mainly in the vast hinterland of the north of Norway, Sweden and Finland (as well as the far north-west of Russia beyond Murmansk). There they led a seasonally nomadic life-style while maintaining many of their pre-Christian beliefs in a pantheon of spirits of nature and ancestors, each of which had his or her benevolent or malevolent side. This religious framework, albeit never forming a unified system, was gradually eroded from the beginnings of Christianization in the fourteenth century. Perhaps the most important of the traditional Saami gods was Veralden-radien (the ruler of the world) who gave fertility and preserved life and to whom the Saami ceremonially sacrificed male reindeer each autumn to ensure his continued benevolence. He it was who gave Madderakka, the goddess of childbirth, the raw material of the soul from which a new person could be formed and he it was also who, upon death, repossessed the soul, carrying it back to 'yabme-aimo', the abode of the dead. Life and death were thus inextricably woven together in a way which made the cult of the dead particularly important to the Saami, especially for its implications for benefits in this life. Usually, its ceremonial functions, involving prayers and sacrifices, were carried out by a shaman, or 'noaide', who was believed to enter the spiritual realm during his trance. The 'joik' of Saami song was also an integral part, in which the rhythm is of primary significance, rather than the monotonic melody. This was normally accompanied by the beating of a drum, richly decorated with mystically significant hieroglyphics, which was the primary instrument of invocation used to influence the spirits of nature and ancestors. These might reside in mountains, hills or, indeed, stones and in all their multiplicity influenced all aspects of human life. Thus, certain areas were considered sacred and in many of these women were forbidden to tread.[73] Diseases, too, were felt to have their own spirits, the three principal ones of which were seen as brothers. The eldest, smallpox, was called 'stuore namma' (great name), in order to avoid calling the disease by 'his' proper name, thereby incurring the affliction. Silence in 'his' presence, was deemed one of the best ways of avoiding the spirit as 'he' marauded about the countryside in quest of victims.[74] Of the higher life forms, however, it was the bear which was most sacred, a beast to be both revered and feared (a reflection of which is also found in much ancient Finnish and Karelian poetry and oral epic).

Alongside such pantheistic beliefs, Christianity also took a slow but growing hold amongst the Saami, in part through the missionary activities of the Norwegian Pietist Thomas von Westen especially in the eighteenth century, and those of the Swede Lars Levi Læstadius (1800–1861), a native of Arjeplog who himself had some Saami ancestry, in the 1840s. He was able to base his work upon a long tradition of pastoral care for the Saami, for whom numerous churches and chapels had been built during the seventeenth and eighteenth centuries, not only for religious reasons but also as a means of better integrating them within the Swedish or Danish state. The relationship of the two cultures in this respect could be symbiotic; the descendant of ethnic Swedes might marry a Saami, whose children might adhere to many traditional Saami beliefs and cultural values. For example, Salomon Tornberg, an eighteenth-century priest in a new parish near Karesuando (Enontekis), where some 64 per cent of the population were nomads, had a son who became a constable and farmer at Naimakka, by the Norwegian border in Finnish Lapland. His son, in turn, married a local Saami woman and became a nomadic reindeer herder, with descendants sharing many Saami beliefs and fully integrated into Saami culture.

Church Towns

During the winter months, despite their nomadic habits during the rest of the year, many Saami retired to huts communally shared with other families in so-called church villages, not unlike those church towns common in the coastal regions of the north of Sweden, in which parishioners living at a distance could reside whilst attending church services, whether at weekends or other holy days (illus. 11). The Saami themselves stood under no legal obligation to attend religious services, but for the non-Saami population attendance at church was a legal requirement, which increased frequency according to residential proximity to the church. Thus, those who lived within ten kilometres of the church were obliged to attend weekly; those between ten and 30 kilometres, every other week and those further away, every third Sunday.[75]

In Sweden, central government in Stockholm was particularly keen to encourage economic productivity in Norrland, the largest if least populated province, and an increase in the number of churches there meant a decrease in the time required to travel to church allowing more time for productive labour from the parishioners. Usually the inhabitants travelled on Saturdays and other feast days to these church towns, where it was customary to spend the night in tiny cabins after a Saturday service, which fulfilled their weekly religious obligation.

Luleå Church Town, Västerbotten, was arguably the most important and closer examination sheds considerable light on the fabric of life there, spiritual and social, since the Reformation. Several hundred one-storey family houses of one or two rooms, with separate stalls for horses, reflected a simplified version of the architectural style of the period, as interpreted by the farmers and joiners who built them. Boasting little in the way of architectural decoration, Luleå Church

11 Vilhelmina Church Town (Lappland), c. 1800.

Town (situated to the west of the site of the new town which had been moved as the coastline shifted eastward as the land rose) became one of the largest and of these church settlements with a population of about 300 on a typical Saturday night during the first half of the eighteenth century.

Its parish church had been constructed on the site of an earlier chapel built in 1339, but greatly enlarged and renovated in 1492. At that time the parish of Luleå had included over a quarter of the territory of Sweden, that is, the whole of Norrbotten. It had thus been geographically larger than many European states and its church had been the largest church in Scandinavia north of Uppsala before the Reformation. Its vaulted interior, with rich Gothic tracery, boasted works by one of the important Swedish artists of the time, Albertus Pictor, and in about 1525, a richly carved and gilt altarpiece had even been imported from Antwerp.

The prosperous local economy based on a trade of dried fish, furs and tar had made such a major undertaking possible and several local merchants, who also possessed large farms supporting animal husbandry, were among the richest men in Sweden. However, it was more the wealth of the Archbishop of Uppsala, who had received the region as a fief from King Sten Sture the Elder, which had really provided the necessary means for the construction and furnishing of the church. With his rights to levy taxes and fish salmon in the Luleå River, relatively large financial resources had been at his command. As a result, the church of Luleå was able to acquire trappings of grandeur which belied the vast parish's meagre population of about 2,500 people in 1559. A significant proportion of these, at least 700, would be absent from church even at Easter and on other important feast days.[76] With the final consolidation of Protestantism towards the end of the sixteenth century the parish suffered a continual financial decline, for the considerable resources of the archbishop were no longer available and trade impositions in the region, which now favoured the merchants of Stockholm to the detriment of the formerly prosperous Norrland merchants, prevented the latter from having direct maritime contact with foreign ports. The economy thus declined rapidly.

None the less, some natives of Luleå did continue to make their way in the world and thrive, especially through the Church which offered a path to both power and prestige even under a Protestant regime. Erik Benzelius (1632–1709), the son of a local farmer, went on to study in Uppsala, six weeks distance overland, eventually becoming its archbishop. Three of his sons went on to succeed him to this high office, in a virtual dynastic succession. The parish was thus not quite such a provincial backwater, occupied by 'primitive Lapps' and reindeer, as some disappointed visitors erroneously expected even during that period. In fact, there were hardly any Saami people living in the coastal regions, though some did visit to trade in the markets.

The parish church situated in old Luleå remained the spiritual and social centre of the parish and even received King Karl XI, who stayed with its dean, as a visitor in 1694. Though the fabric of the church was soon altered to suit the winds of the Enlightenment, the old church cottages with their stalls and related storage sheds remained little changed, still in the ownership of exclusively landed families. Not only were farm labourers and domestics legally prohibited from purchasing church cottages, but, even if their finances had permitted, were usually obliged to look after the homesteads of their masters or mistresses while they were absent, even if they too stood under legal obligation to attend church.[77]

There was an important social significance to such church towns, since for many young people they were marriage markets where acquaintances could be made and relationships deepened on numerous festive occasions. Indeed, as many as 300 people might come together in the nineteenth century when dances were held, outdoors or at times in an assembly room or even a church cottage itself.

While Christmas, Easter and Midsummer's Eve were popular occasions for adults, nubile girls and their suitors tended to assemble for festivities on New Year's Eve and the Thirteenth Day of Christmas during the winter, or on the Feast of the Annunciation of the Virgin, Whitsunday and Michaelmas at other times of the year. Such events could last for several days and it was quite customary for young courting men and women to sleep together in the same bed in order to test their suitability for marriage, an arrangement known as 'bundling' which frequently led to betrothal. Physical liberties might be discreetly taken, but the couple were obliged to keep their clothes on even in bed. Those young men not courting might be conscripted to act as watchmen on guard against the outbreak of fire, the bane of all wooden towns and villages. Often, the church cottage itself would provide the venue for the weddings which were expected to ensue, for churches themselves became popular for the holding of weddings only in the twentieth century.[78]

Increasing population, however, meant that plots of land in the church towns were increasingly in short supply. In Old Luleå alone, by the early years of the nineteenth century, the number of church cottages had risen to 484. As a result, in 1817, P. A. Ekorn, the first governor of the new province of Norrbotten saw that a law was enacted which prohibited those living less than one Swedish mile from Luleå Church from building or acquiring church cottages there. Building permits were also now required and permanent habitation was prohibited. The old parish of Luleå was split into two new ones, Nedreluleå and Övreluleå, in 1826, the centre of which was established at Boden, to which some residents of Nedreluleå moved, taking their church cottages with them in dismantled form.[79]

By 1950, the population was more than seven times that which it had been in 1800. Övre Norrland with a total population of 66,000 in 1800, had grown to almost half a million inhabitants a century and a half later and church building reflected this trend. So it was that whereas some 21 new churches were built in the first half of the nineteenth century in Övreluleå, this number had grown to 40 in the second half of the century, and to 76 in the first half of the twentieth century, making it one of the most important areas of new church building in Scandinavia.

Provincial Church Building in Norrland

As the size of congregations grew, so the splitting of parishes into smaller entities with their own churches provided a means for central government to exert its growing influence. Already, in 1759, responsibility for formal decisions regarding even the design of provincial churches was given to the authorities in Stockholm; indeed, in 1776 they were allocated the responsibility for most of the interior fittings of the churches.[80] Such duties were taken seriously in Stockholm and 'roving ambassadors' were sent out to facilitate decisions made in the capital and to adapt them to local requirements. In 1781, for example, Norrland's Governor Lejonstedt, accompanied by Lector Nordin, later adviser to Gustaf III, both members of the Swedish Academy, and Bishop of Härnösand, spent a couple of months by royal command travelling to remote areas such as Övertorneå in the far north. There he gathered information and laid the groundwork for the building of a new outlying chapel. Frequently, however, local resistance stymied the plans of the central authorities.[81] Away from the urban areas of Norrland it was often possible for local builders to build according to their own wishes, despite the fact that different designs might be sent out from Stockholm for implementation. Thus, local builder Pål Pehrsson at Stugan was able to build a wooden church after his own Baroque designs, despite the fact that P. W.

Palmroth, at the superintendancy in Stockholm, had overruled Pehrsson's designs and provided other ones more congenial to the central authorities. Such local builders even formed their own local 'school' of architecture, straddling both sides of the Gulf of Bothnia and including much of Jämtland and Hälsingland (just to the south of Norrland), thereby providing a regional stylistic unity.[82]

While most churches in Norrland were built in a simple and local vernacular, they did, in exceptional cases, achieve considerable architectural sophistication. Perhaps the most striking example of church-building on a grand scale is the parish church at Skellefteå, by Jacob Thomasson Rijf (illus. 12). At its core it is a medieval building, but one rebuilt with a massive Doric portico, drawing upon inspiration from classical Greek monumental temples such as those at Paestum, in the south of Italy, in the public eye at the time. Rijf was a member of a local family from Österbotten who had worked for years in the building trade and was able to draw upon older Baroque examples of church architecture which he had seen in Stockholm, for example the Adolf Fredrik Church. The result is a grandiose ecclesiastical stage-set, which dominates the surrounding countryside from its majestic seat in a park-like setting by the Skellefte River. Serving the most populous parish in Sweden at that time, it could hold more than 3,000 parishioners and offered a dramatic contrast in scale to the many small red cabins which punctuated the surrounding countryside.[83] Along with the churches at Luleå and Ala-Tornio (Lower Tornio), now in Finland it also marked the first stone church building in Sweden since the Middle Ages.[84]

12 Jacob Thomasson Rijf, Skellefteå Parish Church (Sweden), designed in 1793 and completed in 1800.

A new ecclesiastical vision was now coming to the fore as more and more churches began to dot the landscape of Sweden's northern dominions. Stone, rather than wood, as demanded by government authorities in Stockholm for both practical and stylistic reasons, soon became the principal building material. Windows were enlarged in size and increased in number in order to make the churches airy and bright, the perfect metaphor for the rationally orientated Christianity which was coming into fashion throughout the Nordic world and mirrored the desires of central government to tighten the social and political fabric of the country by means of the church, perhaps the most effective of all the other institutions it dominated.

This new vision of an enlightened order corresponded strongly to the ecclesiastical one of a churchman whose creative bursts of energy were interrupted by acute and recurrent mental disorders. Esaias Tegnér (1782–1846), bishop of Växjö from 1824, was especially keen on altering churches, both old and modern, to achieve architectural forms which would best permit illumination, both divine and temporal, to permeate, thereby helping to bring a Christian order into the world. For him, by contrast, the outmoded Gothic style was the vestigial architecture of a literally darker age when superstition reigned. That Gothic forms had persisted in Swedish and Finnish architecture longer than in many other countries was a matter for lament, particularly when, as late as the 1730s and '40s, wooden churches such as Nordmaling, in Norrland, had been built with ribbed vaulting.[85]

Previously a professor of Classics at Lund University, as well as a noted poet, Tegnér also rejected many aspects of the Romantic movement in his theological works, especially mysticism. Instead, he took inspiration from Johan Winckelmann with his classical Apollonian vision, opting for an ecclesiastical architecture which would express the lucidity and august serenity of Christianity. To this end, religious iconography was to be simplified, so that the Christian message and, in particular, social virtues could reasonably be comprehended by all. Rejected were the bright coloured hellish visions, for example the *Scene from Hell* (1729) in Hakarps Church, near Huskvarna, in Småland, by the Swedish church artist Edvard Orm (1670–1735; illus. 13), which could horrify and chasten the viewer into pious submission. Such primitive visions were soon painted over in white, disdained as symbols of a more barbarous age, with images of divine love and providence now coming to the fore in their place.

The old Gothic churches, with their small windows and restricted space, held few sentimental claims for Tegnér and he used his episcopal rounds to expound on the need to build new churches, commodious and classical in architectural inspiration, with rectangular naves and tunnel vaults. Perhaps the most interesting and opulent expression of his 'enlightened' ecclesiastical vision is to be found in the provinces at Kumla Church (1829–34), in Närke, designed by the Swedish architect Axel Nyström (1793–1868), who had studied in both Paris and Rome. Inspired by classical Greek temple architecture, the nave is rectangular, with two flanking aisles separated from it by fluted Doric columns, elevated upon pedestals. Upon these columns, a rich entablature supports the barrel vault ceiling which, above the altar, merges into an apse, with a heavily embossed ceiling inspired by that in the Pantheon at Rome. Light streams into the church through its wide arched windows, where it is reflected off the white and gilt interior. Totally absent are the high wooden steeples and belfry so typical of churches built in the seventeenth and early eighteenth centuries; a royal proclamation of 1759 (in effect until 1857) had discouraged their construction, partly for fear of fires caused by the striking of lightning, partly because of the new stylistic values.

Such classical values are also reflected in Tegnér's own home, built in 1795,

13 Edvard Orm, *Scene from Hell*, early 18th century, wall painting. Hakarps Church (Sweden).

where he resided from 1827–46 (illus. 14). An imposing two-storeyed house of wood, it sports eleven window bays framed by Doric pilasters and a central pediment featuring a large lunette window, thereby achieving the well-illuminated spaciousness he wished architecture to embody. Such architectural ideals were in sharp contrast to the more traditional Lutheran rectory depicted in *Hellested Vicarage on Stevns* (1847) by the artist Christen Dalsgaard (1824–1907) in which informality and intimacy of scale are the hallmarks (illus. 15). This overgrown cottage seems as much a part of its milieu as the trees and shrubs round about it. Indeed, Dalsgaard's own life reflected the spirit of the rectory he depicted: unlike so many Scandinavian artists of the time he eschewed travels abroad, preferring to remain in his native Denmark, especially the island of Fyn where he long resided.

14 The Episcopal Residence in Östrabo by Växjö (Sweden), 1795.

15 Christen Dalsgaard, *Hellested Vicarage on Stevns*, 1847, oil on paper, mounted on canvas.

For Tegnér, however, such a cosy attachment to a rustic idyll was alien. His was an hierarchical vision which conformed to classical canons expostulated by Vitruvius in ancient Rome. Thus, the rotunda represented the highest classical architectural ideal for Tegnér, even if Scandinavian church architecture in general, especially in the provinces, had neither the financial means nor the vision to realize this form. Yet Skeppsholm Church (1824–42), in Stockholm, designed by Fredrik Blom, did most approximate Tegnér's ideals, for it is a Swedish reflection of the Pantheon, in terms of exterior and interior form with its large rotunda and decorative details, including pairs of Ionic columns supporting the circular entablature upon which the vaulted dome rests. Perhaps, it was a contemporary pedagogue, P. A. Siljeström, who best expressed such values: 'Temple buildings throughout history have been just as important in the generating of religious values as the clergy'; this was a view with which Tegnér could certainly concur.[86]

The Rise of Religious Sects in the Early Nineteenth Century

The demise of the Vasa dynasty in Sweden witnessed the demise, in many respects, of the old orthodox Lutheranism with its demons and hellish visions of the fate awaiting unrepentant sinners in artistic and literary imagery, and also saw the disappearance of rituals now considered superstitious. The formula for the exorcism of evil spirits, for example, was expurgated from the new church handbook in 1811. There was also a strengthening of that wing within the Church of Sweden which felt close affinities to the beliefs of the Moravians and other Pietists, as well as to the growing numbers of adherents of the free churches who had divorced themselves from the established church. This trend was especially strong in Norrland, where powerful evangelical lay movements had developed, usually with a strong emphasis upon temperance, not surprising in a region severely plagued by alcoholism. Indeed, the high prevalence of alcoholism especially in the whole north of the Nordic region, was to lead to the end of the private retail alcohol industry and trade, ending not in prohibition but in the assumption of control by state monopolies in both Sweden, Finland and Norway.

One of the most important of such religious and temperance movements was led by Læstadius, the missionary to the Saami and vicar from 1826 to 1846 in Karesuando (Enontekis), on the Muonio River by the Finnish–Swedish border. His was a religious vision which centred upon the forgiveness of sin, an abhorrence of alcoholic drink and a religious enthusiasm, which he called ecstasy, that seems to have a certain affinity with the trance of the Saami shamans. Sometimes, as at Kautokeino, in Norwegian Lapland, in 1852, a collective religious mania seemed to break out in emotional excesses, but usually its expression was more restrained.[87] The hut in which Læstadius lived reflected his own personal austerity, though it was sufficiently large to accommodate prayer meetings in which Biblical readings and hymns formed the focus of a spiritual life. By contrast, the movement led by Henrik Schartau (1757–1825), from Lund, in the south of the country remained firmly at home within the High Church, with all its ceremonial trappings and formal concepts of architectural and pictorial harmony. It was left to the realm of spiritual literature and Johan Olof Wallin's psalm book of 1819 to attempt to integrate these various Christian movements by drawing on the spiritual and literary strengths of both traditions.[88]

In the realm of the church visible, however, conflicts continued to develop between the High and Low Church movements. Lund University, for example, became a bastion of the High Church in sharp contrast to Uppsala University, where the Low Church movement thrived, whether in spite of or because of the presence of the archbishop. It was the latter, though, which ultimately came to dominate the Swedish church as a whole, being more accessible to a wider population and assisted by a growing deaconate and well-organized missionary movement which involved increasing numbers of lay people in church activities, a significant number of whom went on to spread the Christian message to Africa and Asia.

Methodism, an import from Great Britain, also came to play an important role, particularly in Sweden, where it gave a considerable impetus to the whole free church movement. Introduced to the country by the Scottish preacher George Scott in the 1830s, it appealed to many not only because of its evangelical zeal, but because of its strong commitment to temperance. While its later break with the established church led at first to conflict with local authorities, it had, by 1876, achieved official governmental recognition, if not warm acceptance. Scott eventually returned to Scotland, but his Swedish follower Carl Olof Rosenius (1816–68) helped to spread his own very fiery form of evangelism especially throughout Norrland, where he established the Evangelical Fatherland Foundation in which nationalist and evangelical values merged together.

More radical was the Baptist Church, also deeply evangelical and stressing the importance of adult baptism. Established in Sweden in 1848, its roots were

American, rather than British and it acquired an almost revolutionary notoriety. As a result, it soon found itself in conflict with local authorities who sought to prohibit its members from congregating. Many of its adherents, therefore, emigrated to the United States, following in the footsteps of the communist evangelicals who had left Hälsingland for Illinois in 1846, under the leadership of a fiery evangelical layman Erik Jansson.

Catholicism at first fared worse than these dissenting Protestant sects, despite the fact that King Oscar I's consort, Queen Joséphine, was herself a Catholic. Indeed, so severe was the prohibition on its practice that two native converts to Catholicism in the 1850s found themselves deported from Sweden with all their property confiscated. However, such severe constraints on religious liberty were soon to pass. In 1860, a long debated parliamentary act removed the penalties for apostasy from Lutheranism to Catholicism, enabling other non-Lutheran religious organizations also to achieve official recognition. Jews were henceforth permitted to settle anywhere in the country and to purchase land, previously prohibited to them, on an equal footing with members of the Swedish church. This growing religious liberalism, in conjunction with a worsening social and economic crisis in the Russian Empire led, as the century wore on, to an increasing influx of Jews throughout the Nordic region.

By 1870, public office was available to all regardless of religious persuasion. Thereafter, an increasing variety of free churches blossomed, as sects split and then split again. The upheavals of industrialization in Sweden were also beginning to take effect and these, in turn, made their own demands upon the multiplicity of existing churches as urban populations grew. The introduction of the Salvation Army from England, in the 1880s, especially, provided a militant and more socially conscious evangelical alternative for devout Christians with a keen awareness of the plight of those unable to fend for themselves in Scandinavia's rapidly developing cities and towns, especially Copenhagen and Stockholm.

While the burgeoning of these free church sects occurred throughout Scandinavia among all social classes, their greatest growth took place where the laying of the railways created largely lower middle class communities along the way. This was particularly true of such Swedish towns as Jönköping, in Småland, which came to be known as Little Jerusalem, because of the number of inhabitants who were members of the free churches there. In the large cities, however, the established church continued to maintain its dominant position, albeit modified by a growing emphasis on the role of the laity in religious and social matters. This was also the case in many rural areas where the established church continued to hold sway and church meetings provided important social occasions for village life. This can be seen in a jovial anecdotal work, Tithe Meeting in Scania (1865) by the Swede Bengt Nordenberg (1822–1902) (illus. 16) in which priests and villagers have gathered in a cosy inn, amidst spiritual rejoicing and social conviviality. But, meetings like this could also be sources of bitter acrimony, occasions on which members of the parish might vie with one another for local political influence or prestige and in which bitter enmities might arise.

In Norway, the growth of a free church movement in the nineteenth century was very limited by comparison with that in Sweden but what did develop was facilitated by a sharp decline in the number of Lutheran clergymen relative to the size of the Norwegian population.[89] Despite such a decline the priests continued to exert considerable social as well as spiritual control, often in an official capacity as an arm of the state. For example, anyone failing to submit themselves to religious instruction leading to confirmation was subject to a criminal conviction which could result in a prison regime of hard labour. Such legal obligations were not always empty threats; in the late 1840s, a young gypsy was convicted and imprisoned for the offence.[90]

Yet, in the growing spiritual vacuum which a lack of priests from the established church created after 1800, the evangelical revival could take firm root and blossom as the nineteenth century progressed. The Norwegian evangelist Hans Nielsen Hauge, in particular, attracted perhaps as many as 30,000 adherents, disenchanted with the rationalism of the established church and inspired by his profoundly 'enthusiastic', that is, emotionally vibrant, appeal. A meeting of his followers was dramatically depicted by the Norwegian artist August Tidemand (illus. 17). By contrast with many such movements in Sweden, this Low Church body of adherents largely remained within the established church.[91]

16 Bengt Nordenberg, *Tithe Meeting in Scania*, 1865, oil on canvas.

17 Adolph Tidemand, *The Haugianians*, 1852, oil on canvas.

In Denmark, Jews were granted religious toleration and equality as subjects in 1814, earlier than was the case anywhere else in Europe. Prosperous Jewish merchants like Mendel Levin Nathanson, for example, commissioned works of religious art (see illus. 50). Anti-Semitic riots occasionally erupted, for example in Copenhagen and the provinces in 1819. They were rapidly suppressed by the military on order of Frederik VI, but they cost the king the ironical popular sobriquet of 'King of the Jews' among those who lamented his liberal stance.

The growth of religious toleration continued and rapidly extended to many Christian religious sects. Not only were Baptists and Catholics soon tolerated, but new sects, emanating from America also made their converts, as depicted by Christen Dalsgaard (illus. 18). That the family of an artisan was chosen for the missionary focus of the Mormons is not coincidental, for it tended to be artisans who were most often won over to the new religious sect only recently imported from the United States, though their custom of polygamy was never adopted in Scandinavia.

Bertel Thorvaldsen

The early years of the nineteenth century were a period of traumatic upheaval for Denmark. Copenhagen suffered a great fire in 1807, and was then bombarded by Congreve rockets by the British, resulting in damage to many ecclesiastical buildings in the Danish capital and the destruction of the cathedral itself (illus. 19). It was out of these calamities, however, that some of the most splendid buildings of their type in northern Europe arose. The new cathedral of Copenhagen (illus. 20), The Church of Our Lady, designed by the Danish architect Christian Frederik Hansen (1756–1845) provided a splendid opportunity for an expression of the neo-classical architectural and spiritual values which had come to reign in Sweden and elsewhere throughout Europe and the Americas. Moreover, a commission for a series of individual sculptures of Christ and the twelve apostles enabled one of Europe's most famous sculptors, the Dane Bertel Thorvaldsen (1768–1844), to produce some of his most important works.

Thorvaldsen was the grandson of an Icelandic Lutheran priest whose father, Gotskalk Thorvaldsen, had been a professional woodcarver of figureheads for ships. Trained as an artist and sculptor, he went on to win the Gold Medal of the Royal Academy of Art in Copenhagen for his relief *The Apostles Peter and John Healing the Lame Man* (1793). This prize gave him the means to travel to Rome, where he

18 Christen Dalsgaard, *Two Mormons Attempt to Convert a Joiner and his Family in their Home*, 1856, oil on canvas.

(Right) **19** Jens Peter Møller, *Gråbrødre Square, Copenhagen after the Bombardment*, 1808, oil on canvas.

(Below left) **20** Christian Frederik Hansen, *Vor Frue Kirke, Copenhagen*, 1810–29.

(Below right) **21** Bertel Thorvaldsen, *Christ*, 1833, marble. Vor Frue Kirke, Copenhagen.

remained until 1838, becoming the most sought-after sculptor in residence there. He was fond of expressing figures which evince that dignity and serenity, particularly apparent in his statue of *Christ*, the most important of the thirteen free-standing sculptures made for Our Lady's Church, each of which is some three metres in height (illus. 21). At first, the figure of Christ had been intended for the Chapel Royal of Christiansborg Palace, but its Apollonian grandeur led to its placement in the cathedral above the main altar, where the sculpture became the commanding focus of the whole church, the arms of Christ outstretched in love, the eternal nature of which is underscored by the figure's static balance. With the embrace of Jesus seemingly suspended in time, Thorvaldsen was able to achieve the spiritual expression which he desired, for, as he himself exclaimed, 'Its form has to be simple, for Christ is beyond the millennia of time'.[92]

For Thorvaldsen, commissions flooded in not only from Denmark but from princely houses all across Europe. He was commissioned by Cardinal Ercole Consalvi to erect the tomb of Pope Pius VII (1824–31), the first Protestant ever to produce a monument within the Vatican. Sculpted in marble in an austere neo-classical style, *The Model for the Funeral Monument to Pope Pius VII* (1824–31) includes the figure of the late lamented pope flanked by two ladies with sorrowing countenances, symbolising wisdom and fortitude.

Caspar David Friedrich

Whereas Scandinavia had been influenced by German Pietism, Germany, in turn, was influenced by Swedenborgianism and other Swedish sects, especially in Sweden's German territories, even after they were severed from her after the Napoleonic wars. In particular, the so-called father of German Romantic Painting, Caspar David Friedrich (1774–1840), from Greifswald in Swedish Pomerania, was profoundly affected by mystical Pietist values emanating from both Germany and Sweden. Both these and the mysticism of Swedenborg find reflection in his landscape paintings evincing '[...] a heightened sensitivity to the natural world, combined with a belief in nature's correspondence to the mind; a passion for the equivocal, the indeterminate, the obscure and the faraway [...]'[93] As a devout Christian, Friedrich loathed what were for him the amoral and godless values of the French Enlightenment and felt the military onslaughts of Napoleon to be not merely an attack on the temporal wellbeing and integrity of the German-speaking world, but also an attack on Christian civilization itself. Thus, Friedrich's awesome Tetschen altar piece, *Cross in the Mountains* (1807) is rich in spiritual and temporal meanings, including references to Sweden (illus. 22). On one level its focus stresses the transfiguration of death into life by Christ's sacrifice upon the cross, but since it is dedicated to the last of the Vasa kings, Gustaf IV Adolf, it may also have been specifically conceived by Friedrich to honour the person he considered to be the Protestant hero of the North, a king who was an unrelenting defender of Protestant Christian values; indeed, it has been suggested that the rays of the sun, which beam forth from the eye of God on the frame's predella, may refer to the midnight sun and, indirectly, be emblematic of the Swedish king himself.[94]

In Friedrich's painting *Monk by the Sea* (illus. 23), the German dramatist and poet Heinrich von Kleist (1777–1811) purported to see the influence of the

22 Caspar David Friedrich (frame by K. G. Kühn after a design by Friedrich), *Tetschen Altar or Cross in the Mountains*, 1808, oil on canvas.

23 Caspar David Friedrich, *Monk by the Sea*, 1808–10, oil on canvas.

24 Caspar David Friedrich, *The Ruins of Eldena*, c. 1825, oil on canvas.

theologian Gotthard Ludwig Kosegarten (1758–1818), whose mystical approach to nature was to exert a profound influence on later Nordic culture. A pastor in Wolgast, Germany, Kosegarten expounded the view that an appreciation of the forces of nature would lead to a growing appreciation of the power of God's love, thus enabling divine providence to demonstrate itself in the beauty and goodness of the natural world. Friedrich found a great spiritual affinity with such a view and went so far as to profess that, 'The painter should not paint merely what he sees in front of him, but also what he sees within himself. If he sees nothing within, he should not paint what he sees before him [...].'[95] Many cultural figures of the 1890s, in painting as well as literature, would share this attitude and seek to translate it into the images and imagery of the Symbolist works which they produced.

It is noteworthy that Friedrich often returned to medieval themes, whether of monks or Gothic cathedrals, despite his ardent Protestantism. The ruined cathedral and monastery of Eldena, near Greifswald was one of his favourite subjects: *The Abbey in the Oak Wood* was painted in 1809–10, and later, in *The Ruins of Eldena* (c. 1825; illus. 24), this former Cistercian monastery, largely dismantled by the Swedes in 1665, is used to create a pictorial metaphor for man's own troubled spiritual condition. The Swedes used the reclaimed stones and other building material from the ruins to build both fortifications and the university buildings in Greifswald, after the Swedish territorial acquisitions in Pomerania. Whereas *The Ruins of Eldena* depicts the monastery largely reclaimed by the surrounding woods, other works on the theme, such as Ulrich von Hutten's *Grave* (1823–24; illus. 25), stress more specific historical figures: here, the Lutheran humanist of the Reformation period who glorified not only Protestant spiritual values but Germanic culture and ethnic identity. Just as for Goethe Gothic architecture expressed a unity of the parts in one eternal whole, so for Friedrich an ecclesiastical Gothic ruin, as well as the landscape into which it is set, form a pictorial unity which expresses, through metaphor, the spiritual unity of the natural and divine. This apocalyptic quality is even more overt in such works as *The Cathedral* (c. 1818). Here the natural world is eschewed in favour of an idealised mystical Gothic architectural fantasy that becomes a symbol for the transfigured Christ Himself, the theme to which Friedrich returned again and again.

25 Caspar David Friedrich, *Ulrich von Hutten's Grave,* c. 1823–4, oil on canvas.

Nationalism and Radicalism

For Friedrich, national cultural elements could be interwoven into the Christian fabric, but for some Scandinavians, particularly the Danes, nationalism itself became a primary vehicle for the expression of Protestant Christian values. While the Christian philosopher Søren Kierkegaard (1813–55) was to have an immense influence in the twentieth century on existential philosophy, with such works as *Either/Or: A Fragment of Life* (1843) and *The Concept of Dread*, it was Danish theologians like N. F. S. Grundtvig (1783–1872) who exerted a far more profound influence at the time. For him, the Rational philosophical beliefs of a Danish theologian like Henrik Nicolaj Clausen (1793–1877) were anathema. At the same time, he rejected many aspects of Romanticism as equally destructive, he felt, to the historical roots and traditions of Christianity and the sacraments. What was needed, Grundtvig believed, was a new appreciation of national cultural identity which would enable Denmark to become a new spiritual light unto the world. His three-volume work, *Christian Sermons* (1827–30) expounded these views widely, even though he was obliged to resign his active duties as a priest the year before because of his suspect radicalism, which led also to political censorship of some of his works. His *Handbook of World History* (1833–43), also in three volumes, focuses specifically upon Denmark's national cultural mission to bring a purer form of Christianity to the world. To do this, greater public access to education and literacy was required, so that Grundtvig (along with other churchmen motivated on other grounds) increasingly emphasized popular education as a means to uplift spiritually the common man, especially in the countryside which was for him the heartland of the nation. That Romantic values permeated such a view was irrelevant to Grundtvig and those who shared his democratic vision.

By 1839, Grundtvig's views increasingly came to be seen by the authorities as supportive rather than destructive of the Danish state and so, politically rehabilitated, he was given the parish of Vartov, near Copenhagen. Yet many fellow churchmen and others of cosmopolitan bent opposed his nationalistic point of view. The German-educated Rudebach, for example, in his *Christianity and Nationality* (1847) bitterly rejected Grundtvig's 'egotistical nationalist concept'.[96] He also disliked Grundtvig's preoccupation with Norse mythology and what he considered its covert heathen value system. But for Grundtvig, the sagas of the Norse gods embodied allegories relevant to modern Christian Danes, especially so since the Nordic languages, both ancient and modern, were not sullied, as Latin was, by connection to an alien world and a corrupt church. Indeed, since Danishness and Christianity were mutually reinforcing and since Denmark and the Protestant Church were in harmony, it was a necessity that Danish, rather than Latin, should become the linguistic vehicle used in Denmark for the expression of the Christian message. A national cultural identity was thus, in Grundtvig's view, a God-given blessing to be cherished and therefore one which demanded expression to the greater glory of God. Sometimes, this could lead Grundtvig to take a war-like stance when it came to the preservation of Danish honour and territorial integrity. As he wrote in June of 1848, on the verge of war with Prussia, 'We must destroy the German, showing no mercy, everywhere where we find him in Denmark, if needs be even in our mouth and in our own heart'.[97] For Grundtvig, alien national cultural values, even if deeply rooted in Denmark over the centuries, implied a failure to fulfil Denmark's messianic mission. This was a conviction which even the military debacle of 1864 would prove unable to tarnish.

The resonance of such a view is reflected in numerous paintings of the time such as *A Street in Roskilde. In the Background the Cathedral* by the Danish artist Jørgen Roed (1808–88) (illus. 26). Not the children with a sled in the foreground, but the great dynastic cathedral of Denmark, with its royal tombs, is the focus of the painting, its twin towers rising majestically into the heavens as a symbol of divine munificence. This same focus upon Denmark's glorious historical and Christian past is also evident in another work, painted almost two decades later, *Sorø Church* (1855), by Heinrich Hansen (1821–1890), the first Danish artist to specialize in architectural painting. Though a christening seems at first to be the subject of the work, the actual ceremony occupies only a tiny area of the pictorial space and seems on closer reflection to be insignificant in comparison to the fabric of the church itself. Indeed, here as in the former work, it is the great architectural monument of Denmark's Christian heritage which forms the real theme of the painting and a symbol of the country's true glory. Perhaps not surprisingly, after the conflagration which destroyed Frederiksborg Palace in 1859, Hansen's earlier studies enabled a reasonably accurate historical reconstruction of much of the palace's Renaissance interior.

26 Jørgen Roed, *A Street in Roskilde. In the Background the Cathedral*, 1836, oil on canvas.

For other Danes, such as the philosopher and aesthetician Georg Brandes, Denmark was a mere backwater of bigoted provincialism. Of Jewish extraction, Brandes rejected Christianity and what he perceived to be its constricting conventional morality. In the tradition of Voltaire and Darwin, the contempt he held for Christianity became the focus of much vituperation from both the established church and dissenting Christians. He relished this position, however, and won the admiration of numerous leading intellectuals of his day. The Norwegian playwright Henrik Ibsen (1828–1906), was impressed by his writings and claimed to have found in him a comrade in arms and exhorted him in sympathy to take up the challenge, 'You vex the Danes, and I'll vex the Norwegians!'[98] This he continued to do, deriving enormous inspiration from the works of Friedrich Nietzsche (1844–1900), especially in his work *Aristocratic Radicalism* (1889), which expounds the vocation of the genial intellectual to lead society out of the morass of mediocrity and

27 Harald Slott-Møller, *Georg Brandes at the University of Copenhagen*, 1889, oil on canvas.

complacency into which it has sunk. To do so, Brandes cast himself in the role of an anti-hero, misunderstood by society, assuming a role at once messianic and sacrificial, as evinced in a portrait by the Danish painter Harald Slott-Møller (illus. 27). In this image of Brandes as a firebrand, one can sense both his rhetorical gifts and charismatic personality, characteristics which were employed repeatedly in contrasting the rich intellectual ferment of German culture with the perceived drab banality of the Scandinavian. For, Brandes felt, in contrast to Denmark and indeed the rest of the Nordic region, Germany had not only a richer intellectual culture which produced geniuses likes Nietzsche, but it was also less xenophobic and parochial. After all, he himself had been offered an academic position in Berlin, after his own application for a professorial chair at the University of Copenhagen had been rejected. Yet, Brandes was given the lectern at Copenhagen to expound his views and this he did with great vigour, declaiming that the energies released by nineteenth-century optimism were accelerating in a sterile direction. What was needed, he felt, was a new movement of agitation, or 'Tendens', as it came to be called, which agitated socially to right society's flaws and to shift social values towards an awareness of the need for change through the arousal of social indignation. Those who opposed this growing social consciousness, he felt, were impediments to the true advancement of humanity. As he wrote in 1890, 'What one [...] has condemned as Tendens, is nothing else than the century's spirit, its ideas [...] That which one calls progress is a sick snail'.[99]

Despite such vehement polemic, however, it is less through his own speeches and writings, than through those of such brilliant Danish authors as Jens Peter Jacobsen (1847–1885), that many of his ideas reached a wider literary public.

A leading exponent of naturalism in literature, Jacobsen's atheism, even in the face of death, and rejection of conventional morality, masked a naked yearning for religious values and a deeply moral ethical system. Through such novels as *Niels Lyhne* (1880) and *Maria Grubbe* (1876), Jacobsen was to influence not only several generations of Danes, but generations of Germans as well. His lyrical prose, rich in visual imagery, captures, despite its undercurrent of atheism, a positive spiritual mood which inspired countless readers, disgruntled with the humdrum world of social conventionality in which they found themselves. Yet, as the character of Gerda, wife of Niels Lyhne, lies dying, Jacobsen expounds deeply felt spiritual hopes in strikingly religious terms, for in his mind's eye '[...] the Jordan gleamed like the clearest silver in the morning mist; Jerusalem stood red and sombre under the setting sun; but over Bethlehem there was always glorious night with great stars in the deep blue vault'.[100] With such a melange of elements full of both optimistic mysticism and pessimistic scepticism, it is not surprising that Jacobsen's writings struck profound chords in the enigmatic German poet Rainer Maria Rilke (1875–1926), and reflections of his values can be found throughout Rilke's works, albeit tempered by an infusion of mystical elements derived from Russian Orthodoxy.

Biblical Themes in Late Nineteenth Century and Early Twentieth Century Nordic Art

Despite vociferous and strident atheistic, agnostic and anti-Christian sentiments amongst members of the Danish intelligentsia, most Danes, including artists, continued to adhere to the Lutheran tradition. With the growth of evangelical tendencies within the church and the continued flourishing of Grundtvig's spiritual tradition, Biblical themes continued in vogue as the subject of commissions for religious art providing lucrative work for those artists able to receive commis-

28 Joakim Frederik Skovgaard, *The Angel who Touches the Water in the Pool of Bethesda*, 1888, oil on canvas.

sions in an increasingly competitive market. The Danish painter Joakim Skovgaard (1856–1933) devoted himself to a broad range of Biblical subjects from both the Old and New Testaments. One of his earliest religious works, *The Angel who Touches the Water in the Pool of Bethesda* (illus. 28), is based upon studies he made of a loggia by the Baths of Caracalla, in Rome. In *Christ Leading the Thief into Paradise* (1890), another Biblical theme provides the focus.

(Above left) **29** Niels Larsen Stevns, *The Blind Man by the Road Calls after Christ*, 1910, watercolour.

(Above right) **30** Karl Isaksson, *Jesus Raising Lazarus from the Dead*, 1920–21, oil on canvas.

In the Biblical works of Niels Larsen Stevns (1864–1941) a different sort of spiritual confrontation comes to the fore, one in which the blessings of the spirit offer a heavenly consolation that the world cannot provide, depicted in *The Blind Man by the Road Calls after Christ* (1910; illus. 29). Other artists such as the Swede Karl Isaksson (1878–1922) sought to give their Biblical works a modern social and political context. His *Jesus Raising Lazarus from the Dead* (1920–21; illus. 30) is full of positive symbolic overtones about the situation in Europe after the end of the First World War. Other works, such as *Golgotha* by the Norwegian Ludwig Karsten (1876–1926), however, are less optimistic about a temporal future, in which mankind appeared still unable to make the most of the blessings God gave him and evil seemed to triumph.

The Church in the Nordic Countries during the Early Twentieth Century

While the Nordic churches did not experience a religious revival at the beginning of the twentieth century, the growth of cities, their suburbs and provincial towns necessitated the building of new churches. In the important Swedish mining town of Kiruna, in Norrland, Gustaf Wickman designed the parish church (illus. 31, 32), consecrated in 1912, which together with its belfry (built five years before) forms a masterpiece of National Romantic architecture. Such belfries as those which inspired that at Kiruna had long stirred the imaginations of many romantics. Indeed, as far back as the 1840s, Adolf Törneros, Professor of Latin at Uppsala University and a great aesthetician, had written during a journey in Södermanland, 'In all of European architecture one can hardly find such an extravagant orientalism, a so pagoda-like and mysterious physiognomy, as in our belfries'.[101] With their exotic and picturesque forms adding an alluring note to an otherwise humble rural scene, their revival became a frequent occurrence during this period not only in Sweden but throughout the Nordic region.

In remoter reaches of Lapland, a minor boom in church-building also occurred to cater for the ever-increasing growth in population. Churches in many places in Lapland had existed since the Middle Ages, but most of these were now either rebuilt or moved to locations more suitable for modern needs. Some, in fact, were rebuilt repeatedly, in response to rapid changes in local needs, tastes and resources. For example, the old village of Arvidsjaur had had five churches

(Top) **31** Gustav Wickman, *Kiruna Parish Church* (Sweden).

(Above) **32** Prince Eugen, *Altarpiece for Kiruna Parish Church.*

built since the seventeenth century, each one replacing a former, less suitable structure.[102] The neo-classical church at Risbäck, in the south-west of Lapland, was built in 1858 to cater for people who had formerly been provided only with a chapel, which had been built to provide a local alternative to the parish church at the town of Dorotea (renamed after the Swedish queen). Dorotea church itself had been built in the early nineteenth century to serve those previously attached to the church of Åsele. Its parishioners, in turn, had belonged to the church of Anundsjö, before its erection. Thus, a succession of new churches had been created to cater for the needs of the local population, expanding further and further westwards and northwards.[103]

The growth of rail and other transport links also meant the development of new towns situated in salubrious locations, with easy access to important cities throughout Sweden, and these needed their own churches. A leading example of this type, the prosperous coastal town of Saltsjöbaden, with its smart villas within easy access of Stockholm, had been established in the mid-nineteenth century by Knut Wallenberg, scion one of Sweden's richest families. After the turn of the twentieth century he had a new church constructed (illus. 33) according to the designs of Ferdinand Boberg (1860–1946), architect of Stockholm's Thielska Gallery, who had been inspired by William Morris's Arts and Crafts movement here as in many of his other buildings. Consecrated in 1913 by Nathan Söderblom, who was to become Archbishop of Uppsala the following year, the church also looked back to Byzantine ecclesiastical architecture with its rounded arches and opulent Venetian mosaics, unusual in a Nordic church.

For Söderblom, such an eclectic architectural *mélange* best expressed Christ's Epiphany throughout the history of mankind and was a central feature of Christianity, one which ecclesiastic architecture had an obligation to express, a characteristic apparent even in the funerary chapel adjacent to the altar which was intended for Wallenberg and his wife. The mural painter Filip Månsson (1864–1933) and the sculptor Carl Milles (1875–1955) further embellished it with a marble altar, granite baptismal font and bronze doors, giving much of the decoration art nouveau lines and forms which were a stylistic feature in so many European buildings of the period. The use of native granite for columns and other architectural features gives the building an unquestionable Swedish air, and the subjects of the murals, including scenes from the life of Gustaf II Adolf, and other decorative features merge the religious and the national together into a harmonious whole. Thus, as a physical entity, the Church of the Epiphany reflects the eclecticism which symbolized the increasing breadth of vision of the Church of Sweden at the time, evincing as it did under Söderblom a greater ecumenical openness than ever before, as well as a greater toleration of diversity, both spiritual and architectural, within the church itself. To a certain degree, the theological basis for these changes can be found in the writings of such German Protestant theologians as Karl Holl and Karl Schwarzlose, from about 1890 and into the 1920s. As a result, icons and other eastern religious imagery also became more fashionable and an interest in Russian Orthodoxy grew.[104] This was further strengthened by a renewed interest in symbolism and mysticism throughout the arts in the 1890s, which sometimes sought its roots in the mysticism of the Russian Orthodox tradition. This more open focus was to culminate in 1925 in a great ecumenical congregation of churchmen in Stockholm, in which the common elements of most of the different Christian traditions was stressed. It also set the tone for greater harmony among the various Christian churches, though not, it must be stressed, with the Roman Catholic Church, an institution of which Söderblom remained profoundly wary and unsympathetic.

While this tendency led to a mild decentralization in the Lutheran church, its effects were much stronger upon the free churches which increasingly came to splinter. Many Baptists, for example left their newly established church in order to build another sect, the Örebro Mission Society in 1892. Then, in 1913, the extremely evangelical Pentecostal (Whitsunday) movement was imported from the United States, and shortly thereafter the Baptist congregation of Filadelfia, in Stockholm, joined its fold. Laying claim to speaking in tongues and other ecstatic forms of worship, the Pentecostal movement attracted tens of thousands of mainly urban members, who found its strong sense of community of great appeal. Despite defections, however, there were still over 68,000 adherents to the Baptist Church in 1938; rather, it was the established church which provided the greatest source of members for the new free church sects.[105]

In Denmark, a similar burgeoning of important new church building occurred in the first decades of the new century, benefiting both the established and free churches. Of these perhaps the most architecturally innovative is the Grundtvig Church, by the Danish architect Peder Vilhelm Jensen-Klint (1853–1930; illus. 34), in which elements of the late Gothic merge with a modern architectural fantasy. It was situated in Bispebjerg, a hill in a suburb of Copenhagen with relatively few parishioners, but its construction was more of a national monument to Grundtvig the Danish patriot, hymn writer

33 Ferdinand Boberg, Church of the Epiphany, Saltsjöbaden near Stockholm, 1913.

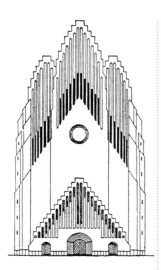

34 Peder Vilhelm Jensen-Klint, *Grundtvig Church* (Copenhagen, 1921–40), drawn elevation.

and founder of the Danish People's High Schools, than to Grundtvig the theologian. His son, the architect Kaare Klint (1888–1954), completed the church after his father's death and it was consecrated in 1940.

In Iceland a new wave of ecumenicism was accompanied by a minor boom in church building for both the established and other churches. The Lutheran church had, as we have seen, dominated all aspects of religious life since the Reformation, but, after the Constitution of 1874, complete freedom of religion was granted and Catholicism began to make inroads in Iceland in the early twentieth century. Yet, even before this date, the role of the Lutheran church seemed to be more social than religious, at least according to some visitors from abroad who commented that only women parishioners appeared to make up the congregations, attending church largely in order to exchange gossip and see friends. Bearing in mind that every village, including small hamlets, possessed its own church, its social importance is not surprising, even if from an architectural point of view these churches tended to be quite humble affairs mainly constructed of turf. However, from the middle of the nineteenth century, imported wood came to replace turf as a primary building material, though the layout of the churches followed traditional lines well into the twentieth century, with only the insertion of side windows tending to provide a modern innovation. Then, by the end of the century, both turf and wood came to be abandoned in favour of modern building materials, usually imported. Artistic embellishments within were also imported, well into the twentieth century. Whereas in the older churches a painting or sculpture based upon a Biblical theme was frequently placed above the altar, it was the funeral epitaphs of ecclesiastic figures and their families which customarily decorated the walls of some of the more prosperous churches, much as they did in Denmark since the end of the Reformation.

In rural areas, small country churches were often indistinguishable from village houses in their form and layout, except for the small white belfry which by custom perched upon the roof of the western end of the building. In the later nineteenth century, however, the dimensions of the new churches increased, often modelled on the cathedral church at Reykjavik with its western towers, crowned by spires.

More radical innovations were to await the twentieth century, when such architects as Guðjón Samúelsson (1887–1950), a deeply committed Christian, devoted much energy to developing ecclesiastical architecture which took heed of the requirements and benefits of modern building materials such as concrete. This he employed in the construction of the churches of Húsavík (1908) and Stóri-Núpur (1909), two leading examples of church building in Iceland of the period. These contrast with the church he built some 30 years later at Akureyri which drew upon an eclectic combination of architectural styles, including classical, traditional Romanesque-inspired Icelandic and Functionalism.

In the Faeroe Islands, churches had for centuries dotted the landscape both urban and rural, even if the priests themselves were few and far between; there were only six in the Faeroes altogether at the turn of the century, three of whom were Danes and the remainder natives.[106] This had meant that most church services were led on Sunday by laymen, rather than priests, and what candidates for the priesthood there were had to travel abroad for their education, either to theological schools in neighbouring Iceland or to Denmark, where the theological school of the University of Copenhagen offered them free tuition. None the less, the role of these churches should not be underestimated, spiritually or secularly. Not only might they serve as meeting halls, but, until late in the century, travellers were sometimes accommodated for the night in them, a usage which persisted well into the twentieth century, and they were frequently used for storage purposes during the week.[107]

In Greenland, elements of Inuit religious belief continued to live alongside Christian ones. Central to this belief was animism; not only people, but all living beings and inanimate objects had their own spiritual essence which could mutually influence one another. A form of reincarnation also played a role in which, in particular, the sacrificial slaughter of animals could be used to encourage living animals to thrive. Meditation between the spirits and people was effected by shamans using incantations and the aid of amulets. Especially important was their role in influencing the female spirit of game and the elimination of disease. A water-colour by the native Greenlander Aron (surname unknown), a kyak hunter who painted in his spare time, was commissioned by Hinrich Rink and is one of a series of four on such themes. It depicts the spirit of the waters clad in a coat of scales with an edging of fur in a benevolent role of encouraging the Inuit fisherman in his kyak towards waters rich in fish. Such an activity was, of course, no mere sport or economic livelihood for the fishermen, whose very lives, along with those of their families, depended on a successful catch for their actual survival.[108] In bad seasons, many Greenlanders starved to death.

The second half of the nineteenth century was a period of growing prosperity, albeit modest, and a minor boom in the construction of churches and chapels occurred which reflected the improved circumstances. For example, a stone church was built at Maniitsoq (Sukkertoppen) between 1860 and 1864 and, in 1869, another church was built at Napassoq, though it had to be reconstructed after a fire in 1896. Provided with three semi-circular arched windows and stairs leading to a wooden gabled area between the slopes of the roof, it resembled the old forge at Julianehåb, built in 1871. Yet this stone church building era, limited as it was, was soon to cease and the little chapel of stone at Atammik in the Sukkertoppen District, built in 1915–16, was the last of its type.[109] Only later in the century would church architecture revive, but then using very different building materials and then in pursuit of a more functionalist architectural vision. In this aspect, it was following general trends in Denmark and, indeed, the rest of Scandinavia, where church building followed in the wake of the growth of new housing developments and suburbs, one in which churches were seen as social amenities, like cinemas and recreational centres.

The Family and Sexuality

The Family Home in Early Modern Scandinavia

Since the beginning of the early modern period the family has remained the central unit of social life in the Nordic region. In the sixteenth and seventeenth centuries it was the principal means by which numerous aspects of life were defined, not only for grand families, for whom the maintenance of political and economic power was a primary familial consideration, but also for humble households, held together by the practical necessities of daily life. The Swedish travel diary of a sixteenth-century German merchant, Samuel Kiechel, a native of Ulm, gives some of the earliest reliable insights into the texture and tone of family life amongst simple peasants in Sweden in the early modern period. Travelling through Scania, north to Stockholm and Uppsala and thence back to Germany through Blekinge during the winter and spring of 1586, he enjoyed the modest hospitality of such families and recorded his impressions of how they lived.

Kiechel relates how farmers and their families, servants and others generally resided in one room, along with a wide range of small domestic animals. As a guest, he was frequently given an honoured place for sleeping, either upon the long trestle table where meals were served, or sometimes upon the floor. Heating, he notes, was provided by a grey stone oven situated beneath an opening in the roof through which the smoke could escape and around which entertainment was provided by his hosts. This frequently took the form of belching (or worse), for not only the noise but also the smell was held by his rustic hosts to be highly amusing, though Kiechel himself failed to appreciate it. Indeed, even without this, the odour in the cabins could be unsettling, he reports, for those accustomed to greater personal space and hygiene than the densely packed presence of people and domestic animals could offer, though it must be added that such close physical intimacy was not ubiquitous.[1]

For most simple farming people these living arrangements hardly altered over the centuries. Long after the fall of the Vasa dynasty in the early nineteenth century, small farmers, with their families and animals, could still be found living together in one room throughout the Nordic region, as depicted in *The Interior of a Farmer's Cabin from Småland* (1801) by the Swede Pehr Hörberg (1746–1816; illus. 35). Such close living quarters might seem puzzling in a country with vast tracts of land, but the need to conserve warmth in the bitterly cold winters was paramount and the materials for building and furnishing were not cheap.

35 Pehr Hörberg, *The Interior of a Farmer's Cabin from Småland*, 1801.

In prosperous northern Karelia and Savolax in the south-east of Finland, however, a rather different set of living arrangements developed. There the extended rather than the nuclear family dominated from at least the sixteenth century. Several families, and others, lived communally during the winter-time in relatively large cabins, where they were allocated different corners to which single people attached themselves. During the summer, these families would retire to their own individual huts (as did many of those newly married even during the winter).[2] Most such familial groups would be composed not only of parents and siblings, but of sons-in-law and others, unrelated to each other by blood, but on the footing of a partner in the economic production of the household. They were very important to those families with few members, providing much needed labour and other forms of assistance. This was especially true among the Saami people of Lapland, where the bridegroom was expected to live with and provide labour for his parents-in-law, as a dowry-service.[3] Since servants were difficult to come by in this land-rich but relatively underpopulated region, such extended families could achieve considerable prosperity by clearing more land and bringing it under the plough. By contrast with the relatively static population in the west of Finland and in most of Sweden and Denmark, where families were linked to the same bit of land from generation to generation, the considerable geographic mobility of Karelian and Savolax families enabled them to take continuous advantage of fresh lands, which then came into cultivation and supported new homesteads.[4]

The actual architectural form and layout of such cottages varied throughout the region. In the province of Setesdal in Norway, for example, at least four different types of cottage had prevailed since the sixteenth century. The cottage with one single room and either a porch or two very small rooms, with a central open hearth was perhaps the most common, continuing an ancient medieval building tradition, as shown in *Room with an Open Hearth at the Sogneskar Farm in Valle* (1848) by the Norwegian artist Adolph Tidemand (1814–1876; illus. 36).

Around Akershus the arrangement was different, for here a fireplace tended to be placed in one corner.[5] In the Trøndelag region, multiple rooms came to prevail with fireplaces in the corners of the two large principal ones. In these last two arrangements the new innovation of the fireplace, introduced from the Continent at the end of the sixteenth century, gradually led to the abandonment of the old ventilation openings and encouraged the use of windows to provide outside lighting. However, the use of a central open hearth fire in cottages, with the smoke expelled through a central opening in the roof, persisted well into the twentieth century in most Nordic countries. In one hovel, in the parish of Vilhelmina in the north of Sweden, for example, a fireplace with a chimney, replacing a hole in the roof, was first constructed as late as 1908, an improvement made possible only because the parish poor fund contributed to its installation.[6]

In Norway, Sweden and Finland, cottage walls were generally constructed of logs, carefully hewn according to the varying fashions of time and locality, but almost always provided with roofs of turf. Only towards the late eighteenth

36 Adolph Tidemand, *Room with an Open Hearth at the Sogneskar Farm in Valle*, 1848, oil on paper pasted on canvas.

century were some painted, a tradition which became commonplace in the nineteenth century as pigments, usually Falun red, a by-product of copper production in Dalecarlia, became reasonably affordable. In Norway, an external gallery was often constructed along the front of the cottage. In the provinces of Setesdal and Telemark this might extend around the whole building, but this was less often the case elsewhere. One particularly intimate view of the principal room is depicted in *Cabin from Kveste in Setesdalen* (1866) by the Norwegian artist Olaf Isaachsen (1835–1893).

By the middle of the nineteenth century, growing prosperity meant that houses such as those Isaachsen depicted often had several floors. Their lofts have become the hallmarks of much traditional Norwegian domestic architecture, with their richly carved timber decorations based upon both traditional and fashionable contemporary designs of the period. Such richness of decoration was not common elsewhere in the vernacular architecture of the Nordic region, except in Karelia. Unlike earlier lofts, the new ones were usually erected on piles rather than stone foundations, in order to hinder rising damp and the infestation of vermin which often plagued such wooden dwellings.[7]

In Denmark, by contrast, houses were usually half-timbered with thatched roofs, but generally more stylishly furnished than those in Norway. Typical of these is the interior depicted by the Danish artist Peter Christian Skovgaard

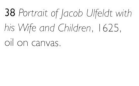

37 *Bjørn Frøysok with his Family,*
1699.

38 *Portrait of Jacob Ulfeldt with*
his Wife and Children, 1625,
oil on canvas.

(1817–1875) in *Cottage in Vejby* (1843). Here he, his parents and siblings are portrayed dining together in their fashionably furnished family home, a small and charming, if cluttered residence, filled with the latest amenities,.

Among the more prosperous segments of the population, images of family life reflected the authoritarian hierarchical focus of society itself. One Norwegian work depicts a farmer from Halling in mammoth format, his figure jutting out from the pictorial space in the centre of the painting (illus. 37). He dominates physically and symbolically his two wives and numerous children, much as prosperous middle class families were coming increasingly to dominate Norwegian society in general at the time. While the image is hieratic and follows the pictorial conventions of the time, the pride felt by the farmer is unmistakable. Indeed, Bjørn Frøysok commissioned the work as a prestigious pictorial epitaph of his family, both living and dead, in the stave church at Gol, in the south-east of Norway.

The *Portrait of Jacob Ulfeldt with his Wife and Children* (1625) conveys how a grand family wished to be depicted (illus. 38). Ulfeldt, ambassador to Holland at the time the portrait was painted, is shown with his high hat, a symbol of authority, seated with his family at a table in a splendid Renaissance Italianate loggia, itself indicative of his great wealth and prestige. In the true fashion of a Lutheran pater familias, his wife and children surround him, like the Apostles surround Jesus in a contemporary painting of the Last Supper, a man to whom his wife and children are subordinated, by virtue of the moral, social and economic order of the times.

Such authoritarian images of the family were gradually to be superseded by a

more tempered vision of family life in which both wives and children were given a more prominent place. Another Danish portrait, painted only a few decades later, by the Netherlandish artist Karel van Mander III (c. 1609–1670) seems to express a more modern image of family roles (illus. 39). No longer is the father, a prominent wine merchant, presented as the central focus of the family in pictorial terms, but instead he is placed to one side. Rather it is his little child, supported by her mother, who is now the focus of the picture. There is a more intimate, relaxed quality about the figures, two of whom are holding wine glasses, which seems to hint at the more urbane values which reigned in sophisticated Danish bourgeois circles in the seventeenth century, by contrast to those in Norway.

39 Karel van Mander III, *Knud Gamborg and his Family*, 1660s, oil on canvas.

Attitudes towards Children

In the Nordic region, as in Europe in general, children were perceived not so much as innocent and sentimental objects of affection, but as diminutive men and women (and as corrupted by original sin as adults). While it was recognized that appropriate training, moral and physical, was necessary to mould them into wise and industrious adults (if they succeeded in attaining maturity), in these times of high infant mortality, they were neither protected nor insulated from harsh adult realities, as would become the case in the nineteenth century. Few vernacular images of children remain from the sixteenth and seventeenth centuries, but one, of a little Swedish girl, *The Portrait of Sigrid Bielke at the Age of Two*, commissioned by a noble family, depicts her in much the same way that her mother or grandmother might have been depicted, underscoring through her dress, milieu and poise, her social status, further highlighted by the rich Turkey carpet beneath her feet, the elaborately bordered apron she wears and the familial coat-of-arms prominently displayed to her left. It is an unsentimental portrayal of a little girl, in static, even hieratic pose, a miniature version of an austere but elegant Lutheran lady, holding a key, possibly symbolizing the household responsibility which in matronly adulthood awaits her.

This emphasis on social roles and status, has an added political dimension in a portrait of 1615 of the Danish king Christian IV's son, the future Frederik III by the Netherlandish painter Pieter Isaacsz. (1569–1625; illus. 40). Here, the small child, strutting in the park of Frederiksborg Castle, which can be seen in the background (it is, in fact, the first landscape portrait ever painted in Denmark), is depicted, with dress sword at his side and holding an enormous rifle, a somewhat ludicrous and even alarming sight for the modern viewer, which is reinforced by the severity of his facial expression. These works emphasized the fact

(Opposite) **40** Pieter Isaacsz.,
Frederik III as a Little Boy, 1615,
oil on canvas.

(Left) **41** Christen Dalsgaard,
*The Stone Corridor at Sorø
Academy*, 1871, oil on canvas.

that, in the seventeenth century, it was social position, even with respect to children, rather than age, maturity or other qualities, that commanded outward respect and obedience from social inferiors.

This so uncompromisingly adult image of childhood is evident in works by the Netherlander Jacob van Doort (died 1629) who was active in Denmark during the early part of the reign of King Christian IV. His group portrait, *Kirsten Munk and her Children* (c. 1623) shows the king's consort (the validity of their marriage was highly controversial), with her three daughters and one son, aged between one and five, comporting themselves as little adults. Such a work had deep political overtones, for it stressed the relationship of Kirsten Munk as mother of the king's children (a relationship he would come to regret when she was later convicted of adultery and condemned to a life-long imprisonment). Their son, portrayed in *Count Valdemar Christian* (early 1630s) by the German artist Reinhold Thim (died 1639), is shown at the age of eleven, while a pupil at the Sorø Academy, where many young Danish cavaliers were sent. He is depicted richly attired with a dress sword by his side and his eyes stare boldly at the viewer. The characteristics of childhood are rejected in favour of his political role, much as his father was portrayed in numerous portraits by van Doort and others.

A radical contrast to this is provided by the nineteenth-century portrait of another boy at Sorø by the Danish artist Christen Dalsgaard (1824–1907; illus. 41), painted when the artist was drawing master there. In the earlier painting by Thim,

42 Johan Frederik Vermehren, *Domestic Chores in a Poor Farmer's Cottage*, 1859, oil on canvas.

the boy has been elevated to a commanding role, but in Dalsgaard's work the boy has an inferior position within the dominating architectural framework, meekly greeting his schoolmaster. Here the message is clear: in the nineteenth century, age and knowledge demand deference, more than wealth or social background.

Of course, a hierarchical social structure still reigned at this time in Denmark, albeit in a varied and weakened form from that of the seventeenth century. A genre painting by Johan Frederik Vermehren (1823–1910) illustrates the persistent presence of poverty and social dependency among large segments of society. His *Domestic Chores in a Poor Farmer's Cottage* (1859) underscores the hardships of life for a mother and daughter in the village of Vindstrup, near to Sorø, eking out their meagre existences while living in grinding poverty in the wretched hovel we see before us (illus. 42). For unfortunates such as these, life changed little between the seventeenth and nineteenth centuries, but for those of the upper classes life had become a very different matter indeed. Already by the late eighteenth century, the uncompromising images of children as small adults in the upper and middle classes of the Nordic region were largely gone, replaced by a new sentimental attitude, one in which neither political power, status nor moral obligations played much of a role.

A portrait by the Swedish artist Per Krafft the Elder (1724–1793) of his two sons (illus. 43) presents the viewer with an intimate and informal portrayal. They are lovingly shown, full of youthful curiosity and tender affection, forming a visual expression of Jean-Jacques Rousseau's image of children still in their virtuous state of innocence, unsullied by corrupting adult influences. Such works evoked great delight amongst many artistic patrons of the time, and Krafft became known as the leading specialist in portraits of children in Sweden at that time. He expressed the new vision of children not as a primary means of asserting a family's social and economic identity, but symbols of domestic order, harmony and contentment.

43 Per Krafft the Elder, *The Artist's Children*, 1783.

Childhood Mortality and the Sentimentalizing of the Family

In order to begin to understand these changes in attitude towards children it is necessary to consider the role of changes in child mortality rates. The proportion of children who died before they reached maturity was fairly constant throughout the early modern period, but began to fall, as it did everywhere in Europe except Iceland during the course of the eighteenth century.[8]

The reality was that hygiene and post-natal care, which had previously been rudimentary in the extreme, began dramatically to improve. No longer would a tragedy occur such as that at Volda, in the west of Norway, where 30 children had died in mid-winter because their parents had insisted on bringing them to church, despite the severe cold, on the day on their birth.[9] With the decline in infant mortality in the whole Nordic region (in conjunction with a relatively stable and high birth rate throughout the nineteenth century), it is interesting to note that child mortality itself, as a subject for pictorial representation, became popular. The Swedish artist Amalia Lindegren (1814–1891) used it as the theme of her sentimental work *The Little One's Last Resting Place* (c. 1860), in which members of the family grieve over the body of the dead child, lying in her cradle, in their snug and cosily appointed cottage. With the child's numerous playthings lying scattered about, the impression is given of a milieu in which love and care have reigned. Of course, childhood mortality had not been eliminated and tragic deaths of children continued to occur, but they were more isolated events which could be used to pull families together, happy in the consolation that most children would now survive.

Another painting, arguably more poignant by virtue of its greater emotional restraint, is *A Child's Funeral Procession* (1879) by the Swedish-Finn Albert Edelfelt (1854–1905). Here the coffin of a young girl, accompanied by her family who are plunged into sombre contemplation of the event, makes its final journey across the fjord at Haikko, near Porvoo (Borgo) in the south of Finland. While its realism is married to an impressionistic painterly style which camouflages the carefully considered composition, thereby successfully arresting a moment of profound family grief, it conjoins it with an image of Finnish nature which seems itself to provide a supra-familial identity. It is as if the grieving family is but a part of the national family and the dead child is borne on the boat, like a dead hero carried back from the war. For child mortality was no longer the deadly reaper it had once been; it was now more a vehicle, at least in artistic terms, for the expression of other societal values.

The Happy Family

Despite such exceptions, Nordic family life was in its most literal sense becoming healthier and more thriving. And, concomitant with this, a growing sentimentality towards the joys of family life and domesticity makes itself obvious in much family portraiture of the second quarter of the nineteenth century. A work by the Dane Wilhelm Marstrand (1810–1873), illustrates this new approach (illus. 44). It is the five playful children, rather than their mother, or absent father, who form the focus of the painting. The message of this work is clear: children belong to a radically different world from adults; their very existence is a source of charm and exaltation.

Such a painting as this may be saccharine, but on other occasions Marstrand could allow himself a bit of irony with respect to depictions of family life and, indeed, marital relations. His anecdotal painting, *A Friend of the House* (1836), for

44 Wilhelm Marstrand, *Portrait of the Waagepetersen Family*, 1836, oil on canvas.

example, melodramatically depicts a woman, cowering, albeit smilingly, behind her lover, who attempts to evict the husband from their presence (illus. 45). Above a corner cupboard in the rather elegant room hovers a statue of Eros, a symbol of the wily and unexpected courses the madness of love can take. For love and familial considerations were two very different matters. Family life even up to the middle of the nineteenth century and beyond was frequently dominated by material and other practical considerations. This was true not only in attitudes towards children but also in the choice of marriage partners, especially among the aristocracy where practical considerations were paramount, and love of secondary value if considered at all.[10] Yet even in these grand families by the early nineteenth century, a more sentimental attitude to children was already creeping in. This is reflected in the portraiture of the time, even in such a regal work as *Crown Princess Josefina holding Prince*

Karl, later to become Karl XV (1826) by the Swedish Court painter by Fredrik Westin (1782–1862; illus. 46). The child, with an angelic smile upon its face, gazes at a miniature of his grandfather and founder of the House of Bernadotte, Karl XIV Johan, whilst his mother looks tenderly upon him, a portrait of her husband King Oskar smiling gently down from behind. Based upon the figures of a Renaissance Madonna and Child, this royal portrait has in fact been given the loving associations of the Sacred Family, quite unlike either the more socially representative or naturalistic works of the previous century.

While many early nineteenth-century family portraits focused upon the well-ordered children of prosperous middle-class industrialists and their wives, Bengt Nordenberg (1822–1920), in Sweden, depicted *The Children of Tobacco Merchant Erik Nordqvist* (early nineteenth century) in a spartan, albeit elegant milieu devoid of luxury or superfluous decoration. It is as though the atmosphere of the portrait was intended to reflect the austerity in which these six children were raised.

Much lower down the social scale, too, children were sentimentalized in a new way. The artist Killian Zoll (1818–1860), from Scania, for example, depicted his own *Two Children* (1848) lovingly embracing each other in the lea of a forest, beyond which a quaint cottage can be glimpsed. Like the babes in the wood of the fairy tale, their hands like angels's wings hover rather than rest upon the small branches lying on the ground.

Towards the end of the century, however, a somewhat different ideal image of the family came to prevail. Carl Larsson (1853–1919), perhaps more than any other Nordic artist, succeeded in capturing the joys of domestic life which few had enjoyed (not even the Larsson family) but to which all could aspire. Born

45 Wilhelm Marstrand, *A Friend of the House*, 1836, oil.

46 Fredrik Westin, *Crown Princess Josefina holding Prince Karl, later to become Karl XV*, 1826.

into poverty in Gamla Stan, in Stockholm, his own mother had been a washer-woman, while his father carted timber for a living, hardly the ideal middle-class parents. Despite having been originally enrolled at a school for children of the poor, his artistic talents, along with his appealing familial themes, made him one of Sweden's most successful artists of the period.

At the Royal Academy in Stockholm, where Larsson was a student, he met his future wife and fellow student Karin, who by contrast came from a prosperous mercantile family. A tumultuous marriage followed in which the Larssons produced eight children who, in the setting of the various homes the family occupied at different times, were the subject of many of Larsson's paintings.

The family house at Sundborn, in Dalecarlia, became the symbol of what almost every middle-class Swede envisioned as the perfect hearth and home. A picturesque eclectic concatenation of multi-coloured wings joined to a typical Swedish cottage painted in Falun red, incorporating neo-classical elements derived from the Gustavian period of the late eighteenth century. This can be seen in *A Home: The Kitchen* (before 1900), in which two of the artist's children are depicted in their cosy kitchen, warmed by a comforting stove, as a gentle breeze blows in through the open window (see illus. 53). Largely painted in the various hues of reds and greens so popular in Dalecarlia, but also in cheerful and spring-like yellows and whites, Sundborn became an icon of Swedish domestic bliss which has persisted to this day.

Yet many elements particularly of the interior decoration derived from Japanese works of art which Larsson had acquired in Paris. Indeed, the use of these Japanese elements married to the influence of John Ruskin's artistic theories and William Morris's Arts and Crafts Movement, as filtered through the Swedish magazine *Studio*, was quite deliberate on Larsson's part. Through this he was able to embody Swedish middle-class ideals of family life in a fresh way. There was even an element of missionary zeal in these images of the wholesome family, which increasingly found its way into all segments of society. Such images served to inspire others, in turn, to improve the health, morals, nutrition and general wellbeing of the humblest segments of the population so that they too could enjoy the blessings of a happy and healthy family life. There was nothing politically radical in such images; nothing socialist or evolutionary. Some such as Theodor Kittelsen may have sympathized with workers who sought to improve their lot by industrial action, as his 'Tendens' work *Strike* (1879) evinces, but Larsson, the working-class lad made good, by no means sympathized with such activities; indeed, he strongly opposed the Great Strike in Sweden of 1909.[11]

In Norway, Gustaf Wentzel (1859–1927) took a less idyllic view of the family in some of his paintings, but, perhaps because of their more matter-of-fact focus, they, too, succeed in capturing a vision of the contented family. In *Breakfast II* (1885) brilliant sunlight streams in upon a breakfast table, where each of the family is engrossed in his or her own activity (see illus. 58). However, the breakfast table and the outstretched arms of the little girl on the left create a unifying effect, as if the breakfast table itself has served as an altar before which the whole

47 Jacob Henriksson Elbfas, *Portrait of Queen Christina as a Child*, c. 1640, oil on canvas.

48 Jonas Dürchs, *The Portrait of Gustaf Fredrik Hjortberg with his Family*, c. 1780, oil on canvas. Släpps Church, Halland (Sweden).

49 August Strindberg, *Inferno*,
1901, oil on canvas.

50 Christoffer Wilhelm
Eckersberg, *Crossing of the Red
Sea*, 1815, oil on canvas.

51 Ernst Josephson,
Fru Jeanette Rubenson, 1883,
oil on wood.

52 Olaf/Olof Fridsberg,
*Ulla Tessin in her Cabinet
at Åkerö*, 18th century,
watercolour.

53 Carl Larsson, *A Home: The Kitchen*, before 1899, watercolour.

54 Anders Zorn, *Midsummer
Dance*, 1897, oil on canvas.

55 Eero Järnefelt, *The Wage
Slaves (Burning the Forest
Clearing)*, 1893, oil on canvas.

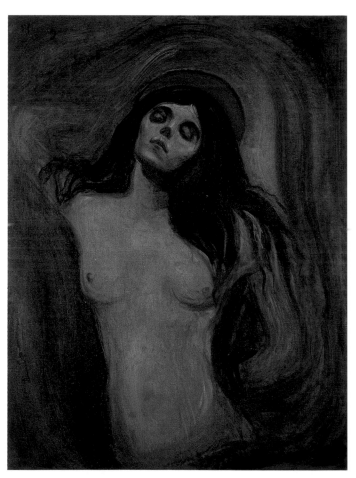

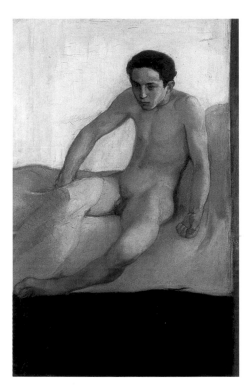

57 Magnus Enckell,
The Awakening, 1894, oil on
canvas.

56 Edvard Munch, *Madonna*,
1893–4, oil on canvas.

58 Gustav Wentzel, *Breakfast II. The Artist's Family*, 1885, oil on canvas.

59 Gustav Vigeland, *Man, Woman and Child*, 1917, granite. Vigelandsparken, Oslo.

family became as one, if only briefly, while above and to the right, the wall clock, like the heart of the household, ticks away in measured serenity.

It is a different focus on the family which reached its zenith in the works of the Norwegian sculptor Gustaf Vigeland (1869–1943). His *Man, Woman and Child* (1917), one of many sculptures of family life to grace Vigeland's Park in Oslo, seems the physical embodiment of the loving, if inward-looking, family unit, a social realist sculptural ode to early twentieth-century family life (illus. 59). It is not surprising, with its robust, muscular image of the family, that it appealed to many Norwegians, like the Norwegian author and Nobel Laureate Knut Hamsun, who yearned for a rugged image of the family that took its roots in the wooded mountains of the north, shunning what he perceived to be emasculating influences from abroad, especially England, which could only serve to weaken the very fabric of the country.

Such a focus upon family roots in the forests found its strongest expression in Finland, where the Finnish sauna, despite the nudity of those who partook, seemed to provide the perfect backdrop to images of the happy family. It was a communal place rich in a familial spiritual imagery, and a place where eroticism was expected to play no role. When Akseli Gallen-Kallela (1865–1931), the great national romantic artist of late nineteenth-century Finland, shattered its sanctity as a boy by a chance remark he made there, it was to cause a shame which reverberated years later in his confessional autobiography; he wrote:

It was still a common custom also in Satakunta in those days for the male and female hands of even so-called gentlemen's farms to bathe together. When I was a brat I once took part in such a sauna and my eye chanced to fall on a fat, naked, red-headed servant girl who in all her splendour was descending the sauna platform. In my innocent indiscretion, I made an impertinent and indecent remark. Bailiff Tuomas who was in the bath rose from his bench and said sternly, 'You ... I'll show you!' I sneaked away ashamed from the sauna, and from that moment on I was awakened to respect the holiness of the sauna and nudity.[12]

For a Swede like the artist Anders Zorn, however, and one for whom the concept of the sanctity of marriage seemed hardly to intrude upon his numerous affairs, such eroticism was by no means to be rejected. On the contrary, he used the image of the sauna as a backdrop for the most erotic of images. His *Girls Bathing in a Sauna* (1906) depicts the sensual aspects of a visit to the sauna by two voluptuous Dalecarlian beauties, seemingly oblivious to any viewer and yet displaying their bodies as if, somehow, they knew that they were being watched. But even in Finland, the old communal sauna, which families, servants, guests and others all shared, was becoming a thing of the past, and nudity became nakedness even in the Finnish forests.[13]

Doubtless, the rise of the popular press in these years did much to foster a more idyllic picture of what constituted family life: The *Swedish Family Journal* was particularly important in this role, drawing upon a readership in the 1870s of more than 50,000, mainly from the lower middle classes of minor civil servants and shopkeepers. In its pages the woman's role as the backbone of the household is stressed, including advertisements for products such as the sewing machine which could assist her to fulfil her maternal and wifely duties. New items of furniture were also beginning to enter middle-class homes and these could become the altar of a new family ritual. This was certainly the case with the piano which assumed an ever growing importance for middle-class households as the focus of cultivated domestic conviviality.[14] Its function can be seen in *The Salon* (1857) a water-colour by the Swedish artist Fritz von Dardel (1817–1901) where, amid all sprawling clutter of furniture and fabrics, the piano has pride of place in the foreground, with the sheet music spread out upon its stand, as if inviting the viewer to join in and play in the bosom of the family.

Other magazines, such as *The Family Friend* (*Familjevännen*) saw the nation itself as one big family. In this context, the status of the royal family, the ultimate family, as the ideal to which the entire nation should look for a role model, was underscored. A lithograph of Queen Louise of Sweden was provided in an edition of the magazine from 1864, accompanied by a poem paying homage to her role as mother, wife and woman. As such, in the truest sense, she is the mother not only of her own children, but of her country itself and the embodiment of Swedish femininity in its most perfect form. Here can be found reflections of Hegel's ethical emphasis on 'moral love' and the importance of the family, in which duty and devotion are the principal ingredients and which had come to inspire the imagination of the popular press.[15] Furthermore, in such magazines as *Before and Now* these images were married to romantic conceptions of the national past in which major figures from history and mythology could anachronistically be taken to symbolize nineteenth-century domestic virtues (as well as vices). Even animals could acquire the anthropomorphic characteristics of the human family, so that paintings of horses and dogs, with their foals and puppies, seemed to reflect not merely the joys given by domestic pets, but allegories of family virtues and relationships themselves.[16]

By the turn of the twentieth century a whole spectrum of social conventions and forms had come to be employed to bolster the growing hegemony of the upper middle classes and their families. Birthdays, wedding anniversaries and jubilees assumed an ever greater role as collective rites of passage in the life of the idealized family.[17] While marriage was still based mainly on practical considerations, popular ideas increasingly held that romantic love would come about as a natural cement which bonded together a dutiful husband and wife to each other. Thus, the old unadulterated pragmatism of both the upper and lower classes was rejected by the middle in favour of a curious, romantic hybrid union of the practical and the idealized, in which extramarital relations would theoretically have no place. Now, the team of husband and wife began to assume a new sanctified importance which was even reflected in attendance at church as, more and more, congregations ceased to be separated into male and female sides, with families and even courting couples now seated together.

Furthermore, the successful moral education of children, as advocated by the Swedish intellectual Ellen Key (1849–1926) in her book *The Century of the Children* (1900), came to be seen as the primary goal of upper- and middle-class parents towards their offspring. This did not mean, however, that parental scrutiny of children or the time devoted to them by the middle classes increased, for the time-consuming and humdrum tasks of looking after their offspring continued to be relegated to nannies and other servants.[18]

Throughout the nineteenth century extended and communal family households themselves became ever rarer, especially in Finland: perhaps the lower rate of infant mortality led to the family becoming more introverted and less communal.[19] The nuclear family unit continued to grow in importance, not only in economic terms but also as the source of social virtues and the building block of national self-identification. This was particularly true from the 1840s when the rising middle classes, and especially the intelligentsia who identified themselves and their family values with those of the nation as a whole, increasingly dominated social, economic and intellectual life. Social problems, including poverty and illicit sexual activity, could both seen as the failure of education within a family and one which was inextricably entwined with both.[20]

Thus, when the perceived dragon of sexuality persisted in rearing its ugly head, the middle classes increasingly tended to view it not merely as a threat to the wellbeing of their children, but of family life and society as a whole.

Masturbation, almost ubiquitous as a practice among young men (such a practice amongst women was not even contemplated), was seen as an odious comportment which threatened the mental and physical wellbeing of the child both in his development and in his future life. The Catholic Church had rigorously condemned the 'sin of Onan' for centuries but it is debatable how seriously this prohibition was taken by boys and their parents in the Nordic region. However, in the early eighteenth century, the publication of a new work *Onania* (1707–17), written by an anonymous Protestant clergyman, sold over 138,000 copies and established a new debate upon the subject and the alleged evils it caused.[21] Other publications soon followed which increasingly emphasized, not so much the spiritual, but the debilitating physical and energy-wasting effects of the practice. These views were adopted almost immediately by Danish medical texts, which rapidly disseminated them throughout the Nordic region. As a result, by 1800, as elsewhere in Europe, they were perceived as forming a scientifically accurate analysis of the 'malady' and therefore considered as fact.

When, by the late nineteenth century, Dr Ruff's *Illustrated Health Lexicon. A Popular Handbook for All* was published in Stockholm in 1888, it won fame far and wide in the Nordic countries not only for his modern approach to health and hygiene, but also for his attempts to eradicate childhood masturbation. He warned the parents of any pubescent boy,

> He must not sleep alone in a room; one must not be shy of going several times during the night to his bed and to removing the blanket without consideration of whether he is asleep or not. Threatened by such visitations a boy given to such an unhealthy habit would not dare to perform his manipulations.[22]

60 Fritz Syberg, *At Bedtime*, 1889, oil.

Perhaps it was the guilt and confusion caused by such 'manipulations' which the Finnish artist Magnus Enckell captured on the face of the youth in *The Awakening* (1894), who stares out with uncomprehending eyes into the empty space before him (see illus. 57). Certainly, it would seem that the youth depicted is tormented by some form of new experience, one with which he has found it difficult to come to terms and for which he himself is perhaps not principally to blame. In his final analysis of the matter, Dr Ruff sees the problem of such 'unhealthy behaviour' as not so much the fault of the child, but that of the parents. As he explicitly makes clear, parents who encourage sensuality in the home also encourage sensual libidinous actions amongst their offspring. Hence, fondling and cuddling of children was to be strictly avoided in favour of a more austere and less physical deportment towards them. He wrote:

61 Edvard Munch, *Puberty*, 1893, oil on canvas.

> It is a habit with many parents to take the child into bed to the enjoyment of parents and child alike. We acknowledge that which is sacred in the love of parents towards their children; we know how to value the enchantment which permeates a father and mother who warmly embrace their beloved child, when it rushes to us in intimate confidence; nonetheless, I strongly admonish against such expressions of love. For in it lies the seeds of sensuality.[23]

In *At Bedtime* (1889) by the Danish artist Fritz Syberg (1862–1939), a mother stands sentinel near her sleeping child's bed, her hands clasped behind her back like that of a sculpture of Patrician Roman matron, static but watchful and vigilant of her child's wellbeing (illus. 60). However, it was not only boys who underwent difficult periods of growing up which left their parents anxious. Girls, too, had their own times of inner turmoil, emotional and physical. In fact, it is just such a time of life for an adolescent girl that Munch has depicted in *Puberty* (1893) (illus. 61). The nude girl sits anxiously upon her bed, her hands and arms jealously covering her pudenda, while a dark shadow stealthily creeps up behind her. Maybe, on one level the work seems to reflect 'eros-thanatos', in which erotic life and death forces struggle with one another for domination (later formulated by Freud in *Civilisation and Its Discontents* in 1930), or the writings of Munch's friend and lauding critic Stanislaw Przybyszewski who wrote on psychological as well as art historical matters. The writings of such 'decadent' Symbolist writers as the Swede Ola Hansson (1860–1925), whose collection, *Sensitiva Amorosa* (1887), also focuses upon many morbid and destructive aspects of eroticism and the human psyche. On another level, however, *Puberty* can also be seen as a pictorial expression of the confusion and angst caused by the processes of puberty for a girl on verge of womanhood. For most women of the upper classes, it was felt, marriage would provide the final solution to any such problems, but for those from less fortunate backgrounds, many pitfalls were seen to lie in wait. Thus, many a mature woman of the upper classes, often themselves unmarried and with much leisure time on their hands, saw the need for a moral crusade, in which the most enlightened values, moral and hygienic (usually

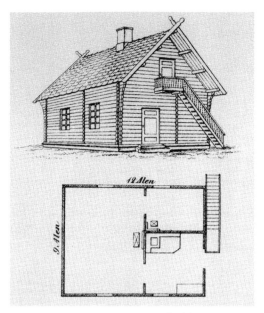

12 Alen

9 Alen

62 Hans Ditlev Frantz von Linstow, *Design for the little house of a working-man's family*, 1851, plan and elevation.

perceived as inextricably linked), could be used to provide those socially and economically (and therefore morally) indigent with the tools for a successful, and, by definition, chaste life.

Unfortunately for these matrons, the sensuality which Dr Ruff had condemned and the inappropriate domestic circumstances in which it thrived did not always horrify the young women (or men) they wished to 'improve', many of whom remained impervious to the exhortations of their 'betters'. Indeed, the sentimental and sexual concerns such as those Dr Ruff dealt with in great detail did not seem to preoccupy the humbler elements of society at all; the very grammar of sexuality differed radically for the two social strata. The concept of the bed, for example, had little of the erotic significance in poorer households (where many family members usually shared a bed together) that it had for the more privileged classes. Rather, it was the haylofts, woods and other hidden corners which best offered the poor the privacy necessary for their sexual relations. Perhaps it was for this reason that, as a contemporary historian of the countryside put it, 'Forests were supposed to encourage immorality, and heathland forest were more immoral than other kinds.'[24] In any case, sexuality did not normally involve for the poor, the intimate foreplay and caresses to which the upper classes were attached. Of course, the rural poor gave caresses and kisses to their children, too, but in sexual terms it would seem that anything other than a brief and purposeful copulation between couples (even kissing) was largely eschewed in favour of a more direct, if less imaginative, satisfaction of need.[25]

This new moralizing approach to the sexuality of the poor (and indeed any possible social discontent they might posses) continued and expressed itself not only through moral exhortations, offers of employment and the criminalization of much sexual activity, but through the architecture itself which was built to cater for their needs, as well. Thus, the Norwegian architect Hans Ditlev Frantz von Linstow (1787–1851) produced an enlightened *Design for the little house of a working-man's family* (1851), in which the ideal conditions would prevail, encouraging the moral edification of the entire family (illus. 62). Built as a traditional log cabin, with sharp overhanging eaves, it had one large room opening on to two smaller ones, one of which served as the kitchen, and an outside staircase leading to the loft above. Published by him in the newspaper *Christianiaposten*, it was, he states, designed to be built by the occupier himself, with functional rather than aesthetic values foremost, and was 'in no way intended to beautify the milieu in which it was situated,' but rather to provide 'a domestic refuge, which can foster morality, not with force or fear, which can only encourage an outward adherence to the law, but through an inner voice which comes of contentment with their position and lot in life.'[26] Already that same year, a tenement for working-men and their families had been built in Christiania, when the initiative for its construction had been taken by the head of police and other city fathers with memories both of the revolutionary upheavals of 1848, as well as the recent cholera epidemics still clear in their minds' eyes. This building included six two-room flats, as well as a large number of bedroom-sitting rooms, each of which had their own kitchens and running water, with a common bathroom and lending library also provided.[27]

When, in 1903, *A Design for a Working Class Residence*, by K. Bay, appeared in the magazine *Egne hjem* (1903), it, too, reflected von Linstow's traditional earlier design, albeit in more symmetrical form. It also allotted more living space per person, since space implied greater respect for the individual and a person respected by himself and others would be more likely to make the right moral decisions. Like its predecessor, it was made of logs, with two windows on one of the longer elevations, and contained three rooms, one of which was a kitchen. Especially innovative, at least in architectural terms, was the introduction of an internal staircase which led to the loft, as well as a veranda reached by a low flight of steps on the front elevation, which would both protect from the elements whilst permitting a greater circulation of fresh air for the residents.[28] Ten years later, Magnus Paulsson (1881–1958) provided an even more radical solution with his designs (also published in *Egne Hjem*), which were used in the construction of working-class houses at Rjukan. These asymmetrical two-family houses were largely timber-clad and were generously provided with windows, even at the level of the spacious loft, as well as an entrance porch. Stylistically, though, their form and design stem more from William Morris and the British crafts tradition of the later nineteenth century than from native Norwegian architectural prototypes, for it was from England that a view of architecture as an important means of facilitating moral and social improvement amongst the poor was actually derived.

Privacy and the Family

It is interesting to note that as intrusion by the upper and middle classes into the most intimate areas of the life of the poor increased, their own need for privacy reached ever greater heights. Bedrooms became almost sacred areas, far removed from the public rooms of their ever larger houses and flats, with the nursery for children and accommodation for servants relegated to the furthest reaches. For the poorer segments of society the architectural arrangement remained quite different, even with a greater allocation of space. Bedrooms and sitting rooms were often one and the same and provided the stage for every aspect of family life. *Morning Reveille* (1893) by Fritz von Dardel helps capture the humorous higgledy-piggledy atmosphere of disarray at morning time in such an overpopulated room in a country cottage in Dalecarlia. Yet, this contrast with middle-class household arrangements was not quite such an ancient tradition as many believed. As late as the early nineteenth century even the bedrooms of middle-class households had been relatively public places, which, as the century progressed, assumed a more and more private aura, just as middle-class family

(Above left) **63** Anna Ancher,
The Girl in the Kitchen, 1883–6,
oil on canvas.

(Above right) **64** Vilhelm
Hammershøi, *Bedroom*, 1890,
oil on canvas.

life itself was becoming more private, something to be experienced in the intimacy of the home, away from the prying eyes of strangers.

Yet, observing others seemed to exert its greatest appeal for the middle classes, a fact of which many artists at the time seemed to have been acutely aware. For example, *The Girl in the Kitchen* (1883–6), by the Danish artist Anna Ancher (1859–1935) focuses upon a quiet and private moment in a little cottage in Skagen, where it seems as if the young woman has been caught unawares, with her back turned to the viewer, while quietly at work with her domestic chores (illus. 63). It is an icon of private domestic contentment, but one which is voyeuristic, as if we, the observers, have taken the place of the husband of the house in stealing this hidden glance. Another Danish artist, Viggo Johansen (1851–1935) was to paint a variation of this theme of women at work in the home in *Kitchen Interior with the Artist's Wife Arranging Flowers* (1884). By contrast to the figure in *The Girl in the Kitchen*, the young woman's back here is provocatively turned towards the viewer, as she gracefully tilts her head towards the activity in hand. For all the gentle femininity of the theme of this work, though, there is a subtle and erotically charged quality absent in the former which seems to imply a male, rather than female, point of view.

In most of the depictions of domestic interiors painted by the Dane Vilhelm Hammershøi (1864–1916), eroticism plays no role. In his pictorial symphony of grey tonalities, *Bedroom* (1890), his wife Ida Hammershøi is portrayed, her back turned, while gazing towards the blank wall to her side, cocooned in an impenetrable solitude (illus. 64). It is as though his wife has been captured not so much by the artist's eye, nor the viewer, but by the very walls of the drawing room in which she is depicted, sealed within it by the constraints of her domestic milieu and restricting social conventions, a state of affairs of which the artist was aware but could or would do little about.

The Marriage Market

That a woman's life might be bleak emotionally was not a primary consideration at a time when the material practicalities of life continued to dominate all aspects of her social and marital role. In Sweden, in the first quarter of the eighteenth century, for example, it was commented by a visitor that 'parents, without consulting their children, match them as they think fit, and wealth is chiefly considered in the affair: the poor girls have not so much an opportunity of being courted or admired or the lover the pleasure of communicating his flame'.[29] Certainly, children were expected to acquiesce to their parents' wishes, whether with respect to marriage, work or other more minor demands. Even for those lower down the social scale, where the members of a household formed a working unit, the ultimate authority in the family remained the man of the house, either the father or eldest male relation. This, in conjunction with the circumstance that the site of work and family life were often the same for both the middle and lower classes meant that the material aspects of a marriage with respect to the partners were of prime importance. This was a state of affairs further condoned by the Lutheran church, which sanctified marriage as a divinely established institution, based more on practicalities than sentiments, and churches were full of pictorial and oral exhortations for couples to lead virtuous lives, with husbands loving and wives obedient.

In some instances, pictorial images were also employed in the home to stress the importance and sacredness of marriage. Mural decorations such as *The Marriage in Cana*, by the Swedish painter Johannes Nilsson (1757–1827), from Gyltige, in Halland, were typical of the grander pictorial imagery which adorned the homes of the prosperous, provincial middle classes, though lithographs of similar subjects might be found in humbler dwellings (illus. 65). Fiddle music, dancers,

65 Johannes Nilsson, *The Marriage in Cana*, 18th century, painted wall-hanging.

66 Balthasar Denner, *The Artist and his Family Playing Music*, c. 1730, oil on canvas.

richly adorned but sober ladies and even a pipe smoker all play a prominent role in this encomium to married life and joyous Christian domesticity. In another mural painting, *The Song of Songs* (1781) by Erik Eliasson (1754–1811), an elegant wife stares entranced at her cavalier husband, whilst the accompanying text above this old-fashioned Rococo painting, confirms their commitment to each other in no uncertain terms. Here, in the country house of Backhansgård, in the parish of Svärdsjö, in Dalecarlia, it is the virtue of mutual devotion so necessary to a successful marriage which is stressed. Yet for all the spiritual exhortations to virtue in such works, it is clear that a common social background for the partners depicted is also of prime consideration. The possibility of a marital partner from a different milieu quite literally does not enter the picture.

Earlier, the artist Balthasar Denner (1685–1749), a native of Hamburg and son of a Mennonite preacher, had drawn upon a very different genre, this time of sophisticated French prototype, to create his pictorial vision of harmony, gentility and culture in Danish family life, as seen in his group portrait *The Artist and his Family Playing Music* (c. 1730; illus. 66). This depicts, in a room of considerable if spartan elegance, his whole family gathered together to play and listen to music. Relaxed, informal, at home in one another's company, it is as if the eighteenth-century Pietistic ideal of cultivated family life has been captured in this Rococo work of muted but delicate colour tonalities.

In another portrait, *The Artist and his Wife Rosine* (1791) by Jens Juel, a different feature of the family is stressed, namely, their social position amongst the gentrified middle classes. In this work the leading Danish portrait painter of the late eighteenth century is depicted in his unquestionably genteel Charlottenborg home, with the *accoutrements* of his art boldly displayed, his fashionably dressed wife seated by his side. No mere artisanal couple; they are a sophisticated and urbane couple who wished to preserve their hard-won status for their descendants. In this they succeeded, by encouraging endogamous marriages for their children within their own artistic circle: indeed two of Juel's daughters married the artist and future professor of the Danish Royal Academy of Art, Christoffer Wilhelm Eckersberg, one after another.

The families of artists, of course, were not alone in their desire to preserve the social status of their children by endogamous marriages. Landowners, priests, merchants, craftsmen, farmers, fishermen – all tended to carry on the occupational status of their forebears by marrying into the families of others who shared their métier. From the late sixteenth century onwards in Denmark, it was expected that a new young incumbent in a parish would marry the widow of the previous clergyman, irrespective of any sentimental inclinations towards each other or the expectancy of children by her. In fact, in the parish of Fakse during the seventeenth century, two wives of clergymen were married to four and three clergymen, respectively, all of whom preceded them to the grave.[30] A more modest example of such a pattern can be seen in a sepulchral painting from Denmark (illus. 67). Depicted side by side, the wife's first husband had died in 1650, followed by her second in 1670. Also included in the representation are her three children from the first marriage, all of whom had died at an early age.

Other groups within Danish society were also rising in the social hierarchy and there, too, marriages would be made from those from a similar background.

67 Bartholomeus Paproczki, *Anne Jensdatter with her two Clergymen Husbands*, 1651, oil on canvas.

68 Christoffer Wilhelm Eckersberg, *Portrait of the Nathanson Family*, 1818, oil on canvas.

This was certainly the case amongst middle-class German-Jewish immigrants to Denmark who married within a small circle of families, often related. They had come both because of the country's policy of religious toleration and because of the economic opportunities which offered considerable financial rewards. The Danish artist Eckersberg, in his renowned painting *Portrait of the Nathanson Family* (1818; illus. 68), focuses upon his greatest patron Mendel Levin Nathanson, an important Jewish merchant of the time and later editor of the leading Copenhagen newspaper *Berlingske Tidende*. Depicted with his wife Esther and seven children, they are elegantly attired in the court dress they wore when granted an audience with the Danish queen. In harmony with the new social and pictorial vision of the time, the individuality of each person in the work is stressed, not only physiognomically but also in terms of their actions and character. That the family portrayed was Jewish is an indication of the liberality which reigned in Denmark at the time; such a work would not have been possible in Norway, where the very presence of Jews in the country after sunset was forbidden constitutionally, a situation only rectified after an embarrassing event involving the arrival of a Jewish philanthropist who had been sent packing during the 1850s, which had led to a constitutional repeal of the relevant prohibitive clause.

Among those in specialized fields like the iron industry, generation after generation of master blacksmiths, usually of Huguenot Walloon backgrounds, also drew their partners from a similar background. Usually married in their early to mid-twenties, they tended to form nuclear family groups, with five or six children on average, smaller families than those of the general population, but typical of most of the Nordic region in containing only two generations.[31] This was also the case in the households of fishermen living in the far-flung Lofoten Islands, in the north of Norway, where more than 75 per cent were nuclear in form. Here, however, farming families tended to be more extended, with spinsters or elderly relations also sharing the family home.[32] This was the exception, rather than the rule, though, in the Nordic region, even in distant Greenland, where nuclear families of four or five members were quite common, and where less than 15 per cent of households had more than two generations living together.[33]

The families of Swedish craftsmen and those engaged in trades tended to be even smaller, with only about three or four members on average, including children. This was less a result of childhood mortality, than an outcome of the fact that most children over the age of fifteen left their homes to seek employment elsewhere, even if they eventually returned to carry on their father's occupation or trade.[34] This was also the case in families with no land or fixed property to inherit, especially those of farm labourers, where children tended to leave at a similar age in order to seek work as domestic servants or farm hands. Employed on a yearly contract, they would frequently move from one homestead to another. Then, only after accumulating a bit of money, would they themselves marry and establish their own homes.

The necessity for many young farmers of inheriting or purchasing a farm of their own before proceeding to marry played a major role in marital patterns throughout the region. It was therefore not surprising that in Norway alone over three-quarters of farmers from a land-owning background married daughters of a similar background who were in a position to provide large dowries or their own farms. As a result, in these situations courtships would sometimes last for years with prospective husbands waiting well over a decade or more for marriage to be entered into, depending upon the age of the wife or the availability of her property. Thus, it frequently happened that a man approaching 40 or more would marry a girl of less than twenty. Similarly, a widow in possession of her late husband's property might take as a second husband a man much younger than herself. Both her property and the working skills she had acquired over the years could prove attractive to a young, and impecunious, prospective husband.

Any opportunity for a attractive match might be seized, with sometimes scant attention paid to social proprieties. As Eilert Sundt, a Lutheran priest and Norway's first sociologist relates, one widowed Bergen matron married the carpenter who had measured up for her late husband's coffin.[35] Of course, such marriages might alter the prospects of inheritance for the children of the first marriage, but this was not necessarily the case, for it was the custom that the second husband of a widow with children from the previous marriage would normally relinquish his rights to a farm upon her death, allowing her eldest child to assume proprietorship.[36] Sometimes, too, with both first and second marriages, the custom of 'home exchange' would be adopted whereby a man would marry a woman in another family, provided that a man in her family married one of his relations. This practice encouraged the deeper consolidation of each family with its respective landholdings, with no loss to either in terms of land or labour.

In Denmark, young men from fishing communities tended to marry within the families of other fishermen, though some also married into those of the cottars. These small farmers, often young, were generally poorer than the fishermen who had more ready cash available from the sale of their fish, since they normally inherited from their fathers at a later age. For this reason, fishermen could generally marry earlier than their farming counterparts and immediately set up independent households.[37] Such was the case also in Iceland where an increase in the fishing industry led to a growth of small coastal towns and villages in the late nineteenth century. The resulting economic benefits led to an earlier age of financial independence and early marriage for many young people.

Other factors sometimes contributed to this trend. For example, an increase in the amount of land under cultivation which occurred in the north-east of Iceland between 1870 and 1900 precipitated an influx of some 12,000 immigrants to the region which also led to a lowering of the average age of those marrying. These were regional exceptions, however, for, despite these local variations, Icelanders generally married later than any other European ethnic group, men being generally over 30 and women 28 by the end of the nineteenth century.[38]

In Finland, too, many rural men married very late or, indeed, avoided the institution altogether. However, here it was the fact that the limited population in this sparsely settled land created a desperate need for agricultural labour, which obliged many farmer's sons to delay or forsake marriage out of fear that laws limiting the splitting up of homesteads would make such a step economically untenable.[39] In part, for this reason, the extended family tended to predominate, often with as many as ten members. Still, once past puberty children often moved away from home, entering the service of other households. This was especially the case in the south-west of Finland where farm labourers and domestics made up more than one-third of the total population. On the other hand, in the south-east and north-west of Finland, fewer than 7 per cent of the inhabitants were so employed.[40] For many of these however, domestic service could provide a quick route to a position of relative strength within the employing family itself.

By contrast with the situation elsewhere in the Nordic region, young female domestic servants in Finland often provided a nubile pool from which marriageable partners for their employers's sons could be chosen, especially in the socially unstratified regions of the north and east. In such close quarters as the physically small Finnish house provided, the character and working skills of the girl (or boy) in question could be assessed and, if found satisfactory, a marriage arranged.[41] By the same token, a propertied widow would frequently marry a farmhand who was employed on her farmstead. It was therefore the case that employment as a farmhand or domestic servant was not so much a long-term form of subservient drudgery but a temporary stage which often led to a more permanently established position within an extended family. Since at least four people were a practical necessity for the running of a typical Finnish farm, such employment of outsiders served several useful purposes, especially in households with few members but much land.[42]

In general, in Scandinavia, however, employment as a domestic servant did not lead to later adoption within a family. Rather, it was a recourse taken for those either just on the threshold of adulthood or young married couples possessed of neither a farm nor the resources to purchase or rent one. For such as these, it was not unusual for both spouses to seek long-term positions as domestic servants, often in different households and away from their native villages. This was an arrangement particularly common in Norway where the children born from such unions would frequently be raised by elderly relations or others back at home; then, only after enough income had been earned to secure a farm through leasehold or purchase, would the family be permanently reunited. As a result, it sometimes happened that a father never saw his child until he or she had reached the age of ten.[43] For those, however, whom misfortune or improvidence had failed to provide with even these sources of income, married life and children were a luxury which could not be afforded and a single life as a permanent farm labourer or domestic servant remained their only option.[44]

Yet here, at the bottom of the social scale, where expectations of social mobility or of inheritance were limited or non-existent, marital and pre-marital relations were the least circumscribed of any social group. In fact, only in the largest houses was domestic architecture so designed as to isolate male and female servants almost completely from one another.[45] Rather, in the vast majority of households, domestic servants and farm labourers tended to sleep in servants quarters, often four to a bed, with limited separation of the sexes, in circumstances which frequently encouraged intimacy, especially on Saturday nights when servants from other establishments made their social visits. This helped to encourage the practice of 'bundling', which was common throughout much of the Nordic region and, as a custom, had a long and venerable history in Scandinavia, providing as it did a means whereby courting couples from humble rural families could become better acquainted with each other. By this arrange-ment, the young man and woman were permitted to sleep together, fully clothed, with younger siblings sometimes sharing the same bed, as the 'night courtship' discretely proceeded. But while fondling and kissing generally occurred between the two parties, sexual intercourse was strictly forbidden, at least among the more respectable church-going families.

Perhaps equally important for courting couples, if less sensational, were the ubiquitous dances held on festive days, like Midsummer Eve, or Saturday nights

69 Alexander Lauréus, *The Dance*, 1814, oil on canvas.

after markets, for they provided useful occasions for prospective partners to make closer acquaintance. One such cotillion in Sweden has been depicted by the Finnish artist Alexander Lauréus (1783–1823), in a work rich in anecdote: *The Dance* (1814; illus. 69). Here rather well-dressed ladies and gentlemen of the middle classes dance away the evening to the music provided by fiddlers in this elegant ballroom of a fashionably decorated hostelry. Since endogamous marriages were encouraged, if not always demanded, guests from different social backgrounds rarely came together at such an event. None the less, even further down the social scale in rural areas, dances, usually linked to seasonal festivities were of considerable importance in fostering social contact. Though of a significantly later date than Lauréus's work, *Midsummer Dance* (1897) by the Swede Anders Zorn (1860–1920; see illus. 54), is without doubt the most poignant pictorial image of an event, repeated in endless villages throughout Scandinavia, and stresses the continued social significance of such dances. Bathed in a symphony of light on a beautiful Nordic summer evening, such a dance could provide the ideal venue for exploring personal intimacies which, if practicalities permitted, might also lead to marriage.

In the Danish Virgin Islands, in the Caribbean, the marriage market functioned much in the same way as at home in Denmark, though there were some noteworthy differences. For one thing, marriages in the colony were sometimes arranged in advance with European residents who first met their future husbands and wives on the eve of their weddings, after the long and perilous trans-oceanic crossing. Their physical comeliness or personal allurements generally played no role in the arrangement. Indeed, missionaries, such as Moravian Pietists, might even find their marriage partners from amongst their own number by the drawing of lots when their spiritual leaders so demanded it.[46] On the other hand, slaves often chose their own partner, since their couplings had little relevance to their masters's and mistresses: slave couples might be split up by sale and even sold abroad, when and if their owners chose. That said, slave women who catered for their masters's personal sexual needs were often obliged to remain unmarried, at least as long as their sexual favours were required, though afterwards they might seek out a partner as they wished or even enjoy manumission as a reward for faithful services.

In the Swedish colony of St Barthelemy, where there were relatively few women of European origins, the taking of black or mixed race women as mistresses was common. Robert Montgomery, a favourite of Gustaf III, who had been exiled there in the late eighteenth century for his role in the Anjala mutiny, commented in his diary that upon his arrival everyone had advised him to take a Negro woman, in order to preserve his health in the hot and languid climate.[47] Such an outlook encouraged concubinage which became the order of the day soon after the colony's establishment. This was not only the case for those taking slave mistresses, but also for the many Catholics there who, in the absence of a priest in the 1820s, were obliged to set up house with their 'wives', until the colony's governor introduced a type of civil marriage to deal with the problem.[48]

In the Danish East Indian colony of Tranquebar, Indian marriage customs persisted among the local population, while Europeans carried on their marriage customs much as they did at home. However, the Indian Hindu custom of 'suttee', that is, the immolation of the widows upon the funeral pyre of their husbands, became strictly forbidden, even if, on occasion, it was still carried out.[49]

Attitudes towards Women

Attitudes towards women, married or single in the Nordic region generally tended to reflect those held elsewhere in northern Europe. There was, of course, a general appreciation of their physical charms and domestic usefulness, but a disdain for their intelligence and loquaciousness underlay general social perceptions in even the highest levels of society. This is clear in the so-called *Hen Picture* (1747) by the Swedish artists Johan Pasch the Elder (1706–1769) and Johan Henrik Scheffel (1690–1781; a native of Wismar, in Swedish Pomerania), which humorously depicts six court beauties of the time, with their attractive heads less than flatteringly attached to the bodies of chickens (illus. 70). Such works, however, were only meant to be slightly contemptuous rather than directly insulting, that is, tongue-and-cheek pictorial jokes, to be appreciated by both sexes, even if the gentlemen were expected to laugh more heartily than the ladies.

Not all such images of women, however, were disparaging of their intelligence, albeit, amusingly so. A limited number of aristocratic ladies were noted for their intellectual sophistication and breadth of literary knowledge. *Ulla Tessin in her Cabinet at Åkerö*, by the Swedish artist Olof Fridsberg (1725–1795; see

70 Johan Pasch the Elder and Johan Henrik Scheffel, *Hen Picture*, 1747, oil on canvas.

illus. 52), depicts the wife of the great Swedish court architect and courtier, Count Carl Gustaf Tessin, at her grand country residence. She is portrayed as a lady of the world, literate, cultivated and a connoisseur of aesthetic excellence, surrounded by her books, paintings and splendid *objets d'art*, imported from around the world.[50] By contrast, an early nineteenth-century Danish portrait painting by Eckersberg of *Madame Schmidt* (1818) depicts this middle-class matron, wife of an East India merchant, with no pretences to intellectual accomplishments. Sombre and monumental, she is seated adjacent to her sewing table, devoid of jewellery and other such frivolous accoutrements, piously carrying out her household task with an august dignity and an unflinching moral conviction worthy of a Stoic Greek matron.

Even aside from individual differences of intellect, generic social statuses among women differed greatly, depending upon both their economic and social background. Thus, while a homogeneity of social status reigned amongst the unmarried daughters of farmers and fishermen, who were called 'girls', those of small tradesmen and the more prosperous farmers had their own status, reflected in the term 'maid'. Further up the social scale, especially in the nineteenth century, unmarried ladies of the upper middle and upper classes lived in a sharply stratified realm, rich in fine nuances of their social positions. For example, the title of 'mamsell', in Sweden, was used to address the unmarried daughter of a priest, common civil servant or merchant, whilst daughters of the aristocracy, in their turn, were addressed as 'miss'. Admittedly, the abolition of the estates in the middle of the nineteenth century led to the a general urban abandonment of the term 'mamsell', but in the countryside its usage continued throughout the century. The use of such terms was not mere snobbery; they reflected an important and sombre social reality: an unmarried woman was sharply constrained, at almost any cost, to circumvent her reduction to a lower social stratum by making an improvident marriage beneath her. For a man, however, the situation was quite different: he could both marry beneath himself and retain his previous status. Indeed, the decline in marriage rates from about 1820 for a century onwards reflects the results of a conundrum which confronted many genteel daughters – either to remain single or to marry beneath themselves and assume their husbands' status. For most the choice was clear – to remain unmarried. In 'Miss Juliana', a poem by Anna Maria Lenngren, for example, an officer's wife admonishes her daughter to prefer the slow withering of a solitary life to the debasement of a marriage of lower status.[51]

As a result, the proportion of unmarried to married women in the population rocketed in Sweden in the nineteenth century: whereas only 10 per cent of all late middle-aged women had remained single in 1800, by 1844 two-thirds of all adult women in the Swedish countryside were single and in Stockholm their numbers reached three-quarters of the adult female population.[52] Almost a quarter of them were unmarried in 1900. Of those from more prominent middle- and upper-class families, 'mamsells' and those addressed as miss, over 40 per cent never married. Can it be then that in C. J. L. Almqvist's *Daughter Maria* (c. 1835), a portrait by the Swedish artist Carl Peter Mazer (1807–1884), the author's own child is wistfully staring before her, wondering whether or not her own future would be spent in spinsterhood as she holds in her fingers a delicate white flower sprig?

This state of affairs is in sharp contrast to the fate of farmers' daughters, nearly all of whom took husbands, not only in Sweden, but elsewhere in the Nordic region, especially in Denmark. In farming families the role of the woman as housewife was virtually the only one available. In *An Old Farmer's Wife* (1832) by Christen Købke, an almost archetypal Danish rural housewife in later life is portrayed, the pillar of the Danish rural family, in emotional and physical, if not intellectual, terms (illus. 71).

Almost all farming men in the Nordic region also married, including the humble 'torpare', since a household without a woman to milk the cow was considered a poor one indeed. There was also the spinning of thread to make cloth, an important occupation invariably delegated to the wife. This is a theme focused upon by the Swedish artist Killian Zoll, in *At the Spinning Wheel*, in which an industrious young mother is depicted, albeit in a humble and sparsely furnished room, but accompanied by a happy child and a contented cat

71 Christen Købke, *An Old Farmer's Wife*, 1832, oil on canvas.

playing by her skirts. The message is clear: a man's chief satisfaction is to have an industrious wife who devotes herself to the material wellbeing of her husband and children. Thus, while rich aristocratic gentlemen might enjoy their bachelorhood, with a paid housekeeper to attend their needs, to be a bachelor in humble financial circumstances was in no way desirable. Bearing this in mind, it is not surprising, that the anecdotal Swedish genre painter Ferdinand Fagerlin (1825–1907) has portrayed the young man in *The Bachelor Mocked* (1883, but the replica of an earlier work from 1864) as a sorry figure, obliged to mend his own clothes, and the butt of scorn for the young woman accompanied by a child on her back who enters his room. Too poor to employ a servant and without a wife to carry out the household chores, the ignominy of doing them himself makes him a figure of derision and a pictorial cautionary tale.

Many professional men and civil servants, however, were able to pay for housekeepers and maids to deal with practical household matters and therefore remained bachelors all their lives, a demographic trend which increased as growing industrialization and increased economic resources provided more men with the means to employ servants. Indeed, among the aristocracy, the frequency of marriage declined, in part, it has been suggested, as a consequence of the increasing sales of their estates, necessitated by falls in agricultural prices, which permitted many men the choice of opting for an urban lifestyle with all the pleasures a city afforded, instead of the more restricted lifestyle of landed married gentleman. For those who did marry, however, especially among aristocratic officers in the armed services in need of capital, many began to take brides from the families of fellow officer cadres who were not of the same background. This meant, of course, that fewer appropriate suitors were now available to women of their own status, so that ever-growing numbers of aristocratic ladies remained unwed, as we have seen earlier.

But there were more pressing issues for many women in Scandinavia where population was increasing by leaps and bounds, especially rural areas. This was particularly the case in Finland where the rural population doubled between 1815 and 1900 and unemployment was increasing.[53] Those not so fortunate in finding household work might go on, like the little girl in *The Wage Slaves* (*Burning the Forest Clearing*) (1893) by Eero Järnefelt (1863–1937), to seek employment in back-breaking manual labour (see illus. 55). The image of a pretty little rural shepherdess, so popular in earlier pictorial representations of rural femininity, has been turned inside out here in a social admonishment to the viewer. Even an unhappy marriage might be a welcome alternative to the gruelling life with which this girl is confronted.

With such existential problems as these with which to cope, issues of broken marriages and divorce remained in the domain of the upper classes who could enjoy the luxury and self-indulgence of such a recourse, albeit one rarely taken. More usual was separation which, at least amongst the upper levels of society, might even be a reasonably amicable recourse, if finances for both sides permitted. For humble yeoman or farm-labouring families, however, the structure and demands of life precluded such options, at a time when the economic requirements of marriages held even the happier ones together more than sentiment. Since nuclear households predominated and, except for the more prosperous yeoman family, elderly relations were not usually available to fill the role of an absent mother, the presence of both partners, contented or not, could not be sacrificed.[54]

The Elderly

Despite the prevalent misconception held today that most families in the past were composed of grandparents and other members living together, most elderly couples in the Nordic countries, as elsewhere in northern Europe, did not live with their children or other relations, but alone fending for themselves as best they could. While some impoverished or ailing elderly widows or spinsters whose options of retirement were limited did find a niche (and quite

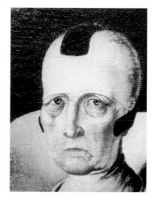

(Above) **72** *Portrait of a Woman*, 17th century. Innvik Church (Norway).

(Left) **73** Michael Ancher, *Blind Kristian as a Nursemaid*, 1885, oil on canvas.

literally not much more, in many instances), most were left to their own devices, particularly if their children (if they had any and of these some had survived) were absent, had migrated or were estranged. Certainly, the morose image of the old seen in *Portrait of a Woman* (seventeenth century) from Innvik Church, in Sogn and Fjordane, in Norway, does not present the viewer with an image of serenity but then the future held few temporal joys for such women (illus. 72). Especially in impoverished Iceland, an elderly woman could be faced with grim choices: she could attempt to establish a place for herself within the household of a relation, she could seek employment as a servant or, at the last resort, she could be placed with a family as a pauper.[55] For elderly men without resources, the opportunities were little better. Sometimes, they would assume the roles normally intended for women. This can be seen in a work from Skagen by Michael Ancher (1849–1927; illus. 73). Touchingly depicted as conscientious in his duty, this elderly man sits close by the little child's bedside, his hand on the frame of the bed so as to be attentive to any disquieting vibration. With its unconventional theme, it stresses the fact that even in this period, divisions of labour between the sexes, at least for those late in life, were not always as sharp as is now generally imagined.

(Above left) **74** Laurits Andersen Ring, *The Grandparents' Sunday*, 1898, oil on canvas.

(Above right) **75** Adolph Tidemand, *The Lonely Old Couple (Household Meditations)*, 1859, oil on wood.

For those elderly people more fortunate or able to avoid familial over-dependence, poverty and ill-health, a serene old age could, of course, be had. The Danish artist Laurits Andersen Ring (1854–1933) showed this happy scenario in his intimate depiction of an aged but content elderly Danish peasant couple (illus. 212). Not only has he been able to capture the gentleness and cosiness of this muted family scene, with the grandfather engrossed in his Bible and the grandmother in her knitting, but he has succeeded in stressing their spiritual communion, which underlies the serenity of the scene. Only the grandson, looking for something in the distance, seems slightly uncomfortable as, if he were striving to break the ennui of a too perfect harmony. Of course, not all such couples found a fulfilling emotional communion with each other. In the Norwegian painter Adolph Tidemand's *The Lonely Old Couple (Household Meditations)* (1859) the title of the painting itself stresses the unfulfilled life and relationship of this aged couple, despite the relative affluence of the room in which they sit, carrying out the hollow rituals of their daily life together (illus. 75).

Illegitimacy

At the bottom of the social scale, many women, often single, entered domestic service or took work in factories or breweries. *The Large Brewery* (1890) by Zorn captures the image of one such industrial establishment (illus. 76). In the painting, the women sit in regimented order along the walls, submerged in funereal gloom, working from dawn until dusk, until marriage and children might release them to exchange the thraldom of the factory for that of the home. For

Zorn himself, the subject was not merely one among many pictorial themes; his own impoverished mother had been obliged to seek work in Stockholm when young and, while there, had encountered a rich German brewer, by whom she had conceived the artist. Though his father never married his mother, he did remit funds for his son's support and continued to be interested in his wellbeing and development throughout his life. For many other illegitimate children in a similar situation, however, the father made no provision.

In general, however, illegitimacy remained a major social problem in the nineteenth century, especially so since the rates of illegitimate births were increasing in the cities and towns of the Nordic region where unwed mothers and children could be swallowed up by anonymous slums. In fact the problem was, at least for the mothers, more one of poverty than morality, since the birth rate of illegitimate children declines as the maternal background ascends the socioeconomic scale. The contrast of illegitimate births in urban as opposed to rural areas is most striking: only one out of twenty children, on average, was born out of wedlock in the countryside in Sweden during this period, but one out of four births in cities and towns there was illegitimate. In Stockholm, where fewer women married than elsewhere in Sweden, almost half of all births were illegitimate. This pattern was also reflected elsewhere in Scandinavia. For most unwed mothers the situation ultimately resolved itself, since some two-thirds of

76 Anders Zorn, *The Large Brewery*, 1890, oil on canvas.

them in Sweden ultimately found husbands by their late twenties. If pregnant women are included among these numbers, almost one-third of Swedish women either had or were expecting children at the time of their marriage. However, a sizeable minority of single mothers remained permanently on their own, obliged to look after their family.[56]

The proportion of illegitimacy also varied from region to region within countries. It was low, for example, in the west and south of Norway, where Pietism and the evangelical movement of Hauge were strong. There in the early nineteenth century only 5 per cent of children born were illegitimate. Similarly, in the Swedish rural areas of Halland, Kronoberg and Jönköping, the illegitimacy rates were very low. On the other hand, in Nordland, Troms and Finnmark, in the north of Norway, and elsewhere in Sweden, illegitimacy remained high.[57]

However, illegitimacy rates in Iceland were the highest in the Nordic region. There, between 1827 and 1830, over 15 per cent of children born were illegitimate, with both the law and the church condoning this situation. This ecclesiastical tolerance is not surprising, bearing in mind that more than 42 per cent

77 Jens Birkholm, *Hunger, Interior with a Woman and Child Sitting*, 1892, oil on canvas.

of priests themselves between 1811 and 1850 had wives who conceived or bore their first child out of wedlock. To some degree, though, this can be seen as a result of the legal situation where any illegitimate child whose parents later married became legitimate, thereby making the circumstances of a birth relatively unimportant.[58]

For a mother and child on their own, though, wherever they were in Scandinavia, there were few recourses available for those in need of social and financial assistance. This was an unhappy state of affairs to which, by the late nineteenth century, many intellectuals, including artists, sculptors and authors, were increasingly turning their attention. Inspired by the new 'Tendens' movement, many focused upon the need to ameliorate conditions for the socially unfortunate and the needy by means of visual images and imagery. At a time when most

78 Laurits Andersen Ring, *Beggar Children outside a Farmhouse in Ring*, 1883, oil on canvas.

social assistance depended on private charitable acts, rather than state-supported ones, the need to produce not always so subtle sentimental tugs at the heart was perceived as the best way of igniting the energies to provide the resources, material and social, to improve the plight of the socially and economically rejected. This the Danish artist Jens Birkholm (1869–1915), one of the numerous artists who worked on the Danish island of Fyn, succeeded in doing with his anguished depiction of poverty: *Hunger: Interior with a Woman and Two Children Sitting* (1892; illus. 77). Focusing upon the three emaciated figures embedded in the unmitigated bleakness of their barren room, the shadowy figure of death by starvation lurking above them on the darkened wall to the side, it taunts us to seek practical remedies. Who, after all, if not the well-heeled viewer, is in a position to take the concerted action necessary to address such evils?

At least in Birkholm's painting, the children could still be comforted and cared for by their mother, but for those unfortunate children alone, without maternal succour, life could be still more harrowing. This was true not only in the town, but in rural areas, where poverty and isolation could be even greater than in a city. Perhaps, the reality of rural poverty for abandoned children in

Denmark in all its bleak banality has been best captured by the Dane L. A. Ring, using an incident which he had witnessed near his own native village (illus. 78). Downcast and with demeanours of despair, the waifs he has depicted proceed on their weary way against the backdrop of a well-tended farmhouse behind, in the prosperity of which they cannot share. The scrawny trees above the stone embankment and the cool greyish tonalities of the paint heighten their desperate appearance and no optimistic note is added. Neither parents, society nor even the church were able to absorb the trickles (sometimes, on occasions of famine or epidemics, streams) of children who meandered their way throughout the Nordic region, in their quest for survival.

Prostitution

While some women could not, others would not submit themselves to the rigours of the institution of marriage. Of these, the vast majority took menial jobs. However, for a small minority, almost invariably untrained and uneducated, the world's most ancient profession provided the only other option. Aside from the very real dangers to health through disease and violence, a life of prostitution offered a practical alternative to marriage (though occasionally also within it), an arrangement which seemed to give considerable independence, and perhaps

79 Edvard Munch, *Rose and Amelie*, 1893, oil on canvas.

even an amusing lifestyle, compared to the other options available. This more jovial side of the profession has been amusingly expressed in *Rose and Amelie* (1893), by the Norwegian artist Edvard Munch (not normally renowned for his humorous paintings) (illus. 79). Two rather chubby ladies of the night happily play cards while waiting for clients, unencumbered by any feelings of guilt or disquiet. However, others in political authority took a grimmer view of prostitution, not least for reasons of health and the finances from the public coffers needed to deal with the problem. As a result, from the 1850s, many aspects of their trade were strictly regulated, especially in major cities and towns, such as Copenhagen, Stockholm and (Christiania) Oslo, but also in smaller ones. In addition to medical and police controls, prostitutes were sharply circumscribed in many aspects of their behaviour, both public and private. In the university city of Uppsala, for example, their discrete and muted comportment was required everywhere. Loitering and accosting in public places was prohibited, along with the entertainment of more than one person at a time even in private. They were also prohibited from strolling on a street after nine in the evening during the winter (or ten in the summer), and they were required to register any change of address with the police.[59] Though, by 1870, prostitutes made up no more than 1 per cent of the female population of Uppsala, it was, none the less, felt necessary to subject them to ever greater restrictions of movement and control, particularly after 1885, when the police took a more pro-active role. A new vagrancy law in the university town enabled the police to condemn convicted women to hard labour for a period of one month to one year, for a first offence, and six months to two years for a second.[60] Similar laws were enacted elsewhere in the Nordic region.

Ironically, it was from those segments of the population where single women were highest, the upper and upper middle classes, that a movement went out to 'save' these prostitutes from sexual vice and the corruption of men, single or married. Many matrons of the upper middle classes felt that proper training as domestic servants for women from humble backgrounds would discourage them from entering prostitution, while usefully providing much needed cheap labour for their vast houses and flats. As a result, many of the benevolent societies founded to improve their lot also sought to provide them with such practical but moral forms of employment. Thus, even the regulation of prostitution now lost its moral footing as one city after another tried to curtail it further, and in numerous instances, to outlaw it. By 1918, even Stockholm had abandoned regulated prostitution.[61]

For many men, the submissive role demanded of women, whether in or outside of prostitution or, indeed, married life, was difficult to separate from their seductive powers. Bohemian intellectuals, like Edvard Munch and his friend, the Polish poet and playwright Stanislaw Przybyszewski (1868–1927) were often fascinated with their alluring vulnerability. The latter was himself married to one of the most charming and enticing women of the Black Boar circle of Berlin's avant-garde, the Norwegian, Dagny Juell. His critique of

Munch's notorious painting *Madonna* (1893–4; see illus. 56) provided the occasion for Przybyszewski's entranced diatribe against the polarized role of vampire which a beautiful woman could assume:

> It is a female wearing a blouse with the characteristic movement of total submission, in which all the bodily organs give themselves over to total lust; a Madonna wearing a blouse of torn cloth with a halo announcing the coming martyrdom, a Madonna captured in the moment, in which the secret mysticism of the eternal forces of creation evoke a sea of beauty pouring out from the face of this female, an epiphany of the depths, where the cultured person with all his metaphysical urges to eternity combine with the lusty destructiveness of the animal.[62]

With respect to Przybyszewski's own relationship with his wife, however, the irony of history confirmed that she was less a *femme fatale* than the victim of the destructive power of men: she was shot and killed by a thwarted student in Tiblis, in the Russian Caucasus, in 1901.

Homosexuality

While the allurement of the female could also evoke fear and loathing, even more frightful to many people was homosexuality, condemned by the Lutheran Church in no uncertain terms. In the years following the Reformation, the crime of sodomy (along with prostitution, adultery and even fornication, all previously subject to the ecclesiastical courts) had become a civil crime.[63] The Appendix to the medieval National Law Codex of 1608 in Sweden-Finland explicitly condemned the sins of Sodom, lumping together both homosexuality and bestiality; this was also the case in the later Law Codex of 1734 though only bestiality was explicitly mentioned. None the less, homosexual acts were understood to be thereby covered and the law remained in effect even after the transfer of Finland to Russia in 1809 even if, legally, a failure to explicitly condemn it as a crime made any legal punishment questionable.[64] This legal anomaly was rectified in 1888 when both male and female homosexual acts were explicitly made illegal, bringing them in line with similar prohibitive laws passed in Sweden in 1864. This, ironically, was at a time when organizations were being established to increase the political rights of women. It was only in the middle of the twentieth century that such sexual activities ceased to be criminal. Many sailors, woodsmen in timber camps and urban bachelors, and some married men, left traces of their homosexual activities in letters and criminal records. Between 1894 and 1919, some twenty men (and two women) were imprisoned in Finland for homosexual acts. Yet statistically these count for but a small number of those Finns who were probably active homosexually and it would seem that the prosecution of homosexual acts was not zealously pursued, if one bears in mind that well over 600 individuals were convicted in the German Reich and about 160 men in Finland in just one year in this period for the crime of bestiality.[65] That said, tolerance for homosexuals seems to have been greatest in Norway, especially Bergen, which was said to be the centre of homosexual life in Norway, at least after independence from Sweden. There imprisonment for homosexuality was quickly abandoned in favour of fines for sexual activity between adults and these were apparently given by the courts only in the event of importuning.[66]

More blatant are the homoerotic references to be found in numerous works of art stretching from the eighteenth to the twentieth centuries. *Faun* (marble, 1774) by the great Swedish neo-classical sculptor Johan Tobias Sergel (1740–1814), for all its Platonic references, clearly reflects a taste in the sensuality of the male form, as well as muscle and skin tone and texture. While no evidence points to any such liaisons on Sergel's part, his monarch and patron Gustaf III was without doubt sexually involved with quite a number of men, from guardsmen to court figures, and found such homoerotic works of art suited to his tastes. In this he was following in the aesthetic footsteps of his probably homosexual uncle Frederick the Great of Prussia, but, doubtless more important, could find a more lofty justification for his tastes in the growing fascination for neo-classical aesthetic values as advocated by Winckelmann, and the classical ruins and sculpture which were such the rage with grand foreign visitors to Italy, of whom he was arguably the most important in 1783.

However, a particularly choice caricature by the Finnish-Swedish courtier Carl August Ehrensvärd (1745–1800) most unequivocally sheds light upon the king's disinclination for women, and, in particular his wife. *Caricature of Gustaf III's Attempt to Produce an Heir* (illus. 80) concentrates upon the desperate measures allegedly required to impregnate his queen Sophia Magdalena, for whom the king possessed a deep aversion. There is also a homosexual element in the work

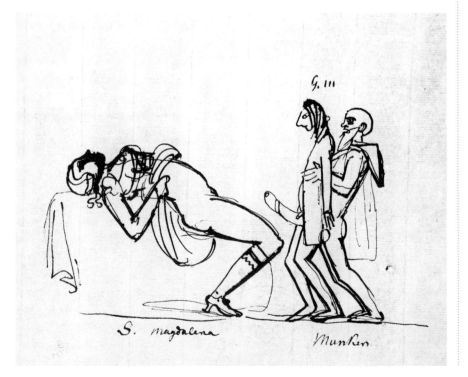

80 Carl August Ehrensvärd, *Caricature of Gustav III's Attempt to Produce an Heir,* c. 1770, pen and brown ink.

81 Eugène Jansson, *In the Baths of the Navy*, 1907.

evinced by the king's clutching of the flanks of his friend Munck. The queen's grand and festive entry into Stockholm as a Danish princess may have been celebrated with a royal procession of horsemen and carriages into Stockholm, but her years of married life with Gustaf remained unhappy ones of considerable isolation and emotional estrangement. Well over 100 years later, another queen, Victoria, the consort of King Gustaf V, was for similar reasons to find it expedient to settle for much of her life in Italy, leaving her husband as free a rein as was possible within the social parameters of his position and time (unfortunately, this did not preclude a sordid attempt at blackmail by a financially greedy guardsman towards the end of his life).

Homoerotic elements are also reflected in a number of nineteenth-century paintings, particularly in such works as In the *Baths of the Navy* (1907) by the Swedish artist Eugène Jansson (1863–1915), in which considerable sensual delight is taken in the depiction of young male nudes (illus. 81). Swimming baths in Scandinavia were favoured gathering places for homosexual men.[67] It is therefore not surprising that, as an active homosexual, Jansson picked up many sailors in these baths, a subject to which he returned quite often in his life. By justifying such works as a celebration of athleticism, he could also extend his admiring public beyond those for whom the beauty of the male form was paramount. Later, artists like Gösta Adrian Nilsson, would take up his mantel, and translate his vision of homosexual allurements into a Cubist painterly vision in which a microcosm of life in Stockholm is amusingly depicted. This is particularly true of GAN's (as he was nicknamed) work in wash and coloured chalk of 1916, *Two Sailors at Bern's Salon*, a popular café by the Berzelius Park, which he frequented, in which the two muscular men are juxtaposed in overlapping planes as if entwined round about one another, their eyes interlocked in a hard fixed stare which hints at both violence and lust. Parks in most European and American cities were haunts of homosexuals in quest of sexual contacts and Scandinavia was no exception. The park behind the military barracks in Helsinki was quite popular, while in Copenhagen Rådhuspladsen (The City Hall Square) was (and is still) a favoured area of promenade for homosexuals in Denmark. It was not only the navy which gained a reputation for a willingness to engage in homosexual activity. The army, too, throughout the Nordic region, provided a reservoir of young men in quest of sex with or without money. It was alleged that Copenhagen in the 1890s had more soldiers available for homosexual encounters than anywhere else in Europe, before a severe legal prosecution against such activity led to a mass exodus of them to Germany. The implication of leading society figures in such activity led to its relaxation and a renewed blossoming,[68] and leading homosexual literary figures like Hans Christian Andersen and later Herman Bang escaped the fate which awaited the latter's contemporary, Oscar Wilde, in England.

In Finland also a number of artists gave vent to works with homoerotic overtones. In Helsinki alone, if Hirschfeld is to be believed, the researcher claimed to have known personally at least 200 homosexual men of the higher classes, out of a total population of about 90,000.[69]

Verner Thomé (1878–1953) in *Boys who Play upon a Sandy Beach* (1903) may have been a part of the fashionable interest in the dynamics of bodily movement, but there is an undeniable erotic provocation in the young boys thrusting their bottoms into the foreground, their legs spread wide. This was a theme to which Thomé returned many times and, like Jansson, justified publicly by references to athleticism. In legal terms, as we have seen, homosexuality remained illegal in the Nordic region, by contrast to the Mediterranean world where it had been decriminalized by the Napoleonic Code in the early nineteenth century. Within the northern European world Sweden and Finland offer an interesting anomaly with respect to the criminalization of lesbian acts. In late nineteenth-century England and Germany, no law was explicitly enacted against such activity, but the parliaments of Sweden and Finland saw fit to prosecute it.[70] Unfortunately, however, as a form of sexuality obviously more deeply disturbing at the time than male homoeroticism, social taboos seemed to have prevented its expression even by indirect allusions in the arts. It was only in the second half of the twentieth century that a significant shift in these attitudes was to occur in Scandinavia, first in Sweden and Denmark and then finally in the last quarter of the century in Finland too, as new, less rigidly structured models of family life and sexuality began to permeate all segments of Nordic society.

Health, Hygiene and Disease

In the Early Modern Period, the Nordic region was probably one of the least healthy in Europe, a region in which the fruits of the soil were not easy to come by and where many people lived close to the existential minimum. Mortality rates were extremely high, especially in cities and towns, where appalling conditions of hygiene and poor diet made them generally double those of the countryside. The arrival of either severely cold winters or hot summers also sharply increased mortality, creating ideal conditions for the spread of disease.[1] The compactness of such cities as Stockholm and Copenhagen, in conjunction with a debilitatingly cold climate, for those already ill or on a poor diet, facilitated the spread of lung infections during winter, while in the warmer seasons epidemic diseases such as plague and smallpox, against which there was little protection, spread with great virulence. Indeed, a city such as Stockholm could only maintain its population level through immigration from rural areas, since child mortality rates exceeded those of births well into the nineteenth century.[2] In the countryside, by contrast, levels of child mortality were considerably lower.

Periodic epidemics of a wide variety of diseases raged throughout Scandinavia well into the nineteenth century. The Black Death which struck the region in 1350 had, by the end of 1351, wiped out some two-thirds of the population in parts of Norway, as well as causing severe devastation in most other areas, while that of 1495 in Iceland, probably a pneumonic strain, also annihilated a large proportion of the population. It continued to visit the Nordic region in waves, wreaking particular havoc in Finland and, to a lesser degree, Sweden, as late as the 1710s, while Copenhagen itself was ravaged in 1654 and again in 1711. Only in 1800 did Denmark's population again approach over 900,000, the level it had attained in the fourteenth century, before the decimating visitation of the plague.[3] The memory of its destructiveness haunted the popular imagination for centuries. It fascinated the Norwegian artist Theodor Kittelsen (1857–1914), who devoted a major series of works to the subject of which *The Black Death Series: The Soaring Eagle* (1894–6), is one of the most powerful (illus. 82). It is as if the awesome virulence of the infection, likened to a predatory, albeit majestic, bird seems to warrant respect. The association of the plague with birds was not merely a pictorial conceit: throughout much of the Middle Ages it was thought to be carried by birds. Other diseases also reaped a harvest of death and misery through the centuries. Leprosy was endemic, while smallpox occurred in many areas at intervals varying from every few years or less, in the south, to several

82 Theodor Kittelsen, *The Black Death Series: The Soaring Eagle*, 1894–6, wash, pen, pencil and black chalk.

decades in the remoter parts of Lapland. There an epidemic might, occasionally, take hold after the important markets held in February and March which brought many people together from diverse areas, with devastating effects.

Smallpox

Few epidemic diseases were given their own highly specific names until the late eighteenth century in Scandinavia or, indeed, in the rest of Europe. Rather, it was usual for the term 'fever' to cover a multitude of contagious ailments of various degrees of acuteness, with possibly the appendage of an adjective to describe its principal symptom. There were, however, two important exceptions to this rule: smallpox and leprosy. While the incidence of leprosy declined from the end of the Middle Ages in the Nordic region, serious outbreaks of smallpox continued to scourge Scandinavia until well into the nineteenth century, and until the introduction of inoculation, the disease made little distinction between great or humble: Queen Christina of Sweden was badly scarred by the disease and Anna Sofie Reventlow, third consort of the Danish king Frederik IV, died of it in 1743. While the introduction of inoculation against smallpox in Uppsala in 1756 soon offered a modicum of protection to those of the upper classes and their dependants who opted for it, it continued to account for 25 per cent of the total mortality rate and up to three-quarters of child mortality during epidemics in the second half of the eighteenth century.[4]

Gustaf III and his siblings were inoculated against smallpox in 1769 by the Prussian David Schultz von Schultzenheim, who had studied the benefits of inoculation in England[5] (the great traveller Lady Mary Wortley Montagu had seen its benefits in the Ottoman Empire, while her husband was ambassador from the Court of St James to the Porte, had been deeply impressed by the immunity it appeared to convey and had popularised it[6]). However, in Sweden generally, particularly in the north, it was rarely carried out, even though many priests increasingly encouraged their parishioners to be inoculated. However, the introduction of vaccination by cowpox in Sweden in 1801 (the Englishman William Jennings had discovered the immunity it provided in 1796) raised expectations of drastically reducing incidences of the disease or even eradicating it.

While most Scandinavians evinced a fatalistic complacency towards smallpox during the eighteenth century, the Saami of Lapland certainly did not. The great botanist Carl von Linné commented in the 1730s that when the disease broke out, they would abandon both possessions and relations, fleeing to the hills with as a great a speed as could be mustered. In 1801 a physician who had practised in Torneå, in Lapland, wrote: 'In the beginning of an epidemic, several Saami families move over to Norway, and it is not rare for them to leave the old people at home and drop those relatives infected on the way, leaving them to their unfortunate destiny'. Even spouses were abandoned in the wilderness, if necessity seemed to require it.[7] The demography of the disease in Lapland was different from that elsewhere in Scandinavia, and the disease more rarely affected the region, probably because of its relative isolation and sparse population density. In

1740 a major epidemic of smallpox was recorded in Jokkmokk, an important Saami trading centre in the far north-west of Sweden and it appears that, like other epidemics in Lapland, it afflicted more the elderly than the young. Usually the disease would enter the region from Finish coastal areas, in close trading contact with Lapland and where inoculation had made few inroads. It then not only seriously affected mortality rates, but exerted a considerable influence upon the demography relating to marriage: victims of smallpox tended to marry one another, possibly because severe facial scaring left them excluded from the more desirable pool of marriageable people.[8]

By the early nineteenth century, however, infection and mortality from smallpox began to decline. Whereas some 41,000 had died of the disease in the 1790s, its death toll in Sweden had fallen by 90 per cent in the 1810s and 1820s, by which time over three-quarters of all children had been vaccinated, a statistic that the clergy were now required to record. Interestingly, though, in Lapland, where vaccination was introduced first in the 1820s, mortality rates for the disease had already fallen radically prior to its introduction, perhaps because the disease had become less virulent.[9] In Finland, too, the incursions of smallpox were being curbed. Severe epidemics having raged in 1754, 1763 and 1771, vaccination was introduced to the grand-duchy by 1802 and by 1820 it could boast of the highest percentage of vaccinated inhabitants in the world.[10]

In Denmark, vaccination was introduced in 1801 and a similarly drastic fall in mortality also followed. In Norway, where vaccination became compulsory in 1810, those failing to avail themselves of it were refused permission for confirmation or denied a license to marry.[11] Later in the century, the activities of disinfectors, employees of the parish who disinfected such household goods as furniture and fabrics in iron ovens (heated by gas to a temperature considerably over boiling point for twenty-minute periods) also helped to lower the incidence of smallpox, as well as of other diseases.

None the less, with some people negligent of or refusing vaccination, smallpox remained a presence in pockets of the country at least until 1915.[12] In the late nineteenth century, the Finnish artist Akseli Gallen-Kallela was still able to depict one victim of the disease, in *A Man from Savo, Scarred by Smallpox* (1893), a unique painterly record of its visual effects (illus. 83).

The far northern colonies of Denmark, Iceland and Greenland, where the isolated populations possessed little natural immunity, were particularly prone to smallpox. During the years 1707–9, a quarter of the population died from the disease.[13] Such epidemics recurred throughout the century, though usually with diminishing severity. None the less, the smallpox epidemic in Iceland which followed the volcanic eruption of Laki in 1783–5, aggravated by severe famine, proved to be one of the worst in the island's history. Even after the introduction of vaccination in 1802, smallpox continued periodically to visit Iceland which

83 Akseli Gallen Kallela, *A Man from Savo, Scarred by Smallpox*, 1893, oil on canvas.

endured a major epidemic in 1839–40 and, to a much less severe degree, its final serious outbreak of the disease in 1899.[14]

In Greenland, a huge percentage of the population had died in the early eighteenth century of smallpox introduced from Denmark. In one summer alone, during the early nineteenth century, 62 people died in the small settlement of Hunde Ejland by Egedesminde, in the west of Greenland. Church records state that an English whaler had sold one Elias Jakob a pair of trousers which turned out to have been infected by the disease and from whom it spread to everyone else.[15] Vaccination was increasingly introduced, hospitals established (usually run by religious organizations), and doctors gradually came to Greenland where they generally assumed positions of great social prominence: *The Doctor's Residence at Godthaab* painted by Mads Lynge (1880), for example, depicts what was arguably the most stately residence in Greenland's most important settlement and underscores the extremely important role medical men played in improving the health and physical wellbeing of Greenlanders as the twentieth century dawned.

Leprosy

From the seventeenth century another major disease, leprosy, greatly diminished in the region, a trend which had already begun towards the end of the Middle Ages. None the less, lepers were not uncommon and it would take many years for its final eradication. The famous seventeenth-century Icelandic priest and poet Hallgrímur Pétursson was himself a victim of the disease, and it afflicted many prominent people. The slow progress of the ailment meant that its victims might live for decades and there was a need to provide appropriate accommodation, which it was thought would hinder the spread of the contagion while providing an asylum for its victims. As a result, a leper hospital would be situated some distance outside a city or town, where it was generally built of wood, together with a chapel usually constructed of stone in the Late Gothic fashion of the times. Life could carry on in a microcosm of life outside, if relatively self-contained and largely communal. In Iceland, however, where the inhabitants were few and sparsely settled, lepers tended not to be isolated from the rest of the population, a major problem over the centuries with respect to the unavoidable spread of the disease thereby fostered.[16]

In Sweden, in the 1600s, the largest leper hospital was at Enköping, where some twenty inmates were accommodated. Before the Protestant Reformation the Church or charitable ecclesiastical foundations were responsible for the establishment and upkeep of leper hospitals, but afterwards, the Crown came to assume their direction, and King Gustaf Vasa was particularly solicitous to protect hospitals and asylums for the poor from private encroachment.[17] Yet, the government, with its eye on greater efficiency, economy and social control, did bring about a significant change in their usage: hospitals increasingly came to be used to accommodate those who were mentally ill with no one else to care for them. Invalids, without family or friends, might also find a refuge in them, though this was usually a last resort. This was also the case in Finland, where the incidence of leprosy had not yet declined so noticeably, and where a leprosarium had been founded as late as the early eighteenth century at Seili in the Turku archipelago, but it even there it soon accommodated more victims of mental illness than lepers.[18]

Despite the reduction in the number of victims of leprosy in the Nordic region, the disease had not died out in Norway or Sweden even in the nineteenth century. There were still some 3000 lepers in Vestlandet near Bergen, in Norway, and about 100 in the provinces of Hälsingland and Siljan, in north central Sweden in the 1850s. A lithograph of *A Thirteen Year Old Boy with Leprosy since the Age of Six*, by J. L. Losting (1847) is illustrated in a medical work *On Leprosy* by two Norwegians, D. C. Danielssen and C. V. Boeck (illus. 84) and shows the ravages of the disease. Only in 1873 was the bacterium which caused leprosy isolated by the Norwegian Armauer Hansen (1841–1912), a doctor at the principal leprosarium in Bergen, enabling new measures to be taken to combat its spread. As a result, numbers fell dramatically in Norway from 2,100 people in 1875, to 300 by the time of Hansen's death.[19]

(Above) **84** J. L. Losting, *A Thirteen Year Old Boy with Leprosy since the Age of Six*, lithograph from D. C. Danielssen and C. V. Boeck, *On Leprosy* (1847).

(Below left) **85** Conrad Djulsted, Järvsö Leprosy Hospital, Hälsingland (Sweden), 1867–89.

Improvements were also made in the quality of life of lepers, especially those who were obliged to remain hospitalized. In 1867, a leprosarium was built by the Swede Conrad Djulsted at Järvsö, in Hälsingland, with accommodation for twenty permanent inmates (illus. 85). The principal building of the complex had the appearance of a typical wooden two-storeyed Swedish country house of the period, with commodious rooms, illuminated by six windows on the ground floor and seven on the first. Visits to the local parish church were now permitted and, by 1889, more spacious accommodation was available for a further 26 residents. The spread of the disease throughout the Nordic region had by now definitely been arrested, in part through the labours of a Danish physician, Edvard Ehlers (1863–1937). From Iceland, in 1898, to St Croix, in the Danish Virgin

Islands in 1904, he helped to establish leprosaria to hinder leprosy's spread. Still, even as late as 1942, one female victim of leprosy, who had contracted the disease locally at the end of the nineteenth century, was still alive in Norway, while the last leper to contract the disease in the Nordic region itself, a Swede, died as recently as 1951.[20]

The social legacy of such asylums should not be underestimated. They provided cradle to grave care, sometimes for whole families. Children were born there and afflicted couples sometimes married within them and remained to live out their lives in the care of the state. In a certain sense, leprosaria can be seen as prototypes of the Scandinavian welfare states of the latter twentieth century.

Veteran Hospitals and the Military

Leprosaria were, of course, not the only type of specialized hospital in Scandinavia. Veteran hospitals, for example, were required to provide long-term care for invalids from the many wars which raged between and among the Nordic nations and their neighbours throughout the period. In Sweden, a hospital for veterans had opened in 1647 at Vadstena to cope with invalids from the Thirty Years War. Largely composed of buildings from a monastery dissolved in 1595, it continued in use until 1783, having been renovated and altered according to the designs of the Swedish architect and courtier Count Carl Johan Cronstedt (1709–1777) from 1763 to 1770. Family members of the invalids were also quartered here, including servants and children, for whom a school was established in 1729.[21] Another garrison hospital at Hantverkargatan, in Stockholm (illus. 86), designed by Carl Christoffer Gjörwell the Younger (1766–1837), a Swede who had studied under Louis-Jean Desprez, opened its doors in 1834 and continued in use until 1969, serving an increasing variety of purposes unrelated to the needs of war veterans. A stately building with a wide central portico of six Doric half-pillars, it was laid out in the form of a truncated

86 Carl Christoffer Gjörwell the Younger, Garrison Hospital, Hantverkargatan, Stockholm, 1834.

'H', the rooms for patients distributed 'rationally' on either side of central corridors running throughout the length and breadth of the building.[22]

Mental Illness

By the early eighteenth century, one of the most important functions of hospitals in the Nordic countries was to accommodate the seriously mentally ill, often with no one able or available to look after them. One of the most famous in the region was Danvik's Mental Asylum, near Stockholm (built 1719–25) by Göran Josua Adelcrantz, one of the largest institutional buildings in Sweden at this time. It included a chapel, with a rectangular nave, surmounted by a clock tower, as the drawing made by J. E. Carlberg in 1733 indicates. On either side were dormitories, containing six windows on each façade at two levels, with stairwells at either end. Each dormitory contained some 42 beds, arranged in pairs along the windows and in groups of four in the centre, on to which arched windows in the nave of the chapel opened.

In Finland, Kronoby Hospital (1743), at Korpholmen, between Pietarsaari (Jakobstad) and Kokkola (Old Karleby), then a major seaport, was one of the most important in the grand-duchy. Mainly of wood, it lay scattered over a tightly but irregularly built area on the left bank of the Kronoby River. In the centre of the complex were two buildings for the containment of those deemed mad, on either side of an enclosed courtyard, each containing a total of 26 cells ('cages'), 1.80 m by 2.40 m in size, ranged around three sides of a much larger room. The 'cages', which housed those most severely ill, generally in chains, were separated from the large rooms by sturdy wooden grating. The less deranged and the simple-minded lived in the larger rooms. There was also a nearby chapel and an adjacent 'spital house' (1670s), both built by local farmers, for the accommodation of lepers who could assist at religious services through a window into the chapel. The complex also housed the chronically ill, blind, lame and those otherwise unable to financially support themselves, including orphans, living in scattered cabins which they had built themselves.[23] With land for the cultivation of crops and animal husbandry to supply the institution's needs, the hospital formed a complete and relatively self-sufficient community, catering for the needs if not of all its inmates, at least of society at large.

In the Danish dominions, mental hospitals such as that based on 'the most modern principles' at Schleswig (1820), by Christian Frederik Hansen (1756–1845), where the Swedish bishop and poet Esaias Tegnér, increasingly plagued by mental illness in later life, was a temporary inmate during the 1840s, became an important Scandinavian prototype. This was, in turn, superseded by others like Sankt Hans, at Bistrup near Roskilde, particularly famed for its enlightened regime. The leading Danish architect Gottlieb Bindesbøll (1800–1856), who had trained under Hansen, produced designs for building work there which was completed in 1859, two years after work was finished on Oringe Hospital (1854–7), which he also designed, at Vordingborg, to cater for the mentally ill of south Sjælland, Møn and Falster.

As time went on, however, the demands of economy as well as the growth of central bureaucratic control from national capitals meant that smaller hospitals ultimately gave way to larger establishments often in small villages within the catchment of major metropolitan areas. In Sweden, for example, Ulleråker, by Uppsala, became one of the most important of these in the 1830s, with other long-established hospitals, such as Vesterås, sending patients there. The nature of the care provided in these new centralized hospitals also changed, based upon the programme of reforms of Philippe Pinel, chief physician at the mental asylum at Bicêtre, in France. He was of fundamental importance, not least for his treatise, *Medico-Philosophical Treatise on Mental Alienation or Mania Cure* (1801), with its novel focus on the need to treat rather than merely contain the victims of mental illness. Pinel abhorred the barbaric custom of the public visiting mental asylums in order to gawk at the inmates for purposes of entertainment and implemented changes to protect patients from such demeaning experiences. By 1820, for example, Danvik's Mental Asylum, near Stockholm, provided 41 cells for only 86 inmates, a radical improvement in the space allotted to each inmate, bearing in mind the number of the mentally ill usually accommodated in dormitories in the early nineteenth century. There were also dining rooms which served as sitting rooms, with workrooms allocated to those able to be employed on useful tasks. Such an improvement was particularly impressive, considering the growing numbers of people during this period classified as mentally ill and given secure accommodation. By the middle of the century, at least 1,000 people were listed as inmates of mental hospitals in Sweden and the numbers of those still requiring accommodation demanded the construction of further hospitals, especially in urban areas. For example, Konradsberg Hospital (1855–8) (now Rålambshovs Hospital; illus. 87) was built on Kungsholmen, in Stockholm, to cope with the needs of the rapidly growing Swedish capital and its suburbs. Designed by Albert Törnqvist (1819–1898), with a façade 140 metres in length, it was a vast building and more space was provided per patient, and hygiene and ventilation were given a new prominence, according to the latest principles.

As the nineteenth century progressed, reformers such as the American Dorothea Lynde Dix exerted a growing influence on hospital building and reform. In Gothenburg, the new mental hospital at Hisingen (1872), with patients' rooms situated within its two long parallel elevations, reflected some of the latest in humanitarian values as viewed from a contemporary perspective. Yet two systems at this time competed as models for the layout of rooms. One was the horizontal arrangement, in which hospital wings were organized with a dining room and patients' rooms on each floor. In the other, popular from the 1880s, the vertical system placed dining rooms on the ground floor, rooms for patients on the first floor, and work rooms on the third floor, largely for reasons of economy.

Whatever the plan adopted, hospitals increasingly came to be situated in large parks, in some cases, as at Lund, newly laid out with over 37,000 plants. There patients could promenade or otherwise occupy their time in serene surround-

87 Albert Törnqvist, Konradsberg Hospital (now Rålambshovs Hospital), Stockholm, 1855–8.

ings, although the strict regime and control of those who lived and worked there remained a sobering hallmark of life within the compound. Not only were patients curtailed in their personal freedom, but even staff were required to receive permission to leave the institution for whatever reason.[24]

Elsewhere in the Nordic countries, a spate of mental hospital construction ensued. Lappviken was built in Helsinki according to the designs of Carl Ludwig Engel, while the German Heinrich Ernst Schirmer (1814–1887) built Gaustad Asylum, near Christiania, opened in 1855. By the early twentieth century the trend was for smaller establishments, at least for the mentally retarded who were felt to still hold some grip on reality. The growing numbers of elderly suffering from senile dementia and other mental illnesses of old age, who survived as mortality rates fell, also required accommodation in smaller residential units in their home communities.

Fashions were not only changing in architectural terms in the treatment of mental illness and related problems of old age, but also with respect to the very ways with which mental illnesses were categorized, as new Freudian and other descriptive terms became popular. Yet, for all these changes, the prognosis of cure remained limited: between 1880 and 1940, only one in three patients in mental institutions was released in Sweden within a year.[25] Without doubt, it is Edvard Munch who has in pictorial terms best captured the unhappy circumstances of the mentally ill as an everyday reality. His *Melancholia (Laura)* (1899; illus. 125) stems from a visit to one of his sisters who was herself a patient in Gaustad. He wrote in his reminiscence *The Yellow House* with veiled references to both Laura's incarceration there as well as his own experiences at a pension in Ljan, a leafy suburb of Christiania, where he was recovering from alcoholism and a mental breakdown.

Elsewhere in the Nordic countries statistics reflecting the low rate of improvement for the mentally ill confirm the poor prognosis for treatment. Compared to the treatment of those entering asylums in the eighteenth century, however, the progress was considerable. In any case, under the auspices of psychiatric professors such as Bror Gadelius at Konradsberg Hospital in the 1890s, cells fell out of fashion for the containment of the mentally ill who were now treated as a matter of course with lengthy warm baths, sometimes for hours, because of their calming effect and given more humane accommodation, often with others.

During the early decades of the twentieth century, the numbers of mentally ill patients in hospitals burgeoned, creating a serious lack of appropriate accommodation.[26] Whether the effects of growing industrialization were dislocating people, mentally as well as physically, or whether it was the case that the toleration of psychological eccentricities by the authorities was diminishing is not clear; perhaps both factors played a role in the increase. In any case, it was certainly true that the growing life expectancy of elderly people increased dramatically that segment of the population which was prone to suffer from senility.[27] Alongside considerable advances being made in the humane treatment of the mentally ill through analysis and medication, others, more disturbing, were also making an appearance towards the end of the 1930s. This was especially true in Norway and Sweden, where intrusive surgical procedures like lobotomy came frequently to be adopted, often under compulsion. As a result almost 50,000 people were lobotomized, while sterilization became the fate of many thousands of others – 'treatments' which would continue well into the 1970s, before a new and less authoritarian approach to mental illness came into fashion.

There were also a significant number of victims of mental illnesses for whom incarceration was considered a necessity in order to protect them from self-destructive impulses. This was particularly the case with those who tried to kill or harm themselves or others, not only by violence, but by alcoholic excesses. This led to a mushrooming of private clinics throughout the Nordic region for those who wished or where obliged by their families to 'dry out'; indeed, the artist Edvard Munch had been successfully cured in one in Copenhagen by Dr Daniel Jacobsen, but for prospective suicides the outcome was more bleak. Strait-jacketing and padded rooms could not the solve the problem of the despairing individual in a society in which suicide remained a major taboo, along with the disease of alcoholism. Indeed, it is as if the virtual absence of Nordic paintings and drawings with references to alcoholism and suicide reflected a social reluctance at the time in the upper middle classes to consider these subjects, even if a temperance movement was in full-swing further down the social scale.

Disease, Diet and Child Mortality

The highest mortality rates in the Nordic region, as elsewhere, affected children, particularly infants. In Sweden, they were especially high in urban areas where a quarter of all babies born died before they reached their first birthday throughout most of the eighteenth century. In the countryside, their life expectancy was greater with six out of seven children surviving their first year. Though mortality rates fell the older a child became, only 70 per cent of children reached the age of 25 in the countryside, as opposed to 60 per cent in cities and towns. Amongst illegitimate children, in fact, well over 30 per cent died before reaching their first birthday, not always to the grief of their parents.[28] As one local general practitioner in Uppsala grimly expressed it, 'The grinding poverty which afflicts the greater part of crofters and agricultural labourers, makes parents more grateful for the demise of a child than their arrival into the world.'[29] Whooping cough was particularly widespread and lethal; more than 40,000 children died of the disease in Sweden between 1749 and 1764 alone.[30]

Only the arrival of the potato crop seemed to offer some dramatic means to enable the poor and especially their children to survive the vicious circle of poverty and hunger and the frightful legacy of famine: low resistance to disease. In the catastrophic famine in Finland of 1699–7, at least one-third of the entire population succumbed. The growth of Arctic pack ice and colder waters had helped to drive Atlantic depressions on to a more southerly course than usual, resulting in severe summer frosts and consequential crop failures.[31] The famine victims died, in the main, not of hunger itself, but of epidemic diseases such as typhus. Famine also encouraged increased movement of population, desperately seeking sustenance from one village to the next, which helped to spread any contagious diseases, attacking young and old with equal severity.[32]

In Sweden and Norway, potatoes were introduced during the mid-eighteenth century from Britain, largely through the good offices of scientifically minded and innovative local vicars, who saw that this crop provided a cheap and easy way of sustaining the mass of their populations. One Norwegian vicar of Gausdal, in Gudbrandsdalen, reaped such a large harvest in 1775 that he was able to provide seed potatoes to all the cottars in his parish. Not only could they be sown in relatively poor soil, but they were more hardy than grains and particularly pleased cottars who could distil them to produce spirits legally after 1816. Moreover, the potato provided a good substitute for corn when wars prevented the latter's importation, as happened during the British blockade between 1807 and 1814 in the Napoleonic Wars.[33]

However, in the longer term, over-dependence on a single crop was to prove disastrous when potato blight struck, much as it did in Ireland, since few alternative foods were available to take its place. In particular, the potato blight of the 1850s in Sweden led to massive emigration abroad, the texture and tone of which is expressed in Vilhelm Moberg's novel *The Emigrants* (1949–59), later made into an award-winning film, with the actress Liv Ullmann. Mass emigration occurred in Norway as well, with many thousands sailing to the United States and Canada. But other parts of the Nordic region also benefited from Norway's loss of population and many Norwegians emigrated to Iceland.

In Finland, another catastrophic famine occurred in 1867, the result of major crop losses of rye, corn and oats in most parts of the country for two years running. 30 per cent of the crop was destroyed in the province of Tavastehus (Häme), while in the province of Savo (Savolax), almost the entire crop was destroyed. Cereal stores maintained for such events were unequal to the magnitude of need created by two years of famine. Despite government admonitions to the contrary, endless streams of humanity made their way southwards, carrying with them typhus and other epidemic diseases which struck down even those in areas where the harvest was successful. As a result, the following year more than

137,700 people succumbed, some 8 per cent of the total population, many in unhygienic camps erected to house the homeless or in areas where it was thought that charitable handouts of food would only create greater problems. Instead, to sustain themselves, 'The population was encouraged to spin and weave, hunt and fish, collect berries, bark, mushrooms and lichen [...].'[34] Large quantities of food, imported from abroad, were ultimately made available, but because of poor transport much of it never reached those who were in need.

Outlying areas such as Greenland were also particularly vulnerable to famine and poor logistics well into the nineteenth century, where large numbers of people continued to live just over the existential minimum and where poor fishing or hunting, in a land with virtually no farming, could result in massive starvation. (This was, in all probability, the major reason for the disappearance of the old Norse population in Greenland sometime during the fifteenth century.) Indeed, even the native Inuit, long adapted as they were to the environment, continued to live on a delicate existential line throughout these centuries. For them, a poor harvest from the sea could easily mean the extinction of a family or group of families until the end of the last century.

In Iceland, matters were little better. The eighteenth century, in particular, was a period of natural catastrophe. In 1702 alone, thousands of Icelanders died of famine, while the volcanic eruption of 1784–5, with its concomitant destruction of arable land and livestock, wiped out one-fifth of the entire Icelandic population.[35] As a result, by contrast with the population growth in the rest of Europe, Iceland's population had declined by some 20 per cent by 1800. Child mortality was double that in Sweden, with many Icelandic children not surviving their first fortnight. Measles usually broke out in gaps of seven years,[36] causing many deaths, while tetanus was particularly lethal. As a result of these and other illnesses, over a third of Icelandic children were dead by their first birthday. By their fifteenth year, fewer than half were still alive.[37] Even in the nineteenth century, a dearth of food could be a serious problem, with malnutrition a major cause of mortality, particularly for men.[38] One visitor, the Marquis of Dufferin and Ava, commented, in 1854, that scurvy, leprosy and elephantiasis also continued to plague the island.[39]

In Iceland, however, mortality figures for children had clearly begun to fall by the second decade of the nineteenth century, and the change became dramatic after 1870, because of improvements in hygiene, pre- and post-natal care and more extensive breast-feeding.[40] Previously, mothers had nursed their children for only a few days after birth, before feeding them on cow's milk, but this practice had come to be abandoned, with considerable beneficial effect.[41] A vicious outbreak of hydatid disease in 1923 created a great uproar but had little effect on mortality rates, though it did lead to the virtual annihilation of all dogs in Reykjavik by some of which the disease had spread in 1923.[42]

Even in periods in which there were no famines, not everyone had enough to eat. This was an unhappy plight which the Norwegian Adolph Tidemand sought to stress in his stridently evocative work *Need* (1874). Elsewhere in the

88 Christian Krohg, *The Fight for Survival*, 1888–9, oil on canvas.

Nordic region, however, especially in Scania and Denmark, relatively rich harvests in grain tended to mitigate against such disasters even in the worst years and famine was unknown.

One of the most disturbing images of hunger, however is that to be found in a 'Tendens' painting by Christian Krohg (illus. 88). *The Fight for Survival* (1888–9), depicts thin children, their faces emaciated by hunger, clamouring for bread outside a charity bakery. In the fight for survival, however, it is the taller and more grown-up throng in front of them who are the victors in grabbing these handouts, a Darwinian cautionary tale.

Typhoid, Dysentery and Cholera

Even when true famine did not occur, mere shortages of food or poor diet could make life for the poor not only miserable but particularly prone to disease. While

SWENSKA QUARANTA[

89 Jacob Forsell, *Känsö Quarantine Hospital*, Göteborg (Sweden), 1818, drawing and wash.

smallpox affected rich and poor alike, diseases like dysentery and typhus were linked to crop failures and the poorer segments of the population. The countryside swarmed with famished migrants seeking succour who spread these diseases wherever they went, especially in the camps sometimes set up to accommodate and sustain them. The diocese of Akershus, including Christiania, for example, in Norway, was devastated by both diseases for over two years, commencing in the autumn of 1808 when the harvest failed, a misfortune exacerbated by the soldiers and sailors returning from the Napoleonic Wars.[43]

In the Danish and Swedish dependencies, too, febrile diseases wrought havoc. Life in the garrisons stationed there was truly precarious. Of the 33 men who arrived in Swedish St Barthelemy between 1805 and 1815, 29 had died by the end of that period[44] and in 1849 about one-third of the population, some 350 people, died of an unspecified fever. In any case, the constant barrages of yellow fever and endemic malaria almost always exacted a horrific toll.[45] The latter is, of course, a mainly tropical and semi-tropical disease, but in Sweden indigenous malaria was not unknown, and between 1875 and 1908 some 60,000 cases of the disease were recorded, mainly in the south-east of the country along the Baltic coast of Scania, as well as along the shores of Sweden's large inland lakes, Mäleren and Vänern. By the mid-1930s, however, malaria in Sweden was eradicated.[46] In Denmark, too, the disease was endemic in the late eighteenth century on the islands of Lolland and Falster, where it came to be treated with quinine. In the 1860s, there were still some four or five thousand cases of the disease in Denmark, many of them on Lolland, though malaria seems finally to have died out even there by the turn of the twentieth century.[47]

The introduction of quarantine in Denmark in the late sixteenth century and elsewhere by the seventeenth and early eighteenth centuries may have helped to preserve northern Europe from the ravages of the plague from the 1720s onwards, but a disease new to Europe, cholera, unwittingly imported from India, was soon to make major inroads during the second and third quarters of the nineteenth century.

Some preparations devised for the prevention of other diseases did exist to hinder its spread, but these did not prove particularly effective. For example, a quarantine hospital (illus.89) which had been established at Känsö, in Gothenburg's archipelago, in order to prevent the outbreak of yellow fever,

INRÄTTNINGEN VID KÄNSÖ.

which it was feared ships bearing salt for the herring trade might carry from the Spanish colonies to Scandinavia. The complex consisted of an infirmary, an observation hospital and two supporting buildings just offshore. These were connected by drawbridges which could be raised in case of infection. A little wooden parlour was also erected for the communications of various parties through a grill which, by means of pipes, emitted cleansing smoke, with vinegar provided to purify documents of any contagion, but cholera was not transmitted like yellow fever.

In fact, when cholera first struck Scandinavia in 1834, the nature of the disease and its means of infection was not understood at all, so few effective measures could be taken to hinder its progress. First Gothenburg fell victim where one in ten of its residents died; then Stockholm followed suit, though the mortality there was down to one in twenty. In spite of the rapid erection of twelve temporary hospitals to deal with victims of the epidemic, some 12,000 people in all died of the disease in Sweden.

Cholera, however, was primarily an urban illness, infection from which was facilitated by poor hygiene. Thus, in the countryside, many areas remained free of the disease.[48] Elsewhere, in the Nordic regions, cholera showed a similar epidemic pattern, with Copenhagen also badly affected. Indeed, the fact that the disease predominantly affected the poorest elements of society led many people in this age of revolutions to conclude, especially in Italy, that a plot was underway by the rich to eliminate the unwanted poor by poisoning. Scandinavian visitors to Italy occasionally found their own movements constrained by the disease. The individuals depicted in *A Group of Danish Artists in Rome* (1837) by Constantin Hansen (1804–1880), for example, are mournfully whiling away the time of day in the studio of the Danish architect M. G. B. Bindesbøll in the Via Sistina, where they had assembled together in order to escape the ravages of a cholera epidemic in Rome at the time (illus. 90). The fact that gravediggers rarely succumbed to the infection, despite the great numbers of dead they buried, while the denizens of slums (though also sailors) dropped like flies, seemed to add credibility to the erroneous arguments of the conspiracy theory. In Scandinavia, however, relatively few gave credence to it, though the revolutionary disquietude which broke out in the Nordic countries in 1848 was genuine enough and not totally unrelated. The reality was that all governments employed old and ineffective techniques for

90 Constantin Hansen,
*A Group of Danish Artists in
Rome*, 1837, oil on canvas.

dealing with the new disease: the erection of *cordons sanitaires*, the use of fumigation and the isolation of those already afflicted or infected.[49]

Another grave epidemic of cholera broke out in the early 1850s, the second and final great visitation of the disease to afflict the region. Most of the major ports of Scandinavia were affected, and it carried away Christoffer Wilhelm Eckersberg, the so-called father of Danish painting, at his professor's seat at the Royal Academy of Art in Christiansborg Palace, Copenhagen. He had failed to heed the admonishments of many of those around him to retire to the country while the contagion raged.

Developments in urban sanitation in the second half of the nineteenth century, including widespread construction of sewers, piped water supplies from more sanitary sources and the general introduction of the water-closet provided the most effective means of preventing cholera epidemics in Scandinavia, even when the disease ravaged nearby neighbours like Russia on the southern and

eastern rim of the Baltic. New and improved quarantine measures also continued. Still, it was only in 1884 that the bacterial nature of cholera and the way it was spread came to be understood, and even then several years would elapse before the benefits of this knowledge could be implemented.

While an epidemic of cholera attacked Iceland in 1882–3, where many were already weakened by famine[50], the severe cholera epidemic which attacked New York, Hamburg and other important cities in 1893 left the Nordic countries relatively unscathed. None the less, other diseases including scarlet fever and diphtheria continued to take their toll, especially among children, and 9 per cent of deaths could still be attributed to their ravages in the late nineteenth century.[51]

In Denmark, as well as elsewhere on the Continent, large general hospitals usually provided accommodation for those suffering from severe febrile illnesses. In Copenhagen, the leading hospital of this order was depicted by Vilhelm Hammershøi, in a mural for the City Hall (illus. 91), a vast complex with numerous ancillary buildings. By contrast, in Sweden, those who fell ill with epidemic diseases tended to be accommodated in small local hospitals, often cottage-like, with half-timbered gables. Such homely establishments, however, tended to be fitted with the latest amenities, including private lavatory facilities.[52]

By the first decades of the twentieth century, continued improvements in hygiene and diet increased living space per person and better hospital treatment meant that diphtheria and other severe contagious diseases declined. The arrival and wake of the First World War, however, had catastrophic effects even for those countries such as Sweden, Denmark and Norway, who were politically neutral: in the influenza pandemic of 1918–19, spread by returning armies and other demographic dislocations, some half a million Scandinavians fell victim to the disease, 85 per cent of them between the ages of seventeen and 40 (illus. 92). Of these, some 34,000 died, despite the fact that all manner of public buildings were turned into hospitals throughout the region to provide assistance.[53] Even in the Nordic periphery, influenza took its harrowing toll, and in Iceland, 486 had died of the airborne contagion by the end of 1918.[54]

Venereal Infections

Other forms of contagious diseases also brought death and debility to the Nordic region. The spread of venereal infections was a serious problem from the end of

91 Vilhelm Hammershøi, *The General Hospital in Copenhagen*, 1902, oil on canvas.

(Above left) **98** Caspar Müller, Larvik Hospital (Norway), 1762.

(Above right) **99** Erik Palmstedt, Monumental gates of the Seraphim Infirmary, Stockholm, 1792.

branches of spruce or juniper trees to hinder the spread of infection. Four nurses lived in a adjacent rooms by the entrance hall, sometimes assisted by medical students acquiring practical training. Though some self-supporting patients were accommodated, funds usually came from a tax on tobacco, lotteries, church contributions and other donations administered by the Seraphim Order of Knights. After 1783, however, the state provided some funds directly, and despite its relatively small size, its appearance was quite grand, for the monumental gates of the Seraphim Infirmary (illus. 99) were built to the design of the leading court architect, Erik Palmstedt, in 1792, who decorated the principal façade with rusticated pilasters and a massive tympanum, including a large royal coat of arms.[70]

Mortality rates in hospitals had always been dreadful, but in the nineteenth century attempts to make them places where cures could be effected, rather than act as transit houses to the cemetery, were made. Thus, modern concepts of hygiene, the importance of good ventilation and the need for greater space per patient exerted massive influence on their construction. More radical changes occurred when the concept of bacteria came to supersede that of miasma, or fetid air, which was previously thought to be the principal culprit of disease.

One of the most innovative of the new hospitals was the Academic Hospital (completed in 1867) in Uppsala, designed by Albert Törnqvist (1819–1898). It allotted 30 square metres of space per patient, and was provided with a complex system of ventilation ducts which were incorporated into the fabric of the building. Side corridors were also provided leading to rooms with internal windows opening upon them.

From the 1870s until the end of the century, pavilions became fashionable: Sabbatsberg Hospital had six. Yet the principal emphasis was on creating and controlling an antiseptic environment. Thus, wood was banished from the wards as far as possible, with linoleum introduced as a floor covering and white preferred as the general colour, a symbol of the purity of milieu to which the medical profession tried to aspire. Under the influence of those such as Emmy Rappe, who had trained under Florence Nightingale at St Thomas's Hospital, London, a new focus was given to the training and care of

100 Seraphim Infirmary, Stockholm, 1792, plan of the first floor after Erik Palmstedt's drawing of 1788.

hospital inmates by nurses, assisted by the wide propagation of Nightingale's writings on natal care. The results of such innovations in hospital care, particularly for those in maternity hospitals, had dramatic results; whereas, for example, 56.1 women out of 1,000 in Sweden had died of puerperal fever in the 1860s in hospital, only 0.7 died in 1896.[71] This optimistic note in hospital health and treatment was captured in *A Hospital Ward* (1920) where Hilding Linnqvist stresses the care and solicitousness provided by the nurses in a milieu of cheerfulness and light (illus. 101). No longer are they gloomy places of death and despair, but life-giving institutions of nurture and comfort.

Hygiene

In the new century, American, rather than British, conceptions of hygiene, with a sharp eye on cost efficiency, came to dominate hospital building. As a result, the space allotted per bed was considerably reduced with no ill effects, while the size of hospitals grew radically, with both the Carolinian and Söder Hospitals, in Stockholm, having more than 1,000 beds each.

101 Hilding Linnqvist, *A Hospital Ward*, 1920, oil.

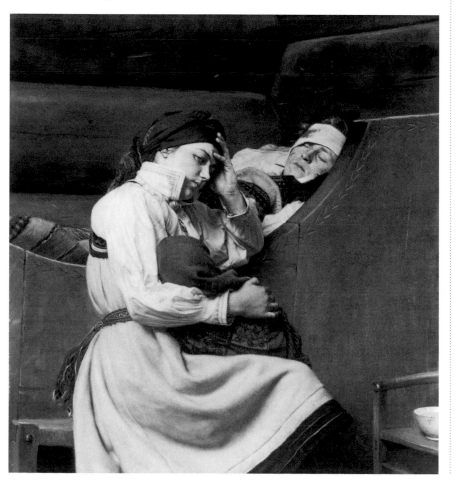

102 Carl Sundt-Hansen, *The Wound*, 1888, oil on canvas.

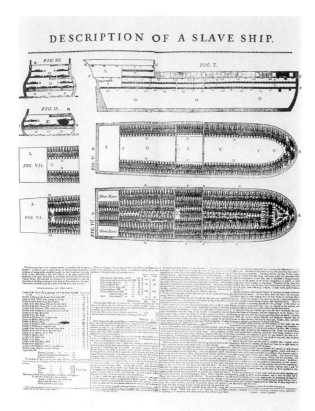

103 'Plan showing how slaves were stowed on the Liverpool Slave Ship "Brookes", a vessel of 520 tons', from *Description of a Slave Ship* (1789).

Yet the prevalence of poverty in both town and country meant that congested accommodation outside hospital walls was invariably accompanied by low standards of hygiene, with filth and stench almost ubiquitous.[72] Folk remedies for disinfecting wounds horrified benevolent late nineteenth-century middle-class ladies, when they came upon humble country women who would urinate on the wounds of their children to cleanse them.[73] Nor was the situation any better for adults. The Norwegian artist Carl Sundt-Hansen (1841–1907) illustrated in his work *The Wound* (1888) a woman from Setesdal, a babe in arms, lamenting her injured husband, whose forehead is wrapped in a dirty and bloody bandage (illus. 102). Even if such an injury proved minor, bacterial infection and blood poisoning frequently claimed the injured person's life.

In the northern periphery of the Nordic countries, hygiene was especially poor. Visitors to Iceland in the nineteenth century often criticized the amount of vermin in houses. In particular, the dormitories of farm labourers left a lot to be desired, for men and women, boys and girls all shared the same untidy quarters, devoid of any partitions and with no privacy or hygiene amenities. Chests situated upon the dirt floor usually served as beds, often containing soiled clothes infested by vermin, so that scabies was quite common. Indeed, on a typical farm only the farmer himself and his wife tended to have the luxury of their own room, though even here cleanliness was not given an important priority. By contrast, the Faeroes were sometimes praised for having a higher level of cleanliness. though good ventilation posed a problem and, except in the capital Tórshavn, the water supply was very unsanitary.[74]

In the tropical colonies, perhaps, more than other territories under Nordic dominion, the maintenance of good hygiene was extremely important because of the speed with which fevers could spread in a hot, damp climate. It was also of the greatest importance during the Middle Passage, when slaves, closely packed together according to size and sex, were being transported across the Atlantic. This required the most careful arrangements for the accommodation of these valuable human chattels. A typical layout is illustrated in a plan from *Description of a Slave Ship* (1789; illus. 103).

As the Danish medical doctor and would-be colonizer of West Africa, Paul Erdmann Isert, wrote of a crossing with respect to hygiene at the time:

> On our ship the greatest cleanliness was undertaken. Every second day the slaves would come up on deck to get fresh air and exercise. Our canvas air-stacks were to catch the maximum amount of wind and send it below.

Before the Negroes were sent back down, the holds were thoroughly smoked out.[75]

Yet such measures were not always effective: as Alexander Falconbridge, a contemporary, put it:

> When the sea was rough and the rain heavy, it became necessary to close the air vents. Fresh air being thus excluded, the Negroes' storage area grew intolerably hot. The confined air, rendered noxious by the effluvia exhaled from their bodies and by being repeatedly breathed, soon produced fevers and fluxes which generally carried off great numbers of them [...][76]

Thus, while a healthy voyage, such as that on the Danish slave ship *Ada*, lost as few as 1 per cent of the slaves on board, an unhealthy one like the *Acras* lost as many as 43.3 per cent of its cargo.[77] This was a worrying state of affairs for slave merchants, concerned for the wellbeing of their financially valuable cargo. However, once on shore, their owners could breathe sighs of relief, for slave markets, situated in the principal towns of the Danish and Swedish colonies, were almost always models of health and hygiene, places where the bodies of most slaves were washed and oiled before public exhibition. Eyes and ears were generally carefully examined, and even body odours were frequently sniffed for indications of ill health. Arms and legs too were usually exercised to test their strength and agility and the sexual parts of the body were thoroughly examined, an event which caused many tears and much consternation amongst the female slaves.[78]

The Water Closet

Along with the advent of greater general hygiene, the nineteenth century also witnessed the arrival of the water-closet. A flushing water-closet had been invented by Sir John Harington, in England, as far back as 1596, but only two had been made, one for Queen Elizabeth I at Richmond Palace and one for Harington himself at his country residence, Helstone, near Bath. In 1775 another Englishman, Alexander Cummings, a professional horologist, patented a flushing water-closet, with a so-called S-trap, which facilitated the disposal of harmful bacteria and made the lavatory pan practical. As a result, over the following century its usage grew enormously, particularly after sewage as a medium for the transmission of many diseases came to be understood. By the 1880s the basic form and functioning of the modern lavatory was complete,[79] and it became a fixture in almost all urban middle-class and upper-class homes, assisting in the prevention of many epidemic diseases.

Even farming families now began to make hygienic improvements,

104 *Consul Blath surprised by Captain Wetterberg, Lieutenant Falkenberg, Major Platen and Dr Fahlman*, pencil drawing from Säfstaholm.

distancing outhouses from kitchens and, where possible, plumbing and flushing water-closets. Special privy outhouses, albeit usually without running water, had been utilized by the landed upper classes in the region for centuries, situated at a safe distance from the house. Yet they were not particularly private places; on the contrary, they were invariably equipped to accommodate several seated visitors at once, even in quite well-to-do households. *Consul Blath surprised by Captain Wetterberg, Lieutenant Falkenberg, Major Platen and Dr Fahlman* (illus. 104) shows one such multi-holed bench, in partial occupation, from this otherwise grand country house in Södermanland, near Stockholm. Typical of its time, there might be different benches for children and adults, with the latter, on occasion, accommodating up to twenty people in the larger yeoman farming households.[80] However, it was only later in the nineteenth century that such specialized privies became general amongst the wider rural population and the arrival of flushing water-closets in most rural homes only came well into the twentieth century. Even today in many rural areas, considerable numbers of houses, particularly those used only in the summer or at weekends still have no plumbing and remain dependent on outdoor privies.

The Sauna

Hygienic lavatory traditions may have been limited in Scandinavia historically, but one Nordic institution has won ubiquitous fame for its efficacy for health throughout the world: the sauna. Possibly utilized in the Stone Age in the wooded areas of southern Russia, Heroditus commented upon its usage by the Scythians who threw water and hempseed on heated stones in order to emit fragrant steam in order to cleanse themselves through perspiration.[81] The Russian chronicler Nestori also records the sauna in writings from the year 1112. It is even documented that in the 1660s the Swedish and Finnish settlers of Delaware built their own saunas, including one communal one on Tinicum Island, in the river itself.[82] However, it was really in the nineteenth century that the sauna was reintroduced into Norway and Sweden, after falling into disuse during the post-Reformation period of the seventeenth century, possibly because of fears for the spread of syphilis.

In Finland, however, its usage continued in town and country throughout the centuries, where it increasingly became glorified in national romantic terms in the course of the nineteenth century as a Finnish social and even spiritual institution of great antiquity, one which seemed to embody the true essence of the Finnish people whilst serving a multiplicity of purposes: saunas were used for bathing, for revitalizing the body, for convalescence in times of illness, childbirth and even for bleeding by leeches. The sick and the dying, moreover, often lay on their death-beds there. As Finnish-Swedish artist Akseli Gallen-Kallela's *In the Sauna* (1889; see illus. 127) expressed it 'The sauna is a ritual, in which a person may participate in various social transformations, cleansing being just one aspect of its total meaning [...] A critical symbolic quality of the sauna is liminality [...] liminality refers to the threshold, the interstitial period between two states'.[83]

105 Viggo Johansen, *The Children are Washed*, 1888, oil on canvas.

The sauna features repeatedly, in a purifying role, in Finnish and Finnish-Swedish nineteenth-century literature, not least in the epic poem *Kalevala*, based upon ancient Finnic folk tales and composed by the Finnish-Swede Elias Lönnrot (1802–1884) (written in 32 cantos in 1835, but enlarged into 50 in 1849). In *Seven Brothers*, the first novel written in Finnish by the 'father of Finnish literature' Aleksis Kivi (1834–1872), it even becomes the focus of central events within the story, a place of refuge, intimacy and revitalization. There the men are cleansed both spiritually and physically, fortified, but when disaster strikes and the sauna, through misadventure, is burnt to the ground, it becomes a symbol of meta-physical and temporal ruin. The prospect of its reconstruction, on the other hand, becomes a guiding star of hope and reintegration into a civilized society.

In Denmark, by contrast, the sauna made little inroads until the twentieth century. As in most of Western Europe, baths altogether were little used there, perceived as they frequently were to be occasions of sin, encouraging both lust and vanity. However, with the advent of the nineteenth century's semi-religious exhortation to cleanse both mind and body, baths became increasingly fashion-able in all segments of the population. Then, bathing became a domestic family ritual, celebrating health and domesticity and a love of children. A painting by Viggo Johansen, *The Children are Washed* (1888) is a veritable celebration of such an intimate family ritual in which health, hygiene and domestic love merge together into a pictorial ode to familial care (illus. 105). It thus becomes a modern secular sacrament, like baptism, but given a homely context, in the most literal sense, in which physical purification by water seems to hint at a spiritual and moral dimension as well.

Nordic Life in the Town and Country

Agricultural Life in the Early Modern Period

Life in the Nordic region in the sixteenth century was based upon agriculture and most people lived in the countryside. Copenhagen, with about 10,000 inhabitants, was the largest of the Scandinavian cities, while Stockholm, with at most 6,000, was the only city in Sweden. Land was divided into aristocratic estates, freed by ancient rights from taxation, and strips of farmland of equal dimension and agricultural worth were allocated to each household in the villages.

Some of the large landed estates of the nobles had been held since pre-Christian times. Others were granted to important magnates by the king when the lands and monasteries of the Church were confiscated at the time of the Reformation. Still others had been given their lands when they came from Germany or Scotland in return for military and other services. The nobles jealously attempted to guard their privileged freedom from taxation well into the nineteenth century, with ever declining success, except in Denmark, where taxation of the aristocracy had been introduced at an early stage. The landowners, often in possession of several or numerous estates and freed from financial concerns, ran local government and the courts, by the consent of their fellow peers, if not of those they ruled. In Denmark an allotted number of men were conscripted for military service from their lands until 1788.

A unique record of country life is provided by the sixteenth-century *Court Roll of Councillor Jacob Ulfeldt* (illus. 106). One of the great magnates of Denmark, Ulfeldt consolidated his lands and rebuilt a number of his country houses, scattered about Sjælland and Fyn in the latest Italianate Renaissance style. In one vignette, the ridge and furrow of one of his fields can be seen, including the figures of two men with their tall hats and a boy. One of the men is sowing seed, whilst the other follows the plough, drawn by a horse, spurred on by the boy and his whip. Others show the manor houses themselves, their courtyards full of the everyday activities of a Danish agricultural estate of the time, a unique pictorial insight into the functioning of a grand Scandinavian manor.

However, the allotments belonging to the common villagers were of greater importance to the king than the big estates, since it was they which provided the crown with the taxation required to support the king and his administration with the financial resources required to rule the country and wage war, either directly or indirectly as in Denmark, where the landlords themselves were responsible for the taxes of their tenants. Since such family farming strips historically had been

106 *Court Roll of Councillor Jacob Ulfeldt*, 1588, drawing and wash.

scattered higgledy-piggledy around the countryside, a trend developed, supported by the crown, to construct centralized villages and hamlets so that travel for farm workers to the fields was the same distance for all families.

Hedgerows, also, were introduced to enclose large village fields in which each family had its strip, thereby encouraging communal responsibility and allowing for the establishment of village councils which decided upon matters of common interest. In combination with the reduction of the aristocracy at the end of the seventeenth century, a principal result of Sweden's involvement in costly wars, and the death of a disproportionate number of aristocratic military officers during them, both the monarch and the common farming population acquired a greater degree of autonomy than had previously been the case. There was, however, a concomitant beneficial effect for noble households, since the land which remained in their possession henceforth became, for all intents and purposes, an inalienable family possession, rather than a fief granted to them by the crown. With their rights of property firmly established, their judicial rights were also maintained, so that almost a third of the farming population remained subject to the authority of their aristocratic landowners.[1]

Finland and the Wild East

In Denmark and to a lesser degree in much of south and central Sweden the primeval forest had long since disappeared. Late sixteenth-century Denmark saw almost a quarter of the land still covered by forests and woodland.[2] This had declined to about 10 per cent by 1750.[3] In Finland, however, the vast majority of the country remained a largely uncultivated tract of forest, swamp and scrubland well into the eighteenth century, and as late as the early twentieth century two-thirds of the country was still forested. Relatively little of the cultivated land had belonged to the aristocracy – only some 215 households in the early sixteenth century – with perhaps 90 per cent of the land in the hands of yeoman farmers. That said, the aristocracy strengthened its position when the Swedish monarchy was strengthened and made hereditary, especially after they themselves were liberated from their onerous obligation to bear arms.[4]

Even in the south-west, around the ancient episcopal seat of Turku, farm-steads and habitations were few and far between. But with a population of about 500,000 in 1690, one-third of whom owned no land, it is not surprising that a gradual colonization of the land to the east and north continued apace,[5] a trend which was intermittently disrupted through the occasional arrest and displace-ment caused by the incursion of Russian troops during the wars which broke out between Sweden and Russia each century. When these occurred, many Finns retreated into Sweden herself, where, from the late sixteenth century, the Swedish province of Värmland offered a refuge, as the names of many villages to this day confirm. None the less, Savo, Karelia, and Ingermanland (where St Petersburg was established after it was permanently lost to Russia) to the east, and Norrbotten, Kajani and Lapland to the north, all at one time or another attracted 'colonial' immigration. Here, by contrast with the south-west of the country where aristocrats made up 14 per cent of the population in 1805, there were hardly any at all.[6]

In Savo and Karelia, in particular, the use of the slash-and-burn method of bringing land into cultivation brought rapid returns. The production there and in Ostrobothnia of almost all Europe's tar and pitch, both necessities for the maintenance of ships, had attracted many immigrants from all parts of Finland in desperate search of work.[7]

Internal opportunities were also available to those without land and keen to make their way in the world. War, famine and disease forced the abandonment of many farmsteads throughout the country, few of which were ever reoccupied by the original family. After Russian occupation in the early eighteenth century, many Finns had been carried off into serfdom or military service by the Russians, never to return, while others had fled to Sweden, where the establishment of new farmsteads made their return to Finland less attractive. As a result, many abandoned farms in Finland were taken into possession by others in quest of land, who, if successful in establishing themselves, were granted new patents of ownership. None the less, many farmsteads remained unoccupied long after the upheavals of war and plagues had abated, and this land was eventually distributed between the crown, aristocracy and the yeoman farming population.[8]

During the nineteenth century, the north and east of Finland increasingly attracted settlers from elsewhere in the grand-duchy. In the closing years of the century in particular, large numbers of people migrated to Savo and North Karelia, with its vast forests and lakes, many connected to the Gulf of Finland by the Saimaa lake system and Canal, built in 1856. Unfortunately, for many of these, like the pauper depicted in *The Old Woman with a Cat* (1885) by Gallen-Kallela (see illus. 130), Savo and North Karelia were not the lands of opportunity they had envisioned, for overpopulation by those without land or special skills condemned many to a life of severe poverty unknown, ironically, in the south-western provinces of Finland where large aristocratic estates predominated. With the rise of urban industrialization, however, many thwarted new settlers were to eventually find employment in Finland's rapidly growing cities and towns.[9]

The Allure of Lapland

The north of Scandinavia had its own appeal, although of a different kind. The growing preoccupation among many European intellectuals with 'natural man', unfettered by the demands of civilization or any social contract, meant that the northern reaches of Norway, Sweden, Finland and the extreme north-west of Russia, geographically known as Lapland, attracted considerable interest as Europe's last wilderness. In the late seventeenth century, the well-travelled French dramatist Jean-François Renard visited Lapland. Then, in 1701, Olof Rudbeck the Younger (1660–1740) published his lyrical ode to the region in *Lapponia illustrata*, which had been influenced in its turn by the *History of the Northern Peoples* (1555), set down by the Swedish Roman Catholic cleric Olaus Magnus (1490–1557). In this work, Archbishop Magnus evokes a rosy vision of the region which was to

be echoed in the writings of others over the next two centuries and beyond. A cosmopolitan humanist, his writings not only absorbed wider European influences but in turn cross-fertilized those of Continental scholars, introducing exotic elements into mainstream European culture.

When the eccentric Swedish confidence man Nicolaus Örn arrived at Versailles in 1706, claiming to be the Prince of Lapland and attired appropriately, he caused a considerable stir among the jaded aristocrats of the French court.[10] Of more lasting importance, however, in the awakening of interest in the region was the extensive travels in Lapland, in 1732, made by the Swedish botanist and explorer Carl von Linné (1707-1778), who was depicted in Saami (Lapp) attire in Martin Hoffman's picture of 1737 (illus. 107). Though painted in Holland, Linné is shown dressed in the garb he wore in Paris during his visit in 1738, along with a typical Saami drum decorated with mystical symbols, not long after the results of his visit to Lapland were published in *Flora Lapponica* (1737). A richly illustrated work, it sang the praises of the Saami people, indigenous in the region for several thousand years, nomads, Linné felt, who lived a free and easy existence, uncorrupted by the stresses of civilization.

Soon he was followed north by the French academician and astronomer Pierre-Louis Moreau de Maupertuis, who led a scientific expedition in 1736–7 in order to measure the length of a degree along the meridian. As a result of these literary works, the exotic charms of Lapland and the Saami people became known to a wider European audience who travelled there, as it were, through richly illustrated books. The sort of image of Saami people which delighted the imagination of so many at the time can be seen in *Lapps in Front of their Summer Tents*, by Pehr Hilleström the Elder (see illus. 128), one of three pictures on ethnic themes he carried out in the nineteenth century (the other two including images of Dalecarlians and Karelians).

Most Saami people were engaged in reindeer herding, fishing or farming, or a combination of all three. However, it was the reindeer herders who especially captured the European imagination. The Frenchman, Reginaud Outhier who journeyed to Lapland in the 1730s, published the exotic illustration, *Renne attelé au petit Traineau* (Reindeer pulling a Lapp sleigh) in his travel diary, *Journal d'un Voyage au Nord en 1736 et 1737*, which appeared in Paris in 1744. The reality of Saami life, however, was that while one or two members of a family might be exclusively occupied with reindeer herding involving on average some 200 reindeer (a third of which would be milked during the summer), the others would be occupied with fishing and farming and have little to do with reindeer.

That said, it was customary for the Saami in Sweden and Finland to migrate to Norway at the end of April, where taxes on reindeer, fish and game provided a sizeable source of income to the government. They would then return at the beginning of November. *A Reindeer Herd on the Drive* (1875) by the Dane Carl Bøgh (1827–1893) illustrates such a migration, in this instance in the mountainous passes of Trøndelag, in the north of Norway, through which they proceeded to their milking place (illus. 108). In between, an extended period of time would

(Opposite) **107** Martin Hoffman, *Portrait of Carl von Linné in Lapp Costume Carrying a Lapp Drum*, 1737, oil on canvas.

108 Carl Bøgh, *A Reindeer Herd on the Drive*, 1875, oil on canvas.

109 Wilhelm von Wright, *Lapps*, 1832, watercolour.

be spent in adjacent forests, until the end of January, when the snow became encrusted and made such activity impossible.[11]

The trading or sale of brandy, though illegal for long periods, also occupied many Saami people, as well as the preparation of reindeer horn for sale to cover tax obligations, the manufacture of glue from reindeer antlers or the trapping of foxes, all lucrative enterprises. Additionally, the home production of sledges and skis, along with other household items such as cradles, domestic utensils and the like, took up a considerable amount of time.[12] Such goods might be sold at the important Saami markets, like the one held annually at Karesuando (Enontekis), on the Finnish-Norwegian border, in the middle of February, which lasted ten days. There, too, Saami women could sell the flax, wool and hemp that they produced during the long winter months.

The life was arduous, but some Saami were able to amass considerable resources which they could pass on to their children; in the late seventeenth century one even became governor of Västerbotten in the north of Sweden.[13] Exceptionally, however, by contrast with the rest of the Nordic region, it was not the eldest who inherited through the legal system of primogeniture, but the youngest.[14] The Finnish artist Wilhelm von Wright (1810–1887) depicted some of these exotic but prosperous Saami wearing furs in a watercolour he painted during his voyage to Lapland (illus. 109). By that time, however, most residents in Lapland were not Saami at all, but immigrants or their descendants from other parts of Norway, Sweden and Finland, seeking new opportunities much as the

Saami themselves had come to the region millennia before. Many new settlers to Swedish Lapland had come during the late seventeenth century when the crown had granted tax relief in order to open up the hinterland. Most of the newcomers, unlike many of the Saami, lived a settled life as farmers or woodsmen, with some, especially in Kemijärvi, earning a reputation for considerable wealth in the late 1800s.[15] Erik Gape, a rector of Karesuando, in Lapland, gave an interesting account of life there amongst the farming population:

> The Farms contain both cattle and sheep, each averaging from four to ten cows and between fifteen and forty sheep [...] To stretch out their food, lichen is at times included in their winter feed. From June to mid September the cows are sent into the woods to graze. On summer evenings smudge fires have to be lit in order to protect them from the plagues of mosquitoes [...] Barley is the only grain sown [...] Of the last thirty years only six have seen fully mature harvests, but four others have been reasonably rewarding. From the church village northwards only turnips are cultivated, since the prospects for corn are so poor. The priest normally has eight cows and a horse, as well as smaller livestock.

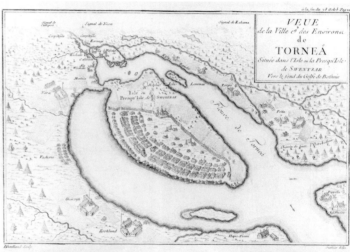

In the peasant homes bread is often replaced by dried whitefish, normal meals consisting of fish, milk, meat or porridge.[16]

On the northern coasts of the Gulf of Bothnia, in particular, Swedes and Finns had long been established in Luleå, Piteå and other coastal towns since at least the sixteenth century. There, the social order corresponded to that found elsewhere in south and central Sweden.[17]

Increasingly, however, in the interior, large farms had begun to spread out along the valleys of the River Torne and other northern rivers. Here, unlike the coastal populations, families lived in considerable isolation from one another, with church and market days providing rare occasions for social intercourse.[18] Reginald Outhier, in his copper engraving, *A Large Farm near the Torne River* (1736; illus. 110) from his travel diary, informatively depicted one such domestic and economic conglomeration: a quadrangle of rectangular log cabins with pitched roofs, their walls broken here and there by only a few windows. Inward-looking and austere, these buildings seem to reflect the character of the Finnish-speaking farming families who lived there in prosperous and self-reliant isolation.

110 Reginaud Outhier, *A Large Farm near the Torne River*, 1736, copper engraving.

Population Increase and the Growth of a Prosperous Peasantry
With the vast bulk of population spread about the most southerly quarter of its land mass, Sweden (with Finland) was a poor and overwhelmingly rural country

in the eighteenth century, with a population in the 1750s of about 1,800,000. Of these, 70,000 lived in Stockholm, the capital and only large city;[19] still smaller than Copenhagen, the region's largest city with a population of 85,000.[20] However, improvements in agriculture, as well as peace, had improved the lot of the peasantry, many of whom had suffered earlier in the century, especially in coastal areas, from Russian military incursions. In 1721, for example, Russians had devastated some 214 farms in the northern coastal parish of Umeå alone.[21]

Sweden remained an overwhelmingly rural country,[22] with small metropolitan centres: Gothenburg and Karlskrona had no more than 10,000 inhabitants each, while elsewhere in the rest of the country public amenities were few indeed. In Gävle, in Gästrikland, only a short distance north of Stockholm, there was, as Linné commented in the eighteenth century, the last apothecary's shop and medical doctor until the North Pole. Indeed, even in the middle of the nineteenth century, Gävle, one of the largest of the towns of Norrland, still had a population of only just over 2,000.[23] In Swedish Finland, the proportion of the population which lived in the countryside was even greater, and Turku, the episcopal seat and largest city, had only 9,000 inhabitants. By contrast, Swedish Pomerania, only a fraction of the size, but relatively highly populated with its old Hanseatic cities, had more than 100,000 subjects.[24]

The farming population made up the vast bulk of Swedes, with those of aristocratic or gentry status forming only five per cent of the population. Each social order formed an estate: the aristocracy was the First Estate, the clergy the Second, the middle classes the Third and the peasants the Fourth, each of which chose their own speaker to represent their interests. The speaker of the Second Estate was invariably the Archbishop of Uppsala, but those of the other estates varied. The highest offices of government were reserved to the First Estate, but increasingly military officers and significant figures from the upper middle classes were able to achieve positions in the state bureaucracy, and a significant number were themselves elevated to the aristocracy.[25]

Language often helped to bond the aristocracy and gentry together, linking those of similar background throughout Europe. Having frequently been raised by French governesses, many privileged Swedes spoke French with such remarkable fluency that it frequently became the private languages of families (including the royal family), whether at home or in correspondence.

The speaking and reading of French also made the literature of Europe more generally accessible to a wider audience. In most of the Nordic region where winters seemed so intolerably long, reading assumed an importance unrivalled in countries in warmer and more southern climes. Avid readers might be aristocratic, such the De Geers of Leufsta Bruk, in Uppland, in Sweden, or the Armfelts of Åmine Gård in the south of Finland, or L. H. von Nicolay, at Monrepos, near Viipuri, in Karelia, who amassed a vast library of thousands of volumes in various European languages. They might also be craftsmen or merchants with only a few cherished works, such as the Bible, to read. Yet, irrespective of what they read, educated Scandinavians became some of the most learned people in

Europe. Johan Tobias Sergel's pen and ink drawing, *A Reading Aloud at Court by the French Lecturer Dechaux* represents not merely an activity of the few but one which was repeated in the many humbler households all over Sweden and Finland.

The Great Change in Agriculture

Farming was, of course, the principal occupation of most people in the Nordic region, especially in Sweden and Finland where farmers made up nearly half of the entire population. In Finland, during the middle of the eighteenth century, yeomen and peasant farmers with relatively small holdings enjoyed a degree of political representation not vouchsafed them elsewhere in Europe. That said, however, not only did occasional enemy military incursions, famines and disease threaten their lives, but feudal obligations and the insecurity of land tenure often put their economic existence under threat. Only in Scania, where the aristocratic estates were especially large, was the so-called English fashion adopted in the late eighteenth century, under the influence of Physiocratic ideas, whereby land was let by the great landowners to tenant farmers in return for goods or money.[26]

But the most dramatic upheaval to affect rural life in Sweden and Finland at this time was the promulgation of a new government policy whose goal was to increase agricultural production. This was the 'great change' (*storskiftet*), a Scandinavian variant of the enclosure movement occurring throughout northern Europe, which commenced in Sweden in 1757 and continued for well over a century in outlying areas. The general farming population was obliged by the government to uproot themselves from their homes, in order to re-establish themselves and their families on new lands organized according to more 'rational' and efficient principles. The theoretical groundwork for this policy had been laid by the Swede Jakob Faggot, in his book *The Obstacles and Aids of Swedish Agriculture* in 1746. In it he pointed out the many benefits gained in British farming by the new system which successfully eliminated the inefficient cultivation of bits and pieces of farmland, scattered about the countryside, in the possession of small farmers. Yet many farmers did not wish to alter the habits of a lifetime. This was not tolerated by the government, which, while not resorting to armed force to ensure the implementation of the new system, did not hesitate to disseminate propaganda and otherwise coerce farmers and their families in many villages and hamlets. The wish of just one farmer in a village to go over to the new system was considered sufficient grounds to impose it upon all. As a result, the ensuing real-location of much larger areas of farmland conjoined in single ownership than had previously been the case, with their varying degrees of fertility and ease of access, created endless disputes wherever it was implemented between those dissatisfied with their new allotments and those who were content.

None the less, most farming communities ultimately accepted the change, not least because considerable efforts were generally made to allot equal shares of both good and bad land to every farmer.[27] The system encouraged the expansion of arable land and for some farmers brought about considerable prosperity. By the end of the eighteenth century, significant numbers of farmers were financially secure enough to be able to purchase estates previously entailed only for the aristocracy (though estates freed from land tax or 'frälsesäterier' remained reserved to the aristocracy until 1864).[28]

The cottars or 'backstugubor' who had paid neither rent for the plots upon which their hovels were built, nor fees for pasturage or household fuel suffered under the new arrangements, based as they were on a cash economy in which the value of woodlands increased dramatically. As a result, they, too, were gradually obliged to pay rents and fees. For the owner of woodlands, however, the charming and vigorous image of the timber industry depicted in *The Big Felling of Timber* (1795) by Hans Wikström, showing lumberjacks enthusiastically going about their business amid the snow and wind, could be taken as a symbol of new-found wealth. It was from such roots as this that families like the Wallenbergs were able to secure a financial basis which, in the nineteenth century, would make them arguably the most important timber barons in the Nordic region.

The hegemony of the aristocracy, however, was clearly declining, not merely in political, but financial terms as well. With the arrival of the nineteenth century and the opening of new American, Asian and other agricultural areas, a slump in agricultural prices occurred and deepened as the century progressed. This obliged more and more members of the aristocracy and officer class to sell off their land and estates, from which they often retired to the city.[29] The ancient social world of aristocrats, priests, burghers and peasants, largely rurally based, was slowly breaking down, assisted by the growth of cities and towns and, in particular, national capitals. By 1815, both Copenhagen and Stockholm had more than 100,000 inhabitants each, less than one-tenth the population of London but by far the largest cities in the Nordic region and large even by European standards.[30] Their growing multitudes spread their influence well beyond city limits in a variety of ways: much of the human waste of Copenhagen was used as manure on the surrounding fields out to a radius of ten kilometres![31]

Still, even in the nineteenth century, the outward forms and structures of gentrified life seemed not to be overly affected by life outside. In mid-nineteenth century Finland, for example, the typical country house was still the low rectangular building of wood, painted Falun red, on one or two floors, introduced in the 1690s everywhere in the region except Scania and Denmark where the traditional Danish courtyard farm persisted as a model.[32] In Finland such houses were generally concentrated geographically in the south-west of the country and in coastal areas, where the aristocracy and gentry had their seats, though there were exceptions to the rule in Karelia and Savo.[33] Indeed, there were over 100 country houses in Savo, usually belonging to owners enjoying military or civil office.[34] However, the agricultural crisis of the 1860s obliged many resident landowners to sell their estates. As a result most of the long-established Swedish-speaking families were obliged to leave, and Jorois, in Savo, remained one of the few parishes in the province where Swedish-Finns kept their estates.[35]

In Denmark during the eighteenth century, rural society consisted principally of aristocratic landowners, yeoman farmers and serfs. In 1733, serfdom (*stavns-baand*) had been re-established, after a lengthy period of interruption. There, as elsewhere in Scandinavia, the farming population had grown considerably in number, making labour less valuable at a time when many major landowners had continued to undergo the financial difficulties which had persistently confronted them since the 1660s.[36]

By the late eighteenth century, however, serfdom was permanently abolished in Denmark, an event of considerable importance, but by no means the only significant change. The movement of the farm-labouring population out of villages and into the countryside, as occurred in Sweden, proved more significant in the short term. The increased amount of land brought into cultivation, mostly remaining in the possession of aristocratic or yeoman families (from whom tenant farmers could lease their land), and the breakdown of traditional village life, led to day-labourers or cottars living a more precarious economic existence than was previously the case in the days of serfdom. The growing importance of money and a wider market economy exerted enormous changes in its own right, as the relative economic stability which underlay country life became more subject to the vagaries of the market economy, often beyond Denmark's own frontiers.[37] That the traditional Danish half-timbered courtyard farm came to be idealized as the image of a more secure and happy world is therefore not surprising and its image was taken up by countless artists during the course of the nineteenth century. Perhaps, however, it was Vilhelm Hammershøi who has most poignantly depicted such a homestead, in all its simple dignity, in *Farm at Refsnæs* (1900; illus. 111), creating the impression of an ideal world on the verge of slipping away. Such images were also explored by Ring and Oluf Høst, each of whom focused upon vernacular buildings in their own home villages, in Sjælland and Bornholm respectively, as the embodiment of a rural domestic world still whole and vibrant.

As late as 1850 in Denmark, 80 per cent of the population continued to live in rural areas.[38] This was a lower percentage than elsewhere in Scandinavia, but still significant. It is therefore not surprising that the establishment of parliamentary democracy in Denmark at the time led to the enfranchisement of farmers, promoted by conservatives like the theologian Gothard Monrad (1811–1887), who saw the political power they might be expected to yield. Whereas the poorer urban population might be radical, poorer farmers, he felt, cherishing their smallholdings, could bolster the established order.[39]

The importance of agriculture itself as an economic force in nineteenth-century Scandinavia should not be underestimated, but neither should the harsh conditions under which the majority of the population lived, especially when times were difficult. While Nes and Ringsaker, on the banks of Lake Mjøsa, formed the granary of Norway and the country was normally self-sufficient, in times of war and famine other recourses had to be taken.[40] During the Napoleonic Wars a quarter of Norway's agricultural needs had to be met from abroad, a difficult feat to accomplish for a poor country.[41] By 1865 there were

111 Vilhelm Hammershøi,
Farm at Refsnæs, 1900,
oil on canvas.

some 113,000 farmers in the country living in reasonably prosperous circumstances, but a further 60,000 crofters and cottars who, with their families, provided an important source of labour for agriculture, fared less well. They were to disappear altogether as an economic force by the early years of the twentieth century, as their farm lots, previously unrecorded and so untaxed, were registered with the authorities and sold.[42] In addition, farm servants accounted for more than another 100,000 people, and for them, too, often young and single, life could be arduous, with low pay, long hours and little freedom.[43]

Innovations in techniques and machinery affected agriculture itself. The potato was introduced to the Nordic countries in the late eighteenth century as a cheap means of sustaining the farm-labouring population, and its longer growing season and use in the distillation of brandy gave it other important advantages over traditional crops. The growth in the production of oats, assisted by the introduction of the iron plough in the late eighteenth century, which had increased the cultivation of most crops, meant that the surplus could be processed for export.

For all the benefits of these developments, however, there were unfortunate consequences as well. Over-dependence upon the potato had dire implications when blight struck, leading to famine and starvation. Furthermore, more efficient machinery meant that many farm labourers became redundant, with neither the skills nor other means by which to support themselves.[44] Many of these moved to urban areas, facilitated by the introduction and growth of the railways.

Elsewhere in the Nordic region, even for members of the farmer's family, life was by no means easy. In *The Daughter on the Farm* (1902), by the Swede Carl Wilhelmson (1866–1928), a typical prosperous farmer's daughter is depicted, but with an awareness of the strength of character and energetic disposition she would be obliged to demonstrate (illus. 112). In a household of perhaps four or five family members, she would have been expected to cook, clean and milk the family's cows, with the help, perhaps, of elderly spinster relations, or even hired

112 Carl Wilhelmson, *The Daughter on the Farm*, 1902.

only in Dalecarlia, but in the provinces of Uppland, Närke and Västmanland as well. Iron mining had become Sweden's most important industry during the eighteenth century, having been developed in the previous century by Walloon Huguenot refugees, and iron supplanted copper as Sweden's greatest export, forming 85 per cent of her exports during the middle of the eighteenth century, half of which went to Britain.[51] Then, the development of a native British iron industry made Swedish imports redundant, while Russian iron increasingly supplanted her remaining northern European markets. On the other hand, Sweden's iron exports increased to the Mediterranean countries, where Bordeaux in particular proved a welcome market for the iron bands needed in viniculture.[52] Swedish iron exports to the United States also continued to grow, assisted by a deregulation of the industry with respect to the quantity produced. As a result, some 75,000 tons of iron were shipped abroad in the 1840s.[53]

Many of the Walloon families active in the iron industry from generation to generation continued to be employed there well into the nineteenth century. A watercolour by the Swedish artist Fritz von Dardel (1817–1901) depicts one such a workplace (illus. 114). Each was run by a forgeman, assisted by his hammer crew, one per hearth, which in turn was divided into two units. Not all forges were run according to Walloon traditions; a minority were run in the German

114 Fritz von Dardel, *The Walloon Forge at the Gimo Works*, 1838, watercolour.

fashion, with each worked by a master forgeman, forge hand and apprentice.[54]

Such industrial establishments could lead to the owners amassing considerable wealth. For example, the proprietary ironmasters in Gästrikland during the late eighteenth century reorganized their production and built entirely new ironworks, often incorporating a country house and park in the neo-classical style for their use adjacent to one side of the forge. On the other side of the forge, perhaps, 100 metres away, would be the cottages of the forgemen and their families, compactly situated in rows, on either side of neighbouring streets, creating the appearance of a little manor.

Their workmen were paid wages according to the quantity of iron bars they produced, but extra income could be earned for the additional production of pig-iron and charcoal. Often, as elsewhere in rural areas, where cash was a rare commodity, they were paid in credit for food and other items, granted them at the general store, owned by the ironmaster, as well as free accommodation, pasturage and firewood. While the ironmasters and their families lived quite grandly, accommodation for the workforce, including the master forgemen, was quite humble, usually consisting of only two rooms.[55]

Women played an important role in this industrial household unit. Few forgemen were able to live on their own; either they were married or they lived with sisters or other relations who kept house, tended the animals and spun cloth. However, circumstances changed radically in the second half of the nineteenth century, when the Lancashire method of forging was introduced. Increasingly, forgemen became itinerant and the ironworks larger. The individual home became more of an industrial dormitory, while communal bakeries, breweries and baths were introduced, making the family unit less important.[56]

Crucial to the development of the iron industry in Sweden were entrepreneurs like the Englishman John Jennings, long resident in Sweden,who spent a considerable time in Paris for the purpose of gathering information during the 1760s. A member of the Swedish Academy of Science, as well as an active politician, he introduced important technical innovations relating to iron at his estate, Forsmark, enabling him to strengthen his position as Sweden's largest exporter of iron. Other important centres for the iron industry included Österby Works, near Uppsala, for a large part of the second half of the eighteenth century in the ownership of the Grill family who had originally made their money in the Swedish East India Company.

The middle years of the nineteenth century ushered in a new era in the iron industry in Sweden, when the Swede Gustaf Ekman introduced important technical innovations. These enabled bar-iron to be rolled, making possible the implementation of the more efficient Lancashire method for the production of iron, which enabled greater profits to be made. As a result Sweden's iron industry continued to prosper, especially the export of cast iron cannon well into the 1880s, when steel supplanted iron in cannon manufacture.[57]

Norway, too, had its own mines, albeit not of the order of those in Sweden and the number of Norwegians working in the industry was small, only 24,000 in 1865.[58] Copper mining at Røros was of note, though mining there had not made it an image of a grimy and ashen industrial wasteland as sometimes happened. On the contrary, it remained one of Norway's most picturesque little towns, glorified in paintings by the Norwegian artist Harald Sohlberg (1869–1935), as his *After the Snowstorm* (1903) demonstrates. The mines of the Norwegian territory of Svalbard, however, in the High Arctic, were anything but picturesque and corresponded more closely to the ecologically destructive image of the industry which has been prevalent since the nineteenth century.

The Industrial Revolution

Sweden was, at the beginning of the nineteenth century, on the verge of its own industrial revolution, and its government was keen to seize the initiative, witnessing the boons that accrued in Britain, a nation that took technical innovation seriously. With its wealth of natural resources, it became the Nordic region's first and only major industrial power in the nineteenth century, a primacy it has maintained to this day. In 1801, the Swedish government sent abroad Abraham Niclas Edelcrantz, a government employee (as well as theatre director), for the express purpose of gleaning the latest in technical and other related developments. This resulted in the improvements he made upon both the optical telegraph, originally developed by the Frenchman Claude Choppe, and the steam engine, four of which he imported into Sweden. One was used to power a textile mill at Lidingö, near Stockholm, two others provided energy for the distilleries elsewhere in the capital, and the fourth provided power for a mine at Dannemora. He had considerable assistance from Samuel Owen, an Englishman, who had emigrated to Stockholm where he saw considerable economic opportunities, and who had worked with James Watt, the inventor of the steam engine. Soon, a fifth engine had been ordered, which provided power for the first steam-driven mill in the country, situated on Kungsholmen, in Stockholm.[59]

115 Eugène Jansson, *The Outskirts of the City*, 1899, oil on canvas.

There were important technological developments in other industrial sectors, as well. In the early nineteenth century, machines for the production of paper were introduced, based on that invented by Luis Robert, in France, in 1799. The textile industry witnessed a considerable blossoming of cotton mills at Norrköping, Gothenburg and Borås in the 1830s and 1840s, which depended upon cotton grown by slaves in the plantations in the Deep South of the United States. The introduction of the sewing machine in 1872 also made its impact felt and soon considerable numbers of women were employed as seamstresses in the textile industry.[60] When Christian Krohg painted *Tired* (1885), he was focusing upon what was probably a very typical occurrence at the time.

Many seamstresses worked at home, carrying on their craft for long hours, but industrial and technical developments led to larger and larger industrial establishments, replacing the cottage industry. This was to lead to further immigration, usually from the countryside into the cities, especially to Stockholm and Copenhagen. There endless new tenement blocks were constructed to house the newly arrived urban poor, like these depicted in *The Outskirts of the City* (1899) by Eugène Jansson (illus. 115). Of course, such tenement blocks were not restricted to Stockholm. In Copenhagen, the largest city of the Nordic region at the turn of the twentieth century, similar tenements accommodated the urban proletariat. *Interior Courtyard on Holmensgade* (1907) by the Danish artist Aksel Jørgensen (1883–1957), shows how grim such barrack-like blocks could be (illus. 116). Even within its courtyard, the direct light of the sun hardly penetrated in the colder months and in such ill-ventilated and congested blocks epidemics of typhoid frequently took their toll.

116 Aksel Jørgensen, *Interior Courtyard on Holmensgade* [Copenhagen], 1907, oil on canvas.

Even in those parts of the Nordic region like Finland, industrial innovations made themselves felt. Though the timber industry remained of great importance, other traditional enterprises such as the production of timber, tar pitch (in the seventeenth century a virtual Swedish monopoly), cordage, flooring stones and the procurement of animal skins gave way to the production and export of other commodities. Agricultural exports became important: improved technical innovations in transport served during the summer months to facilitate the export of produce before it spoilt. This was especially true of exports of perishables like butter to a hungry and undiscerning market like St Petersburg; however, attempts at exporting it to England, where the quality of local butter was much higher, were less successful. With the introduction of ice-breaking ships which came into service throughout the winter in 1891, more and more agricultural products could be exported to distant ports.[61] Thus, by the 1920s, the export of butter and cheese from Finland accounted for some 10 per cent of total exports.[62]

Furthermore, with the territorial annexation of Petsamo by the Treaty of Tartu, Finland gained an Arctic port which remained more or less ice-free throughout the year, unlike the grand-duchy's other long-established ports on the Gulfs of Bothnia and Finland. This was a short-lived benefit, however, as it was permanently ceded back to Russia during the Second World War.

Technical innovations in communications affected Denmark's mercantile economy. In 1828, for example, a steam-powered mail-boat established a connection between Korsør and Nyborg, on either side of the Great Belt, whilst a post-boat linked Bornholm with Denmark in 1841. Other maritime connections followed and the amount of post distributed in Denmark increased from over two million letters in 1833 to twelve million in 1871.[63] Such ease of communication exerted a major effect on trade, not least foreign ventures. In fact, the late nineteenth century in Denmark witnessed a particularly rapid growth of industry involving business ventures abroad and brought in considerable economic benefits. The development of the telegraph, in particular, was of major importance in this respect for, in 1872, the Danish Great Nordic Telegraph Company was granted the rights to lay and maintain the telegraph through Russia to the Pacific, as far as China and Japan, bringing in huge returns for the shareholders.[64]

In Norway, the industrial revolution only began to make a major impact from the 1860s and life there remained overwhelmingly rural.[65] Most Norwegian towns had no more than a few thousand inhabitants each. What industrial establishments there were, at least up to the middle years of the century, remained

117 Edvard Munch, *Workers on their Way Home*, 1913–15, oil on canvas.

118 Edvard Munch, *Evening on Karl Johan Street*, 1892, oil on canvas.

small and dispersed, and dependent on water power. They tended to be most active in the winter months when fewer hands were needed on farms which could then be turned to other occupations, such as fishing or domestic industry. This was to change, however, when the development of larger urban industries, costly to run, required full-time commitment for all to be cost-effective. It was then that such images as Munch's *Workers on their Way Home* (1913–15) become commonplace all over Norway (illus. 117), with a regimented work schedule and some suburbs and villages becoming virtual dormitories for factory workers. Munch was acutely aware of the malaise which many, both working- and middle-class people, were experiencing, in an industrialised world in which a sense of community and belonging was becoming a thing of the past. *Karl Johan Street in the Rain* (1891) by Munch might depict the city in a joyful and dazzling display of light, splashing amongst the raindrops, but other works by him, such as *Evening on Karl Johan Street* (1892) could show it transformed by dusk into a horror of personal isolation verging on autism, in which the regimentation and conventionality of the modern industrial world had removed all signs of human warmth and communication (illus. 118).

In Norway, the growth of industry especially made itself felt in shipbuilding, always important for a country with an immense coastline and vast supplies of wood. Such geographical recourses also led to the development of the sawmill

119 Edvard Munch,
Lumberjack, 1913,
oil on canvas.

industry. But here Munch eschewed anguished images of a tortured humanity in favour of a vision of dynamism and thrust, hallmarks of the burgeoning timber industry. In *Lumberjack* (1913) his compositional focus upon the foreshortened logs heightens the compressed energy of the picture and makes it a metaphor for the timber industry itself (illus. 119). And where there were loggers, there was also brandy; its distillation became an important industry itself, not only in Norway but throughout the Nordic region.

Iceland also underwent a dramatic transformation through industrialization during the late nineteenth and early twentieth centuries. It became increasingly urbanized, with much of the population, male and female, employed in the newly mechanized fishing industry, in which fish processing was as important as fishing itself. The introduction of Iceland's first bank, the National Bank, in 1885, along with the growth of the Co-operative Movement facilitated industrial developments and the introduction of modern technology. The first fishing trawler was brought into use in Iceland in 1906, and by 1915, twenty were in use because of the fishing boom caused by the First World War.[66] Urbanization continued apace and the proportion of the Icelandic population living in towns and villages increased from 12 per cent in 1890 to 50 per cent by 1930.

Canal Building

A by-product of the industrial revolution throughout Europe was the building of canals to facilitate transport, and first Sweden, followed by Denmark and Finland, benefited in this regard. The Göta Canal Project in Sweden linked the country's North Sea coast with that of the Baltic, running from west to east for 347 miles. Based upon English prototypes, it was directed by Thomas Telford, the Scottish civil engineer, supported by the Swedish government because of its military as well as commercial importance. Its inauguration was celebrated in a painting by Johan Christian Berger (1803–1871), *The Opening of the Göta Canal on 26 September 1832* (illus. 120). As the painting indicates, the number of men employed on the project, which lasted for almost four decades, was enormous. Several hundred workers alone worked at the Motala factory which had been set up in 1822 to produce the machines needed to help construct the canal. For all the vast scope of the endeavour, however, the enterprise was not a great success; with the canal frozen for five months of the year transport came to a standstill, while the introduction of railways soon made it totally redundant.[67]

The Saimaa Canal, built in south-east Finland in 1856, also froze in winter; however, it was to prove very useful to the logging industry during the summer, linking this otherwise isolated part of the country to the Finnish coast and the world beyond. It also brought considerable prosperity to the eastern coastal city

of Viipuri, the fourth largest city of Finland and its most important port for the export of wood, wood pulp and paper.

Finally, the Kiel Canal, in the former Danish province of Schleswig-Holstein, was built between 1887 and 1895 by the German government to facilitate naval transport between the North and Baltic Seas in its newly conquered territory. Unlike the Göta Canal, however, the Kaiser Wilhelm canal, as it was originally christened, was never frozen and was of great maritime importance, especially in time of war.

Shipping and Fishing

Shipping was, of course, a mainstay of the Nordic countries, with numerous vessels from Denmark and Sweden, both naval and mercantile, plying the Atlantic and Indian Oceans out of Copenhagen, Stockholm and Gothenburg. Indeed, one of Copenhagen's most important docks, the Navy Dock at Christianshavn was still in use until after the First World War. An ocean-going vesssl such as that depicted in *The Navy Dock at Christianshavn with the warship Fridericus Quintus under Construction* (1755; illus. 121) normally travelled westwards between the Shetland and Faeroe Islands, and then southwards off the west coast of Ireland before proceeding either west

120 Johan Christian Berger, *The Opening of the Göta Canal on 26 September 1832*, oil on canvas.

121 Johan Jakob Bruun, *The Navy Dock at Christianshavn with the warship Fridericus Quintus under Construction*, 1755, gouache.

to America or south and eastwards down the coast of Africa and round the Cape of Good Hope. By the later eighteenth century, however, better navigational aids enabled ships to shorten their voyages by cutting through the English Channel, far more difficult to negotiate than the more northerly route.[68] But the Baltic was also an important area of shipping and a virtual Swedish lake until the Treaty of Nystad in 1721 allowed Russian territorial hegemony to increase and permit the concentration of shipbuilding there. The fortress island outside the harbour of Helsinki, an important centre of activity is depicted in *Sveaborg (Suomenlinna). The Galär Dock being Built as Seen from the South* (c. 1765) by Elias Martin (illus. 122). Costing some 67 tonnes of gold, it and the other docks there were largely paid for by French subsidies to Sweden and required the labour of some 6,750 people for its construction.[69] The west coast harbours of Finland, along the Gulf of Bothnia, also grew in importance in the second half of the eighteenth century and beginning of the nineteenth, as the production of ships boomed. However, the introduction of iron in shipbuilding in the 1850s sounded the death-knell for large wooden ships, and most of this rural ship-building industry soon disappeared with them.[70]

122 Elias Martin, *Sveaborg (Suomenlinna). The Galär Dock being Built as Seen from the South*, c. 1765, oil on canvas.

Not everywhere in Finland, however, was equally affected. The Åland Islands, by the entrance to the Gulf of Bothnia, continued to survive as an important area of shipbuilding, while new centres of steamship building sprang up in some of Finland's major coastal cities in the early twentieth century. Furthermore, as was the case elsewhere in the Nordic region, fishing became a full-time occupation in Finland from the 1850s, with Russia and the Baltic countries providing her most important market. Unfortunately, this dependence upon the east, for neither the first nor last time in Finnish history, was to prove disastrous after the Russian Revolution, causing a collapse of this market. As a result, many fishermen left coastal areas, especially the archipelagos, to seek employment elsewhere, with only those enjoying a variety of seasonal employments able to remain.[71]

Karlskrona, in the south of Sweden, site of an important naval base, was prominent in the production of warships at the end of the seventeenth and beginning of the eighteenth centuries, especially under the direction of the British shipbuilder Charles Sheldon. In his time more than 70 ships were built, but Sweden's sudden demise as a major power vastly diminished the need for such vessels. None the less, Karlskrona remained an innovative naval centre, and Europe's first dry dock was built there in 1763.[72]

Norway, of course, with its vast coastline, was particularly suited to growth in the shipping and fishing industries.[73] In particular, herring and cod fishing were important, with many farmers fishing when their labour were not needed in the fields. Drinks such as wine, spirits, coffee and tea, comestibles such as fruit and olive oil, and fabrics like silk and cotton, were all imported by ships in increasing quantities and many a ship's captain became rich in the trade, enabling them to build houses of considerable stature, like the one depicted in *A Skipper's House on Nøtterland at Tønsberg* (1822) by Jacob Munch (1776–1839), with their new-found wealth increasingly making them pillars of their local towns and villages.

The employment of local men in both farming and fishing was especially characteristic of maritime regions like the Lofoten Islands, in the north of Norway, where young men would generally be engaged in fishing during the winter months, while the more elderly members of the extended family were occupied in farming. Only in the early twentieth century, when fishing became a motorized industry, did it offer a full-time life-long employment for all age groups. In Iceland, where in 1880 fishing provided the primary source of income for less than 10 per cent of the population, the numbers were to increase several-fold during the next few decades in the wake of industrialization.[74]

Women and children rounded off the division of labour in these communities by looking after both the animal husbandry and the harvest, as well as the home, when their men were away.[75] Captured with an unsentimental dignity as statuesque and strong, in *Fisherwomen Coming from Church* (1899) by Carl Wilhelmson (1866–1928) (see illus. 132), they often formed the backbone and source of moral strength of the fishing communities in which they lived. Indeed, frequently they had to cope for both themselves and their children during the lengthy periods when their menfolk were at sea, and sometimes for the rest of their lives in those households where the man was lost at sea.

In some areas, such as that of Kragerø, it was traditional for young men to spend a few years at sea before settling down. This, in the view of the artist Edvard Munch, helped to give them a broader and more European perspective on life than their fellows who stayed at home.[76] It also meant that if they drowned

123 Michael Ancher, *The Lifeboat is Taken Through the Dunes*, 1883, oil on canvas.

(not having settled down), they would not leave a wife or children to fall upon the goodwill of the parish.

In Denmark, fishing had for centuries provided an important component of the economic livelihood of many men, especially on the coasts of Jutland, though usually in combination with farming and other forms of employment, as elsewhere in the Nordic region. Yet earlier than in many other parts of Scandinavia, and well before the advent of industrialization, year-round fishing began to develop there in the seventeenth century, causing the establishment of fishing villages and hamlets all over the country.[77]

Perhaps the archetypal fishing village was Skagen, situated on Jutland's most northerly tip, where the Baltic meets the North Sea. Chartered in 1413, it was visited in the early nineteenth century by such literary figures as the Dane of Jewish extraction Meir Aron Goldschmidt (1819–1887). He was to write romantically of 'Denmark's Sahara' at nearby Råbjerg Mile, and its sand dunes, projecting it into the national consciousness as a place both exotic and archetypically Danish at the same time. So popular did it become that by the second half of the nineteenth century even exotic potentates like the King of Siam came

124 Edvard Munch, *Heredity I*,
1897–9, oil on canvas.

125 Edvard Munch,
Melancholia (Laura), 1899,
oil on canvas.

126 Edvard Munch,
Death in the Sick Room, 1893,
oil on canvas.

127 Akseli Gallen Kallela, *In the Sauna*, 1889, oil on canvas.

(Opposite above)
128 Pehr Hilleström the Elder, *Lapps in Front of their Summer Tents*, late 18th century, oil on canvas.

(Opposite below)
129 Pehr Hilleström the Elder, *Gustaf III Visits the Great Copper Mine at Falun on 20 September 1788*, 1788, oil on canvas.

130 Akseli Gallen-Kallela, *The Old Woman with a Cat*, 1885, oil on canvas.

131 Edvard Petersen, *Emigrants in Larsen's Square*, 1890, oil on canvas.

(Opposite)
132 Carl Wilhelmson, *Fisherwomen Coming from Church*, 1899, oil on canvas.

133 Akseli Gallen-Kallela,
Waterfall at Mäntykoski,
1892–4, oil on canvas.

134 Prince Eugen, *The Forest*,
1892, oil on canvas.

sailing by in their royal yachts, in order to enjoy the picturesque idyll of a Danish fisherman's life by the sand and sea. But the sand dunes themselves (like the real lives of the local fishermen) hid a darker reality: they were not the product of natural erosion but the result of a centuries-old agriculture and the deforestation of a land in which the forests had previously extended to the water's edge.[78]

In reality, too, for the impoverished fishermen and their families, the sea often showed a harrowing and destructive face. Intrusions of the sea had forced the demolition of Skagen's original Gothic church in 1810, with only the old tower left standing, a navigation mark for sailors and a symbol of the devastation the sea could cause. The herring industry, which had thrived since the beginning of the sixteenth century, with thousands of workers employed, disappeared with the vanished schools of local herring which had supported it, leaving destitution in its wake.[79] Other types of fishing continued, but the fisherman's life remained one of considerable risk and times were frequently hard. This can be seen in a work by the Danish artist Michael Ancher (1849–1927) (see illus. 123), who was married to fellow artist Anna Brøndum, a native of Skagen where her family kept the local hostelry (still in existence). The painting shows a common event in an area where countless ships and boats went down in treacherous seas.

Education in the Nordic Countries

Already in the early seventeenth century, popular education had begun to take root in Scandinavia, especially in rural areas. Even in Swedish Lapland, a school for the education of young Saami children had been established at Lycksele in 1632 through the offices of the privy councillor John Skytte, through private donations and subscriptions from himself and others, and four Saami students went on to attend Uppsala University over the next 90 years.[80] In the eighteenth century more concerted efforts were taken to educate large numbers of the population by both the church and the state itself. In

135 Johan Joachim Reichborn, *The Nykirken School for the Poor in Bergen* (1742), 1768, drawing.

1721 a decree was promulgated for the establishment of 240 elementary schools in Denmark, which resulted on royal initiative in 1739 in a new law obliging all Danish children to attend school. There reading was taught, paid for by the state, as well as writing and arithmetic, if additional fees for tuition were paid by the parents. Similar schools were also built in Norway, a Danish dominion, such as *The Nykirken School for the Poor* (1768) in Bergen depicted by the German architect Johan Joachim Reichborn (1715–1783), who had come to the city in 1757 (illus. 135). In all these schools, however, it was not the provision of knowledge leading to a free expression of opinion or political choice by those educated there which was the goal, but the creation of a popular consensus, that is, a commonly held religious, political, ethical and social belief system which would support social and political order.

The cost of such education was largely borne by local landowners and other

136 Oscar Björck, *In the Village School*, 1884, oil on canvas.

notables many of whom often grumbled at the financial burden, and were not convinced of the benefits of literacy for the children of their labourers. Thus, though a sufficient knowledge of the Lutheran Catechism was imparted for the obligatory confirmation (recently re-introduced), by no means all pupils were even taught to read.[81] Later on, in the early nineteenth century, however, the growth of industry was to increase the demands for schools, not so much to educate the common man in classical thought or even general knowledge, as the children of privileged households were educated, but to instil order, discipline and a co-operative spirit, along with the necessary skills for accomplishing basic tasks, especially in factories. *In the Village School* (1884) by the Swedish artist, long active in Denmark, Oscar Björck (1860–1929) depicts a typical smaller educational establishment for younger children (illus. 136). Many political and religious figures realized that a well-educated common man or woman was a necessity in a modern cohesive, democratic nation.

By the 1820s, the Danish king Frederik VI came to take a keen interest not only in the school curriculum itself but also in gymnastics as an integral part of education. *The View of the Gymnastics Field in Gjerrild*, set in Grenå, on Jutland, illustrates the facilities provided (illus. 137). The drawing shown had been made by the local pastor, Nicolai Kamph, not as a decorative work of art but rather as part of his application for the governmental position of academic advisor, a post which he succeeded in acquiring. In such activities, youth were trained not only for the duties of adulthood, but, most importantly, for those of military life. As Nordic governments increasingly stressed the importance of national military might to protect their interests, the role of gymnastics as a part of education, as well as a popular activity for young men, came to the forefront of the educational programme.

137 Nicolai Kamph, *The View of the Gymnastics Field in Gjerrild*, 1826, drawing on paper.

Another man of the cloth, N. F. S. Grundtvig, was to play a particularly important role in not only Danish nineteenth-century education, but in that of the whole of Scandinavia. His principal success was in the establishment and organization of the Danish People's High Schools, based upon the collegiate system with which he had become acquainted during visits to England. This new type of establishment, dedicated mainly to the education of young men from farming backgrounds, was soon taken up everywhere in the rest of Scandinavia even for those from a non-farming background and continues to thrive until this day, providing a liberal arts education for those of non-academic background.

In Sweden and Finland, state education may have lagged behind that in Denmark, but it too was in the course of development. Elementary schools for reading, writing and arithmetic were established there in the 1760s, remaining largely in the hands of the Lutheran clergy, who often frowned upon alien intellectual influences. This was especially true of the French language, which, until the arrival of Marshall Bernadotte upon the Swedish throne, incurred considerable moral opprobrium amongst the clergy as encouraging decadence and could therefore only be learnt privately. For those of means, however, private education was thriving. In Stockholm itself, by 1800, there were 100 private schools, catering to the children of prosperous families. In the state sector, by contrast, there were only twelve schools and, whereas in the former French literature and language thrived (already encouraged among their charges by the ubiquitous French governesses), in the latter it did not.[82] Only when state-sponsored education was widely introduced in 1842, did basic skills in literacy develop in all segments of the population.

In Finland, literacy had become widely spread, not only among the privileged orders and clergy but amongst the broad farming population from the late seventeenth and early eighteenth centuries. This was made possible by local religious education which, in preparing the young for confirmation, helped to disseminate basic reading skills, along with sound Lutheran values. In remote Lapland, education normally rested with the catechist, who lived in the church-village, under the eye of the Lutheran priest. He was paid by the church for his livelihood, but travel expenses to the nomadic Saami encampments, usual until 1792, were paid for by the Saami themselves. Thereafter, most teaching was provided in the towns and villages.[83]

With such a literate population, it is not surprising that some 10 per cent of students who matriculated at the Åbo Academy in Turku (Finland's most prestigious institution of higher education) between 1640 and 1700 were of farming stock, and between the 1760s and 1680s this proportion had doubled. Most of these, in both periods, came from the south and west of Finland where the population density was greatest and the social structure most hierarchical.[84] For many literate people, though, who did not proceed to higher education, the benefits were not inconsiderable; for reading the Bible and other spiritual literature sustained and edified many a family, isolated in the woods, during the long and cold winter nights, even if writing was a rare skill among the vast majority of the Finnish-speaking population until well into the nineteenth century.

Nevertheless, there were practical difficulties in acquiring education for those at the lower end of the social scale, especially in times of economic hardship. The needs of an impoverished economy in many parts of Finland during the early nineteenth century, for example, meant that fewer farmers were willing to lose their children to school when their hands were needed for work at home. Among the aristocracy and gentry, on the other hand, education was prized and virtually all such families employed private tutors for their sons (if not their daughters), many of whom resided for at least two years with their charge's family, occupying a social position midway between dependent family member and servant. When their charges went off to Helsinki, Turku or Viipuri, they would generally depart for another household.

Renewed progress in popular education was eventually made in Finland later in the century, not least through the efforts of Uno Cygnaeus (1810–1888), a Lutheran priest and educator who became known as the 'father of the primary school'. Influenced by the Continental educational philosophers Johann Heinrich Pestalozzi and Friedrich Froebel, like his fellow educationalists elsewhere in the Nordic region, he introduced both handicrafts and other manual training into schooling, winning the applause of Tsar Alexander II, Finland's Grand-Duke. As a result such training became compulsory in rural schools in 1866 and, by 1872, in urban ones as well.

In 1891, folk high schools, along the lines of those already set up by Grundtvig in Denmark, also came into being in Finland, where they served to educate the wider farming population, some of whom continued on to university. In fact, as the early decades of the twentieth century wore on, such schools provided the means by which a majority of farmers's children, both men and women, were able to break away from lives spent in arduous rural labour and to join the rising urban middle class which was changing the nature of Finnish society.

Of the Arctic and North Sea dependencies, Iceland offered the greatest educational opportunities. There, throughout the eighteenth century, the famous Icelandic sagas of the twelfth and thirteenth centuries continued to exert an enormously important influence, and despite the intense poverty, the Icelandic population of the time was probably the most literate in Europe. While the first primary school in Iceland had been set up on the Westman Islands in 1745, with others following elsewhere shortly thereafter, the fact remained that a large minority of the inhabitants had been literate since the Middle Ages. After the Reformation, Lutheran priests had played a key role, especially in the education of children of the privileged classes.[85] Many landowners and other prosperous government officials would send their sons out to the homes of churchmen, where they would reside for two to three years, to prepare them for higher education. They formed up to 27 per cent of the entire population of children in foster homes at that time, not an insignificant number in a society where the fostering of orphaned or impoverished children was quite usual.[86]

Even in humbler households in Iceland, many children in this predominantly rural country were taught reading at home by the clergy. As a result, almost universal literacy had been achieved by the end of the eighteenth century, despite the contemporary onslaughts of famine and disease, an achievement of which no other nation could boast. Writing, however, was not so widespread, especially among women.[87] By contrast, on the Continent less than half of Europeans were literate as late as the second half of the nineteenth century.

By the nineteenth century, there was a Latin grammar school in Reykjavik (consolidated from two smaller ones in 1801), as well as a small medical school. There were also various schools of theology scattered about the island, where ordinants to the priesthood were trained, but no native university. For those particularly gifted students, however, the University of Copenhagen offered an inviting alternative at the time to Iceland's own provincial establishments. Not only were Icelanders exempted from university tuition fees there, but board, too, was frequently provided.[88] Little changed over the following century, but by the 1920s and 1930s, Iceland began to experience a boom in the growth of educational establishments. It was at this time that Guðjón Samúelsson, the official State Architect, designed large numbers of schools throughout the country, appropriate for a nation on the verge of its political independence.

The importance of the Icelandic sagas to Iceland's literary life continued into the twentieth century. This was true not only with respect to twentieth-century Icelandic writing, but even in terms of everyday life, before radio and the television largely put an end to such a tradition. As late as the 1920s and 1930s, it was not unusual for an entire family to come together on a winter's eve to hold a 'kvöldvaka' (evening wake). A contemporary described such an event thus:

> [...] one of the men, generally the father of the household or the one who can recite best and most clearly, sits near the lamp and begins to read, often deciding first by common agreement what saga to choose. If there are several good readers in the house they take turns in the entertainment, following each other in regular order, on successive evenings, for there is no change of reader in the same evening. After the reading the different characters of the saga may be discussed, sides taken for or against, etc.[89]

In Greenland, general education was undertaken largely by religious authorities, whether orthodox Lutheran clergy, or Moravian or Catholic missionaries, using whatever buildings were available. Sometimes schools would be built, like the stone schoolhouse erected at Julianehåb in the middle of the nineteenth century – unusual in a colony where almost all buildings were of wood, and indicating the importance placed on education there.[90]

By contrast, public education in the Faeroes, by the turn of the twentieth century, had made only modest inroads. Primary education there was carried on in Danish, rather than native Faeroese, but many parents preferred not to send their children to school. None the less, if most residents had decided to maintain a primary school in their village, parents were under a legal obligation to send their children to the school. The schoolmaster's salary would then be paid by the local government, but the villagers themselves had to provide for pasturage for his cow, among other mildly onerous obligations. With respect to higher education, those few students wishing to pursue professional careers were obliged to move to Copenhagen, in order to attend university or train for the priesthood, though a small teacher-training institute did open in Tórshavn during the course of the nineteenth century.[91]

138 *Portrait of Rector Hans West*, early 19th century, oil.

In the tropical colonies of the Caribbean, schools began to open in the eighteenth century. In 1788, for example, a little white schoolhouse was erected in Christiansted, in the Danish Virgin Islands, under the leadership of Rector Hans West. For West, the educational goal of his establishment was not orientated towards later work, but was rather intended to make genteel planters: men who were manly, modest, magnanimous and, most important, courtly to the ladies, and to this end they learnt the works of the classical poets Homer, Virgil and Catullus, as well as useful foreign languages.[92] As can be seen in *Portrait of Rector Hans West*, by an unknown artist, he is a genteel Creole resident of St Croix, a classical humanist in the manner which became characteristic of planter society in North America, whether in the Caribbean or the American Deep South (illus. 138). In West's school, the pupil was to be exercised in a labour of the mind, but not the body. The actual hard labour in the colony was to be done by the slaves, as in Ancient Greece and Rome, without whose constant import the Danish Virgin Islands would not have been able to carry on at all.[93]

Even slaves were to be educated. The nineteenth-century governor-general

Peter von Scholten visited Herrnhut, seat of the Moravian church, in order to establish the best type of education suitable for young slaves. This resulted, in 1839, in the promulgation of a law which founded a whole series of new schools in the Danish Virgin Islands, eight on St Croix, five on St Thomas and four on St Jan, dedicated to the education of slaves and focusing on practical skills and moral education.[94]

In the Swedish colony of St Barthelemy education was also taken seriously. There a schoolhouse was built in stone in the early years of the first decade of the nineteenth century, but the heterogeneity of the population and debilitating effects of the climate on intellectual pursuits was used as an excuse to abandon the project. The building was probably then used as a gaol. However, private tuition was given by Catholic monks and nuns sent out by the bishop on the nearby French colony of Guadeloupe. These were supplemented by teachers of the Swedish Missionary Society, who established private schools for children of prosperous families, one for boys and one for girls. But the children of humbler folk, some hundred or more blacks and mulattos, were also catered for by teachers of the Methodist Society, an organization based in London. The colony's governor Norderling who examined them in 1824 was pleased with their progress.[95] None the less, for all such auspicious endeavours, less than one in 20 inhabitants of St Barthelemy could read or write in 1866, a state of affairs which contrasted sharply with that in Iceland and Sweden at the time.[96]

Throughout the Nordic countries and their dependencies the subscription library and its successor the public library was introduced from the United States in the late eighteenth century. In the fledgling republic, such eminences as Benjamin Franklin and Thomas Jefferson had stressed the social benefits to be gained by them at a time when the price of books made their purchase impossible for all but the prosperous middle and upper classes. Such ideas were soon disseminated to Scandinavia where, by the 1780s, Norrköping and Karlskrona, in Sweden, had established their own subscription libraries, with related discussion groups. Then, in 1794, the members of the Vaasa (Vasa) Court of Appeal, in Finland, established a library society, 'for their own amusement and diversion', holding frequent literary discussions.[97] While such societies were limited to the more educated members of society, the libraries of the early nineteenth century, aimed to appeal directly to the average person. As a result, by the second half of the nineteenth century, countless libraries, for the public at large, as well as for working men, had been set up all over the Nordic region, soon to join forces with the Folk High School movement, emanating from Grundtvig in Denmark, during the middle decades of the nineteenth century.

Orphans and the Care of Children

Educational needs of the general population in the Nordic countries may have been increasingly well tended compared to much of Continental Europe, but the care provided for young orphans was limited. The absence of religious confraternities or monastic orders to care for them created a state of affairs whereby life for children without parents or guardians could be bleak. Christian IV of Denmark had built an orphanage in 1619, but it was situated by a house of correction built a few years before in 1605, not a very salubrious environment for children.[98] In Stockholm, the situation was similar, with the orphanage at Norrmalm (illus. 139) also located adjacent to the House of Correction. While distinctions between orphans and criminals may have been limited, sharp distinctions were made between those children deemed legitimate and illegitimate, especially with respect to education; while the former were taught useful trades, the latter were merely groomed for domestic service or other menial tasks. Yet, cleansing of the mind and body, through religious instruction and baths, were provided fortnightly for both and there was a resident chaplain who, together with the chapel, served the local community as parish church.

Originally built to house 150 children, the Orphanage at Norrmalm actually had more than the double that number of inmates by 1756. Then, a reform of the care of children was introduced in 1785, which attempted to place orphans in foster homes in the country. It was motivated not merely by the growing ideological vogue, inspired by Rousseau, of giving children a more 'natural' upbringing, but also by the reduced ongoing costs with which the authorities would be lumbered. Thereafter, the Orphanage increasingly provided accommodation for infants and sick children.[99] Changing circumstances led to the demolition of this establishment and provided the subject of a painting for Anshelm Schultzberg (1862–1945; illus. 140). Few lamented its demise; rather its disappearance seemed to many humanitarians to be a sign of progress, a casting away of the bad habits and conventions of centuries in favour of the new, scientific and more humane regime which they were introducing. The Swedish playwright August Strindberg best expressed their sentiments, interjecting words of warning for those who were quick to see the flaws of the old way while offering no remedies themselves. He wrote ironically in his poem 'The Esplanade System':

139 The Orphanage, Norrmalm, Stockholm, 1638, as illustrated in a newspaper from 1886.

> Oh! The practice of the time is to tear down houses!
> But to rebuild? That is frightening!
> We are tearing down to get air and light;
> Is not that enough?

As the nineteenth century progressed, reforms took place in orphanages and other institutions for children, especially those which were formed to support the handicapped, be they deaf, dumb, blind, or merely difficult to manage. One such establishment, opened in 1840, was Råby Räddningsinstitut (Råby Salvation Institute), designed by the Swedish architect Carl Georg Brunius (1792–1869).

140 Anshelm Schultzberg, *Pulling Down the Old Orphanage in Stockholm*, 1886, oil on canvas.

King Karl XIV himself gave the bricks for its construction, which was carried out under the direction of Baron Axel Gustaf Gyllenkrook, whose own son had fled abroad to escape a conviction for theft. Twelve boys, aged eight to thirteen and formerly in Malmö Prison, were brought there, where they remained for up to ten years before being released. By 1860, their numbers had grown to 30 and other institutions throughout the Nordic region were established. Among these, Holsteinsminde, near Næstved, in Denmark was arguably the most important, using as prototype Das Rauhe Haus, near Hamburg. In turn, it influenced the Hall agricultural colony, in Sweden, built in 1876, to the designs of Johan Fredrik Åbom (1817–1900), where discipline and religious instruction set the tone, not always to the lasting wellbeing of its boys. Indeed, Knuth Becker, a previous inmate, wrote his semi-autobiographical novel *The World is Waiting* (1934) about the tragedy of a boy with little self-reliance or internalized sense of order, who was unable to cope with the outside world after leaving.[100] None the less, the intentions of many of the authorities who ran Hall were of the most noble order, even if the practical benefits were limited. As a contemporary wrote in 1879, 'The whole of the care given to the institution's interior and exterior condition is such that every day and every hour it speaks without words to the mind of the child and through silent encouragements educates them'.[101]

Poor Houses

For those unfortunate adults in Scandinavian society unable to support themselves in both town and country various recourses were available, according to

141 Josabeth Sjöberg,
*Drottninghuset, the room on the
lower floor*, 1832, watercolour.

their sex and station in life. For aristocratic ladies and their gentrified cousins, special establishments were privately provided in many places in the Nordic region by benefactresses or others to accommodate and sustain them for the rest of their lives. In Stockholm, the widows and daughters of officers, priests and the gentry had Drottninghuset (The Queen's House), built in 1689 by Mathias Spihler (c. 1640–1691) and which overlooked the churchyard of St Johannes. It proved extremely popular and to accommodate increasing numbers of inmates a third floor was added to the central elevation in 1775, designed by the architect Carl Fredrik Adelcrantz (1716–1796). It is depicted in a watercolour *Drottninghuset, the room on the lower floor* (1832) by Josabeth Sjöberg (illus. 141), whose grandmother in later life had lived and died there. Each of the twenty persons who resided there catered for herself. Richert von Koch in his novel *The Old Woman of Drottninghus* (1879), has his character describing a visit there so: 'At first sight, he thought that he had never seen such an assemblage of people and objects in one place. It was so full of domestic objects that the whole room looked like a wardrobe of clothes, with hardly an inch in which to manoeuvre. It seemed to him momentarily to be pure chaos'. And so it was, more or less, to remain until 1924, when these rooms were subdivided into smaller ones on either side of a central corridor, to accommodate more inmates in greater privacy.[102]

Gentlemen of a similar background also had their own establishments. There was, for example, in Stockholm, the Borgerskapets gubbhus (The Bourgeois Old Men's Home), providing reasonably comfortable accommodation for those fallen upon hard times. For those of humble background, Sabbatsberg Poor House was founded in 1752. It offered asylum to some 300 inmates and was the principal place of refuge for the urban poor in Stockholm during the 1870s. Elsewhere in the continental Nordic region, major urban centres had their own counterparts, while in rural areas, each parish had its own social responsibilities towards the poor. In Sweden, in 1734, all parishes were obliged to provide refuges for the poor and homeless. As a result, just under 1,400 poor houses were constructed in the provinces to serve this purpose. Maintaining their function well into the twentieth century, they were generally financed either by a local major landowner or the parish itself, mainly for the benefit of impoverished women. Poor men, on the other hand, were expected to take on the role of cottars to sustain themselves. In exchange for their occasional labour, they would be given their own hovels on a farmer's land and a prosperous landowner might have some two dozen hovels on his land, accommodating several dozen men in this fashion, sometimes including their families.[103]

As the century progressed, however, alternative ways of dealing with the poor came to be employed. The Danish reformer C. L. Børresen was particularly influential in this regard throughout the Nordic region, and, from the 1860s poor farms, such as that in Blekinge, near Karlskrona, opened their doors to the poor, in which inmates were put to work in farm labour, giving them full-time gainful employment. Some, such as Ljusnarsberg near Örbebro, in Sweden, incorporated a school for children, an infirmary and an idiot asylum. There those who were neither ill nor handicapped resided in six bedrooms on the two principal floors of the farmhouse. Other rooms included a communal dining room, where prayers were regularly said, as well as a large porch, and residential accommodation for the director and a servant. Sometimes whole families were born and lived on these poor farms and grew in number from year to year, with young and old mixing together.[104]

142 The Dihlström Work House, Stockholm, photograph of c. 1900.

Only in 1918 did children cease to be integrated with adults in poor houses, when it was perceived as more enlightened to separate the old from the young and children increasingly became accommodated on their own, especially those who had been considered susceptible to 'moral corruption'.

There remains one other institution to consider, the least hospitable of all, which embodies the worst aspects of nineteenth-century ideas regarding poverty and the unemployed: the workhouse. Here, the most recalcitrant poor, mostly men, were set to work washing, chopping wood or employed in other menial tasks in extremely austere conditions. One of the worst examples, the Dihlström Work House, in Stockholm (illus. 142), had 414 inmates in 1863.[105] This bears comparison with the corresponding institution in Copenhagen, depicted in Vilhelm Hammershøi's *The Workhouse* (1902) (illus. 143). While the interior here may have been grim, at least the exterior presented a more congenial appearance,

143 Vilhelm Hammershøi, *The Workhouse*, 1902, oil on canvas.

so that its inmates could be suitably chastened to a life of work and productivity, without offending the aesthetic sensibilities of ordinary citizens walking by on the outside, confident that those in authority over society were protecting their interests, aesthetic as well as economic.

Retirement

Traditionally, in Scandinavia, an ageing farmer with land, but no longer able or willing to run his farm, would hand it over to his eldest son, or, perhaps, even a trusted neighbour or hired hand, where there no children or other close relations, who would provide him with accommodation and board for the rest of his and his wife's lives in return. For those without land, the future was more bleak. While in theory the church looked after such paupers, for, without any financial or landed resources that is what they generally became, in reality it was the local landowner or farmer who took over the responsibility for them. How well such people fared depended largely on the largesse of the landowners. In the south of Sweden, where large estates prevailed, private poor houses were organized to cater for them, rather than allowing them to continue to live, albeit humbly, in the community, as elsewhere in Sweden tended to be the case.[106]

The age of retirement was rarely fixed and usually occurred when poor health or decrepitude made work impossible. However, the iron industry provided an exception to this rule, for, in the nineteenth century the men who worked the forges generally retired at 56 years of age, some two decades after they generally had become foremen of their crews.[107]

In the late nineteenth century old people's homes in the modern sense became established in the Nordic region. At first, these were only available for those with private means. One of the first was the Old People's Home at Gothenburg, designed by Carl Fahlström, which accommodated only two pensioners per room, in a new building adjacent to the poor house. Often, however, those with means preferred to live independently with help, or to reside with family or friends. Rather it was those with little alternative, for whatever reason, who sought refuge in such homes,[108] and with the advent of social democratic values and governmental financial support, it became the public sector which increasingly provided care for these elderly people in the Nordic region.

In Iceland, one of the poorest parts of the Nordic region, the care and welfare of the elderly was particularly precarious. Since most farmers leased, rather than inherited their land on a short-term basis and virtually no sheltered accommodation was available, the elderly were often left to the mercy of fate and the kind hearts of relatives or neighbours, not necessarily the most reliable base to enable them to secure a comfortable old age. Here, too, though, social amenities for the impoverished elderly increasingly became available as the twentieth century progressed.

Migration from Country to Town

Travel in the Nordic regions in the early decades of the nineteenth century remained much as it had been for centuries. Winter was the best season for the internal transport of both goods and people, by means of horse-drawn sleighs over fjords, rivers and lakes.[109] In the outlying coastal regions of Finland and Sweden, however, inhabitants might be cut off during those two to three months a year when the Gulf of Bothnia and Baltic Sea froze over, preventing travel by boat. On the other hand, during the warmer months, travel by boat to Turku, Stockholm and Tallinn had improved and links amongst these cities were well-established, even before the advent of the steamship.[110]

Roads were of little importance for the transport of long-distance freight in Scandinavia, but they did enable people to travel more easily between rural areas and towns, where opportunities of employment were greater. The introduction of steamboats in the 1820s, running on regular timetables, made travel even easier, especially true when steamships began to ply the waters of the Baltic between Stockholm and Turku in 1836. Fares were high, however, so that most seeking employment travelled to the nearest urban area. Ease of movement was further facilitated by a relaxation of the poor laws in the 1840s, which removed restrictions on place of residences and movement.[111] Women might find work in domestic service, factory work or even prostitution and those with the requisite skills could teach or nurse. The relaxation of regulations in 1846, which had prevented women from entering other craft occupations, also opened up a whole range of other career opportunities. For men, a whole range of employments, casual and fixed, was available. Indeed, until well into the nineteenth century, both Stockholm and Copenhagen were unable to sustain their populations without an influx of people from the country, so that immigrants were welcomed. This was also true of some provincial cities. Uppsala, the archepiscopal and academic seat of Sweden, which in 1800 had had only 5000 inhabitants, had grown by 1900 to more than 15,000, and many other urban areas in the Nordic region had grown by similar dimensions.[112]

Seasonal migration from interior agricultural areas to coastal or mountain ones also occurred. During the month of August, many people, especially in Norway, moved either to the coast, from which they could fish, or to the mountains, where their animals could find rich pastures.

Many men of farming families also sought seasonal work if opportunities where they lived were limited. They might work, for example, in the sawmill industry, which could take them anywhere in Sweden, Norway or Finland. Bachelors, in particular, were drawn to this migratory work, and they were obliged generally to reside in large barracks, each of which might accommodate natives of one particular region or even country.[113]

In Lapland, whether Norwegian, Swedish or Finnish, seasonal migration among the Saami population was an integral part of their nomadic lifestyle based on reindeer herding. Many Saami migrated to coastal regions, usually on the shores of the Arctic, where fishing could bring in considerable financial rewards.

In Iceland the population was particularly mobile. Fewer than 20 per cent of Icelanders owned their own farms, and most leased their farms annually. The rural population was almost by definition migratory, with children rarely leasing the same farms as their parents.[114] The mountainous terrain, frequently jutting into the ocean, meant that travel and communication in country areas was generally poor. Only in parts of the lowland interior were villages and farms more accessible and there migrant labour was at its highest.[115]

Gypsies were the most migratory of the ethnic groups in the Nordic region. Poor, more violent and frequently perceived as criminal, they were often

144 Akseli Gallen-Kallela, *Kaisa*, 1906, drawing for *Seitsemän Veljestä*.

upbraided for theft, kidnapping and other forms of anti-social behaviour and, as a result, were subject to growing social control especially from the 1840s. In Norway, where the census of 1845 had demonstrated that 3.5 per cent of the population, some 46,000 people, received some form of state financial benefits, political hostilities towards the migratory habits of the gypsies became particularly acute. Political and social scrutiny immediately fell on the lifestyle of the gypsies, obvious in their distinctiveness, and means of circumscribing their movements were actively sought.[116] In Finland, in particular, gypsies developed an especially strong presence, where they were easily recognizable by their dark colouring and vivid and flamboyant clothes. Stigmatized there too as thieving and violent, they were generally disdained by the local, more sedentary population. Just as the gypsy brood of Kaisa was held in contempt in the novel *Seven Brothers*, by the 'Father of Finnish literature', Aleksis Kivi (1834–1872), so the Finnish artist Gallen-Kallela has depicted her as a wild but wily woman, able to hold her own against the hostile social forces pitted against her in *Kaisa*, one of a set of illustrations for the novel he carried out in a humorously affectionate manner (illus. 144). Gypsies were, however, by no means always social parasites: many provided important labour needed to harvest crops, such as hops, in areas short of manpower, while many stalls and entertainments at fairs were maintained by gypsy families.

The rise of industrialization also increased migration. In Iceland it drew many people to the coastal towns and villages, at first seasonally, but gradually on a permanent basis. Of these a disproportionate number were women, at least in the beginning,[117] a trend not unlike that elsewhere in Scandinavia, where urban industry attracted more and more full-time female labour.[118]

In Finland, many were drawn either south to Helsinki and Turku, or west to the coastal towns of along the Gulf of Bothnia. There, the collapse of the ship-building industry in the third quarter of the nineteenth century led many Finns to emigrate to America. Frequently, in the late nineteenth century, the son of a farmer in early manhood might work in the United States for a few years, accumulating work experience and money before returning to Finland to take over the family farm. This trans-Atlantic emigration declined in the inter-war years of the twentieth century; the United States introduced sharp quotas on the acceptance of immigrants after the First World War, while the creation of an independent Finland required more workers for its developing industrial infrastructure.

Permanent emigration was also an important alternative, especially for single men. As had been the case two decades before in Ireland, Norway by the late 1860s, despite having doubled its arable land area, could no longer support its burgeoning population. As a result, vast numbers of Norwegians emigrated, mainly to the United States. Denmark, too, witnessed the permanent emigration of many young men and a large number of families to America. The Danish artist Edvard Petersen (1841–1911) successfully captured the final moments in Denmark of one such emigrating family on their way to America, in his sorrowful work *Emigrants in Larsen's Square* (1890) (see illus. 131). The United States often proved to be a land of considerable opportunity. There, poor Scandinavians with initiative and enterprise could achieve a degree of financial prosperity not usually possible at home, where social stratification and the lack of free land often prevented social and economic advancement.

Criminality, Public Order and the Legal Code

The Nordic countries in the early modern period witnessed the development of strong central political and administrative bureaucracies. In Denmark, the comprehensive legal code initiated by Peder Schumacher, later Count Griffenfeld, was promulgated by Christian V in 1683, introducing less brutal penalties than had previously been the case for a number of crimes. Theft, for example, had ceased to be a capital offence, becoming punishable by flogging and branding. The burning of witches was also forbidden, though witchcraft itself remained a serious crime. Weights and measures were standardized by Ole Christiansen Rømer (1644–1710), whose greatest fame lay in having devised astronomical instruments, including a planetarium, which had astounded the Emperor of China.[119] None the less, an authoritarian legal system continued to prevail, in which serfs could be whipped, incarcerated and otherwise punished as landlords saw fit. The most frequent punishment, however, for numerous minor crimes was the pillory, in use well into the nineteenth century. In the painting *Man in a Chain Pillory*, by the Finnish artist Juho Rissanen (1873–1950) (illus. 145), its mode of deployment is carefully depicted, though when Rissanen painted the work the pillory had ceased to be used. Fines and imprisonment had, by the late nineteenth century, become the penalties for almost all crimes, minor or serious.

In Sweden and Finland, not only aristocrats on their estates, but even yeoman

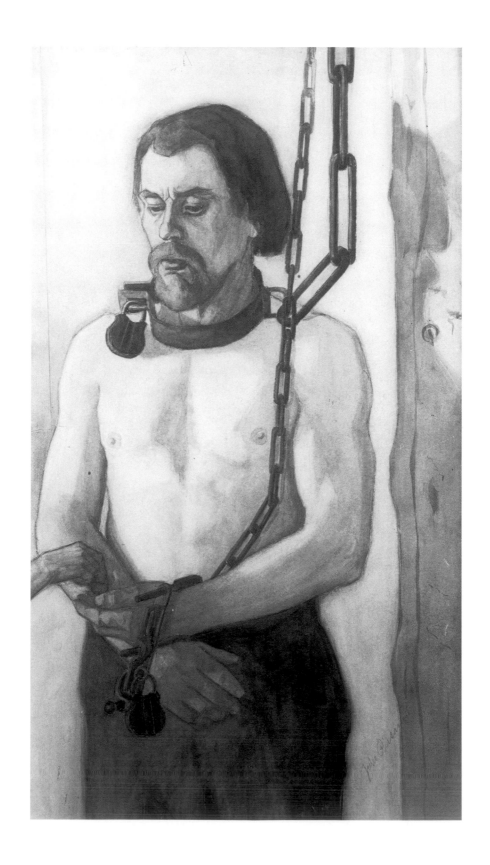

farmers, acted as magistrates in their own households, an arrangement which had been given the force of law in 1671. Their servants and labourers could be beaten, locked up on bread and water for a month and fined for criminal behaviour, as the master deemed appropriate. However, public discontent amongst the clergy, burghers and peasants in the House of Estates, forced the rescinding of the law within four years. In many households, though, such a regimen continued.[120]

Transportation to the Swedish colony in Delaware was also an option for the punishment of criminals and vagabonds during Sweden's brief dominion there during the mid-seventeenth century. For serious crimes committed in New Sweden, however, a culprit would be sent back to Sweden for a review of the trial and punishment as happened to a Swedish gunner, Sven Vass, accused of causing a fire which laid waste to the settlement at New Gothenburg. He was transported back to Sweden in irons after a makeshift local trial.[121]

As today, the vast majority of crimes committed were by men. Violence was especially endemic amongst those engaged in more rugged occupations, frequently erupting, for example, among loggers of different provinces or national origins in the seasonal sawmill industry. It was often exacerbated by drink. Gang fights between the youths of neighbouring villages also frequently occurred. The Swedish coastal fishing villages of Halland were particularly noted for such 'warfare', with village youths frequently goaded on by their elders.[122] In the poorer areas of Stockholm and Gothenburg urban street fighting was common, while in Lapland violence would occasionally break out, usually aggravated by drink, at the annual fairs or feast day celebrations, with ethnic antagonisms between Saami, Swedes, Finns and Norwegians producing occasionally murderous results. Some crime, however, was economically motivated. Along side burglary and theft, relatively infrequent crimes, there was also profitable smuggling in spirits and other commodities. While the former two were usually punished by long years of penal servitude at hard labour, those found guilty of smuggling usually ended their lives upon the scaffold. Public execution was the penalty for most capital crimes and the gallows remained a common feature on principal crossroads well into the nineteenth century.

Lesser criminals, however, might be condemned to prisons like Karlstens Fortress, by Marstrand, on Sweden's west coast. There as many as 30 prisoners were accommodated in vaults some four metres thick where they would cook, eat, sleep and fulfil their bodily needs, with only work providing a relief from their confinement. However, a movement developed for the reform of prisons in the late eighteenth century, taking its inspiration from Britain, in particular, John Howard's *The State of the Prisons in England and Wales*, published in 1777.

Spearheading this movement in Sweden was David Schultz, a native of Prussia who had introduced smallpox inoculation to his adopted country in the 1750s. He supported the designs for a new model prison, by the Swedish architect Gustaf af Sillén (1762–1825), built on three floors, with hardened and lesser criminals separated from one another, and a chapel in the centre. Many reformers

(Opposite) **145** Juho Rissanen, *Man in a Chain Pillory*, 1900, watercolour and pencil on paper.

201

146 C. F. Meijer, Karlsborg
Fortress (Sweden), 1845.

considered that the Karlsborg Fortress (illus. 146), designed by C. F. Meijer in
1845, with its round end towers and monumental elevation of barrack-like
accommodation, provided the optimum arrangement for security, containment,
punishment, work and reform based upon the latest foreign theories. In reality
such functional arrangements, especially the separation of different types of pris-
oner were not new. In the seventeenth century vagabonds and petty thieves had
been locked up for short periods at the House of Correction, with a penal smithy,
formerly in the old Tre Kronor Palace, situated nearby. This smithy was composed
of two rooms, one for men and one for women, with an adjacent prison yard,
but its use was reserved for serious political offenders. One such political convict
was Lars Ulstadius, a Finnish priest, who was incarcerated there for over 40 years.
It was to remain in use until 1850, though its attractively styled Rose Chamber,
in reality a torture chamber, ceased to be used for such gruesome purposes after
Gustaf III abolished torture in the beginning of his reign, thereby winning the
loud approbation of Voltaire and other eminent Enlightenment thinkers.[123]
The gaol erected within the walls of the castle at Kalmar in the early years of the
nineteenth century provided relative luxuries previously unknown to common
criminals, with rudimentary beds instead of a straw and accommodation lit by
windows, rather than a dank cellar.[124] Criminals of the upper classes, by contrast,
fared much better. Not only were they generally provided with apartments suitably furnished according to their station, but they were allowed to keep little
libraries and, on occasion, tame birds.[125]

Generous treatment to those convicted of political crimes was especially noteworthy in progressive Denmark in the nineteenth century. Orla Lehmann
(1810–1870), a liberal reformer who keenly supported the rights of the peasantry,
had incurred the wrath of the government for his strident attack on absolute
monarchy and was imprisoned. However, his 'cell', situated near the Town Hall,

147 W. Koch after P. E. Lorentzen, *Portrait of Orla Lehmann in Prison*, 1842, lithograph.

depicted in *Portrait of Orla Lehmann in Prison* (1842), by P. E. Lorentzen (illus. 147), shows such amenities as a secretaire bookcase full of books, a potted plant on the sill of the barred window and a comfortable arm chair, in which Lehmann lounges in a silk dressing gown, an open book upon his knees. Eventually released, he himself became a lawyer with Denmark's High Court in 1844.

General prison life was, of course, quite different and it is from Denmark that the most monumental and powerful pictorial image of a prison exterior in the Nordic region comes. *The Prison by the Town Hall and Palace of Justice* (1831) by Martinus Rørbye depicts this early nineteenth-century neo-classical edifice (illus. 148), rebuilt after the bombardment of Copenhagen during the Napoleonic Wars in a way which uses a rigid geometry and heavy rustication to emphasize the severe judgement of the law which awaited the those who dared to offend the social order. The fact that it housed both prison and judicial chambers was quite usual. Only later in the century, in major capitals, would prisons come to be separated by considerable geographical distance from the courts.

148 Martinus Rørbye, *The Prison by the Town Hall and Palace of Justice*, 1831, oil on canvas.

Perhaps the most important innovation in prison architecture during the nineteenth century was the introduction of cells, first introduced into Scandinavia in the 1840s, and deemed to be more wholesome, humane and, in particular, suited to the reform of the prisoners. In Sweden alone, by 1877, there were some 2,243 cells which housed two inmates each, though some prisoners continued to be accommodated in the old style gaols. There prison reform was keenly supported from above by the future King Oscar I, who himself was the author of a pamphlet on the subject and took an avid interest both in the latest prison reforms abroad as well as in methods of how to reduce criminality itself. Whether the policies introduced proved to be more effective or whether the frequency of custodial sentencing dropped is not clear but the fact remains that the actual prison population of the country fell to a record low of 2,293 in 1899.[126]

The model prison of the new regime was Stockholm's Remand Prison, built in 1852 to the designs of Axel Nyström (illus. 149). The central prison at Långholmen, designed by the Swedish architect Vilhelm Theodor Ankarsvärd (1816–1887), was built between 1874 and 1880 for long-term prisoners. Based on

149 Axel Nyström, *Exterior View of Stockholm's Remand Prison*, 1852.

the innovative plan of Eastern Penitentiary in Philadelphia, ranges of cells fanned out from the central block, where they opened upon balconies. In the furthermost ranges, new prisoners were incarcerated in solitary confinement for two years, except for an hour or so of outdoor exercise, in cells seven metres square. There they would eat, sleep and be employed in cobbling or making matches. The innermost ranges housed those who been in prison longer than two years. These cells were only three metres square, but generally were occupied just at night, the daytime being spent by prisoners at work in the corridors, in the central areas of which Sunday services would be held, whilst prisoners attended from their cells, doors ajar. In this regard the arrangement was based on that already implemented at Auburn Prison in New York State. Security was, of course, not forgotten, with cells varying slightly in size, so that cell doors were never directly opposite one another on the corridors, which might have facilitated communications between the prisoners when they were opened.[127]

As the nineteenth century drew to a close and the twentieth commenced new prisons continued to be built, but by 1914 further prison construction had ceased altogether. Only in 1939 did the construction of such buildings begin again; that year a new establishment was built at Skenäs in Östergötland.

From the late eighteenth century, minor miscreants, that is, those convicted of begging and debts, came to be seen as distinct from other criminals and so were imprisoned in special establishments erected for the purpose. Beggars, both adults and children, though usually women and the elderly, were sent to so-called spinning houses, where they could be made to be useful in the production of wool. One of the most notable was the Spinning House, built by C. F.

150 Carl Sundt-Hansen, *In Custody*, 1875, oil on canvas.

Adelcrantz in 1784, at Norrköping, a city which was noted for its textile industry. In Stockholm, debtors, who were mainly men, were incarcerated in a former merchant's house, built on three floors. It contained six rooms for men and one for women, as well as a chapel. As was the case elsewhere in the prison system, though, aristocratic or gentrified prisoners were usually treated differently, being accommodated separately in the guardhouse of the Royal Palace of Stockholm.[128]

In Finland, criminality took much the same form and frequency that it did in Sweden and Denmark, where violent crimes were relatively rare. There was, however, one major exception. In the rural south of Ostrobothnia, around Vasa, murders and serious assaults amongst men took on a frequency which made the area one of the most violent in Europe, especially during the nineteenth century.[129] This has led some people to label the ensuing century the 'knife junker period' in this western region of Finland. Young men would gather with knives in pockets and go in pursuit of fights with those of other villages, or, indeed, even their own. However, most violent crimes were not committed with knives, which accounted for only 16 per cent of murder weapons, but cudgels, bottles or other objects that came to hand. Weddings, dances, fairs and other entertainments, often in the Christmas period, at which vast quantities of brandy, often home brewed, were served, provided the venues for some three-fifths of these violent crimes.[130]

For most of the 'knife junkers' convicted of murder, hanging was the penalty. This was in line with the penalty for murder elsewhere in Scandinavia. However, from 1825 and in line with legal custom in Russia, now joined to Finland within the Russian Empire, felons were henceforth transported to Siberia. Whatever the penalty, though, convictions were not always easy to come by, for two witnesses to the event were required for conviction in situations in which the culprit did not admit his guilt. All that could be done in those circumstances was to incarcerate the suspect at Viapori (renamed Suomenlinna in 1918 and known as Sveaborg in Swedish) Fortress, in the harbour of Helsinki, and subject him to the regular admonitions of a priest, until he confessed, or to release him, if the authorities ultimately felt he was free of guilt.

Processes of interrogation, whether by a priest, lawyer or policeman, could be a long and arduous affair in the Nordic region. The Norwegian artist, Carl Sundt-Hansen (1841–1907) succeeded in poignantly depicting the interrogation of a suspect by the authorities in his painting In Custody (1875; illus. 150). While such a work exerted considerable sentimental appeal by virtue of its melodrama, it also attempted to capture the stark reality of legal confrontation with a wealth of anecdotal detail.

Police forces had long been established in the major Nordic capitals, but the outlying areas of the Nordic world also had to deal with occasional crimes, especially in growing urban areas. A police force, for example, had been established in Tórshavn, in the Faeroe Islands, in the nineteenth century, but although their numbers reached some two dozen by the end of the century, no more than two or three were on duty at any one time. Those not active at first served as a crew for the official boat allotted to the use of the prefect of Tórshavn. This arrangement proved unsatisfactory, and during the early years of the twentieth century the police force there was abolished, with local people informally taking over their duties. This was possible only because felonies were few, with most criminal acts caused by drunken seamen, often foreign. While these were summarily dealt a rough form of justice by locals, the rare perpetrators of serious crimes, as was usual in such outlying areas, were shipped to Denmark for punishment.

Even Svalbard, Norway's seasonally populated northern island outpost in the High Arctic was not immune to crime. There violent crimes, often exacerbated by drink, were particularly rife amongst the Russian population. Exceptionally severe there, though, was the murderous Russian mutiny of 1851 which resulted in the Russians being expelled from the island by the Norwegians for an extended period of time.[131]

In the tropical colonies of the Scandinavian countries, where much of the

151 Execution of a slave, engraving.

populations were slaves until well into the nineteenth century, the maintenance of public order was, of course, paramount. This meant that the prevention and draconian punishment of slave revolts and flights became salient features of penal codes and practice. Governor Philip Gardelin, in the Danish Virgin Islands, promulgated particularly severe laws in 1733 which were to remain in effect until the end of the century. Serious crimes invariably led to execution of the slave, since, it was felt, public cautionary examples always had to be made and for this reason owners who thereby lost their 'property' were almost invariably reimbursed from a general kitty created for the purpose. One such unfortunate victim, his arms amputated, can be seen in a grisly depiction by an unknown artist, *Execution of a slave* (illus. 151).

In the Swedish Caribbean colony of St Barthelemy, anyone of African or mixed descent who was neither a slave nor in possession of papers declaring him to be free, was deemed a property of the king and subject to incarceration. Thus, it was deemed legally appropriate for a boy, one Richard Crump, to be sold, in 1815, 'for the benefit of the King, if not claimed, or his freedom legally proved within Three Months from this date'.[132] Perhaps the most prevalent of crimes committed by slaves in the colony was theft, particularly of petty items from their masters or mistresses, crimes which often could only with difficulty be proved. This was to lead to the prohibition on ladies from taking their attending slaves with them to balls and other such public entertainments where 'Hats, Handkerchiefs, Fans, Gloves, Earrings and other Jewels have been entirely lost'.[133]

Whites too sometimes offended against the criminal code in the tropical colonies and the penalties were severe by modern standards. Most serious was murder, a rare occurrence. Far more typical of criminality in the Caribbean islands, as in Scandinavia itself, were the numerous fights and other aggressive acts, usually precipitated by too much drink, the sorting out of which occupied most of the time for the one policeman resident in the capital Gustavia.[134]

Finnish Cultural Identity and the Importance of Images of Nature

Historically, in the Nordic region, as elsewhere, outlaws often took refuge in forests. For that reason, and also because of the wild animals such as wolves and bears (and even fearsome spirits lying in wait for prey as many dreaded), such areas could seem very threatening to the more peaceable general population. Yet, woods and other natural geographical features within them could also have many positive features. For example, since the Reformation in Scandinavia, certain aspects of Nature, such as springs and certain trees, were often considered to be imbued with healing properties.[135]

In Finland perhaps more than elsewhere in the Nordic region, the forest became a key symbol of both personal and national independence and refuge. With forest covering some 65 per cent of Finland, it could offer Finns a haven both real and symbolic from Swedes to the west and Russians to the east, both of which nations dominated Finland by political settlements and force of arms over the centuries. Here it was felt the Finnish virtue of 'sisu' (a stubborn persistence in asserting one's own identity and values) could thrive in glorious isolation, away from foreign intrusions or dependence upon others and 'sisu' became central to a Finnish ethnic identity which few could really define precisely. As the German historian at the University of Göttingen, August Ludwig Schözer, wrote in his *Algemeinen nordischen Geschichte* (General Nordic History), in 1771, about the 'Aborigines' of Finland, 'If the Finns are neither Scythians, nor Samoyeds, nor Huns, nor Hebrews, who then are they? Well, they are just Finns, and that is where I have to stop, my family tree for them does not go any further, and between the Finn and Noah, I do not know of any ancestral links'. Schözer in no way meant such a comment disparagingly. On the contrary, he saw Finland, as 'Europe's Canada', a forested land offering many opportunities for the future for a growing population which, between 1754 and 1769, had increased by one-third, as he stated when the Finnish cultural historian Henrik Gabriel Porthan came to visit Göttingen.[136]

Such questions of identity were complicated by the co-existence in Finland of two different groups, Finnish-speaking Finns and Swedish-speaking Finns. In 1865, when the Finnish language was made an official language on a par with Swedish, the Swedish-speaking population made up some 14 per cent of the population. Yet it was the Swedish-Finns who were at the forefront of the movement to make Finnish an official language, in particular, Johan Vilhelm Snellman (1806–1881), a political philosopher and professor at the University of Helsinki, who was a native of Stockholm. In any case, by 1920, the numbers of Swedish-Finns had fallen to only 11 per cent of the entire population and later this rate would fall to only about 6 per cent, a small proportion of the whole population, though larger than the tiny Russian population which had settled in Finland. Despite Russian political hegemony for over a century, Finland had maintained its own political and social culture and there were still only 7,300 Russians resident in 1910. By 1920, three years after Finnish independence, this number had fallen to only 4,800.[137] Finland had remained a land largely reserved to Finnish-speaking Finns, albeit with a Swedish-speaking minority with the rights and privileges rarely accorded to an ethnic minority in any other country.

The role of winter as a natural phenomenon also exerted considerable symbolic impact in Finland, with that frightening face of the Nordic winter, the 'kaamos' (winter murkiness) often reinforcing Nature's less benign character. Reconciling these two contrary images of Finland's cultural inheritance, Nature as nurturing and Nature as threatening, with growing industrialization and the dramatic increase of urban life in the late nineteenth and twentieth centuries, became one of the principal fault lines of the Finnish cultural and social psyche. Thus, for many Finns, a summer house in the countryside in the twentieth century meant more than sun and fun away from the noise and smoke of the city, but rather an atavistic re-establishment of ties to the natural world. It is for this reason that the Finnish institution of the sauna is much more than merely a bathing house. It is also why both the forest and the sauna are central to the imagery of Kivi's *Seven Brothers* (1870), the archetypal novel of life in the Finnish countryside. Situated near the homestead but on the edge of the forest, the sauna is the link between civilization and the wilderness. As has been said, 'Metaphorically, the sauna is nature; going to the sauna is going back to nature; going back to nature is a return to "real life", a refuge from society, a revitalisation in mythic time'.[138] As such it was the ultimate sanctuary, the opposite pole to church, school and the other constraints of life in a community, where regimentation and order became the hallmarks of their 'civilizing' influences.

In Dalecarlia in the late nineteenth century, the independently minded yeoman farmer and his family became the ultimate model for the happy and prosperous middle-class Sweden, rather than Scania, where the land was far richer and many landowners lived in considerable state. Poets, like Erik Axel Karlfeldt (1864–1931) sang Dalecarlia's praises in *Songs of Wilderness and of Love* (1895) or *Fridolin's Songs* (1898), while the artists Anders Zorn and Carl Larsson expressed their enchantment with rural life in their paintings. Such positive folk values were further reinforced by the popular revival of interest in folk songs and dances, as well as the anecdotal tales about folk culture to be avidly read in such popular magazines as *Allers Familjejournal*. Reconstituted model museum villages, such as that of Skansen, in Stockholm, became hallowed goals of pilgrimage for families from all over Sweden and beyond and further reinforced this trend. As the Swedish poet Gustaf af Geijerstam succinctly put it at the time, 'It is the primitive, which we city dwellers seek in the summer life of the countryside, its primitive qualities and its peace'.[139]

This interest in 'nature', as well as the transport links provided by rail, trams, buses and motor cars, led to the development of prosperous villa towns throughout the Nordic countries, some of the most prosperous conveniently situated adjacent to the capital cities. Saltsjöbaden and Lindingö, near Stockholm, as well as Kulosaari in Helsinki, and Gentofte and Hellerup, near Copenhagen, all became havens of the upper middle classes seeking a sanitized and comfortable return to their idealized rural roots.

Such a trend was not restricted to major urban areas. Even in remote areas, the newly prosperous beneficiaries of the rise of forestry prices, who had not foolishly succumbed to selling their land earlier when prices were low, built prestigious wooden villas, richly embellished with towers, turrets and balconies, imposing if not practical in the frequently harsh climate of Scandinavia. In the little village of Skyttmon, in Jämtland, alone, some ten grandiose villas were built between 1874 and 1914, the last one by the architect Elov Frid, which included no less than seven balconies.[140]

Pantheism in Nature

Well into the nineteenth century and beyond, folk beliefs in the Nordic region, especially in thickly wooded Norway, Sweden and Finland, persisted in perceiving nymphs and sprites in the almost ubiquitous woods and bodies of water, and many artists and literary figures took up this theme. A work by the Swedish artist Ernst Josephson captures such a mythical being, his *Water Sprite (Näcken)* (1884). Such beings were frequent subjects of poetry and novels, such as *Pan* (1893) by the Norwegian Nobel Laureate Knut Hamsun (1859–1952), which takes its title from the Greek mythological figure who embodied many facets of wild nature. Indeed, because of the spiritual presence of Pan in the forest, the hero Glahn is never really alone, living away as he does from his fellow man out in the wilderness of the far north, where even the rocks and boulders are alive.

Such pantheistic attitudes are also evident in the Finnish epic *Kalevala*, compiled and adapted by Elias Lönnrot (1802–1884) (published in two versions, a shorter one in 1835 and a longer one in 1849) and developed in the music of the Finnish-Swedish composer Jean Sibelius (1865–1957) who frequently took the *Kalevala* as his theme, of which the tone poem *The Swan of Tuonela* (1893) is one of the most notable. Not surprisingly, Gallen-Kallela was to pick up on this with his own visual image of the musical elements in his painting *Waterfall at Mäntykoski* (1892–4), in which a musical scale is vertically superimposed over the picture (see illus. 133). As such, it echoes the musical connotations given to such waterfalls in various Nordic novels, not least the Swedish author Tor Hedberg's *At the Torpa Farm* (1888). In the novel, Hedberg likens the roar of a waterfall to the deep tone of an organ, but living and characteristic of the essence of the farm itself.[141] Such pantheistic attitudes were not merely literary conceits, they were incorporated into the life of ordinary people in everyday situations, in such countries where the overwhelming majority of homes remained rural well into the twentieth century.

Stanislaw Przybyszewski (1868–1927), the Polish literary figure, friend and early admirer of Edvard Munch was particularly taken by the relationship of the individual to the landscape. He wrote:

> Two People look at a landscape. One sees it with a simple brain: impressions of light, colours, forms, lines, a well-ordered conglomeration, flat, dull and boring. Another sees this landscape with an individualistic consciousness. The colours become glowing and hot and intense; lines with a child with chalk could draw, become full of pulsing life, they stand in relationship to the most intimate life of the soul, they merge into the forms of the soul and one becomes one with the landscape and lives in her and through her.[142]

This image of nature is obvious in many works by Munch. Yet other Nordic artists were also aware of this. In *The Forest* (1892; see illus. 134) by Prince Eugen, brother of King Gustaf V of Sweden, the lines and colours of the Swedish woods assume a life of their own, almost as if they allude to some alternative reality whose presence we can only sense, while even in *Søndermarken in Wintertime* by Hammershøi this suburban park near Frederiksberg in Copenhagen is transformed into a mystical wood in which signs of human life are nowhere to be found.

Germans, Xenophobia and the Growth of National Identities

Hanseatic Expansion

German links with the Nordic regions had been well-established by the end of the first millennium, focused around the trade routes which brought furs, wood, tar, copper, iron ore and herring to Continental Europe, and southern and eastern commodities to the north. From around 1250, German traders gained increasing control of the important Baltic and North Sea trade. After the formal consolidation of their power through the Hansa League in the middle of the thirteenth century, Germans, over the next 200 years, came to dominate important cities in the Nordic region, bringing with them an urban culture not previously found there. Visby, on the Swedish island of Gotland, in the middle of the Baltic, was by the early thirteenth century a thoroughly German city of considerable riches, with some 56 merchants who had come from the Rhineland and Westphalia.[1] Hanseatic might was a power to be reckoned with. When the Danish king Valdemar IV tried to exert his own authority in the Baltic in 1368, the Hanseatic League vanquished him and, by the Peace of Stralsund two years later, compelled him to acquiesce to the league's Baltic supremacy. Many Germans assimilated with the newly urbanized Swedes, but others, for example the inhabitants of the city of Kalmar, maintained their ethnic identity well into the modern period.

This German identity was also to be found in urban architecture, both religious and secular, which sprang up as the merchants settled. Ecclesiastical architecture, for example, clearly demonstrated its Rhenish and Westphalian origins not only stylistically but even in terms of the materials used. Brick became popular in those areas where stones suitable for building were not available and was the primary building material both in the Cistercian church at Sorø and the cathedral of Roskilde, in the thirteenth century, and in the Maria Church at Sigtuna and Strängnäs Cathedral, in the fourteenth. In towns such as Visby where building stones were plentiful, stone masonry was also largely in the hands of German craftsman, often from Saxony, who travelled to the far reaches of the Nordic region in pursuit of work.

Considerable ecclesiastical authority was vested in the hands of Germans, who were sometimes given sees in the region, such as that of Turku, in the fourteenth century. This German connection increasingly led Nordic seminary students to study in Germany, rather than in Paris, as had previously been the case. In fact, by the fifteenth century, the Pomeranian cities of Rostock and Greifswald (where a university was established in 1456) became the more

152 Jørgen Sonne, *The Arrival
of Norwegian and Swedish
Students in Copenhagen on 23
June 1845*, 1847, oil on canvas.

favoured centres of study. This meant that many German theological points of view found their way into Scandinavia through students who had returned home, assisted by printers from Lübeck who had established themselves in Denmark and Sweden, possibly as early as the 1480s.[2] By the 1500s, even German lawyers and scholars were coming to Scandinavia, where they took up positions in the new centralized government bureaucracy of Sweden, which was extremely important in enabling its autocratic monarch, Gustaf Vasa, to consolidate his hard-won power.[3]

Swedish Expansion Across the Sea

The centralization of political authority and the development of an effective bureaucracy facilitated Sweden's political and military ascendancy in the region, for it meant more effective and abundant taxation and tolls could be put to the service of the state. It was also to have major implications for Germany, especially in the mid-seventeenth century. The king, Gustaf Adolf, though he himself fell upon the field at the Battle at Lützen, helped Sweden to achieve victory in the Thirty Years War over the Holy Roman Emperor Rudolph II and his Catholic allies (even if the principal gains of the war were soon lost). From Lapland in the north to Estonia (Danish during much of the Middle Ages), Latvia and Ingermanland (where St Petersburg is now situated) in the east, from the mouths of the rivers Oder, Elbe and Weser in the west, to the frontiers of Brandenburg in the south, Swedish hegemony held sway, with Denmark the only serious threat to its position. Denmark was vanquished in the following decade, with the resulting acquisition of Scania to Sweden. Long gone were the days of the Kalmar Union (1397–1523) which had united Scandinavia and much of the Baltic under Danish hegemony.

Such a vast imperium brought about its own administrative and social problems. Large numbers of continental Germans and other ethnic groups now became Swedish subjects. One proposed solution to this difficulty was a unitary kingdom in which the Baltic would have become a Swedish lake. Another, advocated by the Swedish Count Axel Oxenstierna, envisioned two separate state entities, the west, governed from Stockholm, and the east, from Narva. As a result, Narva (together with Kalmar) on the south coast of the Gulf of Finland, became one of the Swedish dominion's most imposing Baroque towns, the lavish architectural embodiment of a political vision never realized. Opposition by landed vested interests in the new provinces, motivated by a fear of losing some of their feudal privileges, not customary in Sweden, may have prevented its integration into the Swedish kingdom.[4] In any case, dynastic machinations of the great European powers and a desire to preserve some balance of power also played a role, and the German provinces now ruled by Sweden continued to remain integrated with the Holy Roman Empire, an arrangement that gave Sweden an ongoing direct interest in Central European political affairs as well as financial benefits.

Swedish Pomerania

Shortly after the sovereignty of Swedish Pomerania passed to Sweden, Stettin was established as its administrative capital. Though the German Holy Roman Emperor did remain nominally in supremacy, with the Swedish king his de jure vassal as Duke of Pomerania, rights relating to the raising of taxes, granting of lands and administrative appointments were now reserved to the Swedish king, his 'statshållare', or general governor, and ministers. German (except for the Treasury, where Swedish was adopted) remained the language of administration and common usage, while existing law, coinage and measurements remained legally in force. The highest Swedish court, however, superseded the old German one, and a new courthouse was constructed, which symbolically underscored the new political order. Otherwise, few other civil architectural works were commissioned at the time in Sweden's new territory. Swedish financial and administrative commitment was devoted instead to erecting numerous military fortifications throughout the region, very costly endeavours, without which Sweden could never hope to maintain its political hegemony. To this end, the architect Erik Dahlberg undertook to construct an iron necklace of fortresses which came to embrace the entire southern and eastern perimeters of the Swedish domains, the most imposing of which was at Wismar. Usually triangular, these bastions linked Stade by Bremen in the west with Nöteborg on Lake Ladoga in the east, and were to leave a permanent stamp on urban layout in these towns and cities. The Weapons Magazine (1700) in Stade, built as a magazine for the storage of timber, is one of the few architectural vestiges of this grand military vision.

Swedish dominion also made itself felt in official domestic architecture. In the Wrangel Palace, in Stralsund, for example, built towards the end of the seventeenth century, Nils Eosander (1636–1705), introduced the use of a sloping roof to an urban street façade, a Swedish innovation. Previously, local buildings had always been crowned by gables on the street elevation.[5] Eosander also exerted an influence in rural architecture, carrying out important work on Schloss Spycker, the governor general's summer residence on Rügen around 1670. Originally surrounded by a moat when it was built in the sixteenth century, it is a small castle, with flanking corner towers, and was painted Falun red in characteristic Swedish fashion. Forming a picturesque architectural unity, it became a favourite residence of Governor General Wrangel who died there in 1676.[6]

No sooner had the frontiers of this great overseas Swedish imperium been secured than it was assaulted by Denmark and Brandenburg. First, Wismar was captured by Danish troops, allies of the margrave of Brandenburg, in 1675. Sweden's traditional ally, France, successfully demanded its return to Sweden. In 1679, however, Sweden was less fortunate and much of Nether Pomerania was ceded to Brandenburg for good. Then, Stralsund was conquered in 1715, and five years later Swedish territory was reduced to only a sliver of Hither Pomerania, north of the River Peene. That said, Stralsund was permitted to remain a part of Swedish Pomerania and, indeed, took over from Stettin as the new administrative

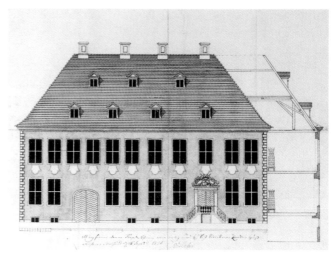

(Above left) **153** *Swedish Military Commander's House in Stralsund, c. 1750, drawing.*

(Above right) **154** And Fischer, *Post Office, Stralsund, 1736, drawing.*

capital. In consequence of the province's political and economic significance, a considerable amount of civil architecture was also undertaken.[7]

It was imperative that Swedish administrative and other governmental buildings in Stralsund reflected the high status of Swedish Pomerania. First and foremost, the construction of a new palace for the Swedish governor-general Count Meijerfeldt was undertaken. The Netherlandish architect Cornelius Loos (1686–1738), who had spent some time in Turkey during the imprisonment of Karl XII at Bender, provided the designs for this. Built on three floors, the typical red façade was decorated and proportioned in a classically inspired Baroque style common in Sweden at the time, with its entrance built of limestone imported from Gotland. The important official rooms were situated upon the first floor, including the governor general's private apartment and servant's accommodation, as well as the public administrative offices, including an archive. On the second floor, at the top, was the apartment of the governor's wife and service accommodation, and there was also a library for Meijerfeldt's use.[8] Other buildings included the Swedish Military Commander's House (c. 1750; illus. 153), and the Post Office (illus. 154), in which Swedish and German elements come together as potent symbols of Swedish hegemony in this corner of Germany.

The Awakening of Danish National Identity

Sweden's foot in Europe was new and tentative but Denmark, by contrast, had always been an integral part of continental Europe, not only through its geography, but because its king, as duke of Schleswig-Holstein, was a vassal of the Holy Roman Emperor. Denmark had been intimately involved in European political and military affairs. As far back as 1460, Christian I had acquired the Duchies of Schleswig and Holstein, proclaiming the inseparability of these German–Danish marches from Denmark, an event later commemorated by Abildgaard in *Christian I Elevates Holstein to the Status of a Duchy in 1460* (1778–7). By 1501, a condominium had been established, with two dukes of the Oldenburg family, the Danish royal dynasty, governing the duchies, one in his capacity as king of Denmark. Though Danish and German speakers were interspersed throughout the region, Danish predominated in Schleswig, in the north, with German the native language in Holstein, in the south. Though this linguistic mix often led to violent ethnic and political friction, it also germinated rich cultural fruits. The establishment of the University of Kiel, for example, in the enclave of Gottorf, in Holstein, educated generations of students from the lands adjacent to the Baltic Sea in German, the *lingua franca* of north-eastern Europe. Its importance as a university became great not only in Schleswig-Holstein, but even in the rest of Denmark: from 1768, anyone seeking to hold office in the duchies was required to have attended the University of Kiel for at least two years, which helped to nurture a sense of Germanic cultural identity.

The gradual economic and social rise of the Danish middle classes and gentry in the eighteenth century increasingly put them in conflict with the established interests of the largely native German-speaking aristocracy, especially in Schleswig-Holstein. Cultural figures, such as the playwright and historian Ludwig Holberg (1684–1754), assisted in this process. Previously, little other than religious works had been published in Danish, but Holberg opted to write and publish a variety of other subjects in Danish. His *History of the Danish Realm* (1732–5), in three volumes, focuses upon Danish history from the origins of the nation until the death of Frederik III, the first monarch who laid claim to his throne by divine right, in 1670. The birth and development of the Danish nation was depicted as a progression toward political and cultural unity and prosperity, under the auspices of her benevolent absolute monarch. Other works by Holberg, such as *Moral Thoughts* (1744), stressed the importance of the individual's responsibility for himself and the position he occupies in society. Deeply influenced by the views of the English political philosopher John Locke, Holberg felt that absolute monarchy provided the best form of government, maintaining that the monarch must act in concert with the will of the people who have given him his authority, otherwise they might remove their consent to his rule. In order to encourage such views and with the considerable financial support of Holberg, the Sorø Academy was refounded, in 1747 (it had originally been founded in 1623 but had later closed its doors) to inform young minds in preparation for entering ministerial roles in the nation's government. The young aristocrats enrolled at the academy could, it was hoped, imbibe Enlightenment values, in a milieu which also stressed discipline and obedience, precisely those characteristics enlightened monarchs wished to encourage.

The remains of the old medieval monastery of Sorø provided the foundations for the college, which was designed in a flamboyant Baroque style by Court Architect Laurids de Turah (1706–1759). An engraving, *The Sorø Academy*, from Pontoppidan's *Danish Atlas*, illustrates the contemporary appearance of this revived academy (illus. 155). Its architectural style provided a radical alternative to the University of Copenhagen, with its hodge-podge of university buildings from different periods in the old centre of the capital. The curriculum, too, was unlike

155 Sorø Academy, engraving from Pontoppidan's *Danish Atlas* (1763–4).

that in Copenhagen, for at Sorø, it was not Latin but Danish that was to be stressed. Nor did it cater so heavily for candidates to the priesthood who, even in 1810, made up some 40 per cent of the student population in Copenhagen.[9]

Another academic, Ove Høegh-Guldberg (1731–1808), engraved by J. F. Clemens in 1782 after Jens Juel (1745–1802), was appointed Professor of Rhetoric and focused upon the relationship between the use of language and cultural identity in his lectures and writings. Appointed tutor to Prince Frederik in 1764, he later went on to leave the academic world for politics, becoming a confidant of the Dowager Queen Juliane Marie, Prince Frederik's mother. This enabled Høegh-Guldberg to assume increasing political power and, after becoming cabinet minister in 1774, he became the most powerful man in Denmark, until his downfall in 1784 when the crown prince seized control. However, he then returned to the academic world and continued his researches into language and cultural identity.

Other academic institutions which stressed Danish identity at the increasing cost of the Continental German, with its taint of cosmopolitanism, also flourished. One such body, the Royal Danish Society of Science, was established in 1742. Throughout the middle years of the eighteenth century it propagated an interest in Danish history, geography and, most importantly, linguistics. While the language of the University of Copenhagen was Latin, a lexicographer, Christian Eilschov (1725–1750), attempted to devise new Danish words in place of the Latin ones then in use so that Danish would become the language of academia in Denmark. Soon, even musical librettos came to be written in Danish instead of Latin or German as previously, though the Church of St Petri, in Copenhagen, which served the long-established German merchant community, continued to publish religious literature in German (illus. 156). The choirmaster

156 Frontispiece of the Petri Church Psalm Book, 1741, engraving.

of the Chapel Royal, the Italian Giuseppe Sarti, went as far as to use a libretto written by the Norwegian lawyer Niels Krog Bredal for his opera, for which the design by the Danish theatre artist Peter Cramer (1726–1782; illus. 157) was made, based on the *Gesta Danorum* (*Exploits of the Danes*), by Saxo Grammaticus (mid-1100s–early 1200s). Written in sixteen volumes under the impetus of Denmark's Archbishop Absalon (c. 1128–1201), Saxo's work had started with the legendary King Dan and had concluded with Canute IV's conquest of Pomerania in 1185. Thus, 2,000 years of Danish history and legend had been woven together into a fabric which could be used by eighteenth-century literary figures to glorify Denmark and her monarchy. Since the Danish language and its vernacular form could also be used to symbolize the spirit of the Danish people, a fact of which the royal family was aware, they too were keen to make use of it in political terms. For this reason the British-born wife of the future Christian VII, Caroline Matilda, a sister of King George III even made a point of learning and speaking Danish with her children, a habit that was happily noted by Holberg.[10]

Opfunden af P. Cramer. Stukket af O Hv. Lode det Kongl. D. S. Kobbr.
Konig GRAM, forklæd som en Læge, spaaer den förbittrede
Kong HENRIK en ond Skiæbne, hvorover Printzæsse SIGNE
forundrer sig; men Kong SUMBLE bliver nedslagen.

157 O. H. de Lodes, *Gram and Signe*, or *Masterpieces of Love and Courage*, 1756, engraving of a painting for a stage set by Peter Cramer.

In such an atmosphere of rising ethnic and linguistic consciousness, it is not surprising that xenophobia was increasing in Denmark from the 1750s with many social groups perceived as foreign, in particular Germans, whether native or foreign. Of the king's four counsellors, three were of German origins, including the most important of them, Privy Counsellor Count A. G. Moltke (1710–1792). His successor on the council, Frederik Danneskiold-Samsøe (1703–1770), became a leader of the government faction most hostile to German influence, whereas the German-born Count Andreas Peter Bernstorff (1735–1797), the foreign minister, became a butt of anti-German sentiments. Born in Hanover, he was viciously attacked by Danneskiold-Samsøe for filling important administrative posts in government with Germans, while contemptuously blocking the advancement of Danish-speaking Danes, sentiments shared not only by middling aristocrats but by many of the Danish middle classes.

Upheavals in the Rheinland and German Immigration to Jutland

For all such anti-German sentiment at court, Denmark was, in many ways, remarkably pro-German with respect to those without political aspirations. Since Denmark's contemporary needs required an increase in population, Germans were warmly welcomed by the government. In 1759 Frederik V invited immigrants, displaced by wars in the Rhineland, to Jutland where many succeeded in establishing villages. These generally consisted of half-timbered houses, closely clustered together, which architecturally resembled those of their German homeland. They also introduced the potato from Germany, a vegetable which conspicuously failed to win an immediate following among ethnic Danes. As a result, the immigrants were labelled 'Potato Germans'. In the long term, however, the establishment of these Germans was not successful, since many of them did not come from a farming background. Most had been artisans and the transition to farming in Denmark proved too great – only some 50 new German immigrant families from this group remained in Denmark after a few years and of those who did remain, quite a few gave up village life, settling instead on remote fields, often newly won from the heaths of Jutland.

Political Factions, Xenophobia and Crisis

With the ascension to the throne of the eccentric and increasingly mentally unbalanced Christian VII in 1766, a battle for political control ensued amongst court factions. The court doctor and confidant to the Queen, Johan Friedrich Struensee (1737–1772), a German from Prussia, rapidly consolidated his position as leader of the Germanophile faction. Having eliminated many of his opponents from the vicinity of the King and Queen, his political machinations led to his ennoblement and appointment as Privy Cabinet Minister in the summer of 1770, making him one of the most powerful men in the Danish realm, able to revamp governmental administration as he saw fit. Within a matter of months he had abolished the Danish Council of State and the office of Governor of Norway. Then, the following year, he reduced feudal obligations on the peasants and granted freedom of the press, earning him the accolades of Voltaire and other French Enlightenment philosophers. He also reformed the legal system and abolished torture. Conservative members of the Royal Family, however, as well as a significant number of Danish courtiers, felt growing animosity towards his more and more autocratic rule, which by inducing the king to permit him to issue cabinet orders without the latter's signature had made him a virtual dictator. To combat growing opposition to his authority in Copenhagen, Struensee established himself at the Royal Palace of Hørsholm a few miles north of the capital, where, in close proximity to the queen, he could live in relative freedom, away from the constraints of the capital and its hostile Court.

Not surprisingly, the Dowager Queen Juliane Marie (1729–1796), the half-English step-mother of Christian VII and widow of Frederik V, loathed Struensee and used every opportunity to undermine his position, in the hopes of unseating him. In the *Portrait of The Queen Dowager Juliane Marie* (1776), by the Danish painter Vigilius Eriksen (1722–1782; see illus. 206), her strength of character and skill in the handling of court intrigues can be sensed. These were qualities which enabled her to weather not only Struensee, but most of the other crises which plagued her regency during the minority of the future King Frederik VI, when the king's state of mind deteriorated further. Though the Danish Dowager Queen was a German by birth (she was a daughter of the Duke of Brunswick-Wolfenbüttel), she tended to ally herself self-consciously with Danish court factions. This was in contrast to the ways of her own mother-in-law, Queen Sophie Magdalene, who had been much castigated for her pro-German sympathies. Juliane Marie went as far as to support plans to enact a law restricting governmental offices to native Danes, to the special exclusion of Germans.

With such powerful enemies as the Dowager Queen, Struensee's days were numbered. His adulterous relationship with the queen was uncovered and he fell. Terkel Kleve's engraved *Portrait of J. F. Struensee* (illus. 158) deliberately depicts the German, tortured and disgraced with a countenance caricatured yet recognizable to all. His coat-of-arms and the Order of Mathilde, presented to him only a few months before, are depicted lying dashed on the scaffold upon which his life was ended at Østre Fælled, on 28 April 1772. To press home even further the didactic

158 Terkel Kleve, *Portrait of J. F. Struensee*, 1772, engraving.

message, a Latin explanation has been provided: 'Mala multa struens se perdidit ipse' ('Through having perpetrated much evil, he brought misery upon himself'). The Hørsholm Palace, despite its royal status, was abandoned to the elements and eventually razed to the ground by Crown Prince Frederik, shortly after his accession to the throne in 1810. Some of the building materials left after demolition were later used to erect a parish church for Hørsholm in neo-classical style, situated on an island in a lake in the centre of the old park.

The adulterous queen was summarily divorced and banished to Celle, near Hanover, in Germany, a territory belonging to her brother George III of England. For a while, a confrontation between Denmark and England over the matter seemed likely, but this was avoided. Incarcerated, stigmatized and forgotten, an embarrassment to both Denmark and Britain, the exiled queen remained in Celle, separated from her children, until her premature death from a mysterious fever (some said she was poisoned) in 1775.

The repercussions from the affair for Danish–German relations were enormous. Xenophobia raged feverishly throughout Denmark and, for the first time in over a century, courtiers of non-Danish political extraction were almost totally excluded from important decision-making councils and bodies. Except in German-speaking Holstein and a number of small enclaves, Danish now became the sole official language of government administration, the courts and the whole of the armed forces. From 1776, office-holders and candidates born abroad were also excluded from all government posts.

The enactment of this law was celebrated with considerable pomp and ceremony. The Royal Copenhagen Porcelain Factory produced a porcelain figure group entitled *The Law with Respect to Natives*, in 1780 (illus. 159). Based upon a commemorative medallion of four years previous, a protective mother watches over her three beloved children, symbolizing Denmark, Norway and Schleswig-Holstein. Such associations were not restricted to works of art and craft: even a new ship of the line was christened *The Law with Respect to Natives*, in commemoration of the event!

Yet, draconian though this law might appear on the books, in reality its severity was mitigated. For example, foreigners already holding government office, landowners, priests and missionaries were all to be considered in the same light as those native born for the purposes of the law. Furthermore, no language test was instituted, at least not until the early nineteenth century, which could have verified the implementation of the Danish language in the way in which the law required. None the less, the new law did have immense implications: it strengthened the unity of the kingdom under its absolute monarch, while the king's German subjects increasingly felt themselves marginalized. Bernstorff, for example, became politically undermined, even though he himself was entitled to retain his office. The new law also increased the political power of the lower aristocracy, gentry and middle classes who made up the government's bureaucracy,

159 Jacob Schmidt for the Royal Copenhagen Porcelain Factory, *The Law with Respect to Natives*, 1780, porcelain group.

giving them the upper hand over the relatively small group of grand aristocratic families which derived both their language and culture from Germany.

The overthrow of the Struensee faction and the new law also had indirect implications for relations with Sweden. With the strengthening of the unity of the Danish realm, including the incorporation of the German enclave of Gottorp, in Holstein, the Swedish king Gustaf III's fears of a Danish-Russian alliance and encirclement seemed to be justified and the two countries only narrowly avoided war in 1773.

Danish Consolidation in the Arts

Even the arts in Denmark were not immune to the repercussions. Increasingly, in artistic terms, the Rococo came to be associated by many rising stars in the Danish political constellation with unwanted foreign elements, either German or French. On the other hand, the neo-classical more and more became associated with the native Danish, and the fledgling Danish Royal Academy of Art encouraged this trend. It had been founded in 1754, with the Frenchman, Professor Jacques-François Saly (1717–1776) as its first director, in order to educate native Danish artists and sculptors. Yet, all but three of the academy's professors were foreign during its first fifteen years of existence. The Danes were Carl Frederik Stanley (c. 1738–1813), who was born in England of a native-born Dane whose father had been English, but had become naturalized during the mid-1770s, before producing his patriotic sculpture *Amor Patriae* (illus. 160), upon his acceptance to the academy in 1777; Johannes Wiedewelt (1731–1802), author of the *Monument to the Prosperity of Denmark, Norway and the other Danish Territories* (illus. 161) and Peder Als (1727–1776).

160 C. F. Stanley, *Amor Patriae, Allegory symbolizing Patriotism*, 1777, plaster.

161 Johannes Wiedewelt, *Monument to the Prosperity of Denmark, Norway and the other Danish Territories*, wash and watercolour.

Saly himself had originally been invited to Denmark in 1753, when he was commissioned by the East Asia Company to produce a sculpture commemorating King Frederik V, for the square amid the splendid Rococo pavilions at Amalienborg Palace, designed by the Danish architect Nicolai Eigtved (1701–1754). One of these pavilions had recently become a principal residence of the Danish royal family. Commissions for sculpture in Copenhagen were rare, and this was an extraordinary opportunity. His work was a masterpiece, and he had been the most logical candidate for the academy's directorship.

After 1772, even the Danish Royal Academy of Art underwent a period of cleansing from alien elements. Foreigners such as the Swede Carl Gustaf Pilo (1711–1793), the Court Painter, lost their posts with the scantiest of justifications. It was alleged, for example, that Pilo had compromised himself not only by having been offered the Vasa Order by Gustaf III, during his visit to Copenhagen while Crown Prince in 1770, but also through the accusations levelled against him by Christian VII's Swiss doctor, Elie-Salomon-François Reverdil, and the Marshall of the Court Johan Bülow, who maintained that Pilo had led the Danish king into a life of moral dissolution, which facilitated his mental breakdown.[11] That said, his work was also deemed old-fashioned, for new fashions demanded the services of new artists conversant with the more austere and naturalistic neo-classical taste in portraiture, like Als and Juel, both native Danes increasingly patronized by the court. The introduction of the so-called 'Law with Respect to Natives' four years later, completed the reorganization of the academy under almost total Danish administration and artistic direction to the great satisfaction of the anti-German elements in government.

Denmark: One Nation or Three Realms?

Despite the new political alignment, projects already commenced, such as the sculptures for Nordmansdal, by the German sculptor Johann Gottfried Grund (1733–1796), on Norwegian folk themes, in the park of Fredensborg Palace, continued to be officially supported. One of the most important of these sculptures and in some respects a forerunner of the national romantic works of the next century is Grund's *Fisherwomen from Fasnes on Karmøen* (1760s; illus. 162) in which he stresses the natural dignity and worth of the Norwegian peasant archetype and, by extrapolation, the important position of Norway within Danish-Norwegian union. Yet the focus of this project soon changed. Grund's figures had been modelled on an earlier series of small ivory figures of Norwegian peasants by the Norwegian sculptor Jørgen Garnaas (1723–1798). Soon, however, they were supplemented by sculptures depicting both Icelandic and Faeroese figures, thereby emphasizing the king's authority over these island possessions, as well. Strangely, sculptures of Danish tillers of the soil were themselves absent from this garden (originally commissioned by Frederik V) since it was felt that Danish serfs, by contrast with the free peasantry of Norway, Iceland and Faeroes, were unworthy subjects for sculptures in a royal pleasure garden.[12]

162 Johann Gottfried Grund, *Fisherwomen from Fasnes on Karmøen*, 1760s, sculpture. Fredensborg Castle Garden, Copenhagen.

The absence of references to Schleswig-Holstein here is also striking. However, because of the increased meddling by Russia in the affairs of Schleswig-Holstein, a firm political statement, emphasizing Danish sovereignty with respect to the duchies came to be desired and this omission was soon filled by other works. Future sculptures on national themes now tended to include Schleswig-Holstein, depicting the united duchies as an integral part of the Danish realm. One design for a mural in the Knight's Hall at the Palace of Christiansborg in Copenhagen, by Nikolaj Abildgaard (1743–1809), commemorated the new legislation. *Jus Indigenatus, Allegory over the Law with Respect to Natives* (1790; illus. 163) depicts Denmark, Norway and Schleswig-Holstein as three lion cubs, suckled by their mother. In another version on the subject with the same title three women, their hands entwined, seem to allude to The Three Graces, here forming a united Danish Realm, a use of neo-classical subject matter for modern political ends.

IUS INDIGENATUS

163 Nikolaj Abildgaard, *Jus Indigenatus, Allegory over the Law with Respect to Natives*, 1790, oil on canvas.

Growing Idealization of the Danish Yeoman

Such neo-classical references are typical and ubiquitous in the work of Abildgaard. Arguably the most literate of Nordic artists, he had spent considerable time in Rome where he had amassed a vast classical library and took to heart the avocations of the German art theoretician Johann Joachim Winckelmann (1717–1768), to adopt the artistic ideals and values of the ancient Greeks.

Others, however, preferred to look at an idealized Danish peasant life for their national inspiration. For many, including Crown Prince Frederik, it was politically important to stress the value of the common man. Growing numbers of important political figures, in particular Bernstorff, considered it necessary to abolish serfdom. From their point of view, the depiction of the Danish peasant as responsible and worthy of dignity had political implications for the stirring of public opinion. It was not so much that the established powers were desirous of heightening patriotic feelings amongst the peasantry, but rather that such virtues as loyalty, thrift and industry, could be nurtured among a wide public and utilized to help to build a productive state, with loyal and enterprising subjects.

Though such pictorial conversation pieces as these look back to seventeenth-century Dutch masters, they none the less have a very contemporary flavour: *Several Farmers at a Haystack* (1778), by Cramer, for example, depicts free, but productive, peasants, surrounded by the agricultural fruits of their toil, from which the whole nation will derive the benefits (illus. 164). They are shown in the parish of Gentofte, north of Copenhagen, whose church tower shimmers in the background, an area in which Bernstorff himself had sold his peasants their land, successfully enabling them to set up their own productive farms.

While Cramer had never travelled abroad, Juel had visited France,

164 Peter Cramer, *Several
Farmers at a Haystack*, c. 1778,
oil on canvas.

Switzerland, Germany and Italy where a close knowledge of both Rococo and neo-classical stylistic elements enabled him to successfully bridge both the cosmopolitan and Danish in his art. Already, as a young man, his enigmatic portrait *A Holstein Girl* (1766–7; see illus. 205) had dignified this hypnotically alluring German maiden to a veritable icon of spiritual intensity. Then, almost two decades later, he would turn these skills, which reflected lessons learnt from both Jean-Baptiste-Siméon Chardin and Thomas Gainsborough, to glorify the new Danophile political order. In his *Landscape from Egnen at Jægerspris* (1784), Crown Prince Frederik's country seat is depicted in the distance with gentle naturalism, benignly surrounded by the small farms of productive yeoman farmers. There is another dimension as well, for the historical union of Christianity with the nation is hinted at through the symbolic inclusion of the column commemorating the towering theological figures of Ansgar who brought Christianity to Denmark, and Luther. Numerous joyful anecdotal scenes are also included, making the painting a visual ode of thanksgiving for a benevolent absolutism which was enabling a prosperous and contented people to thrive.

Revolutionary Rumblings and Danish–German Political Confrontation

As the rumblings of revolution began to be audible in France, so a different sort of political confrontation, albeit non-violent, broke out in Denmark in 1789. Pro-German and pro-Danish subjects, both loyal to the crown, entrenched themselves with a radically different vision of what the Danish realm should be, with respect both to the cultural and social groups it contained, in vociferous debates, political and literary. The former, liberal in regards to emancipation of the serfs, censorship and the fostering of Holstein and the role of its prominent citizens in the Danish kingdom, were opposed by the latter, deeply conservative and suspicious of alien influences and fearful of social upheaval and dislodgement of landed interests. Battle lines between the two factions, however, masked in both camps a remarkable consensus of opinion, in which seemingly hostile political bedfellows were brought together.

With respect to the eruption of the French Revolution itself, Danish opinion was largely united. Both sides welcomed the storming of the Bastille with considerable enthusiasm. Indeed, even some members of the Danish Royal family, like Frederik Christian, Duke of Augustenborg and his wife, the Crown Prince's step-sister, were known to be sympathizers.[13]

Indeed, for most Danes the French king was seen as a symbol of despotism and bigoted Catholicism, despite the fact that he had introduced religious toleration for Protestants. Not only was Louis XVI considered unenlightened, but the political support the French king and queen had given to Gustaf III, Denmark's arch-enemy, who had led Sweden to the edge of a military confrontation against Denmark, in Norway in 1788, had won the Bourbons no friends even in Danish royal circles.

By contrast, the waxwork displays of the National Convention, exhibited in the town hall of Viborg, in Denmark, in the winter of 1793–4, attracted an admiring audience, even if, perhaps, this was more for the cleverness of the models than the political views which they represented. Liberal attitudes found particularly strong expression among many ethnic German residents in Denmark, not least because of their perceptions of social and economic exclusion, prohibited, as they were, from joining craft guilds, among other professional organizations. Some German craftsmen were also keen to establish the right to strike. Two German carpenters, for example, demanded higher wages from their employer and refused to work until their demands were met. As a result, a strike of fellow artisans erupted, which led not only to imprisonment for some 120 of them, but to a complete reform of the guild system as well. Here the motivation was clearly economic, but not all supporters of the liberal German faction were themselves liberal in all senses. Cultural and linguistic attachments led many large landowners who spoke and read German at home, to support the Germanophile side. Denmark's richest private citizen and statesman, Ernst Schimmelmann (1747–1831) not only possessed vast sugar plantations in the Danish Virgin Islands, with hundreds of slaves, but also manufactured the guns bartered to the ruling Asanti tribe for slaves on the Danish West African coast. These activities did not prevent his salons both at his townhouse on Bredgade, in Copenhagen, and his summer home Sølyst, at Klampenborg, from providing the occasions for expression of the latest liberal German political views in an ambience of the latest neo-classical style. He was elevated to the peerage as a count, appointed Finance Minister and given membership of the Privy Council in 1788. In 1790, he received the coveted Order of the Elephant, an indication of the power he wielded and a royal acknowledgement of the wisdom of his views. In fact, the German subjects of the realm, generally richer than their Danish counterparts, often wielded greater power than their numbers might suggest. The inhabitants of Schleswig-Holstein paid considerably more taxes into the governmental coffers than either Denmark or Norway, despite their much greater size.

Some Germans in the Danish realms, however, went over to the extreme Danophile side. Cosmopolitanism and the lessons which could be learnt from elsewhere in Europe filled a minority of Germans with contempt, despite the arguments of those who saw the whole of humanity as one great family. One such person was Werner Abrahamson (1744–1812), raised in Denmark since early childhood, who became one of the leading polemicists of the Danophiles, in the spirit of Tyge Rothe (1731–1795), whose philosophy drew inspiration from Montesquieu, Rousseau and Johann Gottfried von Herder (1744–1803). Abrahamson's laments have a curiously modern ring; in particular, his criticism of foreigners who live in a country for many years without learning the language of the majority of its citizens and refuse to assimilate, an issue still alive in Denmark today.

Sometimes, Norwegians and those from other parts of the Danish dominions joined in the mêlée. In fact, of the leading campaigners on both side, most were not Danish by birth. The Norwegian Christen Pram (1756–1821), for example, campaigned in Copenhagen on behalf of many of the Schimmelmann faction's

165 F. L. Bradt after Jens Juel,
*Memorial to the Emancipation
of the Serfs*, c. 1800,

liberal political views in the journal *Minerva*, while rejecting the more extreme pro-German stance. This minority viewpoint held, with Professor Martin Ehlers, that not only Schleswig-Holstein but all of the Danish realm should enjoy German as an official language, thereby enabling the kingdom to reap the benefits of a culture Ehlers deemed more civilized than the Danish. But, on his side, Pram did not advocate the Danification of all of Schleswig-Holstein. Rather, he felt that Holstein should remain German, but with Schleswig strengthened in its Danish national identity, a division within which the two duchies would be divided naturally from one another by the River Eider.

By the spring of 1790 tensions eased, in part due to the work of Bernstorff, the wise elder statesman, who had succeeded, with his supporters, especially Crown Prince Frederik, in bringing about a relative consensus for political reform. As a result, the emancipation of the serfs was successfully promulgated in 1788, and Denmark proceeded upon a path which a half-century hence would lead to the voluntary abolition of absolutism and the establishment of constitutional monarchy. In celebration of this freedom, a committee of citizens in Copenhagen, commissioned the erection of the *Memorial to the Emancipation of the Serfs* (illus. 165) just outside the west gate of the city, an obelisk in sandstone from Bornholm, resting upon a base of Norwegian marble. Flanked by four figures, with an inscription commemorating Frederik and his wisdom in granting emancipation, the monument was unveiled on the Crown Prince's wedding day, 31 July 1792, to the German aristocrat Marie Sophie Frederike, daughter of the landgrave Charles of Hesse-Kassel. So successful in some respects had this revolution from on high been that by 1814, about 60 per cent of the farming population owned their own land.[14] It was as if xenophobic fears, at least temporarily, had been channelled into a constructive movement for lasting social change which could unite all segments of Danish society.

The reaction against the inroads of German culture in the Danish realms had not been stemmed. As a result, the last decade of the eighteenth century witnessed the demise of a lively German literary production there. Such great bards as the anti-rationalist epic and lyric poet Friedrich Gottlieb Klopstock (1724–1803), who had resided in Denmark for twenty years, were no longer to be found. A schoolmaster at the Sorø Academy, Klopstock's writings had been instrumental in helping to introduce Shakespeare's plays to both a Danish and German audience at a time when, even in England, Shakespeare's literary output was disdained by many. Also absent were the works of playwrights and aestheticians like Johann Elias Schlegel (1719–1749), the uncle of August Wilhelm and Friedrich von Schlegel, whose writings, especially on the concepts of Romanticism, were first published in the journal *Atheneum* (1798) and were to inspire the German Romantic movement.

On the other hand, the growing importance of Denmark for north German artists in the 1790s cannot be overestimated. Caspar David Friedrich (1774–1840), the most important of the German Romantic painters, studied at the Royal Academy, in Copenhagen from 1794 to 1798. It was there that he drew his self-portrait in about 1800 (illus. 166). From Greifswald, in Swedish Pomerania, his early training in the arts had largely been self-taught. Then, he had studied for four years at the University of Greifswald under Johann Gottfried Quistorp (1755–1835), Professor of Drawing, who probably encouraged him to apply to the Danish Royal Academy in Copenhagen. Among other influential figures in this Greifswald circle was the theologian, Gotthard Ludwig Kosegarten (1758–1818), whose poetry, sometimes illustrated by Quistorp, expressed the mystical fusion of emotions and nature which became so thematically important in much of Friedrich's works. Also important was the Uppsala historian and philosopher Thomas Thorild (1759–1808), later librarian at Greifswald, whose pantheistic concepts of the natural world found a resonance in Friedrich and who, together with Ernst Moritz Arndt (1769–1860), a native of the Swedish-German

166 Caspar David Friedrich, *Self-portrait, c.* 1800, black chalk.

terriotry of Rügen and a patriotic supporter of Swedish rule and culture, and a professor at Greifswald whom Thorild had also influenced, were extremely important for the development of Friedrich's aesthetic vision.

In the year of Friedrich's departure from the Royal Academy in Copenhagen, another young German artist, Philipp Otto Runge (1777–1810), also enrolled there. A student at the academy from 1799 to 1801, Runge went on to become one of the leading members of the Nazarene school of painting, but he became acquainted with Friedrich not in Denmark, but in Greifswald in 1801. Thereafter,

167 Caspar David Friedrich, *Bohemian Landscape with Milleshauer*, c. 1810, oil on canvas.

the two remained closely associated, especially after they both, first Friedrich and then Runge, settled in Dresden, where their artistic training in Denmark served them in good stead in helping them to form the new national romantic school of art that was developing there.

Denmark's legacy on Friedrich was especially noteworthy in providing him with artistic models in which nature was used in a particularly emotive way. In fact, Jens Juel, then professor at the Royal Academy in Copenhagen, was arguably the first of many Nordic artists to focus upon 'stemming' (mood and atmosphere) in his landscape paintings. His *Northern Light* (see illus. 208) was the first work which focused upon the Aurora Borealis, a peculiarly Nordic phenomenon in Europe; it was also the first Nordic painting which stressed the romantic and mystical qualities of light and nature in the north. Friedrich, in turn, through works such as *Bohemian Landscape with Milleshauer* (c. 1810; illus. 167), succeeded in embodying a northern landscape devoid of physical grandeur but with a deep spiritual content. This and other works by Friedrich were to inspire many later artists, like the Swedish painter Prince Eugen (1865–1947), whose great symbolist work, *The Cloud* (1896; see illus. 209) is related in both mood and content to Friedrich's own pictorial visions, utilizing a sweeping landscape vision to express an allegory of the human spiritual condition.

The Rise and Fall of Swedish Hegemony in Pomerania

The political and intellectual links which bound Swedish Pomerania to Scandinavia and, in particular, Sweden were not new. By the third decade of the eighteenth century, the University of Greifswald had become the leading centre of academic and intellectual life in the region. With its principal building constructed between 1747 and 1750 on the site of the original fifteenth-century university, it had been re-christened in honour of the Swedish king not long thereafter. Its German architect, Andreas Mayer (1716–1782), professor in mathematics, had employed a very symmetrical North German Classical Baroque style for the seat of the university. More specifically Swedish in design was the landscape garden (1763) behind, laid out by the Swede Samuel Gustaf Wilcke, a former apprentice to the great Swedish botanist Carl von Linné in Uppsala, who clearly had derived considerable formal inspiration from the botanical gardens of his old mentor there.

Sweden lost Wismar to the Grand Duchy of Mecklenburg-Schwerin in 1802, through a hundred-year leasehold, signed the following year, but control of her other German territories appeared to be strengthening in the first decade of the nineteenth century. Swedish law, criminal, civil and ecclesiastical, had been introduced in 1806 and serfdom was rapidly abolished, earning the praise of Arndt. Furthermore, the devotion of many Pomeranians to the Swedish crown also seemed to be increasing. During the coup d'état in Stockholm in 1809, which overthrew the Gustavian dynasty in favour of the French Bernadottes, the Pomeranian guards alone of all the king's military regiments took sides with the deposed monarch.[15]

Many civilian Pomeranians, among them Friedrich, also remained loyal to the Swedish throne. Perhaps for this reason, Friedrich pointedly dedicated his Tetschen altar piece, *Cross in the Mountains* (1807–8; see illus. 22) to the old king Gustaf IV Adolf.[16] Both anti-Jacobin as well as hostile to Napoleon, Friedrich admired the Swedish king, in his role as Duke of Pomerania and Prince of Rügen, whom he perceived to be a defender both of Pietistic virtue and the established God-given order. Resident in Dresden after his departure from Copenhagen, Friedrich would have witnessed Gustaf's presence there during the numerous arduous negotiations with England which took place from 1803 to 1805. Does the sun whose rays are radiated from the frame's predella represent Gustaf IV Adolf as the midnight sun, as has been suggested?[17] Bearing in mind the Swedish monarch's traditional association with the North Star, this is rather doubtful, but Friedrich's commitment to Sweden, its monarch and culture is beyond question. For even in a work as late as *The Stages of Life* (c. 1834; illus. 168), he depicts his son, christened Gustaf Adolf, proudly holding the Swedish flag, with the Baltic Sea, the 'Swedish lake' spreading out behind, a wistful pictorial ode to a political order long departed. Ultimately, the Napoleonic Wars had brought traumatic upheavals to Swedish Pomerania which had led to it severing from Sweden. First, Swedish military forces were defeated by the French at Lübeck in 1806. Then, a successful Russian attack on Finland in 1808 and Denmark-Norway's assault on

168 Caspar David Friedrich, *The Stages of Life (Die Lebenßtufen), c.* 1834, oil on canvas.

Sweden shortly thereafter hindered any attempt by the latter to regain lost territory.

In Finland, moreover, the establishment of German political hegemony strengthened the ties of many Germans living there with Germany, offering as it did the only viable alternative to a Russian political and cultural model. After all, Viipuri, Finland's third largest city situated on the Karelian coast, was very much a multi-cultural port which, in 1812, included large populations of Russians, Swedes and Germans, as well as Finns.[18]

Thus, the close of the Napoleonic period witnessed the de facto demise of Swedish Pomerania. Wismar and Neukloster remained Swedish territory throughout the nineteenth century, leased to the grand-duchy of Mecklenburg, with its own laws and flag of intersecting red and white bands. Only in 1903 was this strange territorial anomaly resolved when these final enclaves of Sweden in Germany were legally absorbed into the Second Reich, as parts of the grand-duchy of Mecklenburg-Schwerin.

The Growing Rift between Denmark and Schleswig-Holstein in the Early Nineteenth Century and the Rise of Danish National Identity

The loss of Norway to Sweden after the Napoleonic wars left Denmark truncated and also increasingly susceptible to German political and cultural incursions. As a result, Schleswig-Holstein assumed an even more important role politically and culturally in the Danish realm than its already large economic power might seem to justify. Such a situation had implications for many aspects of life, not least that of higher education. As the importance and wealth of Schleswig-Holstein increased, so did the academic and political importance of the University of Kiel. Although a Danish chair had been established there in 1811, it was soon reduced to a lectureship, and Danish speakers frequented the university less and less, though Germans came to it from far and wide. An imposing establishment architecturally as well as intellectually, it can be seen in *A View of Kiel* (early 1800s; illus. 169), with its modern buildings which look to Germany rather than Denmark for their architectural inspiration. Not surprisingly, it became the 'hochburg' of German cultural and political studies in the Danish dominions.

When elections were made to academic positions, ethnic Germans often continued to take the leading university offices, not only at the University of Kiel but also in Denmark itself. As a result, the disgruntlement of Danophiles in Denmark itself, as well as in Schleswig-Holstein, increasingly made itself felt. They were also irritated by the fact that close social contacts were now re-established with German universities, which led to many students from Kiel joining in the great German Romantic student festival held at the Wartburg in Thuringia in 1817. The situation was further aggravated by academics like Nicolaus Falck (1784–1850), a Professor of Law at Kiel, who published polemics which emphasized the German identity of not only German-speaking Holstein, but of Danish-

169 *A View of Kiel*, early 1800s, engraving.

170 Johannes Senn and Gerhard Ludwig Lahde, *A Cemetery Dedicated to the Fatherland*, 1814, engraving.

speaking Schleswig as well. For Germans such as these, Hamburg and other North German cities, rather than Copenhagen, increasingly became a Mecca, economically, socially and intellectually.

Thus, more and more, in Denmark and her dominions, political and social loyalties came to be linked with nationalist concepts. The cosmopolitanism which education and transport improvements might have seemed to encourage had not proven itself adequate to stop the rising tide of a new sense of ethnic identity, linked to the concept of language and the nation.

This growing emphasis on ethnic identity, as linked to a nation-state, was occurring within Danish ethnic circles too, for many Danes were recovering from defeat in the Napoleonic Wars. Since 1802, when foreign mercenaries ceased to be hired and two-year military service for Danish nationals was introduced, further reinforcing their national identity. They also experienced other parts of Denmark at the military's expense which helped to diminish narrow local allegiances. This process of creating an ethnically Danish national identity was further helped by the disappearance of Germans from almost all major government posts in Denmark itself. From the North Sea, in the west, to the Øresund, in the east, Denmark underwent a cultural homogenization, assisted by a growing national economy which encouraged trade and the accumulation of capital throughout the kingdom, with each part mutually dependent upon the others.

German intellectual thought lurked in the shadows, for, as throughout Europe, it was the writings of Johan Gottlieb Fichte (1762–1814), among other Germans, which provided the philosophical abstractions and polemical framework upon which the modern nation-state was so much to depend. His *Speech to the German Nation* (1808), presented to university students in a Berlin occupied by French troops, proved, in reality, to be a call to the young of all nations to assume their personal responsibility to foster the wellbeing and strength of their own nation-family. Fichte himself had visited Denmark during the summer of 1807, meeting in Copenhagen a number of Danish literary figures, including the man of letters Adam Oehlenschläger (1779–1850) and the scientist Hans Christian Ørsted (1777–1851), in whose house he stayed. The writings of Herder also reinforced such nationalistic exhortations in Denmark, by further associating the vehicle of language as a means to express the national soul. Such a nationalistic phenomenon as that depicted in *A Cemetery Dedicated to the Fatherland* (1814) by the Danes Johannes Senn (1780–1861) and Gerhard Ludwig Lahde (1765–1833; illus. 170) was another means of expression for this new consciousness. Such works also served practical purposes; this engraving was sold to raise money for those injured or disabled by the Napoleonic Wars.[19]

In Denmark, *On the Sacredness of the Language of the Nation* (1815), by the Danish historian Christian Molbech (1783–1857), reinterpreted Herder's ideas in a Danish context. Even Herder's political views served to support the unitary concept of a Danish nation-state, since, for Herder, multinational empires were political monstrosities, not forming a unified and whole national body, but with limbs unnaturally attached which really belonged to others.[20] Such opinions were to have important implications for Schleswig-Holstein, with regard to the attitudes of both the Danish and the German-speaking segments of the population. The relationship of the two duchies at this time was made rather more complicated when, in 1815, Holstein was admitted to the new German Confederation, by order of the Congress of Vienna, at the same time as it was being integrated into a unitary Kingdom of Denmark. Since this arrangement specified that all member states of the German Confederation were to have their own Estates General, the Danish king's own wishes were thereby contradicted, an issue which was never to be peacefully and satisfactorily resolved.

In the field of history, poets, like Bernhard Severin Ingemann (1789–1862) took inspiration and focused upon historical themes which glorified the ancient Danish kingdom and its political and cultural legacy. In particular, his historical novels like *The Battle for Valhalla* (1821), focusing upon a medieval Denmark rich in glory, caught the imagination of a relatively large and prosperous reading public. Appointed in 1822 to a teaching post at the Sorø Academy, Ingemann was in a good position to influence the many young Danes from prominent families who studied there and would go on to assume important posts in government, the military and the world of commerce. Significantly, too, Ingemann was able to provide them with an attractive model of what it meant to be Danish, an image which was to exert a lasting influence on many Danes. As he wrote in one of his lectures:

> The people have a characteristic historical-poetical spirit – an individualistic mixture of deep earnestness and a good-humoured temperament – of inner contemplativeness and deep feeling, which is often bound together with amusing irony towards life and humanity – a deep sense both for the tragic and the great, as well as for the genuinely comical and ridiculous.[21]

Pan-Scandinavianism

Nationalism was not the only model to provide inspiration for young men wishing to make sacrifices and struggle for a better world. A regional vision, too, could also provide many young men (women played little role in the movement) with an alternative noble ideal for which to campaign. The Nordic countries had

been united in the fifteenth century within the Kalmar Union under the Danish crown, and even in the nineteenth century, it could be argued, the region shared a common cultural, religious and linguistic heritage which gave the Nordic countries together a strength and richness of which no single Nordic state could boast. Thus, the great Danish educationalist, poet and churchman, N. F. S. Grundtvig, depicted in this portrait of 1862 by Constantin Hansen (illus. 171) could write *Is the Unification of the Nordic Region Desirable? A Word to the Swedish People* (1810), on the occasion of the change of dynasty in Sweden. However, whereas the Kalmar Union, four centuries earlier, was based on military strength, Grundtvig envisioned a pan-Scandinavian union, which looked to the spiritual, literary and artistic for its coherence and success, and one which would be cemented by a liberal political outlook, drawing its support from an enlightened yeomanry. Was there not the common Norse mythology, equal in value to that of the Greeks, and had not the Danish Scandinavian

171 Constantin Hansen, *N. F. S. Grundtvig*, 1862, oil on canvas.

Society of Literature fostered its memory even in the dying years of the previous century? Certainly, his *Nordic Mythology* (1832) saw an ancient cultural-historical world stretching from Iceland and England in the west to Finland in the east, a rich and viable alternative to that of the Mediterranean in the south, and certainly superior to the Germanic, sandwiched in between. There was also a religious dimension, for to Grundtvig, as he expostulated in his four-volume journal *Danne-Virke* (1816–19),[22] German culture was polluted by an anti-Christian rationalism. Since the idea of a unified scientific system of reason which governed the world was anathema to Grundtvig, Goethe, the German Voltaire, as Grundtvig styled him, left the theologian with a contempt even greater than that which he felt for the Frenchman, and considered his writings no better than pornography.[23] Danish culture, by contrast, embodied by its very nature Christian spiritual values and this was a culture to be found, neither amongst aristocrats, nor the German yeoman farmers of Holstein, nor even the urban classes of the cities, but among the small farmers of the Danish heartland, unsullied by alien values or ethnic admixture.

Adam Oehlenschlæger (1779–1850), a Danish Romantic dramatist, as well as poet, also concentrated upon Norse themes which glorified the ancient cultural heritage of Scandinavia. In particular, his *Nordic Poems* (1807), which included historical tragedy such as 'Earl Haakon the Great', based on that Danish national hero, and 'Baldur the Good', taking a subject from Norse mythology, awakened interest in many old cultural traditions of Scandinavia. Later, Oehlenschlæger would produce a modern version of the *Edda*, in his epic work *The Gods of the North* (1819). Such works inspired not only Danes, but Swedes and Norwegians as well, and fostered communications among the Scandinavian peoples, at least on the level of students and the literary minded.

The king of Sweden himself was much taken by Oehlenschlæger and awarded him a medal in commemoration of his pan-Scandinavian attitude and writings, while the University of Lund, in the former Danish province of Scania, awarded him an honorary doctorate. As a result of his writings, Danish, Swedish and Norwegian intellectual societies established close contacts with one another, many of which continue to this day. *The Arrival of Norwegian and Swedish Students in Copenhagen* on 23 June 1845 (1847) by the Danish artist Jørgen Sonne (1801–1890; see illus. 152) captures the mood and atmosphere of such a pan-Scandinavian festivity. The scene depicted is that at Nytoldbod, where the ships carrying the students docked after their journey across the straits from Malmö, and stresses their heterogeneity, both in terms of national background and social milieu. Together they form one throng, the cream of Nordic youth, a veritable army of the north who would lead the world to new spiritual and cultural heights.

Such a pan-Scandinavian focus as advocated by Grundtvig and Oehlenschlæger also had important political implications. By the end of the 1830s, there were those who envisaged an economic union of the Scandinavian countries, which might foreshadow a concert of political action. Some went even further and contemplated the possibility of a common defence pact and foreign policy. While only a few actually expressed the wish for a complete political union, the fact that the Danish crown prince, divorced from his wife, had no direct male heir, gave a sense of political urgency to the growing number of discussions and articles which dealt with the issue.

Despite the increasingly vociferous affirmations of pan-Scandinavianism by its ardent supporters, like the Danish politician Orla Lehmann, the foundations of the movement were by no means as solid as they seemed to many intellectuals

172 Constantin Hansen, *The Constituent Assembly of 1848*, 1860–64, oil on canvas.

at the time. For one thing, support was greatest in those areas of Scandinavia in greatest proximity to German language and culture. Norway, for example, though its students enjoyed the festivities to which they were invited in Denmark and Sweden, seemed little inclined to pursue any political goal which limited Norwegian political autonomy. In Schleswig-Holstein, where pan-Scandinavianism went largely unheeded or at worst feared, students and other intellectuals looked to German culture for their inspiration. Ethnic Danish farmers in the duchies, also, remained largely unmoved by the movement, not really surprising, bearing in mind the otherwise minimal contact which existed between Denmark and Sweden, despite the upsurge in student exchanges and a literary output which romanticized it. Ultimately, even the Danish king Christian VIII (1786–1848) himself disdained the movement, which he perceived as deepening the cleft between his German-speaking and Danish speaking subjects to the detriment of the monarchy and the unity and wellbeing of the state itself.

In January 1848, Christian VIII died and his son Frederik VII (1808–1863) succeeded to the throne. Revolutions were erupting in France and Germany, and Denmark, too, was touched by political and social disturbances. On 5 June 1849, absolutism was abolished and the new king became a constitutional monarch with a new bicameral legislature and independent judiciary, an event commemorated in *The Constituent Assembly of 1848* (1860–64) by Constantin Hansen (illus. 172). Important as the results of such governmental changes were, however, a yet greater issue of political immediacy cast its shadow upon the proceedings. For Prussia, under its king, soon to be Kaiser Wilhelm I of the Second German Reich, demanded the partitioning of Schleswig (1848) and the ceding of its German-speaking southern half to her. The Danish response was uncompromising. Not only did Frederik refuse Prussia's demands, but, with support from the National Liberals, he enraged Prussia which was rapidly gobbling up so much of the north of Germany, by incorporating the disputed areas directly into the Danish realm. This further antagonized the latent hostility of much of the German population there who, with Prussian assistance, rebelled. Danes and Germans were now polarized, with figures such as Grundtvig, though generally averse to military intervention, so incensed by the misconduct of the Prussians that he lambasted them as 'the detritus of a motley hodgepodge of German and Slavic people'.[24] Since for him a just war was better than an immoral peace, an aggressive military stance on Denmark's behalf was the only recourse. For Grundtvig, Denmark was a feminine nation and Prussia a masculine one, and the rape of the former by the latter could not be tolerated.

173 Lorenz Frølich, *Freia*, 1845, in the commemorative journal for the Nordic celebrations of 13 January 1845.

Such a viewpoint had long been propounded by Grundtvig. In 1832, in his *Mythology of the Nordic Regions*, Grundtvig had seen the goddess Freyja as the embodiment of Danish femininity and admired the illustration *Freia*, by the Danish artist Lorenz Frølich (1820–1908), for the publication which commemorated the Nordic celebrations of 13 January 1845 (illus. 173). That said, such feminine gender associations did not prevent him from drawing upon quite different figures in Norse mythology when they suited different polemical purposes. For example, when two important Danish sculptors, Herman Vilhelm Bissen (1798–1868) and Jens Adolf Jerichau (1816–1883) presented their sketches for a sculptural monument celebrating the Danish victory, at Fredericia, on 6 July 1849, Grundtvig took sides with the latter, though the sketch of the former was ultimately chosen. Bissens sculpture was of a simple army private from the countryside; Jerichau had chosen the heroic figure of Thor, a mythological archetype in both Norse and Old Germanic mythology. Thus, for Grundtvig, the Danes could be either hermaphroditic, vulnerably feminine or heroically masculine, all according to the allegorical needs dictated by the current political, cultural or social situation.

Racial notions also played a role in Grundtvig's view of nationality, since to him national identity went deeper than mere ideas and consequently the Jews did not fare well in his ethnic scheme. When the Jewish Danish author Meïr Aron Goldschmidt (1819–1887), publicly identified himself with native German

174 *The Citizen's Life*, 1841,
in the weekly newspaper
Corsaren, published by Meïr
Goldschmidt.

elements in Denmark, Grundtvig took him to task, maintaining it was presumptuous of a Jew to intrude upon purely Danish issues, even if he were a native. Goldschmidt himself examined the difficulties of being a Jew in Denmark during the growing turmoil of the 1840s, in his first novel, *A Jew* (1845). Neither fish nor fowl, Dane nor German, the Jew was frequently held in contempt by both ethnic groups. Goldschmidt also irritated the censors with such satirical engravings as *The Citizen's Life* (1841) in his journal *Corsaren* (*The Corsair*), which parodied absolute monarchy, symbolized by the sun, doling out medals with one arm and threatening the whip with the other (illus. 174). The anti-Semitic view held by leading members of the Danish cultural pantheon persisted into the twentieth century, when, like so many of their German contemporaries, the Danish authors Jakob Knudsen (1858–1917) and Johannes V. Jensen (1873–1950) stressed the importance of good racial background, and lamented the role that Jews, especially the intellectual radical Georg Brandes (1842–1927), had played in Danish culture over the previous century.

War in Schleswig-Holstein: 1848–50 and 1864

Given the increasingly confrontational nature of the Danish–German political debate, it is not surprising that war finally erupted between the two countries. In March of 1848, 300 Germans under the leadership of the Prince of Nör, a Germanophile relation of the Danish king, having arrived in Rendsborg by train from Kiel, marched on the fortress which they occupied without a fight, an event commemorated by German supporters in *The Streets of Rendsborg* (illus. 175). Elsewhere, however, fighting did break out in the first Prussian-Danish war in which some 4,500 Swedes and Norwegians supported the Danish cause in battle.[25] The Prince of Nör and his brother the Duke of Augustenborg were immediately vilified in Danophile circles and viciously caricatured in broadsides such as *The Traitor Brothers* (c. 1849) which depicted the two princes facing each other, as they hang from a scaffold (illus. 176). The image became so popular that it was even used inside a mass-produced chamber pot, accompanied by the words, 'Traitors surely are you two! So every Dane must piss on you!'[26] Almost two decades later, even the Prussians would treat these princelings little better, excluding them from any benefits from the final pro-German peace settlement.

Danish artists such as Niels Simonsen (1807–1885), who with his brother Jørgen made studies during the battles themselves, afterwards composed magnificent battle scenes, glorifying Denmark's military might. Most noteworthy is Niels Simonsen's *Battle of Fredericia* (illus. 177) which focuses on the Danish assault on the insurgents by this eastern Jutish town, on 6 July 1849, where one of the military commanders, the Norwegian general Olaf Rye, had fallen on the battlefield, thereby becoming a Danish national hero. When peace was concluded in 1850, Denmark had maintained its territorial integrity, but little of the under-

lying discontent in Schleswig-Holstein was resolved. An international agreement to continue to link the two duchies with the Danish crown was concluded, with a clause requiring the maintenance of the constitutional separation of Schleswig from Denmark, but the Danish king and parliament persisted in cherishing hopes of jettisoning this arrangement. The childlessness of the king created further problems, since Frederik named Christian, Duke of Glücksburg in Schleswig, as his successor.

Two days before the king's death, in 1864, the joint constitution for both Denmark and Schleswig was finally ratified by a Danish parliament hoping that Prussian involvement in quashing a Polish rebellion would prevent intervention. This, however, proved false and Prussia and Austria together declared war. The Dannevirke had newly been strengthened by massive ramparts, as can be seen in one of the woodcuts, *View of the Dannevirke on the Western Flank*, published in the *Illustrated London News* (illus. 177). But the Danish armies had completed few logistical preparations for their maintenance and the prospect for the successful outcome of war with Prussia was not rosy.

Christian IX (1818–1906), a native of ethnically German Gottorp, in Schleswig, was left to pick up the pieces. German-educated himself, he spoke Danish with a German accent. However, despite his own personal disinclination, popular sentiments compelled him to pursue an anti-German stance by supporting the November Constitution. This antagonized the other three great powers, France, Russia and Britain. At the same time, pan-Scandinavianism also held little appeal for him. Rather, he desired a strong and unified Denmark.

175 *The Streets of Rendsborg*, 1848, lithograph.

176 *The Traitor Brothers*, c. 1849, illustration from a broadside inside a chamberpot.

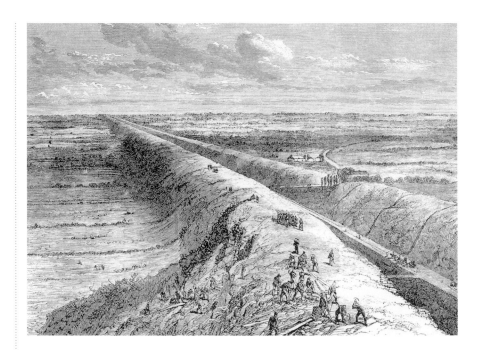

177 *View of the Dannevirke on the Western Flank*, woodcut from *Illustrated London News*, January 1864.

Military confrontation was unavoidable and a short but devastating war ensued, in which both Prussian and Austrian forces, totalling some 57,000 troops, thoroughly crushed Danish defences, with their 38,000 strong resistance, under the geriatric General Christian de Meza.[27] This time, Russia supported the Germans (though some Finns did volunteer to fight for Denmark), not least because of German assistance to Russia during the Polish uprising, and even Sweden-Norway stood officially mutely by (even if some Swedes and Norwegians also volunteered to fight for Denmark), the empty words of pan-Scandinavianism dashed to pieces by German guns.

The Dannevirke was breached and Danish troops were obliged to retreat to Dybbøl, as Niels Simonsen's grey sketch *Retreat from the Dannevirke* immortalized (illus. 178). There a devastating battle occurred on 5–6 February 1864, a subject focused upon in novels such as *Tine* (1889) by the Danish author Herman Bang (1857–1912). The slaughter was considerable and a contemporary woodcut, published in the *Illustrated London News*, showed a wide readership the gloomy task of counting the dead on both sides in the aftermath (illus. 179). Not only was Denmark crushed militarily, but Jutland was occupied up to Limfjord in the north. By October 1864, a devastating peace was concluded and the whole of Schleswig-Holstein, including both German- and Danish-speaking areas, was ceded to the victorious powers.[28] But the Austro-Prussian War (1866), with its defeat of Austria after only seven weeks, removed it from the political equation. Prussia was therefore free to totally absorb the duchies into the ever more greedy German state. The fate of Holstein was, thereby, satisfactorily resolved for most of its inhabitants. That of Schleswig was less satisfactory, for more than 200,000 Danes now lived, unwillingly, in the new German province.[29]

178 Niels Simonsen, *Retreat from the Dannevirke*, 1864, grisaille.

For intellectuals like Grundtvig, however, the deeper wounds perpetrated on the Danish people were more intellectual than physical. As he stated, 'German language and German books have done us much more harm than German weapons or soldiers'.[30] Whether he meant also to reject the German philosophical literary basis of his view on the Danish nation is doubtful. In any case, not all scholarly Danes shared his view of Denmark and Danish culture, nor the outcome of the war. The Jewish-Dane Georg Brandes, for example, took a pro-German stance. He rejected a view of Danish culture cut off from its German and French roots. Though he won the support of such leading literary figures as his fellow Dane the novelist Jens Peter Jacobsen, the Norwegians Henrik Ibsen, B. M. Bjørnson, Jonas Lie and Alexander Kielland, and the Swedish playwright August Strindberg, his rejection for a chair by the University of Copenhagen led to a lengthy sojourn in Berlin (1877–83). This and later his later enthusiasm for the writings of the German philosopher Friedrich Nietzsche (1844–1900) deepened his attachment to German culture which he continued to propound throughout the rest of his life. Indeed, he became the medium through which many of Nietzsche's philosophical views entered the intellectual life of the Nordic region, with implications which were to prove sometimes deleterious in the twentieth century.

179 *Task of counting the dead on both the Danish and German sides at Dybbøl*, woodcut from *Illustrated London News*, 7 May 1864.

Aftermath of the War

The economic and political costs of this second war with Prussian were enormous for Denmark. Though the Treaty of Prague (1866) had provided that the

180 Hans Nikolaj Hansen, *Christian X Crossing the Old Danish Frontier*, 1921, oil on canvas.

north of Schleswig would be ceded to Denmark should the majority of its population so wish, this provision was annulled in 1878, by both Prussia's successor, the German Empire, and Austria. That did not prevent considerable agitation in the north of Schleswig, though not in the more southern areas of the duchy or in Holstein, for reunification with Denmark. None the less, nearly 60,000 Danish speakers eventually emigrated from the region during the following decades and the issue ceased to exert much influence on Danish politics until after the First World War, a conflagration in which the country was officially neutral, though it led to the loss of her Caribbean colony to the United States who feared the establishment of a possible German submarine base there (a veiled threat by the United States forced the 'sale' of the colony to them in 1917).

Only after the defeat of Germany were plebiscites held in Schleswig in 1920 on the matter of national self-determination: in the north of the duchy, 70 per cent of the population voted to be reunited with Denmark; in the south, 80 per cent determined to remain within Germany. With the desires of these regional majorities taken in to consideration, the thorny identity of the two duchies was resolved until the present day, a solution successfully surviving even the dislocations of National Socialism in Germany and the Second World War. A contemporary painting, *Christian X Crossing the Old Danish Frontier* (1921; illus. 180) commemorates the return of North Schleswig and the king's first visit there after the German cession, on 10 July 1920. Riding a white horse and warmly greeted by the local population, the allegorical importance of the event seemed justly auspicious for the future of the region. Now ethnic Danes in German Schleswig-Holstein could attend their own schools and preserve their own cultural identity, while Germans in the north of Schleswig were similarly permitted to maintain their 'Germanness', one of the few success stories of post-war European self-determination.

Emil Nolde, German Expressionism and Danish Cultural Roots

The rich mixture of Nordic and Germanic traditions and values in Schleswig-Holstein could, despite confrontational elements and, indeed, sometimes because of them, produce a cultural soil of the most fertile kind. For example, Nolde, or Emil Hansen (1867–1956) as he was christened, who had been born at Nolde, near Tønder, in the north of Schleswig, territory ceded to Prussia in 1864, became one of the most important artists of the twentieth century. Having first worked as a woodcarver, then later in a furniture factory, he went on to study technical design in St Gallen and finally art in Paris, before moving on to Copenhagen in the autumn of 1900, where he set himself up in an a*telier*. There he became acquainted with such leading Scandinavian national romantic artists as the Danes Viggo Johansen (1851–1935) and Vilhelm Hammershøi (1864–1916), as well as Joachim Skovgaard (1856–1933) and the Norwegian Jens Ferdinand Willumsen (1863–1958). There, too, the landscape on North Sjælland, the large island upon which Copenhagen is situated, offered Nolde numerous destinations for short artistic excursions. It was there also that Nolde met Ada Vilstrup, a Danish actress who became his wife in 1902, in the company of Knud Rasmussen (1879–1933), the famous Danish polar explorer, whose expeditions in the north of Greenland were internationally famed.

Though an ethnic German by birth and initially a keen supporter of the Nazis, Nolde soon came to loathe them and they him. (they classified his art as decadent), and he eventually had himself naturalized as a Dane. None the less, he was deeply embedded in German culture, having lived not only in Flensburg, near the new Danish border, but also in Karlsruhe and Berlin, and became one of the principal artists active in *Die Brücke* (*The Bridge*), the association of German Expressionist artists based in Dresden. That said, his German Expressionist 'storm of colour' technique must also, to some degree, have been derived from an artistic emphasis on colour as expressive of mood and atmosphere which he found in many Nordic paintings of the 1890s. Nolde was, thus, in a sense, the cultural embodiment of Schleswig-Holstein at its most fruitful and his art combines German and Scandinavian elements, even if his works ultimately are the creation of his own highly individualistic personality and artistic style. This can be seen in his landscape watercolour *Seebüll Farmhouse* (see illus. 207), showing the 'vierseitenhof' farmhouse so characteristic of the region. With its fireworks of brilliant colour it is a supreme example of German Expressionism, but with a profound spiritual dimension that evinces Nolde's Nordic roots as well. Nolde and his wife settled at Seebüll not far from his birthplace and here he led a reclusive life until his death. A visit to eastern Asia on an ethnological expedition (1913–14), also left its traces on some of his figurative paintings, particularly those in which dancers are depicted. This should come as no surprise, since both German and Nordic elements in his work were themselves intimately affected by impulses not only from Europe but Asia and elsewhere in the wider world. Perhaps, then Nolde should be seen as the ideal embodiment of that symbiosis of Nordic and German elements, which drew upon both native inspiration as well as that from the far corners of the globe.

Regal and Imperial Visions

Victor Hugo wrote that images of society have long been taken from architecture, and depict it as: 'a great edifice of which each part fits uniquely in the total structure; or from the human body as an all-embracing organic whole: or from the life of society as a great hierarchy [...]'[1] Since the days of the Reformation and the strengthening of the monarchies of Denmark-Norway and Sweden-Finland, the purse-strings of these kingdoms were controlled by their kings and central governments and their architectural commissions had definite political and social functions. In the sixteenth century, ecclesiastical wealth, war booty and tax were absorbed directly into the central coffers of government or allotted to those nobles who served the interests of their monarchs. This assisted in the centralization of political power in the capital cities, Copenhagen and Stockholm, to which all fiscal roads led.

While in the Denmark, absolute monarchy held sway until well into the nineteenth century, in Sweden, the estates vied with the king for control of the reins of government throughout that period. In both cases, however, regal visions, sometimes embodied in architecture, were adopted by the kings who sought to foster the interests of monarchical power. Over time, this vision adapted itself to changing fashions and circumstances but its goal remained the same, the consolidation of royal authority and political and social control. Even in Finland, in the first decades of the nineteenth century, given by the Allies to the Russian tsar Alexander I (1777–1825) as a semi-independent grand-duchy, the expression of an imperial vision became a first priority of the tsar himself.

The monarchs of the Nordic countries had long been aware of the important symbolic role of art and architecture, sometimes drawing inspiration from Italian princes and their visions of a secular Jerusalem, a holy city which would reflect the most beatific qualities of their temporal reigns. Symbolism in art and architecture in the Scandinavian countries thus became the principal means of expressing this epiphanous political and social vision, with profound implications for church, government and education.

Christian IV's Renaissance Vision

While the Renaissance in Italy was drawing to a close, Christian IV of Denmark (1577–1648), attempted to imprint upon Copenhagen his own Renaissance vision, largely filtered through Holland. His primary focus was concentrated upon architectural projects in and around the Danish capital. Most important of

181 Adriaen van de Venne,
*Christian IV as an Arbiter of
Peace*, 1643, oil.

STELLÆBURGI
REGII
HAUNIENSIS

AUREA IN SCRIPTIO

Turris fortissima nomen JEHOVÆ: Ad eam curret justus: Et in munito editoq loco collocabitur.
Proverb. XVIII. vers. x.   H.A Greÿs sculp. 1657.

182 H. A. Greyss, *Round Tower* (designed by Christen Longomontanus), 1657, engraving.

these was Rosenborg Castle, built between 1606 and 1634, in the countryside just outside Copenhagen. Christian took a keen personal interest in the building project, whose primary architect was Willum Cornelisz, but involved other architects including Hans van Steenwinckel the Younger, who built the staircase tower. While the turrets and towers of the exterior were incorporated for picturesque rather than practical reasons, the interior created the opulent impression of a powerful Renaissance prince's palace. Gregers Greuss carved the slender Ionic pilasters and the decorative wall panels (1614–15) which decorate the winter salon, perhaps the grandest of the staterooms and the ceiling paintings by Pieter Isaacsz (1569–1625) are particularly rich in allegorical symbolism relating to the monarchy. Elsewhere in the palace, rooms are decorated with many motifs, including a cartouche with an inscribed obelisk, incorporating Egyptian hieroglyphics, an early example in the Nordic region of pharonic reference. A number of these works were also inspired by the paintings Christian IV had seen during a visit to England where his sister Anne was consort to James I.

The most important painting in representational terms *Christian IV as an Arbiter of Peace* (1643), by Adriaen van de Venne, was painted in the Hague (illus. 181). Here the king is depicted as the harbinger of peace and concord amongst the European nations, accompanied by his son in his role as prince bishop of Bremen. Female figures have also been included, representing piety and magnanimity, virtues with which the king wished to be associated. Unfortunately the peace alluded to was to prove short-lived; the Thirty Years War re-opened with diabolical vigour preventing the painting's transport, and it was only after Christian IV's death that the painting arrived in Denmark. In the following year a marble bust of the king, *Christian IV as a Roman Conqueror* (1644), was carried out by the French sculptor François Dieussart (died c. 1661). While many aristocrats of the court were eroding the royal prerogative by every possible means, the king deliberately chose to have himself presented as a Roman hero crowned by laurel leaves, the symbol of victory. An important historical Danish reference is provided by the royal Order of the Elephant which he wears. But the military prowess of both the king and his son Frederick III (1609–1670) was not that of the heroic Roman emperors.[2] Within a decade and a half, Denmark was to lose permanently her richest province, Scania, as well as Halland and Blekinge, to Sweden.

Christian IV carried out other prominent architectural projects to enhance his capital. These include a number of buildings for the city's university, including Holy Trinity Church and Regensen, a university hall of residence. However, his most famous building project was the Round Tower (1642; illus. 182), designed as an astronomical observatory by Christen Longomontanus, a former student and assistant of the Danish astronomer Tycho Brahe (1546–1601); it became one of Denmark's most famous monuments.[3]

The Stock Exchange (illus. 183) was built by Christian IV between 1619 and 1625 on a grand scale, intending it to be the new mercantile centre of Scandinavia and the Baltic. Two architect brothers of Netherlandish extraction, Lorenz and Hans van Steenwinkel the Younger, provided the design. Disappointingly, its function as a dynamic commodity exchange was never realized and it was soon pawned to a local merchant, but its picturesque roof has remained one of the distinctive features of Copenhagen's skyline.

183 *The Stock Exchange in Copenhagen*, 1619–25, engraving incorporating the designs of the architects Lorenz and Hans van Steenwinkel.

Other works for Christian IV, in Copenhagen, include Nyboder, yellow-washed rows of small terraced houses for members of the navy and their wives, an architectural symbol of the great importance the king gave to his navy, as was the great Holmens Church which provided for their spiritual needs (it was reconstructed from a previous building where anchors had been forged). Two centuries later though, when Denmark had ceased to be an important naval power, half of Nyboder was sold off and demolished (1853–78). Still, in his *View of Nyboder* (1912–14), a small corner of all that remained was humorously immortalized in the caricatures of the Dane Robert Storm Petersen (1882–1949; illus. 184). In it, the wives and widows of absent sailors are depicted engaged in the

184 Robert Storm Petersen, *View of Nyboder*, 1912–14, watercolour.

insalubrious professional activities to which they sometimes had recourse in order to make ends meet.

Outside the capital, Christian IV's most important undertaking was the building of Frederiksborg Castle (1602–20) in Dutch Renaissance style, on the site of his father's old hunting lodge, demolished in order to make room for the new royal residence, seen here as depicted by Christen Købke (see illus. 210). Despite the novelty of its form and decoration, it was to become the seat of monarchical power and symbol of historical continuity in Denmark until the present day. All royal coronations were performed there from 1660 until the abolition of the ceremony in 1840, nineteen years before the building was to a large extent destroyed by fire, to be rebuilt later in the century in a mock Renaissance style.

Christian IV also founded a host of towns in outlying Danish territories, including Christiania (now modern Oslo) in 1624, after the old town of Oslo to the west had been destroyed by fire, and Kristiansand in 1641 where he hoped to encourage mercantile development. In the east, he established two new towns in the then Danish province of Scania, Kristianstad (1614) where he built the little palace of Tyggården in 1615 and Kristianopel, both named after him. The Polish King Stanislaw I and his entourage were to reside in the latter from 1711 to 1714 before settling in France after the political upheavals in Poland which removed him from the throne. To the south, in the Danish duchies of Schleswig-Holstein, Christian IV founded Glückstadt (1616) where he had Glücksburg Palace built in 1631–2. But the king's architectural ambitions were not restricted to Denmark; he also established a Danish mercantile colony at Tranquebar, on the east coast of India, where he had numerous buildings erected (see below, pp. 332, 353). All served the primary purpose of defining royal authority and establishing strong fortifications on the periphery of the Danish realms.

The Triumph of Absolutism in Denmark

Christian IV's son Frederik III (1609–1670) reaped the benefits of his father's political and architectural vision, enabling him to establish absolutism in Denmark over his half a million subjects in 1661. It failed, though, to prevent him from permanently losing Scania, Blekinge and Halland to Sweden in war in 1658, after the troops of the Swedish king marched across the frozen Öresund, despite his heroic leadership of Danish troops in the defence of Copenhagen. This loss was in part a product of the political machinations of England and Holland, countries which had no wish to see these important straits leading to the Baltic under the control of one nation. None the less, from the courage and commitment Frederik III had demonstrated to the city's burghers, he had earned their political support in his internal battle against the power of the aristocracy. A panoramic work by the German artist Wolfgang Heimbach (1615–1678), *The Swearing of the Oath of Allegiance in the Palace Square in Copenhagen* (1666; see illus. 211), commemorates this important victory on behalf of absolute monarchy, focusing upon the occasion when, under considerable duress, the Estate of the Nobility

was obliged to swear allegiance to Frederik III as hereditary monarch, thereby losing many of their traditional freedoms and privileges. Denmark now became the first European state to have an absolute monarchical system of government enshrined within a written constitution. When this was promulgated in 1665, only the church and the indivisibility of the state remained above and beyond royal authority.

Frederick III's son, Christian V (1646–1699) succeeded his father in 1670 as king by divine right. The first of the Danish kings to be anointed in the chapel of Frederiksborg Castle, he crowned himself as well, in a gesture of political independence rich in symbolism. A painting of these events, *The Bishop of Sjælland Anointing Christian V at Frederiksborg* (1671) commemorates the occasion with the almost hagiographic focus the king desired (illus. 185). Time was to demonstrate, though, that the king's political acumen and military skills were not up to the power he wielded and his reign was one of political and social decline, a period in which he squandered his energies in a futile war with Sweden to regain the recently lost territories. Despite this failure, he erected a great statue of himself, clad in the robes of Imperial Rome, a Danish Caesar (illus. 186).

His son and successor Frederik IV (1671–1730) proved to be a more efficient monarch and one with a more international political perspective, as his interest in art and architecture demonstrated. As a young man he had gone to Italy to

185 Michael van Haven, *The Bishop of Sjælland Anointing Christian V at Frederiksborg*, 1671, oil on canvas.

186 Replica of the equestrian statue of Christian V, Kongens Nytorv, Copenhagen.

forge political links and acquaint himself with Italian culture and the political constellations there. Travelling incognito he visited, in progression, Venice, Rome, Ferrara, Bologna, Siena, Pisa and Rimini, where in the Palazzo Corbognano (now Sciarra) he was received by Pope Innocent XII. When he returned to Denmark in 1693, after a short stay in Paris, he commissioned the building of a villa in the Florentine style in the park of Frederiksberg near Copenhagen, a rare example of its type in Scandinavia and a symbol which emphasized his future role, as his ancestor Christian IV had desired, of a powerful humanist prince in the Renaissance tradition. Frederik had hoped to return to Italy, but his father's death prevented another visit until 1708.[4] When he finally returned, however, a welcome awaited him worthy of the vision he had of his regal role.

As Danish king Frederik IV was received on the Grand Canal in Venice by the Doge Aloisio Mocenigo, with all the stateliness he could have hoped for, immortalized in *The Great Regatta at Venice Held by the Doge for the Reception of Frederik IV*, painted by Luca Carlevaris (1665–1731) and later presented to the king as a farewell memento (see illus. 212). Frederik can be seen, dressed in red, seated in the gondola in the foreground, his gondoliers sporting the yellow and red of Frederik's dynasty, the House of Oldenburg, the grand focus of the work.

This second visit to Italy provided Frederick with the opportunity to pursue a political alliance enabling him to gather allies in matters relating to the Spanish Succession which would be of use to his political plans to isolate Sweden militarily.[5] He stopped in Dresden on the return journey to Denmark, where he formed an alliance with Augustus, King of Saxony and Poland, as well as the Prussian king Frederick I, deeply involved in political machinations involving the Spanish Succession. The Danish king's goal was to take advantage of Sweden's defeat at Poltava and to drive home a Danish victory, in concert with Saxony and Prussia, which he hoped, in vain, would result in the reacquisition of Scania and other lost Danish territories. Danish troops were even sent to fight during the War of the Spanish Succession, where they served as mercenaries under the Duke of Marlborough who was fighting against the French on behalf of English interests. Ultimately, though, his endeavours proved futile and the succession of the Bourbons, allies of Sweden, to the Spanish throne was not prevented, nor were the old Danish territories ever regained.

When Frederik returned to Denmark, inspired by the architectural glories he had experienced in Italy, he erected two new magnificent palaces on a scale reminiscent of Christian IV. First, the king built Frederiksberg Palace (1699–1703), to the west of Copenhagen, in a splendid Italianate Baroque style. Then, he constructed Fredensborg, the scene of many court festivities, to the north, naming it after the peace settlement which concluded the Great Northern War in 1720. The central elevation, crowned by a dome, was designed by Johan Cornelius Krieger (1683–1755), who also became Denmark's first landscape architect, laying out a magnificent garden here. First Niels Eigtved and then Lauritz de Thurah, added to the palace, providing pavilions at each of the four corners. With de Thurah's embellishments of four turrets on each corner of the dome creating an exotic skyline and the octagonal range of buildings behind, Fredensborg became the Danish king's most favoured residence, a miniature Versailles, nestled in countryside just outside the capital. Moreover, a new government chancellery, The Red Building, also in the style of a grand Baroque Italian palazzo, was built by royal command adjacent to the old Copenhagen Castle.

Copenhagen Castle itself was to give way to Christiansborg Palace built during the reign of Frederik's successor, Christian VI (1699–1746). This palace took inspiration from Austrian and French, rather than the Italian prototypes. It was begun in 1731 and only completed in 1745, when the king took up residence. It was a monumental accomplishment whose foundations alone required some 10,000 beech trees. However, its magnificence was to be short lived; all but the theatre and riding school were destroyed in a devastating fire in 1794.[6]

Karl XII and the Cultural Expression of Military Might

In May 1697, that great symbol of the Swedish kingdom, the royal palace of Tre Kronor (Three Crowns) in Stockholm, was burnt to the ground, even as the body of Karl XI was lying in state. But for the fourteen-year-old king, Karl XII (1682–1718), the devastation appeared more of a blessing than a misfortune. For Sweden was now at the height of her military might and the conflagration offered the opportunity of building a new palace worthy of the kingdom's dominant political and military position within Europe, a suitable endeavour for the country's first (and, indeed, last) monarch born to succeed to absolute power.

The Great Northern War (begun in 1700), which pitted Sweden against Denmark, Russia and Saxony, at first strengthened Sweden and the king's position. Karl succeeded in placing Stanislaw Leszczynski upon the throne of Poland, which previously, under Augustus II, joint monarch of Saxony, had been an ally of Denmark and Russia. However, the war against Russia (1707–9) and the disastrous Battle of Poltava in 1709 crushed the Swedish army, obliging the king to migrate with his forces to the Ottoman Turks, from whom he vainly sought support over the next five years. In exile for four years at Bender, in the company of some 4,000 Swedes, Cossacks and Poles, Karl XII devised complicated plans for a return to the Baltic through Poland. After he did succeed in returning, later manoeuvres in Swedish Pomerania only served to delay the military débâcle and these wars proved an unmitigated disaster for Sweden. When the king, after his release, fell upon the battlefield during the siege of Fredrikshald, in Danish-held Norway, it was the perfect metaphor for Sweden's demise forever as a great military and political power. The Royal Palace at Stockholm remained (still uncompleted), a monument to the absolute regal power her king had once possessed and the attention he had lavished on it, even by means of lengthy correspondence on the project to Tessin whilst at Bender.

Karl XII had been keenly interested in both art and architecture, as well as military prowess. His father, Karl XI before him, had supported the young architect Nicodemus Tessin the Younger (1654–1728) who had studied in Paris from 1678–80. There he became a keen devotee of the North Star as a symbol of the Swedish monarch, an allusion possibly derived from a chance expression of Cardinal Richelieu who had referred to Gustaf II Adolf as a guiding light to German princelings. He introduced the North Star at every opportunity into his architectural symbolism back in Sweden.7 Tessin had succeeded his father Nicodemus Tessin the Elder who, as Court Architect, had built the Baroque summer palace of Drottningholm (1662–86), outside Stockholm in 1681. Commissioned by the Dowager Queen Hedvig Eleonora, Drottningholm was the largest of the country palaces ever built in the Nordic countries, yet another modest version of Versailles.

It was therefore natural that the younger Tessin spent much of his time abroad, pursuing further architectural studies at Versailles itself in 1687, where the importance of the arts and architecture in political terms did not escape him. He contributed his own designs to a competition for new buildings at the Louvre Palace, in Paris, which were exhibited along side those of such notables as Bernini, Le Vaus and Perrault, and in the first decade of the eighteenth century he was to submit two more on the same subject.

Karl XII reaped the full benefits of Tessin's artistic maturity from the 1690s onwards. Initially, the young king planned a whole range of magnificent buildings to make Stockholm a Paris of the north, though even at this early stage the king's lack of funds would have made such a enormous project impossible. He also envisaged a military church on the scale of Les Invalides in Paris and a new magnificent country palace which would surpass Drottningholm, but these remained wistful fancies with no practical chance of realization.

An indication of the sort of magnificent buildings with which Karl wanted to grace his capital can be found in the architect's own Tessinska Palace, completed in 1700, and situated opposite the building site of the new royal palace. The most elegant Swedish town house of its time, it contained a parade of rooms, including a grand salon. *The Ceiling of the Salon, Tessinska palatset* (c. 1700, by René Chauveau after Tessin) gives an indication of the scope of such a work in Scandinavia at that time. Paintings of Apollo and the nine muses grace its centre with other mythological figures, some of which were derived from Michelangelo and Raphael, provided by the Frenchman Jacques de Meaux. There was also a bedroom suitable for a grand levée, more appropriate for a royal palace than the house of an artist. But, with such, it provided a working model of the architectural values Tessin was attempting to embody in the rebuilding of the Royal Palace itself and it greatly pleased the king, who elevated the architect first to a barony the year before its completion, and finally, in 1714, to the rank of count.

The Royal Palace of Stockholm

Work at the new royal palace in Stockholm proceeded at a very slow pace. A lack of financial resources slowed down its reconstruction so that little work was carried out for many years after 1709. Under Karl XII's successor Fredrik I (1676–1751), whose political powers had been sharply curtailed by the Riksdag in 1720, little progress was made until a special tax was levied in 1727 to pay for its further completion. The following year Tessin died, to be succeeded, in turn, by his son Carl Gustaf Tessin (1695–1770), a courtier and future tutor to Gustaf III, who relegated the work to Carl Hårleman (1700–1753). He was then put in charge of the project in 1741. It was Hårleman, a keen Francophile, who saw that the interior was decorated in a French Rococo style, in accordance with the wishes of the king, by workmen imported from France in 1732. Fredrik I was so pleased that he commissioned him to build the little country pleasure palace of Svartsjö, begun in 1735, but enlarged and completed by Carl Fredrik Adelcrantz (1716–1796) in 1770 (illus. 187). It can be seen in *Svartsjö Palace. Garden Elevation* by Hårleman himself, the first example of a Rococo building in Sweden. The Riksdagen were also delighted with Hårleman's work and put him in charge of all of the buildings, ecclesiastical and civil, for which the Crown was responsible.

187 Carl Hårleman, *Svartsjö Palace* (Sweden), 1735.

Drottningholm in the 1760s

Fredrik I's successor, Adolf Fredrik (1710–1771) and his queen Lovisa Ulrika, a sister of Frederick the Great, were finally able to take occupancy of the Royal Palace of Stockholm in 1754, even though it was not to be completed until the 1770s. However, after the failed coup of her husband, in which the king had attempted to reinstate absolutism in Sweden in 1756, the countryside offered a more carefree lifestyle for the royal family away from the pressures and public scrutiny of the capital, while providing all the amenities of a grand palace. Lovisa Ulrika was keen to make it a showpiece for the latest artistic and architectural fashions from abroad. She was especially taken with the English fashion for the erection of garden pavilions playfully inspired by the Orient, a development in landscape gardening in which the Swedish native Sir William Chambers (1726-1796) was to play such an important role. It also enabled the queen to introduce elements at once exotic and informal into the Baroque formality of the gardens at Drottningholm, while preserving its grand and majestic profile. The palace, with its gardens and appanages, had been given to her in 1744 as a wedding gift from the king; but it was only in the 1760s that she was able to give it her full attention, lavishing money and energies denied her in the political arena. The Chinese

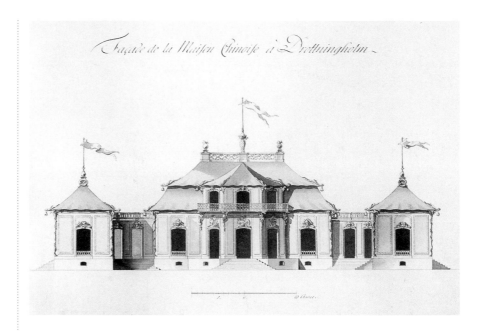

Façade de la Maison Chinoise à Drottningholm.

188 Carl Fredrik Adelcrantz, *The Chinese Palace at Drottningholm*, early 1760s, watercolour and ink wash.

Palace (completed in 1769; illus. 188), designed in Rococo flamboyance by Carl Fredrik Adelcrantz (1716–1796), became the supreme example of its period in the Nordic region, the crowning glory of Sweden's most splendid garden and a worthy stage for displaying the aesthetic wisdom of the House of Vasa.

Such a focus was in no way trivial. The success of absolutism as a form of government depended upon a general appreciation of the monarch as both benevolent and wise. Therefore, it was appropriate that the architectural and artistic vision of the royal couple remained focused upon their need to be at the hub of their country's cultural and intellectual life. Here at Drottningholm, were found local luminaries like Carl von Linné who became a part of a little coterie of intellectuals which the royal couple gathered to themselves for conversation and guidance. It was soon to be formally organized and named the Royal Academy of History and Antiquities in 1753. Lovisa Ulrika also commissioned the construction of a little theatre at Ulriksdal Palace, Confidencen, designed by Adelcrantz and completed in 1753, where her own troop of imported French actors would perform the latest pieces. Of greater importance, however, was the erection of a new theatre. Its principal architectural hallmarks are illustrated in *The Design for the Court Theatre at Drottningholm* (1766), by Carl Fredrik Adelcrantz (illus. 189). There, leading playwrights and could shine before the Court, including Crown Prince Gustaf who expounded his own political and social views, and to glorify monarchical power once he had assumed the throne. He even contributed his own design for a royal opera house, but ultimately chose that of Adelcrantz, allowing his better aesthetic sense to win out over his own inflated sense of his artistic skills.[8]

The queen, however, who had paid for these improvements had financially over-extended herself, and in 1777 Gustaf, now king, assumed responsibility

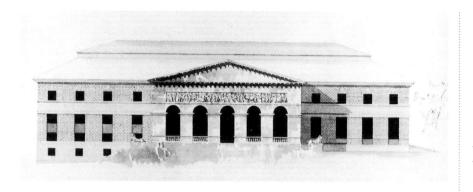

189 Carl Fredrik Adelcrantz, *The Design for the Court Theatre at Drottningholm*, 1766.

himself. He had long been devoted to the visual, as well as theatrical, arts. In 1770, while still Crown Prince, he had commissioned, during his Parisian visit, the leading Swedish artist resident there, Alexander Roslin (1718–1793), to produce a historical painting, *The Duke de Sully at the Feet of Henry IV* (1770), based on a work by Pourbus, of which one version hung in Gustaf's bedchamber at Gripsholm Castle.[9] Even as a five-year-old child, he had taken to heart a letter from his tutor Tessin, 'The most reliable sign of a state's strength can be seen in the degree to which the arts and *belle lettres* flourish there'.[10] Certainly the king never doubted this conviction.

The Tragic Opera of Gustaf III

While the political motives which surrounded the assassination of Sweden's king Gustaf III at the Opera House in Stockholm, in 1793, were later to provide a useful subject for the Italian opera composer Giuseppe Verdi's own political agenda in his opera *Un ballo in maschera* (1859), the very lifestyle and aesthetic vision of the king, Sweden's greatest patron of the arts, was itself operatic in nature even from his youth. Of a profoundly intellectual bent, like his mother, Gustaf admired Voltaire, not least for his rejection of fanaticism and superstition. While in Paris in 1771, he became acquainted with a host of enlightenment philosophers and wrote sardonically to his mother at the time, 'I have become acquainted with almost all the philosophers here: Marmontel, Grimm, Thomas, the Abbé Morellet and Helvétius. It is much more amusing to read them than to meet them'.[11]

The death of his father, Adolf Frederik, cut short his visit to France and he rushed home to assume the throne. Then, with great alacrity, on the 19 August 1772, Gustaf staged his famous coup d'état which re-established absolutism in Sweden, in abeyance since the death of Karl XII. It was a bloodless revolution, but one with profound effects. With the war cry of crushing anarchism and foreign political influence, Gustaf wished to revert to the political system prevalent in Sweden before 1680, though incorporating late eighteenth-century Enlightenment values into his benevolent rule. He also established the Royal Swedish Academy of Music, creating a musical milieu at Court in which poet musicians such as Carl Michael Bellman (1740–1795) were able to thrive. This

190 Johan Tobias Sergel, *Eros and Psyche*, 1776, marble.

was a political gesture of a very different order than the former, but both demonstrated the new king's commitment to enlightened humanist values as preached by France's greatest philosophers.

The king found a coterie of cultural figures keen to encourage his artistic bent. One major Swedish sculptor in particular was to anticipate the megalomaniacal needs of the king, in both artistic and architectural terms. He was Johan Tobias Sergel (1740–1814) who, having won the Gold Medal of the Stockholm's Royal Academy of Art, travelled to Rome in 1767, where he became one of the most important neo-classical sculptors of his generation. Not only was Sergel influenced by the archaeological and other antique Greek and Roman ruins he experienced in Italy, but he was also deeply impressed by the novel and fantastical designs of Giambattista Piranesi (1720–1778). These were classically inspired by ruins, both ancient and modern, and were published from the 1750s onwards until Piranesi's death. As a result, Sergel's own work became increasingly robust and geometric, in line with the growing fashion for stylistic austerity which had developed as a reaction to the now outmoded rococo, with its sensuous curves.

Gustaf III's brother, Prince Fredrik Adolf, visited Rome in 1776, where he purchased a marble bust of Apollo from Sergel, which was followed by a commission for *Venus* (1774–6), in marble, which already existed in a plaster version. Soon commissions were arriving from the king himself. First, a sculpture of a faun was commissioned, influenced by that at the Villa Borghese. Then, Gustaf III took over Sergel's commission for his *Eros and Psyche* (1776; illus. 190), originally commissioned by Madame du Barry, mistress to the late Louis XV, who had died in 1774. Gustaf III intended to place it in a neo-classical temple at his new pleasure palace at Haga, outside Stockholm, for which the Frenchman Louis-Jean Desprez (1743–1804), long resident in Rome, had already produced designs.

The little four-sided temple, with a niche to contain Eros and Pysche, was never carried out, but the subject was so popular with Gustaf III that he had smaller copies of it made which he distributed, one going to his favourite, the Finnish-Swede G. M. Armfelt, at his classically inspired estate Åmine Gård, in the south of Finland. The original work, though, eventually made its way to the museum at the Royal Palace in Stockholm.

In 1778, Sergel received a royal command to return to Sweden to succeed the Frenchman Pierre Hubert L'Archevêque (1721–1778) as Court Sculptor. He was loath to depart, but took his leave of Italy and arrived in Stockholm the following year, where he was immediately made professor of the Swedish Royal Academy of Art.

As far as Gustaf III himself was concerned, Sergel's first contact with the king was not amicable,[12] but he was soon engaged in carrying out a whole range of works to fulfil the king's neo-classical aesthetic vision. Even such smaller objects as candelabras were commissioned from Sergel, who gave his plaster models of these objects an architectural character by modelling them in the forms of caryatids based on those in marble of the priestesses of Ceres which he had seen in Rome. The king was pleased with the grandeur of the symbolism. By 1781 Sergel's salary had been doubled and he prepared to set to work seriously, when Gustaf III demanded his services as cicerone upon a great voyage he was to undertake to visit Italy, for political as well as aesthetic reasons. In 1771, while still crown prince, Gustaf had intended to visit Italy, but the death of his father had prevented this. Now, however, the time was at hand. Karl August Ehrensvärd, whose father had built the fortress of Sveaborg (Suomenlinna) in the harbour of Helsinki, newly made chancellor of the Swedish Royal Academy of Art, had just returned to Stockholm and he, too, was seconded for the king's entourage. Lessons with the noted Swedish artist Elias Martin (1739–1818), long resident in England, had developed Ehrensvärd's not inconsiderable talents for drawing, especially caricatures and he provided an amusing aristocratic companion for the king, for whom he kept an interesting journal of their travels.

Gustaf III's aesthetic vision tended towards the classical. Thus, in the painting he commissioned to commemorate his ascension to the throne ten years previously (before his famous coup d'état), Gustaf III wanted a rich allegorical focus. This was achieved in *The Coronation of Gustaf III* (begun long after the event in 1782) by Carl Gustaf Pilo (1711–1793; see illus. 213) by the use of religious compositional arrangements and other elements to emphasize the divinely motivated nature of the king's ascension to the throne. But such a work was still very Rococo in spirit, in its gauzy pastel colours and swirling forms. Such stylistic characteristics as these, however, would soon disappear from the artistic scene in the wake of Gustaf's travels in Italy and the influence of Sergel.

The king's commitment to the 'ideal' came to synchronize almost perfectly with that of Sergel, though the sculptor was criticized by some for being too doctrinaire in his approach to neo-classical values, too uncompromising in his quest to expressing classical ideals in his works. He was also uncompromising in his rejection of both French Rococo values, especially those of his late mentor L'Archevêque, which filled the sculptor with repugnance, and any attempt to capture the contemporary. When, for example, Duke Karl, the king's brother had sought to influence the bust of himself which Sergel was carrying out (intended as a Christmas gift to the king), Sergel had refused to model the duke with the contemporary English hair style he sported and which he so ardently wished to be portrayed, because it violently jarred with his concept of the classical ideal.[13] This intransigence the king admired, a trait, too, which he possessed in large measure.

Louis-Adrien Masreliez

In this desire to draw upon a strict idealizing classical tradition, Sergel found a like-minded colleague in the artist Louis-Adrien Masreliez (1748–1810). Though a native of Paris and son of the ornamental sculptor Jacques-Adrien Masreliez who had emigrated from France to Sweden while his son was just a small child, the younger Masreliez also came to reject the French Rococo tradition in which his father had worked. His lengthy sojourn in Italy, in Bologna (1770–73), and, of particular importance, Rome (1773–82), gave a profound Italian flavour to his works which were influenced not only by Raphael and the Carracci brothers but by Signorelli and Verrochio, rather unusually at that time. The vogue for the archaeological ruins of the Greeks and Romans also exerted a major influence upon his style, which evoked a resonance not only in court circles but in the aesthetic sense of the king himself who wished to cast himself in a role which would glorify the House of Vasa and provide images to bolster the re-establishment of absolute monarchy in Sweden. Thus, upon Masreliez's return to Sweden in 1782, he was immediately made a director of the Swedish Academy of Art and, in 1783, professor of history.

Most importantly, he was commissioned by the king to decorate the new pavilion at Haga, on the outskirts of Stockholm. Taking inspiration from the archaeological remains of Pompeii and the writings of Winckelmann, Masreliez wanted to create the supreme expression of the king's own neo-classical vision. But even Masreliez's Italianate values could not satisfy the king's aesthetic needs, nor his delusions of grandeur, longings which were enflamed by his travels in Italy.

Gustaf III's Travels in Italy

An injury which the king sustained during his campaign in Finland and the need to undergo an ostensible cure in Pisa provided the public raison d'être for his projected journey, though he did have serious motives of political necessity underlying these plans. He wished to woo the support of the Bourbon powers of France, Spain, the Two Sicilies and Parma for an alliance against Sweden's traditional enemies Denmark and Russia, to enable him to distract these maritime neighbours from his hidden intentions and military preparations for a projected war against them for control of the Baltic, which had been relinquished by Sweden under Charles XII. He also wanted to exploit the cultural riches of Italy to enable him to create, upon his return home, a grandiose new Jerusalem in and around Stockholm. As architecture and art had reflected the glory of the Sun King Louis XIV a century before, so it would, he fantasized, reflect the glory of the North Star King in Sweden.

Therefore, Gustaf III, travelling incognito as the Count of Haga and in the company of Ehrensvärd and Sergel, toured Italy, visiting Venice, Verona and Vicenza in the north, as well as Mantua and Padua, where he was received in great state. They also travelled to the Mezzogiorno, touring Naples and Sicily, paying special attention to the ruins and temples at Pompeii, Herculaneum and

Agrigento. There, like so many fellow aesthetes from the north of Europe, they were attracted more by the recently discovered Greek ruins than by those of the ancient Romans, Renaissance or Baroque architects, though it was not so much the architectural details of these ruins, but the aesthetic spirit which they evoked which entranced them. The most important sojourn of Gustaf III's royal progression was spent in Rome. There a venue was provided for his deepening personal contact with both Sergel and Masreliez, paving the way for an elaboration and development of the king's grand neo-classical vision for Stockholm and its environs.

Louis-Jean Desprez

It was also in Rome that Gustaf III first met Desprez, who was to become the central figure in the king's grandiose architectural designs at home. Desprez, a native of Auxerre, in Burgundy, had studied under Charles-Nicolas Cochin; but, more importantly, he had trained as a theatre designer through the offices of his colleague Charles de Wailly. The theatricality of his architectural vision was already evident in the design for a mansion house which had won him the Grand Prix de Rome, enabling him to establish himself there in 1777 at the Palazzo Mancini, home of the French Academy. Soon he received a commission to assist the Abbé de Saint-Non with his great architectural work, *Voyage pittoresque, ou description des royaumes de Naples et de Sicilie*, and spent about a year in those Bourbon kingdoms. To this enterprise he contributed no less than 136 illustrations of architectural *vedutae*, rich in archaeological and anecdotal detail, as well as dramatic interest. Classical, medieval and Baroque monuments all became the theatrical backdrop to the spiritual and secular life of the local people and earned him considerable fame which opened many doors.

In Rome, Desprez became a close friend of Francesco Piranesi (1758–1810), son of Giambattista Piranesi (1720–1778), who was already acting as agent for the purchase of works of art on behalf of Gustaf III. Whether or not Piranesi had encouraged the king to visit Desprez after his arrival in Rome is not clear; however, it is known that the king paid a visit to the atelier of Desprez in March 1783, after having enjoyed his stage set at the Teatro Alberti. Cardinal de Bernis, French ambassador in Rome, also recommended Desprez to Gustaf.

Desprez's theatrical vision greatly pleased the king who felt he had found another kindred spirit in the young Frenchman. Moreover, his stage sets for the ballet Henry IV, based on Shakespeare's play and rich in political symbolism, intrigued him. Almost immediately, Desprez was commissioned to produce the studies for two panoramic paintings with an extraordinary subject matter for the time: *Gustaf III Witnessing Christmas Mass in St Peter's* (1783) and *Gustaf III Witnessing Easter Mass in St Peter's* (1784; illus. 191). In the former, it is not a realistic depiction of the events of the day which are presented but rather a freely adapted scene in which the king, together with Joseph II of Austria, is shown leading a mass of people towards the high altar, a scene rich in political symbolism, if practically implausible. In the latter, too, the king is given a commanding role, though the finished

191 Louis-Jean Desprez, *Gustaf III Witnessing Easter Mass in St Peter's*, 1784, watercolour, pen and grey ink and brown wash.

oil painting, for which it was intended to be the study, was never carried out. Since the practice of Catholicism was still a capital crime in Sweden at the time, a reference to the king's religious toleration and rejection of fanaticism by virtue of his presence there is inescapable, but it was probably the king's leading pictorial role in the religious drama which forms the real principal focus of these works.

Gustaf III was, however, modest in the number of his commissions and purchases of paintings and other works of art in Italy. A travel purse reduced to only 9,000 Riksdalers precluded too many acquisitions, despite the king's genuine and avowed love of the arts. So Gustaf had to content himself with his departure for home, knowing that Desprez would soon be following him, in July 1784, in order to provide stage decor for royal operatic and theatrical productions in Sweden.

Once in Stockholm, Desprez was put to work producing the stage sets of numerous plays, such as *Queen Christina*, for which his designs for *De la Gardies Garden*, Act One, Scene One, are amongst the most architectonic in his productions of this type (illus. 192). Other works included *Gustaf Wasa* and *Gustaf Adolf and Ebba Brahe*, all glorifying the Vasa dynasty. But Gustaf III had other plans for Desprez relating to his secret plans for a future war with Russia. He took Desprez on a visit to Finland in June 1785, where the artist made sketches of military manoeuvres on both land and sea, as well as of various Finnish towns, such as

192 Louis-Jean Desprez, *De la Gardies Garden, Act One, Scene One, from the Play 'Queen Christina'*, c. 1785, ink, grey wash and watercolour with white highlights.

Turku (Åbo) and Pori (Björneborg). Shortly thereafter, Desprez was elevated to the rank of court architect.

Perhaps Desprez's most memorable paintings on such themes were carried out several years after Gustaf III's death in 1797–8, and based on the artist's own experience of almost a decade before: one, *Larger and Smaller Ships of the Royal Navy Equipping themselves for Battle in 1788–90*, at the Arsenal in Stockholm (illus. 193) depicts Stockholm's Royal Palace on the right, with a tumult of ships and men filling the waterways at the heart of the capital, making it a vast panorama of Swedish royal might.

193 Louis-Jean Desprez, *Larger and Smaller Ships of the Royal Navy Equipping themselves for Battle in 1788–90*, at the Arsenal in Stockholm, 1797–8, watercolour.

The Royal Palace of Haga: Imperial Dreams Unrealized

From 1787, Desprez's responsibilities included all the vast building works intended by the king for the old royal palace of Drottningholm, as well as the new royal palace at Haga, an enterprise planned on such a grandiose scale as might have made it the largest in Europe had it been completed. In 1786, Desprez had been at work creating theatrical scenery for both the festive commemoration at Drottningholm of Gustaf III's coup d'état of 1772 and of the laying of the cornerstone of Haga itself. Both events gave hints as to Desprez's artistic vision with respect to the intended royal palace and can be seen in his *Project for a Temple*

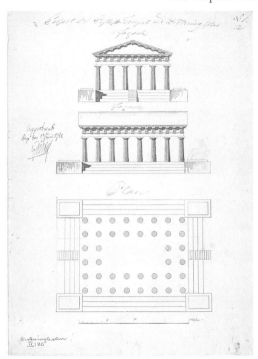

194 Louis-Jean Desprez, *Project for a Temple at Drottningholm inspired by that of Paestum*, 1788, watercolour and ink.

at Drottningholm inspired by that of Paestum (1788; illus. 194). The inspiration and imagery in the props and the temple design were clearly inspired by ancient Roman and Greek architecture, but with the fantastical dimension characteristic of both Gustaf's and Desprez's aesthetic spirit.

Desprez then provided drawings and plans for pleasure pavilions, garden temples, guardhouses and stabling, of which the most memorable is that for a guardroom designed in the form of a Roman military tent. These were, in turn, followed by those for the palace itself. Desprez, however, had not been the first architect involved in the Haga project; Olof Tempelman had already produced his own designs, inspired by that of Palladio's Villa Rotonda at Vicenza, especially his use of a portico for each of the four principal facades of the central pavilion, united beneath a majestic cupola. For this reason, Desprez was obliged rather to incorporate his own ideas into the existing design framework instead of beginning from scratch. First, he included new designs for an enormous staircase, as well as the addition of extensive wings to the east and west. Then, he endeavoured to define the space beneath the cupola by means of a vast unifying colonnade, disengaged from the supporting walls. There was also to be a rotunda, intended to join the two projecting wings, which was to be lit through no less than 62 window bays, with a grand Corinthian colonnade of some 60 columns on the southern end. These, for Gustaf IIII, were to be the ultimate symbol of imperial grandeur and power, much as they had been in classical Rome.[14] Finally, a salon was to be placed beneath the central cupola, flanked by sixteen columns of Siberian malachite, through which light would fall by means of an oculus, resembling that of the Pantheon in Rome. A royal personage standing below would thus be bathed in a dramatic light. Also striking are his innovative designs for a *Salon in the Egyptian Style at the palace at Haga* (illus. 195), which are among the first in this fashion to be produced in the Nordic region, though the salon itself was never carried out.

Gustaf III was ecstatic about Desprez's archaeological vision, which for all its neo-classical elements remained grounded in the picturesque tradition, and included mediaeval elements as well. For example, he embellished some stables

and administrative buildings with Gothic towers, despite their otherwise classic-ally Roman, if ruined exteriors, all to the final effect of creating a supreme architectural statement which would glorify royal authority. With its vast geographical extension, including the whole of the shoreline around the waterway of Brunnsviken, Haga would certainly have presented a panoramic vision of imperial grandeur, as can be seen in *A View of Haga* (see illus. 214). A vast sculptural work was also planned, including a victory column, surmounted by a balustrade and belvedere. This was to be crowned by a sculpture of Gustaf Vasa, the founder of the hereditary Vasa dynasty, which would be visible for miles around, situated on the commanding hilltop at Brahelund.[15]

Work began at Haga after a large granite hill which obtruded upon the intended site was blown up and the foundations laid. Completion of the palace was scheduled for 1796; yet, after six years, little had been constructed. Poor state finances, aggravated by a financially draining war with Russia (1789–90), had emptied the royal coffers and Gustaf III's dreams for imperial grandeur at Haga were to remain forever unrealized.[16] The outbreak of revolution in France further broke the king's spirit, as well as any affinity he might have felt with the middle classes; he preferred instead to seek his allies from amongst the Peasant Estate whose champion he saw himself. As for the bourgeois revolutionaries of France, he could only write contemptuously to his Finnish favourite Baron Armfelt, 'What repulsive people! They are the orangutangs of Europe'.[17]

While Desprez's architectural endeavours for Haga never achieved fruition, other architectural enterprises for the king were successful. He produced, for example, the final austerely neo-classical design for the Botanical Institute at Uppsala University, which had been commenced by Tempelman in a lighter vein, but was completed shortly after Desprez's death in 1807, according to his designs. He also produced a new foyer for Gustaf's beloved theatre at Drottningholm. Even after the king's assassination, supported by the new director of the Royal Museum, Carl Fredrik Fredenheim (1748–1803), Desprez continued to be employed at Drottningholm. There he produced designs for the interior decoration of the entrance hall of the inner gallery of the Stone Museum, which would have glorified Gustaf's military endeavours in the Baltic. While it is true that these and a series of battle scenes which Gustaf had also commissioned came to nought, Desprez's grandiose designs did remain as a lasting legacy of the most majestic and grandiose architectural vision a Nordic monarch had ever cherished.

Carl Fredrik Adelcrantz and the Stockholm Opera House

The successful endeavours of Gustaf's other architects also helped set the stage for the glorification of the Swedish monarchy. Theatres were especially important for these had stages from which the king's political messages could be expounded in carefully chosen plays. The grandest theatre was the Stockholm Opera House, which was built in 1782 and depicted in *The Stockholm Opera House as seen from the Opera*

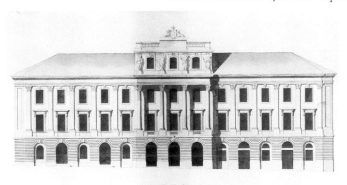

Square, a painting copied after an original by Adelcrantz (illus. 196). For a model, Adelcrantz drew upon Soufflot's theatre at Lyon, which incorporated a similar oval salon to the one he adopted for the audience. It included the latest in theatrical machinery and could accommodate well over 900 viewers. It was thus for Gustaf the ideal vehicle upon which to develop a national forum for Swedish music, theatre and the edification of the common people, all under

196 Copy after Carl Fredrik Adelcrantz, *The Stockholm Opera House as seen from the Opera Square*, 1782, ink wash.

his autocratic but benevolent gaze. While many dramatic operas and theatrical events were staged there, none was so histrionic, nor full of political implications, as that of the assassination of the king himself during a performance in 1792, by a disaffected Swedish aristocrat, Captain Jacob Johan Ankarström. Unwittingly, Gustaf III had become the most memorable tragic actor upon his own majestic stage.

Erik Palmstedt and Gripsholm Castle

The king's architectural fantasies tended to focus around Stockholm and its environs, but even in the provinces Gustaf's theatres became neo-classical monuments to his regal vision. This can be seen in *A View of the New Theatre at Gripsholm Castle*, by the Swedish architect Erik Palmstedt (1741–1803), from 1781 (illus. 197). Palmstedt had already provided festive decoration for Gustaf while Crown Prince in 1766, and had been actively involved with the building of Stockholm's new Stock Exchange in the final years before Gustaf became king. He had published an important literary work for the Swedish Academy of Art, glorifying the ancient ruins he had seen in Italy, *On Antique Monuments in Rome* (1778–80), showing clearly his increasing preoccupation with an austere but melodramatic neo-classicism which greatly appealed to Gustaf III. At the Gripsholm Court

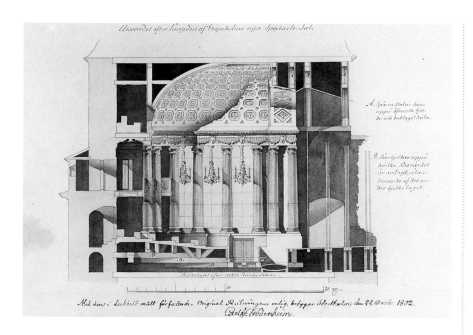

197 Erik Palmstedt, *A View of the New Theatre at Gripsholm Castle*, 1781, watercolour and ink.

Theatre, the Roman Pantheon, including its massive dome and oculus, was again reinterpreted. Theatrical masks upon the architrave above the columns allude to the function of the room, while an interior balcony provided additional accommodation for the audience who enjoyed the rich theatrical and musical spectacles provided by the monarch, and sometimes written by him as well.

Gustavianism in Finland

As an integral part of Sweden, and especially as a frontier province, Finland played a major role in the regal vision of Gustaf III and of his son and successor Gustaf IV Adolf. Both fostered architecture there which drew upon the forms and symbols of antiquity, with all their imperial associations, much as in Sweden itself and here, too, Desprez and others had been employed. Most striking is the parish church of Hämäänlinna (Tavastehus) (designed 1789, built 1795–8) which, with its round nave and cupola decorated with simple neo-classical designs, includes iconographic motifs drawn from the Pantheon in Rome. The Åbo (Turku) Academy (1802–15), by the native Swedish architect Carl Christoffer Gjörwell

198 Carl Christoffer Gjörwell, Åbo (Turku) Academy (Finland), 1802–15.

(1766–1837), a former star pupil of Desprez's, also took inspiration from antique Roman prototypes (illus. 198). The vestibule in the academy is based on that of a classical Roman atrium as described by the ancient Roman architect Vitruvius in terms of proportions and symbolic references to the gods, albeit filtered through the writings of Palladio. The ceremonial hall incorporates a basilican

199 Charles Bassi, Ceremonial hall of Åbo Academy, 1802–15.

nave, completed at one end by an apse (illus. 199). Such an apse, in Roman times, served to frame the centrepieces of grand public rooms, especially imperial ones, in which allusions to both the sacred and profane became entwined.[18] The academy thus became, in the most literal sense, a temple of learning.[19]

The Glorification of Absolutism in Denmark-Norway

Frederik V (1723–1766) of Denmark, though on a more humble scale, was also interested in the arts and architecture and their political implications. He estab-

200 Vilhelm Hammershøi, *Amalienborg Square Seen from the Levetzau Palace with the Equestrian Statue of Frederik V*, 1896, oil on canvas.

lished the Danish Royal Academy of Art in Copenhagen in 1754, thereby ensuring the creation of a future reservoir of artists and architects who could be drawn upon to create works which would help bolster his divine right to absolute power. He can be seen as a conquering Roman hero in *Amalienborg Square Seen from the Levetzau Palace with the Equestrian Statue of Frederik V* (1896), by Vilhelm Hammershøi (illus. 200), who has depicted it against a backdrop of one of the four identical palaces built in about 1750. The sculpture itself had been completed in 1769 by the Frenchman J. F. J. Saly to glorify the absolute monarchy of Denmark at a time when Count Struensee and his followers were attempting to diminish its authority.

Such absolutism was well-established in Denmark – Gustaf III, even at the height of his power, could but dream of realizing it in Sweden – but nowhere in Scandinavia could it be taken for granted. Art, architecture and other cultural media were conscripted to reinforce Frederik's vision of monarchy.

Nikolaj Abildgaard (1743–1809), arguably the most learned of the Nordic men of arts, especially with reference to knowledge of the Greek and Roman classics, was of signal importance in this glorification of the Danish monarchy. He had travelled to Rome in 1772, as the Gold Medallist of the Danish Royal Academy of Art's Prix de Rome, and remained there for a further five years, carefully studying the archaeological remains which were to provide him with inspiration for many of his works throughout his life. This is evident in his painting *Christian I Elevates Holstein to the Status of a Duchy in 1460* (1778–7) which focuses upon the illustrious royal ancestor of the new Crown Prince Frederik, who had assumed the regency for his weak-minded father who had succeeded Frederik V. All the figures, including the king and his two sons, are clearly inspired by some of the antique Roman sculpture which Abildgaard had seen in Rome, but he has given them a non-classical reference as well, by framing them within Gothic architectural forms.

201 Nikolaj Abildgaard, *The Establishment of Hereditary Monarchical Government in 1660*, 1806, oil on canvas.

Central to Frederik's plan for pictorial expressions of monarchical might, after he assumed the throne upon his father's death, was the commission Abildgaard received to provide four paintings for the new throne room at Christiansborg. *The Establishment of Hereditary Monarchical Government in 1660* (1810) was the most important, glorifying the establishment of absolute government in Denmark (illus. 201). However, the king now felt that the work did not possess the historical accuracy that was now fashionable. For this reason, he was convinced, its allegorical significance was lost and the works never assumed their intended place within the throne room.[20] More appealing to him were the fashionable paintings carried out by Jens Juel (1745–1802), who produced more than a thousand portraits of Danish society during his lifetime. His painting, *Crown Prince Frederik with his Family* (1788–9) (illus. 202) portrays the king in younger days amid a naturalistically depicted domesticity, in which the joys and contentment of family life come to the fore. There is, however, an implied reference to Denmark herself as a happy family over whom Frederik, the wise and benevolent pater familias, was to rule as regent and king.

202 Jens Juel, *Crown Prince Frederik with his Family*, 1788–9, oil on canvas.

The End of the Vasas and the Dawn of a New Era

In Sweden, artists and sculptors who had weathered the Gustavian period into the nineteenth century did not fare as well as their counterparts in Denmark. For example, Sergel, though he had even been ennobled by Gustaf IV Adolf in 1808 and was undoubtedly one of the greatest sculptors of his time, found few commissions, especially under Karl XIII, Gustaf III's younger brother who had assumed the throne after the coup d'état of 1809. Having no issue, the new king adopted the former French Marshal Karl Johan Bernadotte (1763–1844) in 1810, and Sergel, like many other artists and architects of the time, hoped for better times with the change of dynasty upon the Frenchman's succession. As he exclaimed towards the end of Karl XIII's reign: 'Would that it could come to pass,

203 Niels Simonsen, *Battle of Fredericia*, 1850, oil on canvas.

205 Jens Juel, *A Holstein Girl*,
1766–7, oil on canvas.

(Opposite)
206 Vigilius Eriksen, *Portrait of
the Queen Dowager Juliane
Marie*, 1776, oil on canvas.

204 Nikolaj Abildgaard,
*Christian I Elevates Holstein
to the Stature of a Duchy*,
1778–9, oil on canvas.

207 Emil Nolde, *Seebüll Farmhouse*, watercolour.

208 Jens Juel, *Northern Light
(Landscape with Aurora Borealis.
In the Background Middelfart
Church)*, c. 1790, oil on
canvas.

209 Prince Eugen, *The Cloud*, 1896, oil on canvas.

210 Christen Købke, *Frederiksborg Castle seen from the North-West*, 1836, oil on canvas.

(Opposite above)
211 Wolfgang Heimbach, *The Swearing of the Oath of Allegiance in the Palace Square in Copenhagen*, 1666, oil on canvas.

(Opposite below)
212 Luca Carlevaris, *The Great Regatta at Venice Held by the Doge for the Reception of Frederik IV*, 1709, oil on canvas.

213 Carl Gustaf Pilo, *The Coronation of Gustaf III*, 1782, oil on canvas.

214 Louis-Jean Desprez, *A View of Haga*, c. 1790, pencil, grey ink and watercolour.

without in the least wishing for the death of anyone, that this Great Man (Karl Johan) may have the opportunity as soon as possible to display to the world the greatness of his beautiful soul!' Despite this optimistic remark, Sergel may even then have realized that Karl Johan was no patron of the arts in the mould of Gustaf III. When, as early as 1811, Karl Johan had sat as model for a portrait medallion by Sergel, the artist was struck by his seeming disinterest in any of the works of art there, or indeed, works of art anywhere.[21] This disappointing event was pictorially recorded by Sergel in *Crown Prince Karl Johan Visits Johan Tobias Sergel in his Atelier* (1810; illus. 215). It may have been the case that Karl Johan found it difficult to be reconciled to one like the sculptor so bound up in the aesthetic vision of Gustaf III and the House of Vasa. For all Sergel's attempts at striving after the ideal, his unwitting emphasis upon 'truth to nature' in over 40 busts and 180 portrait medallions was sometimes considered unflattering to the sitter and unsuitable to the more bombastic style which came into favour after the Gustavians. Simply put, Karl Johan's regal vision was that of the new post-Napoleonic age.

While Sergel and many others after him may have considered this interlude between Gustaf III and Karl Johan's ascension to the throne as barren, the reality was less grim. Sergel's commemorative statue of Gustaf III had been unveiled in front of the royal palace in 1808, when he had famously exclaimed, 'By a thousand devils, wasn't Gustaf III a ray of eternal light!'[22] The artist Carl Fredrik von Breda (1759–1818) was also busy at work on portraits depicting leading members of the Riksdag, from various estates in 1811, the year he was elevated to the peerage. However, it is certainly true that royal commissions of art and architecture were few and far between, compared to the reign of Gustaf III, and that which existed could hardly be said to express any broad regal vision. A resurgence in the world of the arts had to await a new dawn and new visions, which came, albeit in modest measure, after the enthronement of Marshal Bernadotte.

215 Johan Tobias Sergel, *Crown Prince Karl Johan Visits Johan Tobias Sergel in his Atelier*, 1810, ink wash.

The Establishment of the Bernadottes

Bernadotte had arrived in Sweden in 1810, having been adopted by the Gustaf IV Adolf through a complicated Napoleonic dynastic arrangement involving the Allied powers. This enabled him to succeed to the Swedish throne in 1818. Already that first year as king, he contributed some 10,000 Riksdalers to the newly renamed Free Academy of Arts, formerly the Academy for Artists and

Sculptors, a not insignificant sum.[23] Though lacking the aesthetic vision of his predecessors, one could argue that the new king had even greater need of an architectural and artistic vision to help compensate for his relatively humble French origins and few connections to Sweden. Moreover, he never learnt to speak or read the Swedish language. He also realized that the bleak political and debilitating financial circumstances of the reign of Gustaf V Adolf, culminating in a riot (in which Axel von Fersen, Marie Antoinette's Swedish favourite was torn to pieces), had exerted a moribund effect upon the cultural life of Sweden. There was now developing a new focus to the neo-classical, stressing monumentality, rigid geometry and, through these characteristics, imperial and regal splendour, a fashion the king wished to harness.

France provided the principal sources of these developments in architectural and artistic fashions. Charles Percier (1764–1838) and Pierre-François-Léonard Fontaine (1762–1853) were extremely important in this regard, since they had been responsible for the redecoration of the Empress Josephine's palace of Malmaison, outside Paris, which she had purchased in 1799. By 1812, they had published some 72 drawings of their splendid imperial interiors there in *Recueil de Décoration intérieure comprenant tout ce qui a rapport à l'ameublement*, a work which was to disseminate their architectural and decorative ideas throughout Europe and beyond. Such an aesthetic vision of imperial grandeur found a considerable resonance in Karl Johan and his Queen, Desideria, both of whom shared French art and architectural tastes reinforced by their French background. The new Swedish king had visited Malmaison itself, while still fighting under Napoleon, and was considerably impressed by the palace. It is thus natural that such visions should have figured largely in his own architectural and decorative commissions.

The Palaces of Karl Johan

The 'empire style' in Sweden is closely bound up with Karl Johan and the establishment of the Bernadotte dynasty. The Swedish architect Gustaf af Sillén designed a new royal residence at Rosersberg in a style clearly influenced by the earlier designs of Percier and Fontaine, even if the new queen's bedchamber was designed by Gjörwell. Rosersberg became the first 'empire-style' building in the country. Then the king commissioned the building of a new little palace, Rosendal, at the Royal Deer Park on an island just outside Stockholm (1824–31). The Swedish architect Fredrik Blom (1781–1853) provided the designs, but with considerable input from the king himself, who supervised the many aspects of the building work and decoration which combined neo-Classical and Gothic decorative elements, glorifying both Classical and Norse stories.[24] A sculpture of the Roman Cicero sat beside one of Norse Heimdal, the father of mankind in the king's library at Rosendal. In similar fashion, in the Red Salon, where the king received his guests, the sculptural decorations included Marius and Sulla, who helped established the Roman state, as well as the Norse god Odin, figures rich in imperial symbolism with whom the king was keen to associate himself.[25]

Karl Johan and the Arts in Sweden

Karl Johan was active in other architectural projects. He was keen to establish for himself an appropriate seat in his new realm of Norway, transferred from Danish sovereignty to the Swedish king by the Treaty of Kiel in 1814. There was a pressing need for a suitable royal palace in Christiania (now Oslo), the Norwegian capital. Construction was carried out in the 1820s, and a painting by Joachim Frich (1810–1858; illus. 216) shows the neo-classical edifice rising majestically above the rest of the city, and the newly laid-out Karl Johan Gatan, the principal avenue of the developing city, lying below. Elsewhere in Sweden other public buildings were already in progress. The new library *Carolina Rediviva*, of Uppsala University, for example, was being built on a site chosen by Karl Johan while Crown Prince in 1812, and became one of the finest examples of its type in the old university city.

The visual arts were not neglected. The Swedish artist Fredrik Westin (1782–1862), in particular, found favour with the king who commissioned him to carry out quite a number of works. Influenced by the paintings of Gérard and Girodet, artists who appealed to Karl Johan's French tastes, Westin had already painted a work depicting Gustaf III as defender of the arts and sciences in 1803 under the old regime. He had also been involved in decorations for Karl Johan's bedchamber at Rosmersholm and, in particular, his early depiction of the Karl Johan's daughter-in-law, Crown Princess Josefina (the consort of the future King Oskar) for Gripsholm Castle, is rich in allegorical references to a poem by Tegnér

216 Joachim Frich, *The Royal Palace as seen from a Country Vantage Point*, 1853.

283

217 Fredrik Westin, *Allegory of Crown Princess Josefina's Arrival in Sweden*, 1823, oil on canvas.

on the subject (illus. 217). But other works by Westin include paintings based upon themes from Sweden's distant past, as well as family group portraits of the Bernadottes. Such works, often sentimental in their anecdote, pleased the king not least because they succeeded in linking the new dynasty with Sweden's history giving the House of Bernadotte added legitimacy. Rumours of Gustaf III's homosexuality had for decades cast doubt in some circles on Gustaf IV Adolf's parentage. Indeed, as has already been shown above, Ehrensvärd's *Caricature of Gustaf III's Attempt to Produce an Heir* indicated Munck as Gustaf IV Adolf's biological father (see illus. 80). But Karl Johan's claims were even more tenuous, totally unrelated as he was by blood to the House of Vasa. Thus, he energetically encouraged any suitable visual imagery which could be used to bolster his claim to be the rightful king of Sweden.

The works of the sculptor Johan Niklas Byström (1783–1848) also appealed to the Karl Johan. Byström himself gave the king a marble sculpture, *Karl Johan as*

Mars (1816; illus. 218), which glorified the old French warrior's martial past. Mammoth in size, the face of the king is rendered with great realism, capturing many of his facial characteristics, though the sculptor altered his physiognomy radically according to the king's wishes. As a result, Karl Johan valued this work, not least because it appeared as if the king were being portrayed realistically, even if this was not the case. As well as the figure of Mars, a shield was incorporated into this sculpture group, decorated with the Norse mythological figures of Svea and Nore, symbolizing Sweden and Norway, the two realms under Karl Johan's sovereignty. Although it was given to the aristocratic courtier Magnus Brahe, it ultimately found its way, by 1835, to a tower in the Castle of Skokloster, where it became a memorial to the founder of Sweden's new royal house. The classical temple, however, which Byström had wished to erect in memory of Karl Johan after his death, was to remain unrealized, as neo-classical forms increasingly fell from favour.

218 Johan Niklas Byström, *Karl Johan as Mars*, 1816. Skoklosters Slott.

Norse Gods and a French Marshal Turned King

The next generation of artists and architects increasingly came to rebel against neo-classicism, a style they increasingly felt to be alien and exhausted. Instead, they turned more and more to the ancient mythology and history of their own region, real and imagined. The journal *Phosphoros*, founded in 1810, was very important in propagating these new values. It was soon to be followed by the even more influential journal, *Iduna*, to which the Swedish poet Erik Gustaf Geijer (1783–1847), later professor of history at Uppsala University, was a major contributor. Together, they greatly inspired The Gothic Society, recently founded in 1811, whose lecture series held by Per Henrik Ling drew attention to Norse myths, later publicized in Ling's book, *Symbols of the Eddas*. Others, such as John von Breda (1788–1835), son of Carl Fredrik, now looked to such Nordic sources almost exclusively.

Von Breda himself had for a considerable period of time been out of favour with the king. Indeed, the so-called 'Breda squabble' erupted because Karl Johan held suspicions that Breda entertained political circles opposed to him. This had led, albeit temporarily, to the confiscation of his home and atelier. Certainly, Von Breda was a rebellious figure in artistic as well as political terms: he joined together with Bengt Erland Fogelberg (1786–1854) and Johan Gustaf Sandberg (1782–1863) to form a Society for the Study of Art, in opposition to the Swedish Royal Academy of Art, which railed against it. Fogelberg, however, who lived in the same house as Ling, escaped Karl Johan's disfavour. Indeed, the king himself, too, was soon smitten by Norse mythology, especially the fraudulent but cleverly contrived epic poem *Ossian*, in reality written by the eighteenth-century Scottish poet James Macpherson and based on ancient Irish Gaelic ballads. Along with many other admirers of *Ossian* throughout Europe, Karl Johan named his only son Oskar, after the son of the hero of the poem.

219 Bengt Erland Fogelberg, *Karl XIV Johan's Drinking Horn*, 1819, grey ink and brown wash.

220 Bengt Erland Fogelberg, *Odin*, 1818, plaster.

Norse subjects came to dominate the cultural world of Sweden, much as elsewhere in northern Europe. When the Gothic Society held a competition on a Nordic mythological theme, Fogelberg contributed three clay models, respectively of Odin, Thor and Freyr, as well as eight further drawings related to these subjects. A spring exhibition then followed eight days after Karl Johan's coronation, attracting the king's keen attention. Such an appreciation of Norse symbolism by a Swedish monarch was not new. Even Gustaf III had commissioned a theatrical work by Carl Gustaf Leopold (1756–1829), the Swedish Court Poet, on the subject of Odin which linked the Vasas to the Norse god. However, such imagery had left few permanent marks on the visual and decorative arts. This was to change and the king commissioned a drinking horn from Fogelberg depicting the meeting between Odin and the Swedish king Gylfe (illus. 219). This was just one of a number of innovative Norse pictorial and sculptural themes which other artists and craftsmen would take up for several decades to come.

Odin had been a heroic man, a native of Asia Minor, who had immigrated to the Nordic regions, and through his son Yngve Frey had established a new dynasty, based in Uppsala. This could, of course, be seen as an allegory for Karl Johan himself, an immigrant from the south who was establishing a new and powerful dynasty. So pleased was the king with the subject and its dynastic allegorical symbolism, that he soon commissioned the Swedish painter Pehr Hörberg (1746–1816) to produce a painting upon this theme, a subject also taken up by the now elderly Elias Martin. As late as 1828, the king commissioned the artist Hjalmar Mörner to produce a frieze on this and other subjects related to Odin, for the walls of the Red Salon at Rosendals Palace, which he did to considerable acclaim.[26]

In the medium of sculpture, Karl Johan became intensely interested in the final form his alter ego, Odin, would take. In 1826, therefore, the king specifically requested that the realization of Fogelberg's sculptures be done such that *Odin* (carried out 1828–31; illus. 220) be larger than life, while his *Plaster cast of Thor* (1818) and *Plaster cast of Freyr* (1818) were to be life-size. He also wanted Odin to represent a warrior-king, standing with a lance and shield even though Fogelberg had preferred a rather different pose.[27] The fact that Fogelberg used classical forms and poses, albeit with Old Norse attire, for his sculptures, in no way disturbed the king's sensibilities. It was the allegorical significance rather than the actual historical realism of the depiction which was of interest for Karl Johan. So pleased was the king with his flattering sculpture that he rewarded Fogelberg with an appointment as Court Sculptor, despite his former associations with those, like Von Breda, out of political favour.

Tsar Alexander I's Imperial Vision for Finland

Though in 1809 Finland's political jurisdiction was transferred from Sweden to Russia by the Treaty of Hamina, a neo-classical style of architecture continued to be employed to express monarchical authority, now that of Russia's Tsar Alexander I, Finland's grand-duke, instead of the Gustavian monarchs. Henceforth, Apollonian allegorical references were transferred to Alexander I (illus. 221), an Orthodox Russian who had willingly guaranteed Finland's long-established Lutheran Church and sworn to preserve its legal and landed system, in order to secure his primary goal of military control of the Gulf of Finland and Bothnia coast. Other changes, however, were in the offing.

Turku, the old capital of Finland, was abandoned as the seat of government in 1812 in favour of the small fishing village of Helsinki, a town of only 4,000 inhabitants. Originally established on small islands in the estuary of the Vantaa River, by order of King Gustaf Vasa by means of the enforced immigration of burghers from other Finnish towns, it had been re-situated directly on the coast in 1640 where it had shown itself vulnerable to the onslaughts of disease, especially plague in the early eighteenth century. However, its eastern geographical situation made it, at least theoretically, more susceptible to influences emanating from the imperial capital at St Petersburg, on the far eastern shore of the Gulf of Finland, a characteristic which made it of partic-

221 François Gérard(?), *Portrait of Alexander I*, c. 1814–15, oil.

ular appeal to the tsar as his grand-duchy's new capital. Since Helsinki had suffered a disastrous fire in 1808, the need for reconstruction and development provided a marvellous opportunity for the architectural expression of Russian imperialism on a grand scale, made possible by appropriate finances out of the imperial coffers.

In 1811, the tsar was already contemplating a plan for the monumental re-development of Helsinki as part of a clear imperial vision. To this end, a rigidly rectangular Senate Square was designed with the Senate House to the east, the governor-general's residence to the west and a grand-ducal palace dominating the whole square to the north-east, thereby creating an architectural unity of great symbolic import: the cohesion of Finland with the Russian Empire despite its legal autonomy.[28] In this Alexander I had astutely anticipated Victor Hugo's remark that 'not only the form of buildings but also the site chosen for them revealed the idea which they represented'.[29]

An early plan for the new capital was drawn by the Finnish Swede Johan Albrecht Ehrenström (1762–1847), who had been cabinet secretary at the court of Gustaf III in Stockholm. Charges of conspiracy after the king's assassination had almost cost him his head but he was eventually pardoned and returned to Finland. There, after its transfer to Russia, and with the support of the Finnish governor-general, Fabian Steinheil, he produced his designs for a new St Petersburg in miniature, a model neo-classical city, in which Alexander I's munificence as an enlightened grand-duke would be obvious to all. At first, he envisaged a Senate Square on which the tsar's Grand Ducal Palace would be situated. However, in his final plan this building was excluded from what was to become Helsinki's central and most prominent square. The Russian governor-general's residence remained on the square, but a new Finnish Senate House was to be constructed to the east, and the new arrangement would emphasize Finnish autonomy rather than Russian imperial integration. The commanding position would be filled on the northern side by a great Finnish Lutheran church, another symbol of Finland's autonomy from Orthodox Russia.[30]

Carl Ludwig Engel

222 Johan Erik Lindh, *Carl Ludwig Engel*, c. 1830, oil on canvas.

To carry out these grand designs, respectful of Finnish autonomy, the tsar chose the most fashionable architect active in St Petersburg, Carl Ludwig Engel (1778–1840), depicted here in a portrait by Johan Erik Lindh (1793–1865) a Swedish artist who had immigrated to Finland (illus. 222). A native of Berlin, Engel had been a student at the Bauakademie (Academy of Architecture) there at the beginning of the nineteenth century, about the same time as the innovative German architect Karl Friedrich Schinkel; indeed, both of them studied under the powerful influence of Friedrich Gilly's strict neo-classical aesthetic, which Engel took closer to heart than Schinkel, who was more interested in the Gothic.

Engel had settled in St Petersburg in 1814 as an architect in the imperial service and soon earned the tsar's admiration for his monumental neo-classical architectural vision. With his encouragement, he travelled to Helsinki and gained the sturdy support of Ehrenström whose earlier plan for a new city centre was to remain basic to the layout of the new grand-ducal capital. Inspired by the designs and writings of Stuart and Revett in their innovative Hellenophile work *The Antiquities of Athens*, Engel much more strictly adhered to classical forms and elements than did his contemporary Schinkel in Berlin, whose lack of orthodoxy, on occasion, he criticized.[31] Image, rather than function, was paramount in Engel's architectural designs. Even his design for a post office at Eckerö, on the Åland Islands, a Swedish-speaking outpost of the tsar's grand-duchy opposite the coast of Sweden, had an elegant Greek-inspired neo-classical façade, which for both the tsar and Engel was important monarchical symbol, even on this isolated and sparsely populated Baltic island group.[32]

Residence of the Governor-General

Engel's first commission in Helsinki was to provide plans for a suitably grand residence for the tsar's appointed representative, the governor-general. In the end, for a variety of practical reasons, another residence, The Bock House, already situated in the south-eastern corner of the square, was enlarged in 1817, by the addition of a floor, with balcony, and a diminutive portico of four Ionic columns to add dignity to the otherwise discrete façade. A ballroom was also provided. Finished and decorated by 1818, it provided an excellent stage for the arrival of tsar Alexander himself on his name-day, 11 September 1819.[33] He appeared on the balcony to great popular acclaim and devoted a not inconsiderable portion of his time in Helsinki to considering Engel's plans for his new grand ducal capital, down to the smallest detail, in numerous designs and discussions.

The Military School for Orphaned Children

First the tsar commissioned the erection of colonnaded accommodation for guards on the Senate Square. Then he ordered the construction of a military school, the so-called Kantonist School (now the Medical Clinic). Such military schools for orphans were very important institutions throughout the Russian Empire between 1758 and 1856, for they provided highly civilized, if austere, homes for male orphans over the age of eight, in which training for military careers was provided free of charge. Raised at the expense of the state and educated for the army and navy, the boys received a through education in religion, grammar and geometry. Even drawing was taught and training provided on such martial musical instruments as the flute and drums. Most of the boys resided in the school itself, but some were accommodated within private families. For those unsuitable for a military career, apprenticeships as cooks, tailors and shoemakers were available to satisfy the ancillary needs of the military.

Such institutions were central to the tsar's social and architectural vision throughout his empire because of their military usefulness. It was, thus, only fit that Engel's school was to be built on a large scale, one which would accommodate 300 boys from all over Finland. With conscious symbolism it was situated in a street celebrating the union of Finland and Russia, in the heart of Helsinki, just off Senate Square and elevated upon a small hill. By 1824, the two-storeyed building was complete, a mere four years after the original plan had been drawn and a clear indication of the priority its construction was given by the tsar.

223 K. A. Scheele after Gustaf Wilhelm Finnberg, *The Ruins of Turku*, 1827, lithograph.

Helsinki University

For Alexander, academia offered similar scope for an expression of imperial power and magnanimity. A fire which devastated Turku in 1827, the aftermath of which is illustrated in *The Ruins of Turku* (1827), by the Finnish artist Gustaf Wilhelm Finnberg (1784–1833; illus. 223), destroyed 786 buildings. This provided an excellent reason for re-establishing Finland's only university, that of Turku, first established in 1640, in Helsinki. Yet the grounds for such a move were political rather than dictated by physical necessity; the old university building, though damaged, had survived the fire, while Engel's own astronomical observatory, only opened in 1819, and medical clinic were totally unscathed. However, the tsar wanted Finland's academic elite, as well as the seat of government, to be situated more closely within his own geographical orbit, away from a city so strongly linked to Sweden. Therefore, of all Finland's leading institutions, only the episcopal seat of the Lutheran Church in Finland was allowed to remain in Turku.

Inaugurated in 1832 and situated on a site originally intended by Ehrenström for the Governor's Residence, the façade of the new university building was given by Engel the character of a temple of Apollo, with restrained Greek character. The more opulent Roman style was reserved for the façade of the true seat of political forces in Finland, the Senate House.[34] The Ionic columns used for the university were modelled on those of the Erechtheum, on the Acropolis in

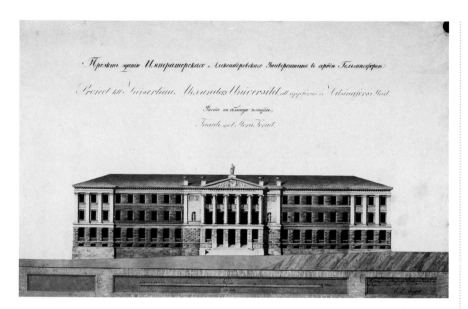

224 Carl Ludwig Engel, *The Final Design for the Imperial Alexander University in Helsinki*, 1828, drawing.

Athens, probably built by the renowned architect Mnesicles in the fifth century BC. Engel had, of course, never visited Greece (few architects at the time had) but he was deeply influenced by Greek architecture, as seen in his drawings (illus. 224). Its position adjacent to the projected Great Church of St Nicholas was well considered. Processions between the university and church, the site of much university ceremonial, could proceed with considerable ease and a minimum of disruption under the gaze of the Senate House across the square.

The interior of the university is formally and symmetrically arranged around a central axis. An external range of steps leads into a large vestibule, which resembles an atrium, the loggia-like corridors on two levels decorated with Doric columns and friezes. This is an arrangement clearly derived from the Thrasyllus Monument in Athens which was destroyed during the Ottoman bombardment of 1826, but illustrated in Stuart and Revett's *The Antiquities of Athens*. The vestibule, in turn, opens on to the great ceremonial hall in which the principal functions of the university are still held. Decorated with Corinthian columns, this vast room, shaped in the form of a Roman amphitheatre, accommodated a bronze bust of Alexander in the garb of a Roman emperor, by the Russian sculptor Ivan Martos, rector of the St Petersburg Academy of Arts. For all its classical references, however, there was a far more recent prototype for the university's architectural layout, from which Engel took inspiration: Moscow University where Domenico Gilardi had used a similar arrangement (later renovated by M. F. Kazakov).

Helsinki University Library

The establishment of the new university also required the establishment of a new library, but the ever present risk of fire and memory of the conflagration in Turku required great safety measures. Therefore, a decision was taken to house the new library separately from the rest of the university. Situated adjacent to the great

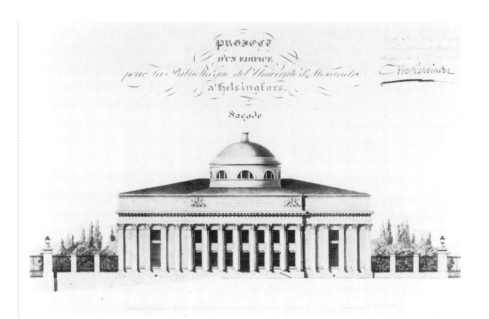

225 Carl Ludwig Engel, *Proposal for the Alexander University Library*, 1833.

church on its east–west axis, it is just off the Senate Square, next to the main university building to the south and the Kantonist School to the north. Together their attenuated façades of over 300 metres give a majestic appearance to Union Street and one suitable for the tsar's Finnish capital.

226 Carl Ludwig Engel, *Principal reading room of the Alexander University Library*, 1833.

The new library can be seen in a drawing by Engel, *Proposal for the Alexander University Library* (1833; illus. 225). The exterior has been carried out in a Roman style. The interior space reinterprets a Roman bath to provide accommodation for over 100,000 volumes, as well as readers and staff. One of the two large reading rooms, with magnificent interior colonnades, can be seen in illustration 226. Situated on either side of a central hall, each was heated in the latest fashion with mechanical apparatuses in the cellars, from which hot air rose into the rooms above, the same solution to heating difficulties which had already been implemented in the main university building.

Here, too, in the new University Library, the tsar took a keen if not intrusive interest in its form and decoration. Engel had been obliged to produce a series of different solutions and Alexander chose the one he himself preferred, even though it was Engel's least favourite.

The Senate House of Helsinki

Engel was given a freer rein with the Senate House which was finally built, between 1822 and 1828, according to his designs as illustrated in *A View of the Principal Façade of the Senate House* (illus. 227). Built on three floors, the façade was richly embellished with the grandest of the classical orders, the Corinthian. The oval throne room was also adorned with Corinthian columns, which formed a half circle at either end and provided a commanding view over Senate Square. Though its ornate Italianate classical decoration has a certain affinity to the works of the Italian architect, Carlo Rossi, who was active in St Petersburg at this time, the three wings of lesser height decorated with Ionic pilasters, and two corner pavilions, obviously strive for a more strict Greek neo-classical correctness.

227 Carl Ludwig Engel, *A View of the Principal Façade of the Senate House*, 1822–8, drawing.

On the other hand, the Pantheon in Rome clearly inspired both the façade and crowning cupola of the building.[35] Engel incorporated his own individuality of thought into the structure and design, even though the original spatial plan was provided by Ehrenström. He included a library, since destroyed, in the East Wing of the Senate House, with no obvious choice of classical prototype. Innovative despite his classical architectural grammar, Engel chose his inspiration from the Baths of Diocletian, a building which, according to tradition, contained books as well as baths.[36] This meant that even the form and spatial arrangements of the library, including its tunnel vault, could express the tsar's desire for a Roman imperial reference.

Military Establishments

The tsar gave his attention to other buildings of importance, especially military ones and attentively followed Engel's progress in their regard. The Military Barracks in Helsinki were vital for the maintenance of public order and defence of the realm in the capital and Engel was therefore particularly lavish in the architectural form and decoration of this monumental building, respectfully situated at a slight distance from the Senate Square. Internally, the principal rooms of these barracks are decorated with military images, including weapons and armour, unequivocally alluding to the function of the building. Externally, using the classical Roman prototype of the Doric order for such a monumental masculine edifice, Engel provided a portico of eight monumental columns, like that chosen by G. Quarenghi for the Italian architect's imposing architectural masterpiece, the Smolna Institute, in St Petersburg.

Engel also designed the residence for the Russian commander of the military division based in Helsinki, built 1822–5, on the southern side of the Esplanade, a great tree-lined avenue designed by Engel, near Senate Square. Built on two floors, work rooms for both the commander and his household were situated on the lower level, with representational and residential rooms above, including an Orthodox chapel.

After the office of military division commander was eliminated in 1840, as part of an imperial administrative reorganisation, the former residence assumed even greater importance as the new seat of the governor-general in Finland. The first incumbent to stay there was Prince Alexander Mensjikov, normally resident in St Petersburg, on his rare visits to Helsinki; however, others such as the later native-born governor-general Alexander Amatus Thesleff actually lived there on a regular basis.

The Esplanade and Boulevard

As a unifying feature of the tsar's grand architectural scheme for Helsinki, Engel's esplanade linked the harbour to the old part of the city, while it underscored the separation of the area around the Senate Square, to the north, from the barracks to the south. Planted with trees along its length and laid out with extensive lawns in 1824, it was ideal for the smarter residences which Engel began to build. These included the two-storeyed Sundman house, which, despite otherwise ornate decoration, remained unadorned by any columns. For Engel, the use of such features, however humble the classical order chosen, were unseemly for the residence of a merchant; columns were to be reserved for the residences of those of noble office or with high public functions, not for use by those engaged in trade.

Initially, all these new buildings were intended to be built of stone, but in Finland, with its abundance of relatively inexpensive wood, this proved to be an impossible demand. Thus, even Engel's theatre, built in 1826–7 at the eastern end of the Esplanade, was constructed of wood, painted yellow. With space to accommodate 400 spectators, it had a traditional horseshoe shaped auditorium, with loges arranged symmetrically on the sides. Two small side wings contained a buffet and cloakroom, respectively, with all but the latter totally unheated.

Another tree-lined avenue, the Boulevard, laid out to the west of the Esplanade provided the setting for Engel's own residence, an elegant, dignified but restrained house on the western outskirts of the capital.

The Astronomical Observatory

The transfer of Finland's only university to Helsinki from Turku meant that scientific buildings with highly specialized purposes, like the Astronomical Observatory, also had to be built anew. Engel collaborated on this with the eminent professor Friedrich Wilhelm Argelander (1799–1875), who provided him with details on the practical requirements of the Observatory, as well as lengthy discussions on how best to achieve them. Such continental observatories as those at Göttingen, in Germany, and Dorpat (Tartu), in Estonia, then under Russian hegemony, with long elevations stretching from east to west, had provided prototypes for the one at Turku and did so again at Helsinki. The observatory has a commanding view over the city, prominent with its three revolving towers. The central elevation included residential rooms for the director, as well as a work room, with the 'meridian' room to the west and a lecture room to the east. For reasons of economy, costly items such as the granite pillars which had supported the astronomical instruments in Turku were removed to Helsinki where they were re-used for the same purpose. For all its technical usefulness, however, the Observatory served another function: it was a symbol of the tsar's beneficence to the sciences in his new Grand Duchy. As if punctuating this point, an oil-soaked cloth would be regularly raised above the central tower, to be ignited at precisely twelve o'clock, the measure of time for all subjects in view by land or sea.[37]

The Old Church of Helsinki

In religious matters, Alexander I had agreed to respect the established Lutheran church of Finland, despite his own growing personal commitment to Russian Orthodoxy. It was thus a Protestant, rather than an Orthodox, church which became the centrepiece of his architectural vision for the Senate Square and the rest of the centre of Helsinki. But long before such a project could be contemplated, it was necessary to build a smaller church as a substitute for a previous one on the Senate Square site which had been removed during the course of redevelopment. To fulfil this short-term need, The Old Church, as it is now known, was built and still survives. Designed by Engel in 1824, its construction was completed by the end of 1826 on a Greek cross pattern, usual for Orthodox churches, but with the external appearance of a traditional Lutheran church, as if it had a long nave. Tunnel-vaulted and furnished with objects salvaged from the old demolished Ulrika Eleonora Church, it was one of the largest wooden structures in Finland at the time. Situated in open countryside beyond the limits of the old town, the classical Tuscan order was chosen as suitable for both its rustic geographical position and humble temporary function. A funerary chapel was also conceived by Engel in the park of the church, as an architectural foil to the church itself, its sombre neo-classical form and decoration reflecting that of the Old Church.

The Great Church of St Nicholas

As early as 1819, Engel commenced work on various designs for the new Great Church, though the episcopal seat of the Lutheran Archbishop in Finland remained at Turku. Although one design was chosen by the tsar in 1822, building work did not start until 1830, the third centenary year of the proclamation of the Augsburg Confession, and was completed only in 1852, during the reign of Alexander's brother and heir, Nicholas I (1796–1855), long after the death of Engel. To Nicholas, for whom St Petersburg's own Senate Square had dreadful associations (the Decembrist uprising in 1825 had erupted against him there and was only crushed with great force), it was particularly important that the Senate Square in Helsinki be associated with the magnanimity of the Russian Imperial house, rather than its military might and, to this end, particular care and resources were lavished upon the Great Church (now the Cathedral of Helsinki).

228 Carl Ludwig Engel, *The West Façade of the Great Church of St Nicholas* (now Cathedral Church of Helsinki; 1830–52), *c.* 1818–27, drawing.

It can be seen, as finally built in illustration 228. Engel drew eclectically upon classical Roman and Renaissance architectural ideals, fused to the modern ecclesiastical architectural solutions current in the best early nineteenth-century architecture of St Petersburg. Though he was no admirer of the Greek cross plan, he employed it so as to be able to crown the church with a great cupola, visible from far and wide. The iconostasis which embellished many Russian Orthodox churches had produced in Engel a powerful emotional effect and he wished initially to include one in the Great Church, though this was never realized. The guards' accommodation on the north side of the square was eliminated, thereby heightening the harmonious integration of the church with the Senate Square, the Senate House and the University.

For all its antique classical features, it included among its most technically advanced innovations a form of central heating, using cast iron stoves located in the cellars, which gave off hot air led by pipes directly into the church. Moreover, the plaster which covered the walls of the church was made of hydraulic chalk, a type of cement which Engel felt would serve to better preserve the fabric of the building against the onslaughts of the intense cold and damp of a Helsinki winter. Similarly, the capitals of the columns and pillars, as elsewhere in Engel's work, were made of plaster and processed with the aid of oil, making it more durable than stone, despite its seemingly fragile composition. Cast iron or granite was usually used for the bases of columns, though use of brick was sometimes made for the construction of the joists and tympanum because of economic constraints and the need to save on labour. Even so the average working day for the labourers, generally Russian, was an arduous fourteen hours.[38]

Though the Great Church became the supreme symbol of Alexander I's imperial vision for his Finnish capital, not all Finns were pleased by its image or symbolism. For Zacharias Topelius (1818–1898), the great Finnish national romantic literary figure of the nineteenth century, the church remained 'a chicken, in possession of neither wings nor a tail'. Indeed, for Topelius, the architectural vision of the Russian tsar was little more than bourgeois, if a comparison were made with such Gustavian commissions as the old university in Turku or the justice building in Vasa.[39]

The Holy Trinity Russian Orthodox Church

Respect for the established church of Sweden did not, of course, prevent the tsar from commissioning the construction of a Russian Orthodox church. Obviously, with an influx, albeit limited, of Russian administrators and courtiers, a suitable Orthodox church was needed. The tsar therefore commissioned the building of the Orthodox Holy Trinity Church, which was situated behind the Great Church and opposite the Kantonist School. It was completed in stone in 1826. With its long nave, it resembled more a Lutheran church than an Orthodox one and was surmounted by a wooden tower to the east, later replaced by one of stone in 1898. Decorated by pilasters and crowned in the Baroque fashion initiated by Andreyan D. Zakharov's Admiralty Building in St Petersburg, it had a much smaller cylindrical tower to the west which took its inspiration from Domenico Trezzini's Peter and Paul Church in the Russian capital. Two small pavilions on either side (later removed) flanked the steps leading up to the church. This arrangement was also to be employed at St Nicholas, where separate pavilions were eventually situated on either side, above the grand flight of steps rising up from the Senate Square.

The Assembly Hall

Engel also produced designs for the Casino (later to become the City Hall), in 1814. Situated by the market, at the entrance to the harbour, the imposing neo-classical building was the first vision of Helsinki to greet a maritime visitor. It included not only the casino itself, for the amusement of gentrified residents and visitors, but also a restaurant, hotel accommodation and ballroom. Originally planned on four floors, it was finally built on only two levels, the lower of which is rusticated, with a relatively austere façade above, decorated by pilasters, which congregate in the centre and at either end.

Another Assembly House was built near the far end of the Esplanade and completed the architectural unity. It opened in 1832, having been paid for by public subscription four years earlier. Normally commencing at half past six in the evening and continuing until eleven, such assemblies were accompanied by music and dancing, for which entertainment guests paid the sum of two and a half rubles.[40] One of the most magnificent integrated neo-classical urban building schemes in Europe, a crowning glory in architectural terms for Finland's imperial grand-duke, had finally been accomplished.

European Arctic Hegemony: Scandinavian Overseas Colonies in the Far North

Norse Iceland and Greenland

To understand many aspects of life in Iceland and Greenland, where old traditions persisted longer than elsewhere in the Nordic world, a knowledge of their early colonization during the Middle Ages is required. In fact, Scandinavian links with Iceland began between 870 and 930, when the island was colonized, largely by Norsemen from the western parts of Norway. According to tradition and an early text of *Navagatio Sancti Brendani Abbatis* (800 AD), Irish monks had already visited Iceland by the end of the eighth century.[1] They fled before the arrival of the Vikings, who were accompanied by others from what are today Denmark and Sweden, and also by immigrants from Ireland and the western isles of Scotland, as both the medieval *Landnámabók* and modern genetic research into blood distribution groups confirms.[2] Patterns of social life, however, seem to have been based on those of Scandinavia rather than Ireland as was the domestic architecture, which persisted well into the modern period.

According to archaeological investigations and literary descriptions, the Viking long-houses, known as 'skali' or 'eldaskáli' (indicating the presence of a fireplace), were frequently up to 30 metres in length and six metres in width. Arranged longitudinally, the interior of such a house often contained two rows of posts supporting the roof and dividing the interior space into three aisles, the central one of which contained the fireplace and was the largest. Along the walls, a 'set' or narrow elevated floor provided space for sleeping and sitting. By contrast with the rest of Scandinavia, this architectural tradition was of extremely long duration and persisted in Iceland throughout the Middle Ages and into the eighteenth century.

During the early settlement period, Iceland's population grew to more than 20,000 and, within a century, the island had become a stopping-off point for those who proceeded on to Greenland.[3] The earliest Norse settlers in Greenland, about 500 in number, had first arrived with Erik the Red in 985, principally from Iceland and Norway, and they established themselves in two colonies.[4] One was in the north-west near present day Godthåb (Nuuk), and consisted of at least 190 farms, twelve churches and two monasteries. The other was further south and east at Julianehåb, and was smaller, with 90 farms and only four churches.[5] There the settlers lived by fishing, animal husbandry and the export of walrus ivory, among other pursuits. Walrus ivory was also used locally and it provided the head of the bishop of Gardar's crosier, now in the National Museum in Copenhagen.

229 Cornelis Claesz far
Wieringen, *Dutch Whaling
Station on Jan Mayen*, c. 1620,
oil on canvas.

As the colony thrived and its population grew to some 3000, its importance to the mother country increased and what had begun as an independent settlement became fully incorporated into the Norwegian kingdom in 1261.[6] In return for acceptance by the Greenlanders of the Norwegian king's right of taxation, he, in turn, ensured that a life-line to the colony was maintained through the annual vessel from Norway which carried much-needed iron, wood and other goods, necessary to keep the colony afloat.

In the following centuries plagues and an increasingly colder climate, along with Inuit attacks, decimated the population. In 1379, an Inuit assault destroyed the settlement at Godthåb, while European contact with the settlement at Julianehåb appears to have ceased in 1408, possibly for similar reasons. By the sixteenth century, the Norse population, totally cut off from Europe, had become extinct. It was said that the forced landing of a Norwegian merchant ship on Greenland in the 1530s discovered the body of a man of Nordic appearance, holding the remains of a well-used knife. The wreckage of a Greenlandic Norse boat was also found, inscribed with the motto, 'often was I weary when I pulled thee', perhaps the final written legacy of the old Norse population in Greenland.[7] It has even been suggested that what remained of the Norse population may have moved to Newfoundland. Whatever the truth, memories of the ancient mercantile ties which had bound Greenland to Europe led to their revival later among princes, courtiers and merchants eager for profit.

Contacts and Exploitation of the Nordic Islands of the High Arctic

Through the impetus of mercantile expansionism in the seventeenth century, a European presence once again began to make itself felt in Greenland. Christian IV, having brought Denmark to the height of her political power, was keen to revive trade with the western reaches of his dominions. These had been under the Danish crown since 1389, when Norway's former territories, including Iceland and Greenland, were incorporated into Denmark. The benefits of gold mining in the Spanish Main were a source of great wealth for the king of Spain, and the king of Denmark, too, was keen to exploit any such mineral resource in his own territory, however remote. He commissioned expeditions to explore these regions, but ones which might also exploit the rich whale stocks, important for the production of oil, in Arctic waters, even if gold were not found.

First the English and then the Dutch proved themselves particularly successful in developing whaling as a profitable enterprise, especially in the seas round the previously uninhabited Arctic island of Jan Mayen. Claimed by Denmark as a Norwegian dependent territory, it became a successful whaling station, as shown in Cornelis Claesz far Wieringen's *Dutch Whaling Station on Jan Mayen* (c. 1620; illus. 229). A typical Arctic scene is depicted with tents made of wood and large pieces of canvas which were so characteristic of an early European whaling station. Though there were, of course, no trees on Jan Mayen, driftwood from Siberia and elsewhere was relatively abundant along the coast.[8] Ovens for the processing of whale blubber can be seen in the background. By the middle of the century, whale stocks in the region were exhausted and ships were obliged to plough the seas further and further north in pursuit of their prey.

In the High Arctic, it was the Dutch, rather than the Norsemen or Danes, who first made their presence felt. The Dutch captain Willem Barentsz, who later left his name to the straits between Alaska and Siberia, is famous for his vainglorious but failed attempt to find a north-west passage to the Orient, and in so doing came upon uninhabited Bear Island and Svalbard. Other visitors included Basques who were frequently employed as harpooners and flensing masters (who stripped off the whale blubber), but as the whales in coastal regions grew more scarce, both they and the Dutch increasingly abandoned their whaling stations.

Others, however, especially Russians, who travelled to these northern parts in pursuit of walruses whose blubber, oil, tusks and leather were such valued commodities at home, had a more lasting presence. These 'pomors', as the visitors were called, were largely the descendants of medieval immigrants from Central Russia who had settled in the coastal regions of the White Sea as hunters and farmers. Financed by mercantile or ecclesiastical bodies, such as the Solovetsk monastery near the White Sea Coast, they usually travelled in their open sailboats or 'lodyas', departing in July by way of the Norwegian port of Vardø. About 50 days later their ships would return home, occasionally leaving hunting parties to overwinter in Svalbard. These early temporary colonists used driftwood and other local materials to construct their primitive huts, sanctified by the characteristic Orthodox crosses, up to five metres in height (a few of which survive today), which were erected nearby.[9] Though their heyday was in the eighteenth century, the pomors continued to be active in Svalbard well into the early years of the nineteenth century.

The Moscovy Company, under the helm of an Englishman, Stephen Bennet, was the major exploiter of the region. With more than 600 walruses killed by his party in just one day in 1606, stocks were exhausted within a few years.[10] Whales, however, continued to abound, encouraging greater numbers of whaling ships to visit the region. As a result, by the 1620s, a de facto division of the islands into national spheres had occurred. This political and social arrangement was to have great implications for the future, especially in Svalbard, where such a condominium persisted well into the twentieth century. The Dutch-controlled north-western corner, Amsterdamöya, became the site of the region's largest whaling station, appropriately named Smeerenburg, 'blubber town'. It had about twenty buildings, most of which were used for the processing of blubber, though some accommodated 200 or so men who populated the settlement at any one time. These would have come from a local maritime population in the Svalbard region of about 12,000 men, sailing on as many as 300 ships. Only a fraction of these ships would have been in harbour at any one time, for this was a seasonal industry, with sailors and hunters generally returning to Europe for the winter. Some Russian hunters had over-wintered in 1630–31, but an expedition there three years later met with disaster and similar attempts in following decades were largely abandoned. As the century progressed, more efficient techniques of whaling and flensing moved the industry offshore. However, its success led to ever greater exploitation, so that, by the end of the seventeenth century, whaling stocks were vastly reduced and Smeerenburg too was largely abandoned.[11]

Renewed Contacts between Greenland and Denmark

An interest was also growing for the economic exploitation of Greenland and the quest for a shorter sea route to the Orient. In 1619, the Danish aristocrat Jens Munk had sailed with two ships and 64 men to Hudson Bay, by way of Greenland, with the hope of establishing a north-west passage to India. The expedition was a disaster, and all but Munk and two seamen died. Munk produced an account of his exploratory voyage, *Navigato Septentrionalis* in 1624, with woodcuts of his encounters with the natives in Canada, and the death of some of crew members by scurvy. This helped to awaken a considerable interest in the economic exploitation of the far north, not least at Court. Christian IV was very keen to find means of satisfying his growing financial needs, but he was to be deeply disappointed with the economic benefits of his maritime forays into Greenland. None the less, an anthropological interest in the exotic natives discovered took his imagination, which, indirectly, led to the capture, quite literally, of some unfortunate Greenlanders encountered by the Danish sailors while exploring parts of the vast island: five native Inuit kidnapped by the king's explorers were taken to Denmark, where they aroused immense curiosity at Court. *Two Women and a Girl from Greenland with the Dutchman David Danell* (1654; see illus. 244) depicts the four captives who survived the journey with the expedition's leader and is the first painting ever made of indigenous Greenlanders. They are portrayed in their native attire, along with a number of their hunting accoutrements. Such exotic subjects whetted the king's appetite to explore further his *terra incognita*. Therefore, another expedition the following year was undertaken, which returned to Denmark with a further three Inuit. However, neither gold nor other resources suitable for exploitation were discovered and Greenland was quickly dropped from the king's vision of economic gain. As a result, for more than half a century further contact between Denmark and Greenland once again ceased.

Iceland and Denmark in the Early Modern Period

By contrast to Greenland and Denmark, contacts between Iceland and the mother country were maintained throughout the Middle Ages and into the modern period. However, Iceland suffered a severe demographic decline, especially after the Black Death ravaged the island in 1402, reducing the population within two years to only about 40,000 people.[12]

In economic and social terms, life in Iceland remained fairly static throughout this long period, a characteristic which Icelandic architecture also reflected. The influence of certain Greenlandic architectural features in Iceland remained and even spread long after the demise of the Norse inhabitants of Greenland. Passageways in domestic architecture, common in Greenland, for example, had probably been introduced to the north of Iceland in the thirteenth century and sometime between 1450 and 1550 they became common in domestic architecture throughout Iceland. According to this arrangement, the old heated, sauna-like bathroom or 'baðstofa' and sitting room or 'stofa' were situated opposite the kitchen, pantry and general sleeping room or 'skáli', a name formerly signifying the old Viking long-house. This proved an extremely functional arrangement and was in use almost everywhere in Iceland by the early eighteenth century. The bathroom, however, had largely fallen out of use by the sixteenth century because an increasingly colder climate and the almost total elimination of native forests meant that wood was no longer available as a heating material. This meant, in turn, that the heating of the oven was reserved only for the most severe weather, and the oven itself was removed to a special new stove room or 'ofnhús'. By the sixteenth century, the old bathroom became a multi-purpose room where the residents could sit, dine or work. In more prosperous houses the original sitting room became a special chamber for the celebrating of feasts and other important events, but in humbler households it disappeared altogether. Other rooms remained unchanged and the sleeping room continued to accommodate most of the inhabitants of a farmhouse, though the farmer and his wife would often have their own bedroom.[13]

For the royal Danish coffers, Iceland continued to be an economic drain. Occasional incursions by Barbary pirates exerted their toll on the king's finances, for Christian IV had to expend considerable financial resources in order to ransom several thousand Icelanders kidnapped by pirates based in Tunis during the early seventeenth century.[14] However, there was a gradual realization with the dawn of the eighteenth century that the situation in Iceland had reached a desperate stage. A General Census of Iceland's population was taken in 1703 which showed that the island had a population of about 50,000. It had been commissioned by the Danish government in Copenhagen, in response to a petition from emissaries from Iceland to the Danish king, eager to find means of ameliorating the appalling economic conditions, exacerbated by the monopolistic trading company which controlled Iceland's foreign trade, a situation further aggravated by a terrible famine the year before which had carried off thousands of Icelanders. As a result, two prominent men, Árni Magnússon, a noted collector of manuscripts of the ancient Icelandic sagas, and a leading man of law Páll Vídalín, were commissioned to investigate matters. They discovered some surprising demographic information: in particular, they found that for every thousand females, there were only 832 males. For a country with little emigration and spared the devastation of war, this was a strange statistic, reflecting a great imbalance numerically between the sexes. They also found that the age of marriage for Icelanders was higher than that in the rest of contemporary northern Europe. For example, only 42.2 per cent of men and 32.9 per cent of women aged over twenty were married. No doubt the large servant class, forming about 20 per cent of the population over the age of fifteen, played a role in keeping these figures low, for the ownership of land was often a prerequisite

230 Lars Moller (Aqqaluk), *From the Dedication of the New Church in Sukkertoppen,* c. 1860, chromolithograph.

for entering marriage, a luxury no servants had. Since another 6,789 Icelanders, half of whom were under the age of 20, were reckoned as paupers, it was not surprising that many, a further 13.5 per cent of the entire population, were not in a position to marry.[15] This did not mean, however, that unmarried adult Icelanders were celibate, for cohabitation was a common practice, especially for those without a farm or other secure livelihood to sustain them. Nor did it mean that the children of unmarried couples were necessarily considered illegitimate, since the offspring of couples who were engaged were also deemed, for all intents and purposes, to be legitimate. But the statistics did demonstrate that all was not well in Iceland and remedies were sought.

However, despite the census and the measures taken by the Danish government to assist the island, conditions in Iceland hardly improved. Epidemics exerted their toll and natural disasters wrought enormous havoc. A volcanic eruption in the south near Öræfajökull, which persisted over a six-month period in 1727, resulted in lava flows and floods from melting ice. Not only did these destroy many farms, but they also ruined the grazing pastures upon which the sheep and ponies depended for their survival. This devastation was augmented two years later, when another volcano, Krafla, destroyed many farmsteads near

Mývatn. On the opposite side of the country, which had been spared these hardships, earthquakes took their own toll. In Rangárvellir, thirteen farms were totally ruined, while a further 40 were severely damaged.[16] It is thus not surprising that as a result of such devastations, an awareness of the latent power of volcanoes became forever embedded in the Icelandic mentality, an awareness even present in the muted depiction of *Mount Hekla* (1909) by Ásgrímur Jónsson (see illus. 247), who saw the volcano, formerly known as the 'Mountain of Hell' not merely as a natural phenomenon but as a spiritual presence of sublime and terrifying proportions. That he did so is not surprising since the 1,491 metre high volcano has erupted no less than fourteen times since the twelfth century, on occasion, as in 1766, with enormous loss of life.

The Recolonization of Greenland

By contrast with Iceland, Greenland, in the early eighteenth century, entered a period of sustained economic and demographic development, albeit with occasional terrifying setbacks. In 1721, the Norwegian Lutheran missionary Hans Egede (illus. 231) arrived in Greenland, with his wife Gudrun Rask, and instigated many changes. He had gone there as a missionary in order to bring the light of Protestant values to a Norse people, whom he feared were either wallowing in 'the darkness of Catholicism' or had relapsed into paganism; however, he failed to discover any living traces of the old inhabitants who had come from Iceland and Norway. None the less, he succeeded in establishing his own permanent settlement at Godthåb, building a small stone residence for himself and his family, and was soon followed by other Danes and Norwegians.[17] During the fifteen years he lived there he managed to establish a foothold of Lutheran Christian civilization in Greenland (illus. 230). This development continued under his son, Poul Egede, who carried on his father's missionary activities. To assist him, the younger Egede learned the Inuit Greenlandic language into which he translated the Bible, and through which he communicated to the natives, some of whom he encouraged to enter the Lutheran priesthood. Many native Inuit came under the influence of the established Lutheran church although, as the century wore on, the Moravians increasingly carried out missionary activities, building a mission station at Lichtenau with a stone rectory.[18]

231 *Hans Egede*, lithograph.

The lifestyle of native Greenlanders changed little at this time. They continued to occupy sparsely populated coastal villages, to hunt whales and seals from their umiaks and to fish from their kayaks, much in the way that they had done for centuries. These were all activities depicted by the elder Egede himself in such sketches as *Whaling and Seal Hunting amidst the Eskimos* (illus. 232).

232 Hans Egede, *Whaling and Seal Hunting amidst the Eskimos*, engraving.

The early Greenlanders who visited Denmark and elsewhere in Europe in the early eighteenth century remained a source of great interest. Elaborate festivities were sometimes held in their honour; occasions which could also be used to serve a mercantile purpose, for the exotic qualities of the Greenlanders could be used to attract money and personnel to various projected colonial enterprises in Greenland. This fascination with the exotic was mutual, for Denmark and the Danes were also most intriguing to early Greenlandic travellers. One young Greenlander, Poq, who visited Denmark in 1724–5, was profoundly taken by the Round Tower, in Copenhagen, which he likened to a mountain whose winding interior passage resembled the inside of a snail's shell. He is depicted with a fellow Greenlander in a portrait by Bernhard Grothschilling (1697–1776), *Poq and Qiperoq* (1724) (illus. 233), painted the year both voluntarily travelled to Denmark. They are shown shorn of their locks, the absence of which was a symbol of status in Denmark at that time, since it depicted them as gentlemen accustomed to wear the requisite wigs so necessary at court. Qiperoq is portrayed wearing European shoes of a medieval style, whereas Poq wears Inuit boots. Paraded throughout the city's canals on kayaks, they were made to fire upon ducks from these vessels, to the great entertainment of the public.[19] This pastime can be seen in a contemporary drawing, *Greenland Cavalcade* (1724), in which the vessels of the Greenlanders are joined by a cavalcade of boats and barges, decked out with sails depicting walruses, fish and other Greenlandic fauna (illus. 234).

Such impressions as the Greenlanders themselves gleaned of Europe resonated not only in their own native region of West Greenland but eventually even in remote East Greenland where in the local oral poetic story-telling images of Europe merged together with native Greenlandic elements from their epic, *Kigutikkaaq*.[20] These tales were sung again and again in the communal homes of the Inuit, who gradually altered them with the telling, through the centuries, as past impressions and the need for modern embellishments demanded.

233 Bernhard Grothschilling, *Poq and Qiperoq*, 1724, oil on canvas.

234 *Greenland Cavalcade*, 1724.

Rays of Light in a Time of Gloom: Iceland in the Eighteenth Century

From the 1750s, the Danish authorities in Iceland began construct important governmental buildings in stone, giving them a more authoritative and prominent profile. Of these, the oldest and most important was the new governor's residence, built in 1753 on the island of Viðey, adjacent to the new city of Reykjavik. However, with only modest funds allocated for this purpose, such official commissions were few and far between.

More common was the construction of new houses, especially for priests, who were usually the most prominent and prosperous members of their communities. Throughout the eighteenth century rectories in Iceland took much the form of the homes of wealthy farmers, based largely on the arrangement of the ridge-farmhouse or 'burstabær', which was focused around the central passage, still a dominant architectural feature, especially in the north of the country. Timber was used to clad the exterior walls, which were made of turf and stone, though in more humble homes no attempt was made to mask the bare turf walls.

Some architectural features, however, did change. For example, in the late eighteenth century the 'skáli' and 'stofa' were rearranged, so that their gables faced the front façade, instead of the sides, and the bathroom was relocated away from exterior walls into the centre of the house, where the heat of the stove could best be preserved, and its ceiling was lowered to facilitate this. This became the new all-purpose room for work, sleep, eating and recreation for most of the household. It also reflected the continuing material impoverishment which afflicted the country at this time.

In the south of Iceland, however, an innovative priest publicized in an Icelandic journal a new architectural arrangement which proved more suitable to the late eighteenth-century fashion for greater space and a larger number of rooms. In this plan, the bathroom was placed adjacent to the main entrance from which an entrance hall led to the kitchen, with other adjoining rooms leading to the 'stofa' or a pantry. The passage was truncated to provide space for three new rooms, with wooden gables projecting from the front façade. Turf and stone were readily available for construction, but wood was not and had to be imported, usually from Denmark, though driftwood, carried by the East Greenlandic current from Siberia to the shores of Iceland was also utilized. Interiors tended to be constructed in wood, in the fashion of Norwegian stave churches, with relatively elaborate carvings sometimes decorating the more prosperous houses.[21]

The second half of the eighteenth century in Iceland was, however, a period of almost unmitigated misery, though certain mercantile areas, like Flatey in the north-west, enjoyed some local prosperity. By the end of the century, the population had declined to a mere 40,000.[22] The volcano Katla erupted in 1755, devastating 63 farms. Then, in the 1760s, four-fifths of the stock of sheep was annihilated by a plague. These disasters were only overtures to a bigger catastrophe: the violent volcanic eruption of Laki in the south of the island, which commenced on Whitsunday in 1783, laying waste over 565 square kilometres, totally destroying two parishes and devastating pasture, animal husbandry and agricultural land, leaving a famine in its wake.[23] Governmental food relief was forthcoming, as was financial assistance, but less than a quarter of the funds accumulated reached those in need. The following year, an earthquake in the south destroyed more than 1,500 homes, including the ancient church and episcopal residence at Skálholt. The Lutheran bishop, Hannes Finnsson, then re-established his seat at Reykjavik, thereby enabling the small village, with a population of only about 150, to acquire the privileges of a city.[24]

At this time most male Icelanders, whether landowners or servants, were employed in agriculture. Potatoes were introduced in Sauðlauksdalur in 1760, and from 1771 reindeer were imported from Norway.[25] During the late winter and spring, many men fished for their livelihood, but the establishment of permanent fishing communities which could sustain relatively young married couples was not encouraged, since it was felt that fishing as a full-time occupation was too precarious for families to depend upon as a reliable source of income. Therefore, local authorities often prohibited migration to coastal areas of settlement and tried to limit opportunities for those wishing to contract marriages there, a state of affairs which persisted until 1880. This meant that fewer than 8 per cent of Icelanders lived in coastal towns or villages.[26]

The Danish king, however, who was consolidating his authority as absolute monarch, needed a native urban bureaucracy in Iceland to assist him, and increasingly urban growth was seen by the government as an essential part of this development. Reykjavik soon became the administrative capital of the island, bound to Copenhagen by an annual mail-boat from 1776, and attracted merchants and farmers as the years went by. It also became increasingly notorious for its drunken revelries in early summer, when fairs for the sale of wool or other commodities were held.

The wooden town houses built in the new capital were similar to the more prosperous Icelandic farmhouses. Shops and warehouses were also constructed by resident merchants, some of whom had moved there from Denmark. Two of the oldest of these wooden buildings, dating from the second half of the eighteenth century, are still to be found at Eyrarbakki and Isafjörður and are of so-called 'block-house' construction, made of timber hewn and cut in Denmark. Mainly single storey, they have sharply pitched roofs and exteriors covered in tar to protect against the elements. It was these houses, both in Reykjavik and elsewhere, which became the nuclei for the building of other residential areas. Later, the founding of a wool-processing factory in Reykjavik would also contribute to its growth and development.

The strict regulation of social life existing in Iceland at this time did not mean that the island possessed a rigid hierarchical society. On the contrary, great egalitarianism reigned both in the choosing of marriage partners and with respect to other practical social relations, well into the nineteenth century. One observer in the middle of the eighteenth century noted that even the Icelandic clergy are obliged to have recourse to manual labour for maintaining their families, or to go fishing like the common people'.[27] Even in the nineteenth centuries, the life of an Icelandic priest had changed little and the lives of these priests, like their rectories, continued to remain largely indistinguishable from those of the larger farmers.

Despite the harrowing events of the late eighteenth century in Iceland, some aspects of life improved. A more prosperous mercantile community on the island was encouraged by the abolition of the Danish trade monopoly in 1786. Henceforth, merchants resident in Iceland, virtually all of whom were Danes, could deal freely with their counterparts in both Denmark and Norway, even if not abroad. This led to an increase in the wealth and status of numerous villages, including Ísafjörður, Eyjafjörður, Reyðarfjördur, Grundarfjörður and Vestmannaeyjar. Foreign ships and traders, however, remained excluded from these benefits and most of the population continued to languish much as before.

Colonial Exploitation in Greenland in the Eighteenth Century

Though few immigrants came to Iceland during the course of the eighteenth century, more and more Danes and Norwegians, amongst them a considerable number of missionaries, did colonize the west coast of Greenland. In 1729 Governor Paars had envisaged the establishment of a populous colony of Europeans on the south-western side of Greenland, to be christened New Denmark and stretching from Godthåb, in the north, to Kap Farvel (Uummannarsuaq), in the south. With his vision of a hierarchical social system adopted in the new colony similar to that in Denmark, Paars conceived that noble proprietors from the home country would be granted land, to be tilled by European peasant farmers imported for that purpose. Paars was aware that not many Danish aristocrats would voluntarily forsake Copenhagen for the rocky and not so green fields of Greenland. However, his solution to this difficulty was ingenious; he would seek out those nobles who had fallen into disfavour at court for some misdeed. In order to exonerate themselves, he felt, they would be permitted to retire to the new colony, accompanied by their serfs and peasants retainers. An alternative plan conceived of immigrants made up of Danish prisoners transported to Greenland for their crimes.[28] Such visionary solutions, though, were never translated into reality and other solutions were sought by government administrators, based upon the economic realities demonstrated in Denmark's Caribbean colonies.

As commercial companies had been established in the Danish Virgin Islands, West Africa and India, so the Royal Greenland Trading Company was established to administer Greenland and, more importantly for its shareholders back in Denmark, to exploit it economically. The company's headquarters in Copenhagen can be seen in: *Greenland Trade Wharf* (1908) by Vilhelm Hammershøi (1864–1916; illus. 235), a majestic establishment which had been granted exclusive trading rights in Greenland, a monopoly it retained until the 1950s.

Administratively, Greenland was divided in 1782 into two regions with

235 Vilhelm Hammershøi, *Greenland Trade Wharf*, 1908, oil on canvas.

authority invested in inspectors, a political arrangement which mirrored the very different conditions of the north and south of the colony. Architecture was also different in the two regions. North of the present-day commune of Sisimiut, where native Inuit predominated, stone architecture developed from an ancient Inuit tradition of building houses of turf and stone for over-wintering. However, to the south, where Greenlanders increasingly had Danish antecedents, and where shared social values were more influenced by Danes, the architecture looked back to that of the old Norse period. In northern Greenland, the stone walls did not support the roofs, which sharply overhung the walls in order to protect them from the elements. In southern Greenland, however, the walls were firmly fixed to and supported the roof, by means of wooden anchors.[29] Such well-conceived houses reflected the expectations of the growing numbers of Europeans who immigrated to this Arctic frontier region and the European tone of the communities.

By 1785, the Royal Greenlandic Trading Company employed some 174 Europeans, mainly Danes and Norwegians, but only 31 native Greenlanders. Most of the Europeans were engaged in a variety of occupations, including trade and administrative work. However, according to the statistics of 1793, only 34 of them were engaged in missionary activity by the established Lutheran church, who were themselves, in turn, assisted by six native Greenlanders. To these numbers must be added Moravian missionaries, as well as the wives and children of the missionaries, merchants and administrators who accompanied them, which made the total of Europeans in the region at this time approximately 250, or 4 per cent of the entire Greenlandic population. By comparison, native Greenlanders made up a total of about 6,000.[30]

Unlike their Norse predecessors who lived in stone houses, the Europeans were mainly accommodated in wooden houses. Wood was a precious commodity in Greenland, but the preferred material for building, and continued an architectural tradition with which the Norwegians of the colony felt at home. By contrast, stone buildings were damp and cold, and the use of turf to insulate their exteriors made them unhygienic and difficult to keep in good order.[31]

The growth of the whaling industry in the late eighteenth century and an increase in number of whaling stations in Greenland encouraged colonists, all requiring suitable housing. One example of this type of construction is the still-surviving house of a whaler at the whaling station complex at Disko Bay, which was constructed between 1777 and 1790. Built of massive timber, imported from Scandinavia, such an establishment took many years to complete and it was far too valuable to be abandoned when functional requirements changed. As a result, many such buildings were taken down and moved about the region as need required. Among the growing towns which benefited from this nomadic approach to architecture were Upernavik, Godhavn, Jakobshavn and Claushavn, to all of which buildings were moved and re-erected at various periods after the whaling station at Disko Bay, for which they had been built, was shut down.[32] Julianehåb, however, one of Greenland's most important fishing and trading settlements, maintained over the years what was, for Greenland, an imposing appearance of stability as seen in the *View of Qaqortoq (Julianehåb)* (illus. 248).

Continued Exploitation of the Islands of the High Arctic in the Eighteenth Century

Jan Mayen remained little visited during the eighteenth century, but Svalbard continued to prosper, even though whale stocks had largely run out by 1800. There were other economic alternatives, however, especially the pursuit of fur. Indeed, Russian trappers came in considerable numbers during the period 1715–20. Arriving in groups of between 100 to 150 men, they would split up into ten or more smaller groups once on land. Each man might earn, perhaps, some 50 rubles, though the group leaders might receive four times that amount.[33] Not all visitors, however, were hunters; scientists also visited the region for their own purposes of exploration. A young Norwegian, B. M. Keilhau, for example, came to study the geology of Svalbard and, in 1758, A. R. Martin, a student of Carl von Linné, also visited there in order to explore the flora, fauna and climate of this far-flung island group.[34] There was even an influx of Russian soldiers in 1764, when an attempt was made to create a military base there. This failed, but Russian attempts at settlement continued, financed by prosperous merchants from Archangel. One Russian monk, Starostin by name, spent 30 years in Svalbard, until his death in 1826, living in a little log hut devoid of windows, on the end of a cape by Grønfjorden.[35]

The End of the Dark Ages: Iceland in the Nineteenth Century

The tide of Napoleonic upheavals in Europe had little effect upon the High Arctic. However, it did reach Iceland. The old now enfeebled Icelandic parliament or Alltinget, perceived by some as an anachronistic institution of the past with little authority, was finally abolished by the crown in 1800, and replaced by a new court of justice based in Reykjavik, with Magnús Stephensen as its spokesman. European-educated and deeply imbued by Enlightenment values, he endeavoured to bring a Continental system of justice and standard of social wellbeing to this isolated island, without coming into conflict with the the Danish king's benevolent but absolute authority.[36]

War between Britain and Denmark in 1801 and then again, in 1807, cut Iceland off from royal control and obliged those in official positions on the island to exert their own authority, in particular in seeking means of alleviating the misery which a virtual blockade by the British had effected. The removal of the island's treasury by the United Kingdom in 1808 (most of its resources were eventually returned) also forced Iceland to see its fate as distinct from that of Denmark. Moreover, the door to British trade was now opened, albeit by force, as a result of which Denmark's total economic hegemony in Iceland was undermined. Indeed, even American ships had come to Iceland by 1809.[37]

However, when the Napoleonic Wars came to an end, the old prohibitions on foreign shipping were re-established and foreign merchants who had settled in Iceland were obliged to leave. There was, though, one important exception now permitted to these stringent regulations: by the payment of an export license, Danish vessels could carry Icelandic goods directly to foreign ports, rather than through the intermediate ports of Denmark, a considerable boon for merchants with markets outside the mother kingdom.[38]

During the first half of the nineteenth century Iceland slowly recovered from the natural disasters of the previous catastrophic century. Fodder for animal husbandry remained Iceland's most important crop and, with the still modest but growing importance of fishing as a part-time livelihood for many, coastal hamlets grew in size and assumed considerable social and economic importance. Garður, on Faxa Bay, for example, in the south-west of the country, had grown from a parish of 421 inhabitants in 1800 to 1,779 by 1875, not least because of its excellent harbour.[39] Such population growth also encouraged social mobility and Iceland continued to be seen by visitors as a relatively egalitarian society.

The typical Icelandic farmstead in the nineteenth century was rustic in the extreme: small mounds covered by wood formed the walls, with small panes of glass inserted as windows. The central door led into the principal passageway which, in turn, led to the kitchen, all constructed of layers of turf and uncut stone. Two smaller passageways to either side led to the other rooms of the house, some of the walls of which were frequently decorated with 'in memoriam' obituaries of deceased family members. On more prosperous farms, one complete mound might serve as a servants' dormitory, in which both sexes would be permanently housed without regard for the proprieties held so rigorously elsewhere in most of the Nordic region at this time. Adjacent, but unconnected to this living area, were the forge, harness room and other service rooms so important to the running of the farm. Turf sheds and winter stables for animals completed the outer periphery of the homestead which they encircled.

The Greenlandization of Greenland

In Greenland, economic and social developments largely reflected the state of the whaling industry which, from the beginning of the nineteenth century, had entered a prolonged period of decline. It was also found more economically rewarding to leave the hunting of sealskins, a sought-after commodity in Europe, to native Greenlanders, rather than for Europeans themselves to attempt to acquire them more cheaply directly. As a result, the number of colonists in Greenland dropped, with many of those already there returning home to Europe. Soon, only administration, general trading and missionary activities remained viable options for Europeans. This state of affairs benefited native Greenlanders, on the other hand, who were now able to take on work in areas previously considered a European preserve.

Once such native able to avail himself of new career opportunities was Hans Zakæus, who became one of Greenland's first artists in the European tradition. Craft traditions in Greenland were well over a thousand years old, but painting, in the European sense, was a novelty. Officially, Zakæus was employed as a translator for facilitating European and Inuit relations, but he also possessed skills in whaling and seamanship, and he was employed in 1818 on the famous Ross expedition, in the quest for a north-west passage. During this lengthy voyage he depicted the Inuit peoples of the high polar regions which the expedition came upon. One such memorable meeting of the ship's officers with the native Inuit is depicted in *The Ross Expedition's Encounter with Polar Eskimos in 1818* (illus. 236). In it Zakæus depicted himself, in a blue jacket with white shirt, a mediator between the two alien peoples who are about to exchange gifts with each other.[40]

As the nineteenth century progressed, opportunities of employment for Europeans continued to diminish[41] and natives now took over jobs in administration, trade and missionary activity, in positions formerly taken by Europeans. Furthermore, while old buildings were re-utilized for different purposes than that for which they had been built, new buildings were built to meet current and projected needs. For example, at Nord-Prøven by Narsaq, an 'outrigger' house, or home on the edge of the community, was built of stone in 1830, one of few early examples constructed since Norse times. The remains of numerous Norse

ruins helped to provide splendid stone building materials for its construction. Two years later, another 'outrigger' house was built at the settlement of Sydprøven, by Alluitsup Paa, of stone and wood, both imported from Denmark.[42]

236 Hans Zakaeus (John Sackheouse), *The Ross Expedition's Encounter with Polar Eskimos in 1818*, chromolithograph.

The Industrialization of Iceland

By 1850, Iceland was once again suffering the debilitating effects of an economic crisis in agriculture, caused in part by a major increase in population. The Danish government responded, albeit slowly, and in 1854 granted local merchants complete freedom of trade, but in 1855 Denmark's new constitution failed to allow Icelanders a sufficient measure of political autonomy. Unlike Schleswig-Holstein (and its little enclave of Lauenburg), which had been granted the right to elect 80 members of the Rigsraad, Iceland had been ignored as a separate identity. This was rectified on 1 August 1874, the thousandth anniversary of the island's settlement, when the defunct Alltinget was revived as Iceland's new assembly. With its two houses, composed of a total of 36 members (six were chosen by the king), it could now make laws and control the island's finances. Final confirmation, however, still depended upon royal assent. However,

Icelanders lost the right to be represented in Copenhagen, though they also ceased to pay Danish taxes.

Some industries flourished in Iceland despite the general economic malaise, including the processing of shark liver oil, used for street lighting throughout many countries in Europe. The herring-processing industry provided new opportunities for many, affecting, for example, Seyðisfjörður, on the eastern coast, where a typical hamlet Dvergasteinn had 141 parishioners mostly employed in farming. Sudden urbanization occurred when the herring industry arrived in 1870.[43] Unfortunately, this boom proved short-lived, for the herring industry collapsed within a couple of decades.

Most rural areas were not so fortunate in being able to provide work for the increasing number of unemployed. As a result, the numbers of those on poor relief increased dramatically, reaching 12 per cent of the entire population by 1870. Similarly, the numbers of those seeking employment as farm labourers or servants also increased during this period, as did the incidence of child abandonment. The final two decades of the nineteenth century did enjoy a modest recovery, since the pressure of over-population diminished with the rise of immigration to Canada, especially after the Askja eruption of 1875, a recourse taken by at least 15,000 Icelanders by the end of the century.

Fishing increasingly provided an alternative livelihood to farming, usually for cod, instead of shark, as had previously been the case. The export trade in fish also thrived, facilitated by growing commercial links with Spain and Portugal.[44] As a result, many Icelanders now immigrated from the countryside to the coast.[45]

The Industrialization of Greenland

Greenland, also, saw a considerable improvement in social and economic conditions. These went hand in hand with the improved communications which linked Greenland to Denmark and the rise in the number of exports of industrial

237 Israil Gormandsen, *Drinking Coffee*, 1840, watercolour and ink on paper

238 Aron of Kangeq, *The Legend of Kannuk*, 1860, watercolour.

goods produced there. European immigration to Greenland also began to rise again, albeit slowly. In 1855, there were 248 Europeans in West Greenland, as opposed to 9,648 native Greenlanders of Inuit extraction, and they introduced some European customs (illus. 237). While this demographic increase can be traced to improvements in hygiene amongst the native population and to their increased immunity to infectious European diseases, it was also related to a lesser dependency on fishing and hunting. Myth and tradition remained strong in the face of westernization.

Most of the resident Europeans were engaged in trade or missionary work at this time, and were often now accompanied by their wives and children. Though many districts had no Europeans at all, immigrant colonists remained a tiny and relatively constant percentage of the entire population throughout the nineteenth century.[46] Furthermore, even this quite modest European population maintained itself largely because of the development of cryolite mining at Ivittuut, one of the few industrial ventures which continued to succeed in the region.[47] Population growth and the improvement in economic circumstances meant that the construction of a variety of public buildings boomed after 1900.

In the second decade of the twentieth century the Royal Greenland Trading Company was active in commissioning bridge, quay and harbour facilities, all of granite, in Julianehåb. A further eight or ten houses were also privately built of stone and, by the 1920s and 1930s, the construction of stone buildings in Greenland reached its zenith, for there now existed a successful body of stone-masons in the region. However, the most famous of the masons at work was not Greenlandic, but a Dane, Carl Andersen, from Bornholm, who possessed a skill which the native Greenlandic stonemasons lacked, being able to dynamite the stone he required from nearby cliffs rather than importing it. He was further able to cut it to the specified uniform size, thereby attracting a high premium for his labours.[48]

Icelandic National Identity and the Growth of the Fishing Industry

In Iceland, too, native industry was slowly beginning to develop, especially industrialized fishing.[49] Economically, though, as elsewhere in northern Europe, workers increasingly became financially dependent on the companies for which they worked. Many fishermen were now employed by large enterprises, with their worldly goods supplied on credit by the company store, a situation poignantly reflected in fiction in the novel *Salka Valka*, by the Icelandic Noble Laureate Halldór Laxness (born 1902). Just like the heroine of the novel, many young women at that time took casual work in the local fish-processing industry, before taking on the obligations of a family.

As a result, by 1901, those on poor relief in Iceland had diminished in number to 7.8 per cent, but for those who depended upon it life remained dreary, a situation aggravated by local government regulations which saw their relief auctioned to the lowest bidder; this was an arrangement which lent itself to much abuse.[50]

As the first decade of the twentieth century progressed, economic and social conditions in Iceland gradually improved. Reykjavik, the administrative capital, now had a population of some 3000, the largest of any town in Iceland. While its cultural amenities were sharply limited, the local newly established Art Society encouraged exhibitions of art, a fledgling activity on the island. These exhibitions enabled the island's first two native artists, Thórarinn B. Thorláksson (1867–1924) and Ásgrímur Jónsson (1876-1958) to achieve considerable professional success. Thorláksson's *Sunset by the Lake* (1905) depicts Reykjavik by the calm waters of Lake Tjörnin, silhouetted against the glowing horizon of an otherwise cloudy autumnal sky (see illus. 249).

Did Reykjavik have a picturesque appearance at this time? A contemporary visitor there at the beginning of the century wrote, 'Taking all in all, Reykjavik is probably the ugliest town in Europe [...] It boasts some streets and a square, but the material of which most of the buildings are made, or to speak more accurately, in which they are encased, is corrugated iron – a substance which does not lend itself to architectural beauty'.[51] By contrast with Reykjavik, Akureyri, Iceland's second city, situated on the Arctic coast, had a higher proportion of wooden buildings which gave it a more charming appearance. By and large, Icelandic towns had much the same character, with a few important establishments like the apothecary shop in Reykjavik, embellished as it was with neo-classical plaster motifs, punctuating an otherwise monotonous scene.

In villages, ancient building traditions lived cheek by jowl with the new forms of construction: in Heimey, in the south of Iceland, for example, tiny houses of piled stone, roofed in turf, with at the most one tiny window, alternated with small two-storeyed houses, sometimes of wood, but more often of corrugated iron, frequently brightly painted, with the names of European cities emblazoned upon them to heighten their status. Usually, the roofs of these more modern homes were of turf; sometimes, however, neatly hewn slates, as was the fashion in Denmark, were used.[52]

239 Thórarinn B. Thórlaksson, *Thingvellir*, 1905, oil on canvas.

In some paintings of the time, it is not the landscape or architecture but the political symbolism which was of primary importance. This is obvious in Thórlaksson's *Thingvellir* (1905; illus. 239) which delights in the hardy and rugged landscape of the countryside. Thingvellir was the site of the foundation of the Althingi or national parliament in 930, an important symbol in the late nineteenth and early twentieth centuries of Iceland's struggle for nationhood and independence. Only in 1904 did Iceland receive from Denmark her own native minister, resident in Iceland, and thereby a certain degree of autonomous expression. Not surprisingly, as in so many parts of Europe at the time, a political movement was growing which supported home rule. Thus, this work by Thorláksson has a very contemporary political dimension and played its own propaganda role in the popular demand for independence which very soon gave Iceland real political autonomy and, in 1944, complete national independence. At the same time, though, in Thórlaksson's painting, geographical details are accurately depicted: the viewer can see the ridge of lava, adjacent to the Almannagjá Gorge, with Mount Skjaldbreiður in the distance to the right.

By contrast, Jónsson's *View of Thingvellir* (1905; see illus. 250) provides a gentler and more intimate view of the church and farmhouse, if a less lofty one, while

240 Ásgrímur Jónsson, *Mount Esja seen from Vinaminni*, 1910, oil on canvas.

still keeping the political associations inherent in the locality. With their bright red roofs and smoking chimney, the buildings have assumed a cosy and endearing aspect totally absent in Thórlaksson's work. Moreover, the greenness of the valley and the presence of two girls, one of whom dangles her feet languidly in the cool water, give the painting a lyrical quality, which makes it also an ode to the delicate joys of an Icelandic summer.

The picturesque charms of rural Iceland notwithstanding, Reykjavik continued to grow in size, as it absorbed the new immigrants seeking employment from the countryside and Jónsson, though mainly a landscape painter, was one of the first Icelandic artists to succeed in capturing such a new urbanized scene. His *Mount Esja seen from Vinaminni* (illus. 240) depicts a variety of buildings, residential and industrial, along the Bay of Reykjavik, with two motorized fishing trawlers majestically ploughing their course up water in the background. These industrial buildings and the considerable increase in housing had all been made possible by a revolution in building techniques and materials. By the late nineteenth century, for example, pre-fabricated wooden houses were imported from Norway by the numerous Norwegian merchants active in the herring trade in Iceland.[53] Then, after the turn of the twentieth century, it was no longer necessary to import wood as the principal building material. Concrete, first utilized in rural Iceland in 1895, was now cheaply available and became the most popular building material in Reykjavik after 1900.

It was about this time that Iceland's first native architect, Rögnvaldur Ólafsson (1874–1917) began to devote himself exclusively to architectural commissions. He was assisted in this by his colleague Einar Erlendsson (1883–1969), who later succeeded Ólafsson as architectural adviser to the government. Though Ólafsson was obliged to break off his studies abroad because of ill health, he was able to undertake a number of important commissions, amongst them, work on the tuberculosis sanatorium at Vífilsstaðir (1910), outside Reykjavik. This building demonstrates his success at adapting to the new medium of concrete, after his earlier mainly timber ones.

So much had the architectural scene changed over a few years that, by 1915, after an enormous fire in the centre of Reykjavik, regulations more or less compelled the use of concrete for virtually all new buildings and wood largely ceased to be used in the country as a primary building material. Despite the revolutionary use of concrete, however, in terms of style and layout, these houses were built in much the same fashion as stone and brick houses then being constructed in Denmark.[54]

The Faeroe Islands and the Advent of Modern Development

Even the Faeroe Islands, isolated in the North Sea between Norway and Iceland, shared in the economic and social development of the late nineteenth and early twentieth centuries, though its capital remained a provincial backwater with the prison the most prominent building on the islands. An ancient territory, belonging first to Norway and then to Denmark, its security had been preserved by Magnus Heinason, a noted naval hero, who had built a fortress in 1588, situated on the eastern coast of the island of Strømø by Tórshavn, the principal town and capital of the island group. Renovated during the Napoleonic Wars to ward off a possible British attack, this fortress was later used as the sole prison in the Faeroes until the turn of the twentieth century, when another one was built expressly for the purpose, intended to cope with unruly sailors from the neighbouring Shetland Islands, who frequently visited the Faeroes, causing the occasional disturbance.

By 1900, the Faeroes had a population of more than 15,000,[55] and of these almost 6,000 resided in Tórshavn, the seat of the Løgting, the elected assembly of the Faeroes in which members were chosen every three years and which convened under the presidency of a senior government official appointed by the Danish king. The abolition of the crown trading monopoly in 1856, imposed during the sixteenth century, had led to an upsurge in mercantile prosperity, creating a thriving port. This, in turn, was augmented by the increasing importance of the town as a port of call for ships plying the sea lanes between Denmark, Scotland, Iceland and Norway, and the growth of tourism towards the end of the century, largely drawn from Britain, also gave Tórshavn considerable prosperity.

Tourists were charmed during the first two decades of the twentieth century by its picturesque appearance, especially on such a rare sunny day as the one captured in Christian Holm Isaksen's *East Bay, Tórshavn* (1920; see illus. 253). The artist, a self-taught landscape painter and draftsman, who was also very active in musical and literary spheres, has depicted his native town as a phenomenon of nature, organically grown out of the rocky shore, where even the turf roofs seem one with the grassy meadows luxuriating in the background.

Houses in the Faeroes were generally built of wood, with roofs of birch bark, coated in tar, but these were not native materials and had to be imported from abroad. Only the roof insulation of turf which covered the birch bark and rough-hewn stone foundations, usually whitewashed, in which the cellars were situated, were local. The residence of the prefect and a few other important buildings, including the town's school, were constructed of stone, with a variety of typical nineteenth-century Danish features, classically inspired but eclectic in style. The Løgtingshús or Assembly House, on the other hand, was built of wood, with its roof thickly clad in turf, in the traditional fashion.

Outside Tórshavn, village life remained largely unchanged. Some 8,000 inhabitants lived scattered about the coasts of the islands, in villages of twelve to 60 households, with another 1000 or so living on isolated farms, linked by a necklaces of boats plying the coasts. These farmhouses, with walls characteristically draped by nets, drying fish and whale meat, were usually small two-storeyed cottages. Typically a dry-house for the preservation of mutton and whale-meat was situated nearby, formed by widely spaced laths of imported wood through which the air could easily ventilate. The houses themselves, however, usually lacked ventilation, and with bedrooms containing box beds, often created a claustrophobic effect on foreign visitors to these far-flung settlements.[56] Their character and remoteness is most successfully captured in Syðradalur Village on Kalsoy (1918) by the Faeroese artist, Jógvan Waagstein (1897–1949; see illus. 246). Like many Faeroese artists at this time he was self-taught, and earned his living as an organist. The houses in this painting possess few windows, heightening the sense of an enclosed atmosphere. None the less, the open vista towards the ocean provides a visual channel beyond the enclosed fjord, much as such a waterway did in reality in the Faeroes, for those who wished to escape abroad or, at least, go beyond the narrow limits of their settlement, sentiments also expressed by the Faeroese writer William Heinesen in his novel Noatun. On the other hand, Waagstein's Morning (1939), with the sky opening up just behind the heavy cloud hovering over the village and shore, is perhaps more a presentment of the advent of the Second World War than simply a timeless vision of life on the Faeroes, in which heavy clouds may suddenly seem to be dispersed by the sun.

Yet such an optimistic pictorial note was far from the reality of a typical interior of a Faroese dwelling. Bleak and with unpainted deal walls, the interior of such a home has been captured in Loss (1934; see illus. 245), a sombre funereal work one of the most important of Faeroese artists, Sámal Joensen Mikines (1906–1979), a sophisticated artist who had trained at the Royal Academy in Copenhagen and worked in France.

By contrast to the arrangement of the Icelandic farmhouse, passageways were largely eschewed in favour of a series of rooms opening one upon another. In the seventeenth and eighteenth centuries some of the principal rooms of the largest ones could be surprisingly substantial, as the great hall at Kirkebø demonstrates. Yet the grandeur of such spacious rooms was not reflected in their construction. The enormous logs of which such a hall was built were employed whole, with no attempt made to smooth their surfaces, so that they possessed an unselfconsciously rustic appearance. The front door which opened into the hall at Kirkebø led to an internal dais, on which a long bench was situated. Devoid of both oven or chimney, though, the room was heated by an open fire on the floor which belched its smoke through a hole opening out of the ceiling. By the early twentieth century, however, an American stove replaced the open fire and the open hole in the ceiling was glazed over. This brought in more light, for the shutter which had sealed the hole off in storms was no longer necessary.[57] Thus, the older more prosperous Faeroese dwelling shared more characteristics with the small medieval European manor house, than anything to be found in Iceland or Greenland.

In late nineteenth- and early twentieth-century large farmhouses, however, the kitchen or dining room came to replace the traditional hall. Lined by benches placed against its walls, it remained the room in which servants ate, slept and even worked, a smaller bench, placed in the centre of the room serving as a trencher for containing the food. Yet despite the architectural distinctions of prosperous and humble farmhouses, a certain homogeneity of lifestyle was maintained. With the exception of a few Danish merchants or the bailiff, a relative social and economic equality reigned amongst the Faeroese outside Tórshavn, even in the second largest town Thrangisvaag, since access to land, fishing and whaling remained open to all, offering relatively plentiful returns, even if seal hunting itself had ceased to be productive.[58]

Developments of the Nineteenth and Early Twentieth Century in the Islands of the High Arctic

Unlike the Faeroes, the islands of the High Arctic had remained relatively undeveloped in terms of a permanent resident community, not least because of the severe climatic conditions. It was the so-called First International Polar Year, 1882–3, which led to a renewed European focus upon these remote and windswept territories when an Austrian expedition undertook a lengthy winter visit to Jan Mayen. Such a prolonged stay required appropriate accommodation to cope with the bitter winter conditions, exacerbated by almost perpetual gales. To this purpose a little settlement was established by the expedition which was called 'The Austrian'. Each hut was built in the form of a ship, turned upon its top, so that its sharply bow-shaped form could better withstand the vicious winds, while the rear wall was embedded in the hillside for added protection. Within the hut, double walls were filled with wood scrapings for greater insulation, the floors were given an underlay of asphalt and the bedroom 'papered' in linoleum. Each room was warmed by a stove, fuelled by imported coal and driftwood. None the less, the rooms of the hut were kept cool with an average winter temperature of 9.7° C, which was never permitted to climb higher than 15° C. With these adaptations to the extremes of an Arctic climate, such a hut was considered by Wohlgemuth, the expedition's leader, to be the ideal prototype of a polar house.

Originally, a room was incorporated in the hut to serve as a larder, but shortly after a separate building was constructed from driftwood for this purpose, after which time the old larder was used as a study. There was also a kitchen and adjacent bathroom which contained a bathtub, enjoyed by the men on a monthly basis, which also served as a darkroom, among other usages. So successful was the construction of the settlement that it was able to survive with little damage until the visit of the Duc d'Orléans in 1909, on his way to Greenland, and remained in occasional use well into the 1920s. Schjelderup's Seal Hunting Company, in fact, initially used the huts as a base, before they built their own hut at Sørbukta. This new hut was an idiosyncratic affair, clad in imported timber vertically placed, with a roof, containing a little window, sharply sloping to one side from the top of a wall to help withstand the winds. Along with a number of huts used by visiting trappers, roughly five metres square in dimensions, they remained the only edifices on Jan Mayen until a Norwegian meteorological observatory and a radio station were built in 1921, eight years before Norwegian sovereignty to the island was internationally confirmed.[59]

Further north, in the region of Svalbard and Bear Island, settlement commenced at a much earlier date. The oldest dwelling still in existence on Bear Island is the so-called Hammerfest hut, built of logs in Hammerfest, in Norway, and shipped in 1823 to serve as accommodation for the first Norwegian expedition to over-winter there. The adjacent windowless log extension was added later by a Captain Tobiesen, in 1865. Then, in 1872, another dwelling was built, this time for the Swedish-Finnish explorer A. E. Nordenskiöld (he is best known for successfully navigating, with his ship *Vega*, the North-East Passage to the Orient, by Siberia), who wished to explore the potential for phosphorite mining in Svalbard. Known as the Swedish House, it is located on Isfjord, near Cape Thordsen, where phosphorite had been discovered. During The First International Polar Year it was further enlarged, under the auspices of Nils Gustaf Ekholm, the year the photograph was taken. Though a thriving new colony had been envisaged, it was never to materialize and little in the way of mining ever occurred there. An observatory was soon built in the vicinity[60] and there were quite a number of huts for trappers on the islands, but these often consisted merely of old boats, turned upside down and resting on narrow vertical timbers, entered by a small slightly projecting doorway.[61]

A ship's captain writing in *Skilling-Magazin* about his visit to Krossfjord, in Svalbard, in the summer of 1835, sheds considerable light on the Russian habitations there at this time. He wrote of one, 'Inside we found a sitting room which was quite functional; it was well built of wood, had a window, four bedsteads, a chimney and a baking oven. In the attic a small air vent was to be found which could be opened, when the flue of the chimney was shut'.[62] Having forced his way through the door of the hut, tied firmly from within to prevent the entrance of wild animals, he found the body of a Russian who had just died of starvation, a sad and all too frequent fate of those who attempted to brave a winter in the High Arctic.[63]

Shipping improved during the nineteenth century and the seasonal population of the region increased, despite the difficulties. Seventy-three vessels sailed north from Hammerfest during the years 1827–30 alone, when seal hunting and other forms of trapping drew ever greater numbers to Svalbard, especially during the slack season in fishing when fishermen sought other forms of seasonal employment to supplement their incomes.[64] However, of greater long term importance to the region was the industrialization which began to make inroads at the turn of the twentieth century. Søren Zachariassen, from Tromsø, commenced coal-mining there in 1899 and in 1904 a British company was established. They, too, invested in mining and erected Svalbard's first town, Advent City, on Revneset. Meanwhile, the American entrepreneur John Monroe Longyear had arrived in 1901. Three years later, he and his colleague Frederick Ayer purchased Norwegian rights on Advent Fjord, which shortly thereafter led to the creation of a stockholding concern, The Arctic Coal Company. So successful did this venture turn out to be that by 1911 some 200 workers, mostly from the Nordic countries, were producing 29,000 tonnes per year for shipment to Norway. This undertaking had already led to the establishment of yet another town, Longyear City (Longyearbyen), in about 1910.[65] Almost entirely composed of one-storey concrete barracks, its bleak walls were only alleviated by the sparse placement of traditional Scandinavian windows with six panes. Later, in 1911, the mining of marble was also undertaken at Camp Mansfield (Blomstrandhalvøya) where a settlement was established for the 40 Scottish miners whom it employed. This venture, however, along with an attempt at gold mining, proved totally unsuccessful and was aborted. Coal mining continued to thrive: supplying Norway and Sweden when the First World War cut off other sources of coal. After the war, however, the Swedish mines were sold to Norway or, as in the case of Pyramiden, in Billefjord, in 1926, to the Soviet Union. The Dutch also sold their mine at Barentsburg to the Russians, who set up an additional one at Grumantbyen, to the north-west of Longyearbyen. Thus, the multi-national zones of activity of the pre-war years increasingly became a condominium of Norwegian and Russian interests.

Life in these early twentieth-century mining towns was extremely regulated by the industrial companies employing the miners. Miners in Advent City were paid four Norwegian crowns per day, of which one and a half crowns was deducted for room and board. Life was austere. The barracks in which the workers lived contained up to 50 men, with little privacy, and of the ten-hour work-day, eight were spent in the mines themselves. Work hazards were considerable: in 1920, 26 miners were killed in an explosion at Longyear City. Not surprisingly, strikes frequently occurred and plans were conceived to bring in Chinese miners to circumvent this problem, though in the end they were not implemented.[66]

Hunting and trapping of seals, polar bears and Arctic foxes also continued in the early twentieth century on Svalbard but, of course, within very different social parameters to those of the previous centuries. Increasing numbers of hunters and trappers began over-wintering after 1900. In the pre-war period, four men would live in a hut, covering a common hunting ground, but after the war these groups were broken up, with men often living alone and covering their own territory alone.[67]

National Autonomy in Iceland in the Twentieth Century

Formerly, foreigners and, in particular, Norwegians had provided both the financial resources and technical knowledge to run Icelandic industry. After the First World War, however, Icelanders came to dominate their own industries, especially the industrial salting of herring, with many men taking summer work as herring fishermen in the north and east of Iceland.[68] In 1918 the Danish government confirmed Iceland's sovereign status as an independent nation under the Danish crown. Increased urban development followed in this wake and a considerable demand for architectural skills was created. The Icelandic architect Guðjón Samúelsson (1887–1950) enjoyed many official commissions after his appointment in 1919 as State Architect. His work included official residences, hospitals and schools. In fact, most public buildings built until the post-war period were designed by him. His work from the early 1920s is neo-classical in style, albeit with a number of neo-Baroque features, as was fashionable in architecture in Denmark and Sweden at the time. His houses at Austurstræti 16 and Túngata 18, in Reykjavik, are characteristic of this. From 1923, however, traditional Icelandic architectural elements began to appear in his work, with the projecting farmhouse gables coming back into fashion in his domestic architecture. The school at Laugarvatn and government residence at Thingvellir, from this period, hark back to the rustic old-fashioned Icelandic farmhouse, despite their official and public function.

Only in the 1930s did functionalism begin to appear in Samúelsson's work, under the influence of his assistants and students who had studied abroad. The primary advocate of functionalism, though, was Sigurður Guðmundsson (1885–1958). Having been a student at the Kunstakadamiet in Copenhagen, he was aware of the latest architectural trends when he returned to Iceland, in 1926. An artist and literary figure, as well as architect, this modern humanist introduced Functionalist principles in the private residence he built at Garðastraedi 41, in Reykjavik in 1930. Yet, even he, one of Iceland's most revolutionary figures of the time, became disenchanted with Functionalism and returned to more traditional Icelandic architectural values, as his Nautical School in Reykjavik demonstrates. However, a number of other younger architects, who had trained abroad in Denmark, Sweden, Germany and England, persisted in designing in the Modernist mould, such as Gunnlaugur Halldórsson (b. 1909) and Ágúst Pálsson (1893–1967), who obstinately turned their backs on traditional Icelandic architectural elements.[69]

Reykjavik, of course, remained the capital of economic, administrative and social life throughout this period, but Hafnarfjörður was also growing in importance because of its harbour and British investment in Iceland's trawler fleet, some of which was based there. When this source of income fell away, however, in the late 1920s and the Great Depression hit Iceland, Hafnarfjörður endured considerable economic hardships.[70] Some smaller towns, however, could boast of greater and more long-term success. For example, Siglufjörður, on the northern Arctic coast of the country, attracted men and women from all over Iceland to its burgeoning fishing industry. But here too boom was punctuated by bust, as fortunes were made and lost in rapid succession.[71]

Growing Autonomy in Greenland

In Greenland, too, considerable economic and social development was occurring, and a variety of new urban amenities became available as buildings were constructed with new techniques and building materials. At Julianehåb, Greenland's first public baths were built in sandstone from Igaliku, while a slaughterhouse for sheep (1929) and a warehouse for the storage of fish (1933) were constructed in concrete and dressed in granite by the Dane Helge Bojsen-Møller, nearby. A native female Greenlandic architect, Pavia Høegh, was commissioned at about this time to build the adjacent harbour warehouse, which was constructed entirely of granite and completed in 1939, demonstrating the technical accomplishments of which a native Greenlander could now boast.[72]

In terms of the sculpture, however, the medium was still in the hands of Danes. Most famous for his work at this time in Greenland was Egil Knuth. His sculptures of native Greenlanders from the east coast in 1936–7 were generally in the form of busts, with blank eyes in the classical fashion: 'I am a head-hunter', he was accustomed to say.[73] Of the more than 30 in clay which he produced, those of a blind man, in the local hospital, and a mother and child are arguably the most famous. In fact, he had come to Greenland first in order to join a French expedition there, but had then proceeded to establish himself as a sculptor in Ammassalik. Previously, he had been in contact with Einar Mikkelsen who influenced his landscape paintings, but these proved themselves too modern in taste for the natives of the area, who preferred a more naturalistic style of painting.

Absorption of Svalbard into Norway

By contrast with Iceland and Greenland and their relationship to Denmark, the outlying Arctic islands, claimed by Norway, had their bonds to the mother country cemented in the inter-war period. Norway's declaration, in 1925, that Svalbard was an integral part of the kingdom was eventually accepted by the world at large, including the Soviet Union. This confirmation of sovereignty did not prevent both the Store Norske Spitsbergen Kulkompani (Great Norwegian Svalbard Coal Company) and Arkitukugol (Soviet State Coal Trust) from splitting the mining on the islands harmoniously between themselves. Each community continued to exist relatively happily together on Svalbard, perhaps because there was little social contact between the two. In fact, the Russian settlement remained more or less autonomous, the Norwegian government administration, in the form of its district governor, exercising only titular authority there.

Coal mining continued to dominate the entire economy of the region. Attempts at cod fishing, however, proved unsuccessful, but hunting and trapping continued to be lucrative. Moreover, a new industry also made its modest appearance in Svalbard, in the years leading up the Second World War: tourism. Svalbard's first tourist establishment, The North Pole Hotel, opened in 1936. Its life, though, was soon cut short by the advent of the Second World War, with its ominous and dramatic implications for all spheres of life in the Arctic region.[74]

A Peculiar Institution: Slavery, the Tropics and Scandinavian Colonial Expansion

The Founding of Scandinavia's Southern Overseas Colonies

Like most other European maritime powers in the early modern period, the kingdom of Sweden, including the province of Finland, and the dual kingdoms of Denmark and Norway, united under the same monarch, were keen to procure for themselves the mercantile advantages of overseas colonies. In the Arctic regions, Greenland and Iceland remained undisputed territories of the Danish crown, with Lapland parcelled out amongst the two Nordic powers and Russia. In the semi-tropics and tropics, however, opportunities were more restricted. The Scandinavian fleets were reasonable in size, but they could not vie with the military strength and political hegemony exerted in these regions by Spain, Portugal, Britain and France. Instead, they had to be content with the few opportunities for expansion with which they were provided by the political and economic situation.

Swedish Settlements on the Delaware

In 1637, two Dutchmen, Samuel Blommaert and Peter Minuit, had succeeded in encouraging the establishment of the New Sweden Company in Sweden, a new colonial enterprise. This was followed in 1638 by the settlement by Swedes of Fort Christina (now Wilmington), in a colony which they named New Sweden (now Delaware), though immigration there was slow. As a result, in 1641, the penal transportation to the colony of Swedish and Finnish military deserters and other court marshalled soldiers (among this number a man convicted of cutting down six apple trees in the royal orchard at the old monastery of Varnhem), as well as poachers and vagabonds, was instituted to supply the necessary man-power. They were often accompanied by their families. Once established in the colony, where the native Delaware Indians had already cleared much of the land for their own agricultural needs, they cultivated tobacco, in contrast to the Indians who mainly planted corn. The tobacco was then exported to Sweden, along with beaver skins acquired by hunting or barter.[1] Shortly after, another Swedish settlement and fort was established to the north on the western bank of the Delaware River, which was christened New Gothenburg, to which the governor's seat was moved in 1643.

Arguably, the most lasting cultural legacy of these Nordic colonists was the introduction of log cabins which American settlers quickly adopted throughout the colonies as a means of building solid but cheap houses. An eighteenth-century Swedish visitor to Delaware, Pehr Kalm, described them:

241 *The View of the Harbour Streets in Gustavia,* 1800, engraving.

The houses which the Swedes erected for themselves, when they first came here, were very poor [...] a little cottage (built of round logs), with a door so low that it was necessary to bend down when entering. As they had no windows with them, small loopholes served the purpose, covered with a sliding-board which could be closed and opened [...] Clay was plastered into the cracks between the logs on both sides of the walls. The fireplaces were made of granite (boulders) found on the hills or, in places where there were no stones, out of mere clay; the bake-oven was also made inside of the house.[2]

The dwellings of the first Finnish colonists were even more rudimentary, somewhat similar to the tents of Indian wigwams, but more closely resembling the tent-like huts of the Saami people (Lapps). Mainly composed of poles, several inches thick and over a foot long, they were joined together at the top and extended diagonally downwards in a circle around a space usually about ten feet in diameter. Moss was used to fill the cracks between the poles, whilst the small entrance was protected by animal skin or cloth.[3] By the mid-1650s, however, the growing prosperity of the colony made possible the building of improved residences, generally of hickory wood and often on two floors. Perhaps the grandest of these was the governor's seat on Tenakongh Island, where Governor Prinz's daughter, married to the Vice-Governor Johan Papegoija, continued to reside after Prinz's departure, before returning to Sweden herself many years later.[4] The diet of the colonists and soldiers at that time reflects their general prosperity: rich in game, beef, pork and fish. It also included cheese and 'English bread', baked from wheat, rye and corn, as well as a copious supply of vegetables and melons. As in Sweden, beer and brandy were ubiquitously drunk in large quantities.[5]

Despite the successful development of the Delaware colony, this Swedish colonial foothold was soon to be broken by Holland which continued to maintain its greater proprietary rights over the Delaware region.[6] After less than two decades, the first and last Swedish colony in Continental North America was seized by the Dutch of New Amsterdam, under Peter Stuyvesant in 1655. Nine years later they were obliged to relinquish it to the English, who renamed it New York. Few Swedish or Finnish families, however, left the colony after the transfer and a census report of five years later gives the European population of the colony at some 500 families, a significant number of whom were also Dutch.[7]

Here, in Delaware, black slavery was first introduced into a Nordic dominion, albeit with the presence of only one black slave who had been imported in 1639. From such a humble beginning as an institution, it was to thrive and then survive for more than 200 years in the other Nordic American colonies.

Early Development of the Danish African Slave Trade

The roots of Danish colonial expansion, based on the slave trade, are to be found mainly in the middle years of the seventeenth century. However, the import of black slaves to cultivate sugar cane for Europeans stemmed from a much more ancient past; already in the thirteenth century they had been imported from

242 *Christiansborg, Denmark-Norway's Principal Fort on the Guinea Coast with the Village of Orsu in the Foreground,* drawing.

Africa by the Venetians to the island of Cyprus, for that very purpose.[8] Later, in the fifteenth century, African slaves were also imported to the Canary islands. In 1658, during the First Northern War, when Denmark and Sweden were pitched against each another (1655–60), the Swedish fortress of Carolusborg, on the West African Guinea coast, was briefly captured by the Danes, and a new theatre of confrontation opened up between these two warring kingdoms. This war was fought for different prizes, with gold, ivory, and sugar now the coveted rewards. As one of the few coastal areas in Africa not under European control, but rich in slaves, the Guinea coast was a region which offered Danes opportunities already available to the British, the French, the Portuguese and the Spanish.

When Sweden repossessed Carolusborg in 1666, Denmark quickly acquired another coastal station where they promptly established a new fortress, on the site of an abandoned fortification called Amanfro. The land was purchased from local Fetu chieftains at Elmina and Accra for 50 gold benda and christened Frederiksborg.[9] The following decade, another trading post was established by the Danes at Christiansborg, adjacent to the important trading capital of Accra, which can be seen in *Christiansborg, Denmark-Norway's Principal Fort on the Guinea Coast with the Village of Orsu in the Foreground* (illus. 242). The Danish flag is flying proudly from the uppermost bastion of the stone fortress, with the Baroque church-like gable and portals of the gatehouse projecting out over the windowless huts, with their palm frond roofs. By such acquisitions as these, the groundwork was laid for the establishment of the Scandinavian slave trade.

The sovereignty assumed by Denmark over the Virgin Islands, first St Thomas, in 1666, and later St Jan, assisted in this process of expansion. Some 324 colonists had set forth with great expectations of colonizing St Thomas, but within six months, all but 64 had died, victims of a climate in which arduous labour meant almost certain death for Europeans. Therein lay the need for the new colonial enterprise, that peculiar institution of slavery which, for better or for worse, was to help solve colonial labour problems in the Americas for up to two centuries.

The prosperity it brought to many white colonists was indisputable. Within a decade of the colony's establishment, 156 colonists, some Danes, but many English and Dutch from other Caribbean colonies, were being assisted by 174 blacks slaves, and one lame native Indian (his left foot had been amputated in punishment for attempting to escape), in farming 45 plantations. New demands in the north of Europe for sugar, indigo, tobacco, and later coffee could thereby be catered for within Danish territory.

Economic rewards were not only to be found on the shores of the Atlantic. Asia, too, proved a rich continent for exploitation and the Danish East India Company was established to secure this end in 1615–16. In particular, spices and textiles, and later porcelain and tea, became increasingly desirable commodities. Between 1618 and 1622, a Danish courtier Ove Gjeddes, later an admiral of the Norwegian fleet, had seen opportunities in India and Sri Lanka. As a result, a small area of the Coromandel coast of India, including the fortified city of Tranquebar, were acquired through leases with local princes, including the Nayak Ragunatha of Tanjore, and so-called loges in Bengal, Java, Borneo and the Celebes, from which trade, including that in pepper, could be conducted with a maximum of security and enormous profit.

By the late seventeenth century, Copenhagen had become the centre of the sugar trade in the north of Europe, allowing Danish merchants to accumulate vast wealth. Some of the profits, especially from the Caribbean, were reinvested in industry in Denmark and a sugar refinery was erected near the Stock Exchange in the centre of Copenhagen, to meet the growing demand for sugar. Sometimes, blacks themselves became the sought-after commodity in Denmark, not so much for their capacity to work in a country where serfdom was still thriving, but rather because of their novelty value. Frederik III and his court specifically requested the governor of the Danish Caribbean possessions to provide 'beautiful and well-mannered Negro children' for their entertainment in Copenhagen. A letter from the board of directors of the Danish West India-Guinea Company, from 1689, specifically required that only those of fine proportions be acquired for this purpose, since 'deformed or crippled blacks were better suited to remain and till the soil'.[10] The West India Company was obviously successful in fulfilling this goal, as A. Wuchters's painting, *Frederik III's Queen Sofie Amalie with her Negro Boy and other Exotic Accoutrements*, shows (see illus. 254). A century later, Frederik VI would also have his own black page boy.

A more important function of the West India Company, however, was to satisfy the need to establish a suitable administrative apparatus for dealing with the economic exploitation of the new Danish territories, as well as their successful integration with one another. To this end, the Danish West Indian-Guinea Company had been jointly organised, in 1674, when it was endowed with privileges that made it one of the Danish-Norwegian kingdom's most powerful institutions, with its own judicial system. It was to survive until the middle of the eighteenth century.

By 1686, the population of St Thomas had doubled to more than 600, half white settlers, half black or mulatto slaves, and numbers continued to grow as the numbers of plantations increased.[11] Particularly instrumental in successfully increasing the number of imports of slaves in the Danish Virgin Islands at this time was Jens Juel (not to be confused with his namesake, the eighteenth-century artist Jens Juel), and younger brother of a famous sea captain. In his post as Vice President of the Commerce College and Director of both the Danish East India and West India Companies, he was in a uniquely powerful position to influence political as well as financial decisions. His imperious full-length portrait, *Jens Juel in the Attire of the Order of the Knights of the Elephant*, clearly expresses his authority and it is easy to imagine the business acumen of a man who had been awarded one of Denmark's most prestigious medals. So successful was he in the increased procurement of Guinea slaves that, by 1733, even St Jan, the smallest of the Danish island possessions, had a slave population of over 1,080 working on 109 plantations.

Danish Slaving Establishments on the Guinea Coast

Large numbers of slaves were continuously needed to make up for the unsuccessful reproduction of the slaves in the Caribbean. By comparison with other European colonies in the Americas, the absolute number and proportion of slaves to the free population was relatively small.[12]

An important Dutch merchant, Wilhelm Vosman, residing at Elmina, not far from Christiansborg Fortress, on the Danish African Guinea coast, has shed much light on the functioning of the trade in the 1690s. Most of the slaves, he writes, were taken as prisoners of war and so were considered lawful booty. Immediately, upon the coast, they were imprisoned in slave prisons, from which they were removed for sale in a large square. There, those over 35 years old and the infirm were separated from the young and fit. Slaves found desirable and purchased by the company's buyers were then branded by a hot iron with the company's coat of arms, from where they were summarily dispatched to the company's own slave prison to await final shipment. Slaves at Christiansborg were branded with the initials CB. In fact, branding was no simple matter, for slaves could be transferred to the accounts of the shippers, the captain, officers and others, each of whom had a part of the slave's upper body allotted for their use in branding so as to indicate for whose account the slave was being sold.[13]

Usually, slaves were shipped from the interior, but sometimes a battle outside the walls of the fortress could provide unexpected benefits, as happened in 1708–09 when the inhabitants of Accra, living under the walls of Christiansborg and thinking that they enjoyed protection by the Danish crown, were fallen upon by the Aquamu tribe. The Danish commandant, Erik Lyggard, refused to come to their defence when the panic-stricken fugitives sought refuge before the fortress. Not only did he thereby avoid an attack on the fortress by the Aquamu, but he was able financially to benefit from the fresh influx of slaves into which these helpless victims of the assault were soon transformed. Historical fate is fickle, and with poetic justice, later in the century, many Aquamu warriors were themselves to fall victim to the powerful warrior Asante tribe, becoming slaves in their turn.

European goods played a key role in the slave trade process. Most slaves were purchased by Europeans with arms, but spirits, especially brandy, were also a very valuable currency. One Danish slave trader of this early period, Ludevig Ferdinand Rømer, has given important insights into the functioning of the trade on the Guinea coast. The needs of an African king and his court to sell thousands of slaves to keep them adequately supplied with drink provoked his bemused commentary. Logistically, such large provisions of drink were not difficult to accomplish, for a typical Danish merchant vessel usually carried upwards of 40,000 bottles of brandy, shipped from Copenhagen to the Guinea coast, along with weapons, textiles and various metals. According to Rømer, a male slave on arrival at Christiansborg was worth two rifles, including 40 pounds of ammunition, two bars of iron, one bar of copper, a barrel of Danish brandy, and various trinkets. Deductions were made for those missing teeth, a good way for a purchaser of reckoning a slave's age, or otherwise 'damaged'. The usual purchase price to the Danish trader for a healthy slave amounted to 96 riksdaler. In turn, Rømer was able to sell the slave at great profit, realizing between 128 and 160 riksdaler, per slave, out of which he was obliged to pay various commissions, albeit relatively small, to others involved in the trade.[14]

Sometimes, African royal families themselves fell victims to slavers. This had implications which could be manipulated for colonial political ends. As one Swedish colonist wrote, 'The emancipation by purchase, of a son of the King of Mesurado, from his "pretended" friend, and which I had then the happiness to effect in London, seemed likely to induce his father, to favour the establishment of our intended colony in his territories'.[15] For slaves of less noble parentage, though, hopes of emancipation on any level remained small.

By the middle years of the eighteenth century, the warlike Asante had successfully subjugated the surrounding regions of Christiansborg, in particular the mouth of the River Volta. This meant that a flood of new slaves, taken from the prisoners of war of the defeated Ada, Awuna and Way tribes, also filled the market and prices fell as a result. For many of these captives, slavery was a lesser evil than what would otherwise have awaited them, since conquered males were normally put to death. Because of the lucrative profits of the slave trade, however, now, only those captured and unsuited for slavery, such as children, were cast into the rivers to drown. For Rømer then, with his eye also alert for profit, these were 'glorious times on the coast, for a man could buy a slave for a bottle of brandy'.[16] An engraving, *Portrait of L. F. Rømer*, depicts this slave merchant after his permanent return to Denmark in 1749, with a decade of very profitable trading in Africa behind him, a man of substance and authority, who had wisely re-invested his considerable fortune in a new sugar refinery at Nyhavn 11, in Copenhagen.

Life on the Guinea coast may have benefited Rømer, but for most Europeans it was fraught with difficulties. White women were extremely rare, with just a few Lutheran priests accompanied by their wives. Even these few ladies had expired in a few weeks, for malaria, yellow fever, dysentery and Guinea worms were all prevalent. To deal with this dearth of women European men often took a temporary mistress during their time on the coast. By the usual arrangement each kept whatever property he or she owned before they 'came together', though the man did support his African mistress. She, in turn, looked after his home and any children that came of the union. So frequent did this concubinage become that a special fund was established for the payment of a permit legitimizing it, the resources of which were used to support the increasing number of children born to these unions. Many of the boys went on to become soldiers at the fortresses, while the girls, on occasion, were taken as wives; more usually, however, they became camp followers.[17] One such woman taken as a concubine was Tim Tam. Her loving master, Wulff Joseph Wulffs, eventually left all his possessions to her upon his death. She can be seen with turbaned head-dress in a drawing, *Portrait of Sara Malm* (illus. 243) labelled by the European name her 'husband' gave her. This approach to a type of native concubinage reached into the highest levels of government and lasted throughout the 200 years of the Danish colonial establishments on the Guinea coast. Even the last governor, Edward Cristensen, had his own native woman, sentimentally christened by him Severine.[18]

243 *Portrait of Sara Malm,* c. 1850s, drawing.

Christiansborg Fortress was neither the only nor indeed the principal focus for Rømer's business ventures or the Danish slave trade itself. Fredensborg Fortress, built in 1736 at Store Ningo, 75 kilometres east of Christiansborg, was the real hub of his lucrative activities, built to supply the increased need for slaves of Denmark's recent colonial acquisition, St Croix, purchased from France for 164,000 riksdaler by the Danish West Indian-Guinea Company.

Frederiksted, the principal town of St Croix, was established in 1751 by a deepwater harbour, on the site of an earlier French settlement. Round about it, sugar plantations had been already parcelled out, at a coast of 1,000 riksdaler, with the less desirable cotton plantations sold for half that price. All were laid out with straight boundaries, according to the most rational principles of the early Enlightenment for the allotment of farmland. As a result, about 250 planter families were successfully established there by the late 1750s, all with a desperate need for slaves.

Keen to supply the market demands, Rømer was not blind to the pitfalls of the trade. Female slaves with children, he found, were a terrible nuisance in the business. For one thing, he states that many slavers held the view that a woman slave with just one baby needed to occupy three times the ship space as one without. Therefore, attempts were made, he candidly admits in his writings, to deceive both the slave merchant and the shipper if their 'goods' were accompanied by young children. Obviously, upon embarkation, the true situation of the slave-mother would become apparent. Sometimes, she was allowed to board, with her child upon her back. Usually, it would die in transit. On other occasions, a child would be slung out upon the beach as the mother was herded onto the vessel.[19] The Danish West Indian-Guinea Company's bookkeeper, however, was more positive about the benefits for the trade of mothers with babies, for, by his accounting, they could bring in up to 800 riksdaler.[20] Children over the age of about three were always sold independently, an added bonus.

Conditions at Christiansborg, where the slaves were accommodated overnight in large cavernous barracks, the so-called 'barracoons', were not very salubrious.[21] The intense heat of close quarters in these tropical climes, with the slaves chained together for security behind locked doors, in conjunction with poor hygienic amenities, could have deleterious effects. By contrast, the breaking up of stones for building, upon which the slaves were employed during the days they remained on the coast, could provide a welcome relief, being carried out in the open air. This stone could be used for building material and some of it, along with sand and clay imported from Denmark, went into making the walls of yet another Danish fortress on the coast, Prinsensten. For attractive female slaves, however, daytime prospects were less satisfactory, for it could be a time of humiliation, in which soldiers often exploited them as they wished.[22]

The most arduous part of the trade, both for the slaves and those transporting them, was the Middle Passage, that is, the Atlantic voyage. Ships which had set sail from Copenhagen generally set a northerly route round Scotland, in order to avoid the often hazardous weather conditions of the English Channel, before bearing southwards down the coast of Ireland towards Africa, with wares in their holds. Once docked at the Guinea fortresses, though, these previously quite ordinary merchant ships were rapidly transformed in order to fit them for their new merchandise. Palisades and other defences were erected upon the upper decks, including cannon and guns pointed towards the slave quarters, with railings heightened by nets. This was a precaution not against revolt but to hinder suicide, the frequent and last resort of a discontented slave.

But even for those slaves keen to live, death often lay in wait. On the maiden voyage of the slave ship *Fredensborg*, launched from Copenhagen in 1779, 143 of the 419 slaves on board died in transit. This loss, however, was not unexpected and insurance rates took account of this. Twenty-five per cent of slaves on board usually succumbed to the rigours of the voyage, though, by the end of the century, this number was reduced to 16 per cent. Specially constructed slave ships had by that time improved hygiene and thereby hindered the otherwise raging rate of infection which could sweep a vessel when an epidemic broke out. Even a ship's crew were not immune; indeed, their death rates could be higher than those of the slaves. In fact, Africans were often less susceptible to infectious diseases than whites, for they had a natural resistance to African ailments, with a moderate resistance to European diseases as well, a long-term immunological

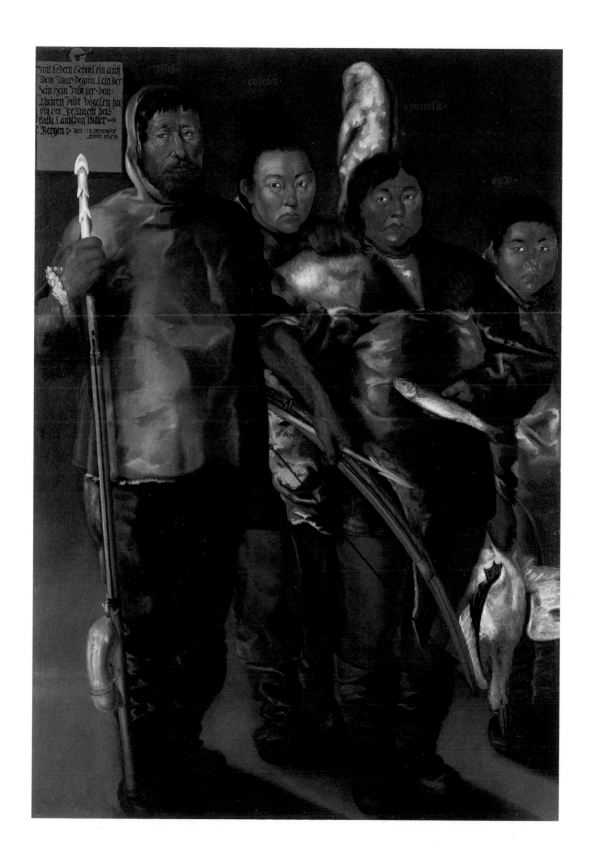

337

248 Jens Mathias Mathiesen,
View of Qaqortoq (Julianehåb),
1830, watercolour.

249 Thórarinn B. Thorláksson,
Sunset by the Lake, 1905, oil
on canvas.

250 Ásgrímur Jónsson, *View of Thingvellir*, 1905, oil on canvas.

251 Vilhelm Hammershøi, *The Asiatic Company's Buildings in Copenhagen*, 1902, oil on canvas.

(Opposite above)
252 Major General Peter Anker, *Frederiksnagore*, oil.

(Opposite below)
253 Christian Holm Isaksen, *East Bay, Tórshavn*, 1920, oil on canvas.

254 Abraham Wuchters,
*Frederik III's Queen Sofie Amalie
with her Negro Boy and other
Exotic Accoutrements,*
c. 1650(?), oil on canvas.

255 Lieutenant Francis Meinell, *View of a Slavedeck on the Slave Ship Albanez*, drawing.

benefit of the trans-Saharan slave trade which had brought them into contact with European illnesses. Whites, on the other hand, had no immunological preparation for African diseases.[23]

Unfortunately, no illustrations exist of the interior of a Danish slave ship. However, a watercolour *View of a Slavedeck on the Slave Ship Albanez* (illus. 255) depicts the middle deck of a Spanish slave ship Albanez, captured by the British after the slave trade had been prohibited in the nineteenth century, and gives a good impression of how a purpose-built slave ship was fitted out. Slaves sit in a variety of postures, on the wooden floors, beams and barrels of the ship, as best they can, with space obviously at a premium.

Life on the voyage was sharply regimented for both crew and slaves. The specified weekly diet of a slave, in 1708, consisted of half a pound of pork, a barrel each of beans, oatmeal, and millet, as well as half a pot of brandy and one-eighth of a pound of tobacco. A quarter of a pot of palm oil, another important commodity from the Guinea coast, was also mixed into the porridge each week to improve the health of the slave.[24] By comparison with the usual diets in workhouses, in England, during this period, the diet was very good; slaves were, after all, valuable commodities. Morale, however, could be a problem on the voyage and some slaves refused to eat. Moslem slaves were sometimes outraged by the provision of pork. Forced feeding apparatuses, therefore, were a necessary accoutrement of any voyage, also useful as implements of torture as and when required.

Because of the grim conditions with which slaves were confronted, attempts were made to mitigate the miseries of the middle passage. Musical entertainment was often provided for the slaves in order to revive their flagging spirits – anticipating the modern cruise ship in a macabre way. As Rømer reported, 'The Europeans are preoccupied with keeping their slaves in good humour. Therefore, they buy drums and pipes on the coast, and bring along lyres and other musical instruments. Furthermore, a part of the ship is given over where they can dance and play'.[25] Such dances must have been rather awkward for chains were not removed for these occasions.

Nevertheless, slave mutinies did occur. In the early hours of 15 September 1709, for example, a revolt broke out on a Danish slave ship, the *Fridericus Quartus*, which lasted some time before it was crushed. The leaders, in this case, were skinned alive or dismembered, but in the wake of a similar disturbance on the *Christianus Quintus* in 1775, the remaining slaves were deposited upon a neighbouring barren shore to save themselves as they could, with the ship then sunk, in order to claim on the insurance. That same year, 400 slaves on the frigate *Christiansborg* succeeded in breaking loose and gaining control of 1,200 firearms, the worst mutiny recorded on a Danish ship. It was crushed only when forces sent out from Christiansborg Fortress arrived on the scene. Sixty-one slaves died in the ensuing engagement.[26]

Despite such setbacks, the Danish slave trade continued. Perhaps, one of the finest of the slaving ships under the Danish flag was *The Count Bernstorff* (illus. 256), which sailed the triangle from Copenhagen to the Guinea coast and then across the Middle Passage to the Danish West Indies, during the 1780s. With unintentional irony, it had been named after the minister who was instrumental in abolishing serfdom at home at about the same time.

Not all of the Danish fortresses served primarily as temporary slave barracks. Kongensten Fortress (1782), one of the last of the Danish establishments built in

256 *The Slave Ship 'Count Bernstorff'*, 1799, coloured drawing.

West Africa along with Prinsensten, served as a multi-tribal fortification dominating the area round Rio Volta, with the Danes, under Jens Adolph Kiøge, the new
general, controlling what had previously been a region of conflicting tribes,
damaging trade in the area. A painting by Albert Eckhout and collected by King
Frederik III, *African Gold Coast Warrior*, depicts the sort of fierce tribal warrior who
would have fought in Kiøge's army of 4,000 men, though the latter would have
a Hellebæk musket, as well as his characteristic broad-bladed sword. In payment
for his services such a warrior would received two skilling for their period of
service, along with tobacco and brandy. Under the nominal command of Otho,
king of the Accra tribe, the integration of the native into the Danish military
defence system involved considerable ceremony. The engraving *Otho's Camp at Volta*
(illus. 257), a work by the Danish doctor Paul Erdmann Isert, who accompanied
General Kiøge on his campaigns, illustrates such an event. Later to become an
abolitionist, Isert wrote *Reise nach Guinea und den Caribbischen Inseln in Columbien*
(Journey to Guinea and the Caribbean Islands in Columbia) (1788), from which
this illustration comes, a work which provides considerable insight at the time
into the organization and functioning of the slave trade on both sides of the
Atlantic, as well as much anecdotal information.

257 Paul Erdmann Isert,
Otho's Camp at Volta, 1784,
engraving.

Administrative Consolidation of the Danish Virgin Islands

The second half of the eighteenth century was a period of economic boom for Denmark, with free trade extended to all Danish subjects in 1754. As a result, the Danish-Norwegian Crown took over direct control of the Caribbean and Guinean colonies and fortresses from the Danish West Indian-Guinea Company, thereby allowing greater independence to the planters and independent merchants. This event is depicted in a painting by Anton Christoph Rüde, *Frederik V and the Directors of the West Indian-Guinea Company* (illus. 258), where the king receives the deeds to the colonies and fortresses of the company, assisted by A. G. Moltke, in the presence of the eminent Danish minister Count J. H. E. Bernstorff who had expected considerable financial benefits to accrue to the government. The exchange proved more beneficial to island planters and merchants than to the crown or the company, for the national debt was quickly trebled and shareholders received only three-fifths of the nominal value of their shares. That said, the crown assumed the responsibilities of government, with local authority, under a Governor General, Baron C. L. von Prøck, based in the town of Christiansted, on St Croix, founded in 1735. *Prospect of Christiansværn* depicts the seat of the governor's military power at this period (illus. 259). The crenellated fortress, containing a two-storey neo-classical building, was important both practically and symbolically, at a time when privateers from without and slaves from within could threaten the security of the colony. During Prøck's tenure, efficiency in colonial local government improved and more humanitarian principles were lauded. Though the governor's written mandate confirmed the status of slaves as private chattels, it limited the circumstances in which they could be executed, maimed

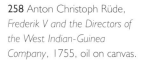

258 Anton Christoph Rüde, *Frederik V and the Directors of the West Indian-Guinea Company*, 1755, oil on canvas.

or otherwise punished. Its benefits remained theoretical, however, for objections about the concomitant intrusion upon private property rights from both governor and planters kept it a dead letter. Moreover, hunting after 'marons', that is, runaway slaves, was and remained a popular sport.

In 1755 the Seven Years War commenced. The hostilities between France and Britain disrupted their sugar trade, enabling the Danish-Norwegian sugar planters and merchants, as subjects of a neutral power, to thrive in their place. Among these were Nicholas Cruger, in whose trading house Alexander Hamilton (c. 1755–1804), later first Secretary of the Treasury in the United States, became an apprentice.

Sugar had become Denmark's white gold. The domino effect in Copenhagen was enormous in economic terms; at its zenith over half

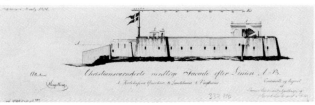

259 V. Gjellerup and V. Friis, *Prospect of Christiansværn*, 1836, drawing.

of the city's exports consisted of refined sugar. Furthermore, an increase in the number of slaves in the colonies mirrored the economic benefits in Denmark. Within two decades the number of slaves on St Croix increased from 12,000 to 24,000, 80 per cent of whom worked the fields. Their days were long, for work usually commenced at four in the morning and ceased at about six in the evening, with the whip encouraging the less sprightly, wielded by a 'bomba'. This was the name given to the slave, freed from menial labour, who held authority over several dozen other slaves, who, together with all other slaves and 'bombas' were subject to the white overseer.

Longevity amongst slaves was rare. The death of slaves, as a Danish government official of the time, Reimert Haagensen, pointed out, occasioned little ceremony: burial occurred the same day, with the body, unencumbered by a coffin, dumped into a hole.[27]

The Jews of St Thomas

Jews, discriminated against in all European countries at the time, had found a welcome refuge in the Dutch and Danish Caribbean island colonies in the seventeenth century. In the Danish Virgin Islands, Gabriel Milan, the scion of a rich Jewish family with connections in Portugal, Flanders and the Hanseatic city of Hamburg, served as governor of the colony from 1684 until 1686, and Emanuel Vass was to negotiate with the French authorities in Martinique over the transfer of St Croix from French to Danish sovereignty.[28] The colony also had other Jewish sons of note. Benjamin Franks, a merchant of St Thomas, was a key figure in the prosecution's case against the notorious pirate Captain William Kidd, who mastered the ship from the Caribbean to New York upon which Franks had travelled. More famously, there was Judah P. Benjamin (1811–1884), of St Croix, who went to Florida, later becoming Attorney-General, then Secretary of War and finally Secretary of State in the Confederate States of America, under the presidency of Jefferson Davis. After the collapse of the Confederacy he fled to London, where he continued to practise law.

260 Hansen, *A View of Charlotte Amalie from Blackbeard Hill,* c. 1850, engraving.

Most of the Jews had come to the island in the eighteenth century. A considerable number had come to the Danish Virgin Islands from St Eustatius, after the British Admiral Rodney attacked the Dutch colony during the American Revolution. A few Sephardic Jews had fled Morocco where they had fallen out of favour with the Sultan, while still others had sought refuge from the slave revolution in Hispaniola, during the French Revolution.[29]

After Denmark became the first European nation to completely liberate the Jews in 1814, a considerable number of Jews flocked to both Denmark and her colonies. By 1837 there were some 400 Jews living in St Thomas alone. An English visitor to the island wrote in 1843 that 'the flock of Israel's fold is thick and fares well at this place; however, one or two houses of eminence are of this class, as also a large portion of the second rate traders, those who keep stores of hardware, glass porcelain and the dispensers of spirit and friperie ...'[30] There were also a few Jewish planters.[31]

Most famous today of all St Thomas's Jewish inhabitants is undoubtedly Camille Pissarro (1830–1903), who was born in the free port of Charlotte Amalie where his father Frederick, who had married his young widowed aunt, Rachel Petit, was a minor merchant. There they lived in a typical townhouse in Charlotte Amalie, including an internal courtyard with a shop on the ground floor and accommodation above. *A View of Charlotte Amalie from Blackbeard Hill* (late nineteenth century; illus. 260) depicts it much as it looked when Pissarro resided there. Such a marriage between close relations as Pissarro's father had forged was frowned upon by the Jewish congregation, because of its violation of Levitical Law, and the couple was obliged to be married in a civil ceremony. Ultimately, though, the matter had gone to the chief rabbi of Copenhagen, who had religious authority over the Jews of St Thomas, and congregational harmony was eventually achieved after several years. Perhaps it was helped by the fact that the familial links of Pissarro's family with the New World were considerable; indeed, it was said that the Pissarros were related to the Spanish conquistador Francisco Pizarro.

261 Camille Pissarro (attrib.), *A Jury of Painting on St Thomas*, c. 1851, black and brown ink and graphite on paper.

Pissarro went on to attend the Pietist Moravian school on St Thomas where a majority of the students were black or mulatto, before being sent, at the age of eleven, to his grandparents in France. He returned to the island however, in the summer of 1847.[32] It was then that he first met the Danish artist Fritz Melbye, who also made drawings of St Thomas, and whom he accompanied to Venezuela in pursuit of artistic themes. A work which Pissarro probably drew in St Thomas before his departure caricatures the philistine reaction of the local burghers of Charlotte Amalie to a painting by Melbye, *A Jury of Painting on St Thomas* (illus. 261). Obviously both artists had not achieved the public acclaim which they felt was their due when they set off for South America. None the less, Pissarro was to reside on St Thomas again from 1848 to 1852, when he drew *A View of Long Bay, St Thomas* (1852; illus. 262),[33] a subtle rendition of the island's enchanting coastline, and from 1854 to 1855.

262 Camille Pissarro, *A View of Long Bay, St Thomas*, 1852, pen and ink.

The Early Development of Denmark-Norway's Asian Colonies

Denmark's trading connections with the Far East were also lucrative, if not on the scale of those with her Caribbean colonies. Of particular importance was the mercantile factory established in Canton in 1720, the only city at all which Europeans could visit and through which Chinese tea, porcelain, silk, mother-of-pearl and lacquer were exported. *The Prospect of Canton* (illus. 263) depicts the European mercantile factories, situated along the riverside with the Danish factory, a large building containing offices and a warehouse, clearly seen on the far left. Two officials could be housed there, though only at certain permitted times and with their movements sharply restricted. Even Chinese visitors were only permitted when necessity required their presence. As the eighteenth-century Icelandic seaman Árni Magnússon wrote, 'No one was allowed into the city, and if our captain had to speak to someone there, two Chinese followed, carrying him blindfolded, to the place appointed for the meeting. After he had accomplished his task, he was once again carried blindfolded, outside the city gates'.[34] This scene achieved such popularity that it still appeared in the latter years of the nineteenth century on ivory fans, produced for export, as an example in the Victoria & Albert Museum, in London, shows. The frigates that plied the seas for China were the largest in the East India Company's fleet, carrying some 600–700 tons of goods, compared to the 300–350 tons of the ships which only went as far as India. Among the provisions which these ships carried on a typical voyage to China were fourteen oxen, thirty swine, fifteen sheep, two rams, two goats and one cow. On one such vessel the cow was renowned for having survived the return journey to and from Denmark no less than three times.[35]

The financial benefits of such voyages could be great, so that in 1783 alone five ships arrived back in Copenhagen from China.[36] For example, Christian Lintrup, the son of a Danish tradesman, made enough on three voyages from the purchase and sale of Chinese goods to eventually purchase the estate of Gjörslev, on Sjælland, along with two further neighbouring estates. Shortly thereafter,

263 *The Prospect of Canton,* late 18th century.

he was ennobled as Baron Lindencrone.

Sometimes, traders or ship captains would have their portrait bust baked in clay and painted with great realism by local Cantonese artists. One such patron of local talent was the portly Zacharias Allewelt, captain of the Chinaman *Kongen af Danmark*. A native of Holland, he had joined the Danish East India Company when trade to China blossomed in the 1720s.[37] The eventual formation of the Asiatic Company to handle the trade led to the construction of imposing neo-classical company buildings in Copenhagen, depicted much later in their cool and austere beauty by Vilhelm Hammershøi in *The Asiatic Company's Buildings in Copenhagen* (1902; see illus. 251).

264 First Lieutenant Gregers Daa Trellund, *A Plan of Tranquebar with Dansborg*, 1733, drawing with wash.

Aside from the physical inconvenience, the expenses of the East India trade were great, but shareholders in the company were already receiving considerable profits in the early years of the eighteenth century. Tranquebar grew and was established as the capital of the Danish Indian territory. With its more than 5000 inhabitants in the early years of the eighteenth century, it was larger than most Danish provincial cities of the time. Only about 300 of its principal citizens were native Danes, but it was they who gave the streets of the city their familiar names, such as King Street, Queen Street and Merchants' Street, names found in every Danish northern European, city and town. The wealth and ethnic diversity of its many inhabitants, as expressed in the city's architecture, can be seen in *A Plan of Tranquebar with Dansborg* (1733) by First Lieutenant Gregers Daa Trellund (illus. 264). The stone buildings there, aside from private houses, included the Protestant Zion Church, built in 1701, a Catholic church for the Portuguese, and various temples and pagodas. Most prominent of all, however, was the Danish fortress of Dansborg, which can be seen rising fierce and majestic in defence of the coast against maritime attack. Such a threat was real: the colony was vulnerable to attacks from both pirates and enemy European warships. Less majestic, though, are the 200 dwellings of straw, 100 houses of clay and 400 smaller hovels which housed the more humble inhabitants of the walled city, including slaves, some of whom were imported from Africa. Three harvests reaped by local farmers just managed to produce enough rice to feed the colony, 60 per cent of which was expropriated as tax by the Danish administration and sold in the city.

While Tranquebar was the first Indian destination for vessels loading pepper, Frederiksnagore, a loge of vast proportions on the Hoogley River, was the port of call for loading of fabrics and saltpetre. It was built upon an otherwise barren ground under the auspices of Lieutenant Colonel Ole Biel. From the third quarter of the eighteenth century until 1805, he reigned as commander-in-chief and principal entrepreneur, laying out the streets and building a panoply of buildings, public and private. Most striking was his extraordinary prison, in which segregation was arranged not only according to sex, as was usual, but according to race and religion. *Frederiksnagore* by Major General Peter Anker, Danish colonial governor in India, depicts this rather grand town (see illus. 252). Anker painted quite a large collection of works depicting the south of India and, on his return to Norway, used them to decorate many of the rooms of his country estate.

The Swedish East India Company

Sweden had established its own Swedish East India Company in 1732. Each of its expeditions was financed by public subscription with rapid return of dividends on the profit, based predominantly on the auction of tea and porcelain, but also of spices, such as cinnamon, ginger and arak (used in Swedish punch which came into fashion in the eighteenth century), as well as textiles, ivory and lacquer. However, exports to China remained insignificant. By the time of its closure in 1807, 132 voyages to the Orient had been made, many to Canton, from its seat at Gothenburg. The grand neo-classic façade of its headquarters was designed by the great Swedish Baroque architect Carl Hårleman. Despite the company's name, only eight ships ever terminated their voyages at India where a Swedish attempt to found a colonial factory at Porto Novo aroused the armed opposition of England and France.[38] None the less, the rewards of China were great enough to lure many a ship and passenger eastwards, including William Chambers (1726–1796), born in Gothenburg of a merchant of Scottish roots, and later knighted by the Swedish king. In 1755 he became architectural tutor to the young George III, still the Prince of Wales, and was allowed to assume the dignity of his foreign knighthood by adopting the prefix 'Sir.' His journey on a Chinaman of the Swedish East India Company to Canton had resulted in an immensely influential work, *Designs of Chinese Buildings* (1757), and a pagoda at Kew Gardens, near London, shortly thereafter. These were to exert enormous influence throughout Europe, helping to establish the fashion for Chinese architectural and decorative features, not least as reinterpreted through the English country house park. Such values were to find their own expression in Chamber's native Sweden, at the Royal Park of Drottningholm and Haga, and numerous country houses, including Forsmark, in central Sweden.

Not everyone was pleased with the success of the Swedish East India Company. Many Pietists felt that the luxurious goods entering Sweden were weakening the moral fibre of the people. Others of a more practical turn, such as the botanist Carl von Linné, felt the trade with China was debilitating native Swedish industry.[39]

The Scandinavian Caribbean Colonies at their Zenith

West as well as east continued to offer vistas of opportunity to many merchants and colonists. As the decades of the eighteenth century wore on, planters in the Danish Virgin Islands grew more prosperous. In 1783, more than 127 ships from the West Indies visited Copenhagen, a good indication of the amount of trade involved (illus. 265).[40] One such prosperous planter, Johan Lorenz Carstens (1705–1747), later ennobled as Baron Castenschiold, wrote charmingly of the life-style of the leisured classes. It was customary, he wrote, for both sexes to awake late in the morning, the ladies afterwards to do their sewing, the men to make their promenades along the harbour. This latter custom can be seen in *A Prospect of the Harbour Square in Christiansted Viewed From the Sea* (illus. 266). The midday dinner was taken after these occupations, after which all retired, Spanish style, for their lengthy siestas. The evening was the most lively period of the day, with cards and billiards providing entertainment until late in the night, with rum and other alcoholic drinks lubricating the lively social intercourse between the sexes.[41]

Plantation life could offer wonderful opportunities to express the wealth and social station of the planter and his family. One of the most splendid of plantation houses in the Danish Virgin Island was that belonging to Johan Sobotker, in its heyday during the 1780s. *Hogensborg Plantation* (1838), by Frederik von Scholten depicts a small but palatial establishment, named 'a city of hawks', amid well-tended gardens (illus. 267).[42]

By the 1790s, Caribbean plantation society had reached its social and economic zenith and the European planters were increasingly joined by a new social group, the slave-owning freedmen, some of whom were notorious for bad treatment of their own newly acquired slaves. By 1800, there were at least 1,500 freedmen on St Croix, many manumitted by the last testament of their masters or mistresses, and required to carry identification attesting to their free status. Manumission, however, was no assurance of the free status of the slave, since creditors with liens on the goods of an estate could seize upon the slave in compensation before freedom was granted. That said, from the 1790s onwards,

265 *Prospect of the Danish Flag Dannebrog Flying from Fort Christiansværn and on the Ships in the Bay of Christiansted.*

266 H. G. Beenfeldt, *A Prospect of the Harbour Square in Christiansted Viewed From the Sea*, 1815, drawing on paper.

British pressure to end the slave trade greatly reduced the number of Danish imports of slaves and, from July 1791, Count Ernst Schimmelmann established a commission to improve the conditions of the remaining trade. As proprietor of two plantations on St Croix, La Grange and La Princesse, as well as two others on St Thomas and St John, all inherited from his father in 1782, he attempted to establish plantation models in which the worst aspects of slavery were ameliorated. He even sent promising young slave boys to Denmark, where they were provided with vocational training.[43] Not surprisingly, when in 1782 he was offered and accepted the directorship of the Danish East India-Guinea Company, he continued to foster a softened image of the slave trade and to ameliorate the conditions of slavery.

Opinion, however, both in government and amongst the public at large, was not totally convinced that the trade had become thoroughly humane and on 16 March 1792 the slave trade was banned, an event commemorated by the minting of a medal. On one side the profile of a young black man is given, surrounded by the legend 'Me miserum' (Poor me), on the reverse the Greek god Nemesis tramples upon a yoke.

For the supporters of abolition, the victory was, at least in the short term, uncertain, for the trade was not to cease on the date of proclamation, but a decade later, in 1802. In the meantime, the slave trade increased in volume, and with the company's trade monopoly abolished, anyone who wished could import slaves, with the assistance of government loans. Furthermore, special benefits for traders who exported to the Danish West Indian colonies were granted, especially for the export of female slaves, capable of reproducing the slave population. While the birth rate of these women remained stubbornly low, the trade did reach its numeric heights during this period.

None the less, alternative usages of Denmark's African establishments were considered and their adjacent ports were opened up to all nations. Furthermore, efforts were made to create an African colony, under Dr Isert, on an island in the River Volta. However, slave traders hindered the development of the fledgling colony, which was then re-established 60 miles from both the River Volta and the town of Accra, all for a rent of only £16 sterling per month, paid to the chief of the Aquapim. Such cash transactions were not always simple matters, for chiefs often demanded multiple purchases of land, since they tended to hold the view that land neither immediately occupied, nor cultivated, reverted to the previous owner. The distances from an important navigable river and major mercantile centre may not have encouraged trade in the settlement, but it did provide the colony with a more salubrious micro-climate and fertile soil, enabling the successful cultivation of Guinea corn, millet and cotton, all assisted by the successful introduction of the plough. The Danish government also supported Isert's attempts to establish his colony successfully. Ostensibly, this assistance was justified as a means to encourage the abolition of slavery by providing alternative economic inititatives, but, in fact, it actually condoned it, for the import of slaves from Christiansborg, albeit seen as a temporary measure, proved itself as much a necessity in Africa as in the Danish Virgin Islands, though not in the same numbers. The inability of white settlers to survive the climate while engaged in hard labour seemed to demand the use of slaves. Isert's failure to respect the rigours of the climate led to his own death and Lieutenant Colonel Roer was appointed to continue his attempt to keep the colony running.

Considerable energies were also devoted to adapting European architectural

267 Frederik von Scholten, *Høgensborg Plantation*, 1838, watercolour.

268 *An Elevation of a Temporary House to be Constructed on the Trunk of a Tree*, from C. B. Wadström, *An Essay on Colonization particularly applied to the Western Coast of Africa with some free thoughts on Cultivation and Commerce...*, pt II (1794).

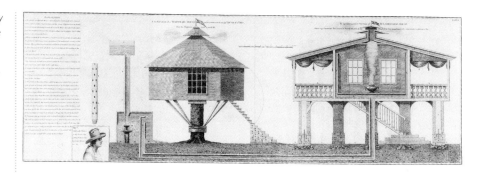

forms to the geographical and climatic demands in Africa. This can be seen in a fanciful illustration, *An Elevation of a Temporary House to be Constructed on the Trunk of a Tree* (illus. 268). On the left, a multi-sided single-roomed house stands upon a tree trunk as on a carousel and a single flight of stairs leads through the centre of the building.

An alternative is provided by 'Mr A. Johansen's Permanent Colonial House Adapted for the Transfusion of a Continual Circulation of Air', in which a house possessing five pillars of brick on each elevation, which rest on stone courses, is illustrated, with arches supporting the single wooden room. This has a Grecian urn in the centre for containing a fire, the smoke from which rises and escapes through the double lantern chimney hole. There are two windows, with two glazing bars, in this room on each elevation and broad verandas, including balustrades of wood, while the gently pitched roof rests in turn on simple pillars, devoid of capitals, an unusual adaptation of classical forms to southern needs.[44]

The Swedish Colony of St Barthelemy and Other Colonial Endeavours

With the Danish Virgin Islands flourishing, Sweden, too, wished to acquire her own place in the sun. To this end, in 1784, the Swedish king, Gustaf III used the opportunity of a visit to Paris, while travelling back from Italy, to make an advantageous exchange with Sweden's ancient ally. In return for giving France the right of an entrepôt for French goods in Gothenburg, amongst other trading privileges, Sweden received the small Caribbean islands of St Barthelemy and St Martin, colonized by the French in 1648 and annexed from the Knights of Malta seventeen years later. On 7 March, 1785, Sweden assumed control of these islands, with their population of 739, 458, of whom most were white, mainly French, English and Dutch settlers, with only 281 blacks and mulattos. Although some agriculture was successful, despite the stony ground and semi-yearly period of virtually total drought, the principal benefit of the island's acquisition was the economic gains expected from Le Carenage, St Barthelemy's splendid harbour. Total sugar and cotton production did not even fill four ship-loads per year, nor were the harvest of fish, quarries of lime and animal husbandry sufficient for anything more than subsistence income for the colonists. The harbour, however, enjoyed a growth of trade of astonishing proportions, serving as it did as an entrepôt, and the population increased accordingly. By the end of 1785, the population of the colony had grown to 950,[45] reflecting increases in islands of similar size in the Antilles.

To administer this new colony, Sweden established the Swedish West India Company in 1786 (its affairs were taken over by the Swedish government in 1806), which shared political power with the new governor, sent out from Stockholm. He established his seat at Gustavia, St Barthelemy's only town, christened after the Swedish king, and site of a fortress, Fort Gustaf. Governmental authority was not onerous, for, though Swedish law superseded the French legal code, local customs were also incorporated into the legal framework. With only 348 inhabitants at the time of the Swedish assumption of government, Gustavia had grown to some 5,000 in 1800, making it one of the largest towns under Swedish dominion, on a par with Uppsala in terms of population at that time.[46]

Colonists were drawn from a range of different European nationalities, including not only Swedes, English and French, but also Dutch, Danes, Americans, Spanish and Germans, some native to the Caribbean, others immigrants from their home countries. To cope with this pluralistic and, indeed, mobile colonial society, it was found necessary to elevate the three most important languages, Swedish, French and English, to an official position in the colony's governmental, legal and economic system. Such a liberal approach to languages, however, did not address the social problems of such a rootless society and some contemporaries complained of the corruption attendant on a colony with people always on the move. One writer of the time lamented the situation writing, 'The West Indian way of living, residing and moving on means that one can never rely on anyone. The urge to make a profit, on the one hand, and fraud, on the other, turns people into a form of currency, circulating in the world in exactly the same fashion as coins do'.[47] A Lutheran church was established in 1787, with morning services at ten, to improve the spiritual and moral wellbeing of the colony. The church also provided a venue for Roman Catholics, who made up the majority of the population, as well as for Anglicans, whether British or American in origin.

Sweden also attempted to establish proper colonies on the West African coast. In this project they were influenced by the voyage of the *Chevalier Des Marchais*, commissioned by the French government with a view to exploring the African Guinea coast and establishing a French colonial settlement there. A society was formed at Nyköping, in Sweden, 'for the purpose of diffusing those principles, and that species of civilisation, which appeared to them best calculated to promote social order and happiness [...] It was concluded then, that there was a probable prospect of establishing in Africa, with little opposition, either from European claims or from the natives, a colony on their own principles, which might serve as a basis for a new and free community [...] beyond the sphere of its political, financial and (especially) commercial influence'.[48] While it was intended for some 40 families to embark, mainly composed of manufacturers and merchants, it was ardently hoped that the pitfalls of the Old World could be avoided, with both private monopoly and imprisonment for debt made illegal in the colony.

This utopian initiative found support in the high echelons of government in Sweden with the senator Baron Liljencrantz, Secretary of State, who induced Gustaf III to grant a charter to these 40 families. They were to be permitted to organize their own government, enact their own laws, and otherwise set up a form of government best suited to their own tastes and largely independent of that of the home country. Idealism was, however, not the Swedish government's prime motivation. For, as Wadström, who had joined the attempt at establishing the colony, wrote after the attempt had failed, '... the truth is, that the King loved gold, my worthy companions loved natural science, and I loved colonisation.'[49]

The colonists journeyed from Sweden to Havre de Grace, on the French coast, from which they set sail with a ship of the French Senegal Company, arriving at the end of the rainy season. However, changes of administration in French West Africa and rumours of war between France and England created difficulties with the company. Also, 'the general war, into which the most powerful negro nations were provoked, by the oppressive monopoly exercised by the Senegal company, to declare against the French, rendered it impossible for us to penetrate to the interior, through the extensive maritime territories of those justly irate princes'. Even the purchase of a parrot, according to this colonist, had to pass through the hands of the company, a fact which made him most irate himself.[50] Cape Verde, it was felt, would have provided the most satisfactory location for the colony, but political considerations had prevented this and other plans from coming to fruition; the colony, therefore, came to naught.

Though in no way as disastrous as the attempt to colonize West Africa, Sweden's new West Indian colony was also assailed by difficulties. For one thing, St Barthelemy was dependent on food imports to sustain its growing population. In the absence of natural springs, cisterns collecting rainwater also had to be introduced in order to provide enough water on this extremely dry island. Furthermore, after the beginning of the French Revolution, privateering by the British against French vessels hindered trade. None the less, new immigrants continued to flock to the island. In particular, many French colonists fled there from Guadeloupe, horrified by the emancipation of the slaves and the grisly massacres that appalled the world in the French colony of St Domingue (now Haiti) after the French Revolution.

By 1793, there were some 1,488 inhabitants in the colony, 568 living in Gustavia alone. By 1800, when 1,330 ships visited the port, the population had reached 6,000, 5,000 of whom lived in Gustavia, a truly dramatic demographic increase. To cope with this quantity of residents, 32 cisterns were needed to provide adequate water, as well as some 871 dwellings of varying sizes, almost all newly built. The population at this time included 40 merchants, two insurance agents, 22 publicans and one watchmaker. Food was purveyed by six bakers and four butchers, with other domestic needs catered for by three goldsmiths, eight builders, eleven joiners, six tailors, three shoemakers, a hatter and a milliner. Six doctors looked after the health of the colony. Despite the island's small size, education of the young was surprisingly well-provided for in five schools, though most of these were very small. Recreation was not neglected in eight public houses for the sociable and the thirsty. Some drinking establishments even provided billiards.[51] Dancing was also very popular and there was a resident dancing master, who supplemented his income by teaching duelling.[52]

Other more sophisticated forms of entertainment were available as well. The New Private Theatre opened in Gustavia, in 1804, established in a former general store. There productions were held using both local talent, as well as groups who came out on tours from London. Concerts, too, were held, using local as well as foreign talent.[53]

Blacks and mulattos, it would seem, were apparently especially fond of dancing. Carlander wrote:

> Male and female people of colour and the better Negroes assembly with the
> Governor's permission and dance their minuets and Conradian dances,
> often with greater skill than the most elegant whites. Each person pays one
> daler for which he receives food, wine and port, to the accompaniment of
> music. English Negroes have only Sundays free, but French Negroes have
> both Saturday and Sunday at their disposal. Even the labouring Negroes
> dance on Saturday and Sunday afternoons, two by two, as is their wont;
> their music consists of one or two drums, open at one end which is struck
> […], whilst a Negress will sing and shake a rattle, during which time the
> others clap their hands and sing, some in chorus, some in solo.[54]

Generally, though, life in the colony was uneventful. As Carlander narrates, baths or promenades, either by foot or on horseback, were taken at seven or eight in the morning. *The View of the Harbour Streets in Gustavia* (1800) depicts the heart of Gustavia upon which such promenades would have been endlessly repeated (see illus. 241). Thereafter, the daily work was carried on. Dinner was served at two or three in the afternoon, after which a little work might be done. At six in the evening, a further promenade might be undertaken or a game of whist indulged. Tea would then be served from seven to nine in the evening, after which a small collation might follow.[55]

The Napoleonic Wars brought some problems to the colony. Many felt that if neutrality could be maintained, the island would continue to prosper, but in 1801 St Barthelemy was briefly seized by the British and its Swedish inhabitants were obliged to swear allegiance to the British Crown. By 1802, however, Swedish sovereignty had been re-established and £900 paid to the island in restitution for misdemeanours perpetrated there during the occupation. Then, in 1807, both British and French privateers assailed the island. None the less, trade thrived. The release of the colony from the trade restrictions the Swedish West India Company's privileges had imposed, in 1806, and the opening of free trade to all Swedish citizens the following year made for a considerable boom, with nearly 1,800 ships visiting St Barthelemy in 1811. The countryside, however, languished in a poverty which contrasted sharply to the prosperity of Gustavia. The years 1812–15 were indeed a period of economic strength for St Barthelemy. No less than 20 per cent of United States exports, from October 1813 to September 1814, passed through the colony, when war between the United States and Britain closed British colonial ports to the Americans.[56] The slave trade was also thriving, for not only did representatives of the Swedish West India Company continue in the traffic, but the Crown itself benefited through the sale by auction of all slaves who had found sanctuary in the island from other colonies during the war.

The Scandinavian Caribbean Colonies in the Post-Napoleonic Period

In the Danish corner of the Caribbean, the period of the Napoleonic Wars, especially 1808–15, under British occupation were relatively uneventful, with British forces and local Danish administration working amicably together for the population of some 40,000. The economy also improved, with sugar cane in particular fetching high prices. Still, the ending of hostilities brought rejoicing in the colony when, in 1815, the Danish Virgin Islands were returned by Britain to the mother country, now shorn of Norway, which had been given to Sweden by the Allies in appreciation of her assistance during the Napoleonic Wars. Though over half the tonnage of the Danish fleet was now reduced, the painting *Prospect of the Danish Flag Dannebrog Flying from Fort Christiansvarn and on the Ships in the Bay of Christiansted* can be seen as an evocation of the joy of the colonists returning to the Danish fold. The colony now consisted of whites, free blacks and mulattos, and slaves. Though a proclamation of 1755 had given whites and freedmen equal rights, only now, some 60 years later, were these rights respected.[57] However, life for most slaves continued much as it had for decades. A watercolour *Scene from St Croix: A Negro Hut* depicts a typical slave habitation, with a pig and parrot in the open doorway lending local colour (illus. 269).

Unfortunately, the end of the Napoleonic Wars meant the end of the Swedish colony's prosperity, as rival British, French and Dutch ports began to thrive. The possibility of such a predicament had already been astutely perceived back in 1788 by the then governor, P. H. von Rosenstein. He had voiced his misgivings regarding the benefits of continued economic growth which had fallen to the colony, for he felt that it would only prosper if there was war between the great colonial European powers. He was thus at pains to find another means to bring economic prosperity: 'The virtual war which has newly erupted between England and France, gave St Barthelemy the greatest expectation on a brilliant future, and left me with great anxiety on how I should deal with this situation'.[58] Almost 30 years later, the tone and content of the governmental secretary was similar: Carl Ulrik von Hauswolff stated in 1816, 'It would be foolish to deny that both the warring colonial powers, as well as their jealous trading partner states, have elevated our cliff to great prosperity, and that the general peace, which will re-establish the former patterns of trade, threatens to destroy the new, rootless colony's very life and to reduce it to nothing'.[59] Population dwindled and the

269 After F. Visby, *Scene from St Croix: A Negro Hut*, 1867(?), lithograph.

price of cotton also collapsed. The tentacles of poverty now reached even into the highest of homes. Governor Rosenvärd, who arrived in St Barthelemy, in 1816, complained in his first report back to Sweden of the lack of space in the Government House, which he shared with his wife and child. He likened its close quarters to that of an English ship and bemoaned that 'there is only one bed, the bedclothes are torn, there is hardly any bed linen and pillowcases, and all the napkins are worthless, though even of these there are hardly any to be found'.[60] The coffers of the colony were empty, as trade moved to St Thomas and St Eustache, the colony's principal rivals. The crown was therefore obliged to take over the financial maintenance of the colony's public order. Matters had so deteriorated that, by 1817, many died of starvation, especially slaves. In desperation, a large number of the colony's inhabitants hoped for a general European war which would boost the island's economy, as the Napoleonic Wars had done, but no war materialized.

In 1818 trade once again picked up, in part because of an increase in trade to the former Spanish colonies. This provided a temporary respite from such economic miseries, while a new and more optimistic governor, Johan Norderling, was appointed. The ensuing modest economic upsurge even allowed the establishment of a newspaper and printing press in Gustavia, run by a mulatto, though a certain amount of official censorship was soon imposed upon it. Epidemics and other natural disasters, however, followed and the government in Sweden considered a sale of the colony, if only a suitable offer could be made. None was forthcoming and matters remained unresolved.

Then a series of disasters struck. In 1819, a hurricane destroyed 56 houses in Gustavia alone. This was followed by drought and yet another severe hurricane which, among many other buildings, destroyed the recently erected Methodist church. Reconstruction could compensate for these ravages, but the destruction of trade caused by the opening of British ports to American trade in 1831 could not be made good, and many foreign merchants emigrated. Agriculture seemed to offer no better prospects, for the cotton crop brought in diminishing returns, 150 bales in 1825, only 80 in 1826. Vines brought in from Madeira also failed to take hold.[61]

Matters were also not going well in the Danish Virgin Islands, where persistent economic decline was increasingly overtaking St Croix and St Jan. In the 1820s, the price of sugar declined by a third, whilst the sugar yield fell by 40 per cent. Making matters worse, sugar beets flooded the European markets and many planters went bankrupt. Of some compensation, though, was the increase of trade which benefited St Thomas. Its principal town, Charlotte Amalie, whose 11,000 inhabitants made it Denmark's second largest urban centre, reaped the benefits of the newly opened trade between itself and the now independent Latin American colonies. Such grand houses as Frederiksberg (1820s) and Cathrineberg (1830), with their commanding views and imposing Doric porticoes were among the grandest in the whole of the Caribbean colonies. This economic upswing was further reflected in the establishment, in 1837, of the Bank of St Thomas, the first Danish private banking house, to meet the town's financial needs. A symbol of the relative wealth of Charlotte Amalie can be seen in the proud classical features shown in *Interior of Riise's Apothecary Shop, Charlotte Amalie* (illus. 270), which had been established in 1838. Despite such proofs of prosperity, popular discontent with the economic conditions increasingly seethed, erupting into great violence in Frederiksted, on St Croix, on 1 October 1878. Danish forces were able to crush the uprising, but the basic economic and social problems of the colony remained unsolved.

As the nineteenth century progressed, it became more and more clear to the Danish government that the Indian colonies, too, could not be maintained. With half the Danish fleet reduced during the Napoleonic Wars, order and provisions could not be easily provided. Therefore, in the summer of 1845, both Tranquebar and Frederiksnagore were sold to The British Company for 1,250,000 riksdaler, with sovereignty assumed by Britain in the autumn of that year. As a contemporary of the time stated, 'Everyone, white and black, Hindus and Muslims were united in their sadness, that their dear flag had been lowered'.[62] Twenty-three years later, the final Danish possession in the region, the Nicobar Islands, where the death rate for whites from malaria had prevented almost any successful colonization, were transferred without payment to Britain.

The Abolition of Slavery in the Scandinavian Colonies and Their Sale

By 1834, the population on St Barthelemy reached 3,720, of whom 2,080 lived in Gustavia, the remainder in the countryside. Severe economic conditions exacerbated the poor relations between whites and blacks. Moreover, yet another hurricane devastated the colony, destroying over 200 houses and killing 40 resi-

dents. Even smuggling ceased to be a lucrative employment, since the former Spanish colonies were now free and could trade with whom they wished. The islands were no longer needed as transit points. Only local petty smuggling of brandy now continued.

Slowly, however, in the 1840s, the situation began to improve. The Swedish Colonial Department was closed down and the colony transferred to the Finance Department. The introduction of yams improved the economy, catering for the British Caribbean market. Now, though, it was more the countryside, and not Gustavia, which prospered.

Slavery, meanwhile, had continued unabated, though new imports of slaves had long ceased, under the watchful eye of the British navy. None the less, it was quite clear to the Swedish authorities that slavery was a social institution which had fallen out of fashion in the colonies belonging to the northern European nations and, more importantly, was showing itself to be economically unsatisfactory. Negotiations, therefore, commenced in the late 1840s to implement the gradual emancipation of slaves. In 1846, 1,800 slaves were purchased by the state and freed for the sum of 19,991 Spanish dollars, with the remaining 282 freed the following year for the much larger amount of 24,699 Spanish dollars. On 9 October 1847, slavery was officially abolished in the Swedish colony, with the last slaves owned in the name of the Swedish crown finally manumitted. By contrast with the Danish Virgin Islands, where the old and the infirm among former

270 After F. Visby, *Interior of Riise's Apothecary Shop, Charlotte Amalie*, lithograph.

slaves remained the responsibility of their former masters, in St Barthelemy they were maintained from public funds. The reduction by a minimum of 50 per cent of free labour wages in this period and the bankruptcy of many plantations, especially those producing sugar cane, meant that the differential between free and slave labour in cost terms for the planter was now reduced. Furthermore, there were other economic benefits from emancipation for impoverished planters, since they no longer needed to support their superannuated or under-used labourers, as had been the case whilst slavery existed.

On the Danish Guinea coast, despite British prohibition the slave trade continued to flourish, with 1,500 slaves each year exported from the Danish colonial settlements well into the 1820s. Local African traders, and in particular the Asante kings, who were at the height of their power, vehemently opposed any abolition of the trade and the military weakness of the enclaves – increased by the disruptions of the Napoleonic Wars keeping military forces occupied else-where – further convinced the Danish authorities tacitly to allow the trade to continue. As the Asante king Osei Bonsus put it, 'Let the King of Denmark do what he will in his country, I shall do what I will in mine'.[63] He also threatened that the abolition of the trade would mean the slaughter of criminals and captives of war. This was worrying, for the Asante king reigned over more than a quarter of a million square kilometres at the time.[64] By the mid-1820s, however, Danish toleration was at an end. War broke out between the Danes and Asante in 1826. With support from Britain and, in alliance with the Akwamu king, Kwafo Akotoh I, a vicious campaign involving the burning of many Asante and Awuna villages commenced, a struggle which was to continue under later British rule intermittently throughout the century. Nevertheless, the slave trade continued and even blossomed. While the export of slaves from Africa before the European prohibition amounted to about 100,000 annually, the numbers doubled after the prohibition. Falling prices also meant that many Africans themselves were now able to purchase slaves throughout the continent and the Spanish and Portuguese colonies remained avid buyers, the legal and naval impediments of Britain notwithstanding.

Prinsensten (illus. 271) remained an importance fortress for Danish military operations, commanded by Edward J. A. Carstensen, last governor of the Danish

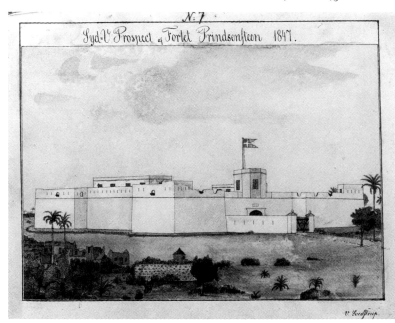

271 V. Svedstrup, *Prinsensten*, 1847, coloured drawing.

Guinea settlements and commander of the fortress, and had been rebuilt by Lieutenant Johan Vilhelm Svedstrup during the twilight of the Danish Guinea colonial period in 1846–7. Shortly thereafter, though, it had to endure a three-month siege, until the middle of October when grenades and other weapons were used to turn the surrounding coconut groves into flaming infernos which engulfed native villages. After five days onslaught, the Danish ultimatum for a final cessation of the trade in that area was finally accepted by local tribes. Inland, however, away from Danish control, the trade continued until, in 1848, all slaves were freed under British pressure. Then, on 31 December 1849 the Guinea colonial settlements, including Christiansborg, Fredensborg, Kongensten, Prinsensten and the small Augustaborg, were transferred to British sovereignty. So desperate was Denmark to rid herself of them that all went for the small sum of £10,000, a tiny fraction of the £285,000 which had been optimistically requested in 1843.

Despite the emancipation of the slaves in the Danish establishments in Guinea, freedom for existing slaves in the Danish Virgin Islands was first planned for the end of the year 1859, as Christian VIII had put it in the summer of 1847, 'with the motives of justice and humanity'.[65] Newborn children of slaves were deemed to be free already from the date of this proclamation, but the existing slave population, impatient for emancipation, rose up during the following summer, and threatened to overrun the colony. Taking matters into his own hand, the governor, Peter von Scholten, whose mistress was a mulatto, then issued his own proclamation, emancipating the slaves throughout the colony, in 1848. The seat of his government, where both the governor and his administration were accommodated is depicted in *Government House in Christiansted* (illus. 272).

As a result of this bold act of emancipation, von Scholten himself was returned to Denmark and brought to trial for his unlawful emancipation and failure to crush the uprising. However, the Danish High Court refused to overturn his decision and crushed that of the lower court. Thus ended all slavery in the Danish dominions, more than half a century after serfdom had been abolished in the mother country, an event commemorated in Emancipation Park, in Charlotte Amalie, opposite the fortress, on one side, and the two-storied Grand Hotel (1843), with its imposing first floor loggia, on the other. Altogether some 50,000 slaves had been transported on Danish ships, just under half of one per cent of the approximate total of 11,000,000 Africans who survived the Middle Passage over the centuries until abolition of the Atlantic slave trade.[66] Of these two-thirds had been male, for female slaves had generally fetched two-thirds less in the Americas. Since the internal African slave trade sought females rather than men, the two trades had a proven complementary arrangement. Yet even this was by no means the end of slavery, for when the Atlantic trade was abolished, the internal African one expanded, and continued to survive well into the twentieth century, in some areas to the present day.[67]

In St Barthelemy, too, slavery was soon abolished, yet many problems remained. In the 1850s a catastrophic fire destroyed 135 of Gustavia's houses.

272 *Government House in Christiansted.*

Charity collected in London and New York rather than the Swedish government came to the assistance of the colonists. More and more, the threads that bound the colony to Sweden were loosening. The basis of the economy was also changing. Cotton, except for the brief period of the American Civil War, ceased to be cultivated, with pineapple taking its place; soon, it became the colony's most important export commodity, with well over a million exported in 1858 alone. Economic growth, however, was not reflected in the population.[68]

Some new industries did open up on St Barthelemy. The export of salt was of growing importance, with salt dams established on the eastern side of the island, against which the winds usually blew. Lead was also discovered in 1868, near the village of L'Orient. In addition, some 1,000 acres stood under cultivation, with another 1,000 used for animal husbandry. Still, emigration was the only option available for many on St Barthelemy to sustain themselves economically. For those who remained, spiralling debt was often the price of their lifeline at home.

Sweden had now become long weary of a colony which increasingly drained its economic resources. Therefore, in the hopes of getting rid of the island, negotiations were opened, first with the United States, in 1868, and then with Italy, in 1869, but with no results. However, in 1876 negotiations were commenced with France and, on 10 August 1877, it agreed to take over control. In a referendum at that time in the colony, 351 inhabitants voted for the transfer of sovereignty, with only one against. Final arrangements were agreed in April 1878 and the treaty of transfer was signed at Paris. Sweden was given compensation of

320,000 francs to provide pensions for former Swedish civil servants in the colony, along with an additional sum of 80,000 francs, which would be donated by Sweden to St Barthelemy for the establishment of a new hospital at Gustavia. Swedish residents were to be permitted to continue to reside in the colony and to maintain their Swedish nationality. Finally, on 16 March 1878, the Swedish flag was lowered on the island and the ultimate governmental authority for the colony, with its population now of only 793 inhabitants, passed to the governor of the French island of Guadeloupe, the former rival of St Barthelemy for trade in the Antilles. As rapid as the population had risen in the days of Gustaf III, so had its decline over the last half century been gradual. Moreover, whereas in 1787 there had been 115 Swedish speakers on the island, by 1860 there were only six, a clear indication that what ethnic Swedish identity the island had was on the verge of extinction.[69]

Denmark, however, retained her Caribbean colony into the twentieth century. The upheavals of the First World War were to exert their own political impact, though, for neither Britain nor the United States wanted the islands used as a base for German subversion, should Denmark tow a German political line. Denmark, therefore, realizing that she had neither the military power nor the will to resist this Anglo-American pressure, acquiesced in the demand for a settlement. Thus, during the summer of 1915, negotiations were opened for the sale of the colony to the United States, with $25,000,000 the price finally agreed. A Danish referendum at home (none was held in the colonies themselves), on 14 December 1916, was overwhelmingly in favour of the sale. Therefore, on 31 March 1917, the colony became a possession of the United States. The retreat of Nordic political presence in the Caribbean was complete.

The Danish Virgin Islands, Swedish St Barthelemy and the other southern Scandinavian colonies, though their direct contact with one another was rather limited, had shared an exceptional characteristic: only among the European colonies, was a tiny minority of nationals in a position to dominate, not only black and mulatto slaves, but also the whites of other foreign nations, who made up the overwhelming majority of the population. Another unusual feature of these colonies was the religious toleration which had been in practice since soon after their establishment. Perhaps only British rule in Quebec bears comparison in this regard. Less favourably, these colonies also differed from the other colonies of the European great powers in that they were never successfully integrated into a larger imperial framework, which could, in a complementary way, fulfil the needs economic and social of both the mother countries and the colonies. Isolated, the economic success of the colonies always tended to depend upon relatively brief periods of hostility between the other European colonial nations, enabling them to reap the benefits of a sudden upsurge in trade with their neighbours. Thus, in the long term, their political and social links to their mother countries were doomed, for neither Denmark nor Sweden was able to sustain their economies or their social fabric at such a distance and with such differing needs.

Some Conclusions

If there is one trend which can be perceived in the history of the Nordic region over the last half millennium, it is the movement away from tyranny towards a social world in which the voice, desires and efforts of the individual have increasingly played a significant role, one in which the maintenance of a prosperous, modern democratic nation has been crucial. In this development, the benefits of growing public education and literacy have been of primary importance, even during the long centuries in which the lot of the common man and woman was dominated by poverty. Yet it was precisely this material dearth which demanded literacy and encouraged greater equality in education and training for both men and women, in a sparsely populated region in which the physical labour of both was a necessity. It is therefore no quirk of history that important educationalists like the Uno Cygnaeus came precisely from a poor country like Finland, nor that the idea of manual training which he developed first spread to Sweden and thence to the rest of western Europe and the United States, where it has now long since been integrated into the curriculum of most schools in one form or another. Nor is it a coincidence that Finland became the first nation in Europe to grant women the franchise and the first in the world in which women became eligible to stand for parliament.[1]

The brutal impositions of nature and climate have gradually been subdued or accommodated, even as the authority of church, monarchy and aristocracy has been eroded in the interests of society as a whole. Such developments, of course, have not come about smoothly, but have proceeded at an uneven pace, often demanding the sacrifice of other important benefits. There can be no doubt, however, that Norden has been tamed since the beginning of the Reformation; religious tyranny has given way to toleration, and a growing acceptance of 'otherness' has occurred, as expressed in racial, sexual or even mere stylistic eccentricities, even extending to those institutions previously proscribed. The Roman Catholic Church has risen up like a phoenix since the second half of the nineteenth century to become the fasting growing religious institution in the Nordic region, while in our own time an international communion has been established between Lutherans and members of the Anglican/Episcopalian Church, thereby joining together diverse peoples not only in Europe but in Africa and the Americas as well. Perhaps, the visit of the Pope to Uppsala Cathedral in 1989, in which he, the Lutheran Archbishops of Uppsala and Turku and the King and Queen of Sweden all prayed together is a symbol of that new-found harmony.[2]

Such changes, however, have not been brought about without a price. Religion and spirituality have increasingly made way for a secular, mechanistic view of the world, with little time for contemplation of the meaning of life other than in terms of pleasure and economic wealth. An earlier quest for spiritual and moral improvement, aided by the Church as a purveyor of reading skills, has been supplanted by one which strives for continual technical and medical developments. In such a world as this, qualities which cannot be measured by graphs and statistics seem weak and intangible to modern politicians and other pillars of the community and therefore are largely ignored. This is particularly dangerous in a region where, unlike Germany with its contemporary fear of governmental authority or Britain where a rich and historicist cultural tradition is considered the fountainhead of the good, national governments, especially in Sweden but also elsewhere in the Nordic region, are considered the wise and benevolent hermaphroditic deities serving the interests of all in a society in which the wellbeing of the collective identity is perceived to take precedence over individual rights and desires to a greater degree than elsewhere in Europe or the Americas. This has led to a greater emphasis upon conformity than perhaps anywhere else in the western world and a great adherence upon 'Jente Lagen', an implicit social law in which the individual who stands out from the general run of humanity is made to feel a culprit, guilty of self-importance and egotism, however productive of benefits he or she might be.[3] This has been especially the case in Sweden, where a more highly centralized administration, in both government and church has led to fewer local initiatives being taken than elsewhere in Scandinavia, while subjecting even the most personal aspects of life and the family to close scrutiny and control by central government and its rigorously enforced regulations.[4]

But the benefits of this approach have also been obvious. Traditional ethnic divisions, for example, between Germans and Danes or Swedish- and Finnish-Finns have definitely waned. The national romantic zeal (albeit sometimes tempered by an eye for the social and practical benefits) which has led many Swedish-Finns to adopt a strictly Finnish cultural identity, has also led some Finnish-Finns to adopt the Swedish one, making the situation almost unique for the ease with which members of one ethnic group can join those of the other. This has no doubt been facilitated by the fact that religious differences here and with respect to Denmark and Schleswig-Holstein, all of which are nominally Lutheran, have played no role. Even the arrival of large numbers of new ethnic groups, such as Poles and other Baltic peoples, during the post-war period, has been happily accommodated. Indeed, the Saami people, now some 50–60,000 in number and, to a lesser extent, Greenlanders and gypsies, formerly the social pariahs of Scandinavia, have come to achieve a certain cultural and economic recognition. For prosperous Saami reindeer herders, surveying their herds by private aeroplane, a complete integration into the international economy and world of the jet-setting rich can be said to have sometimes occurred. None the less, it must be added that this harmony has been accomplished at a cost, namely that of growing assimilation and an increasing loss of native ethnic identity of significant numbers of people.

The relatively recent arrival of non-European ethnic groups, often refugees, such as Kurds, Iranians, Turks, Somalis and Albanians, has not always produced the degree of harmonious integration into Nordic society which was desirable, perhaps precisely because they have been less amenable to assimilation, though the fact that Vietnamese refugees, granted asylum in Iceland, were obliged to take Icelandic names, may indicate an overzealous desire to absorb the newcomers. On occasion, murderous assaults have occurred in Sweden and Denmark, though the success of such right wing and anti-socialist political parties as that of the Progressives, founded by Mogens Glistrup in Denmark, has been limited. It may well be so that a few decades are needed in order for their successful integration to be completed. Whether that will permit a certain maintenance of their own separate ethnic identity or demand a complete assimilation, remains to be seen.

Serious inter-Nordic conflict has, however, been totally eliminated. In fact, even if, or perhaps in part because, no unitary Nordic political union has been achieved on a social and cultural level, the nations of Scandinavia have achieved a viable and continuous peace with one another since the Napoleonic period, a period of almost 200 years, whereas previously an almost endless series of wars had plagued relations between Denmark and Sweden, with Russia and France, the big powers behind the scenes, jockeying for supremacy in their geographical spheres. It is true that political hostility between Norway and Denmark did erupt briefly this century, over Greenland and Svalbard, largely for the control of oil fields, but this was peacefully resolved. More serious were the difficulties of the Second World War, when neutral Sweden permitted the transit of German troops to occupied Norway, a cause of resentment among the older population even to this day. The wealth accumulated by certain companies, individuals and indirectly even the government through the sale of iron ore and scrap metal also left a residue of resentment, leading some to see the financial basis of the Swedish welfare state as in part secured through such nefarious means.[5] On the other hand, Sweden welcomed refugee Jews from Denmark and elsewhere with open arms, while the humanitarian efforts of the Swedish diplomat Raoul Wallenberg enabled many thousands of Hungarian Jews to escape the German SS with Swedish passports, winning him an almost legendary fame.

Without doubt, though, it is in terms of health and hygiene that the taming of Norden has been especially successful. Not only has the mortality rate plummeted to among the lowest in the world, but the great epidemic scourges – bubonic plague, leprosy, smallpox, malaria and cholera – have been totally eliminated, while others such as tuberculosis have been reduced to a minute number of cases, usually contracted abroad by foreign immigrants. Even AIDS, which arrived in Scandinavia in the early 1980s, while taking its toll amongst the sexually active, has failed to make the harrowing inroads into Nordic society which had at first been predicted. Moreover, the establishment of hospitals to care for the victims of the old epidemic diseases can in many ways be said to have served as microcosms of life and precursors of the welfare state, providing as they did cradle to grave care for those unable to cope on their own. However, a pessimistic note must also be added. Recent economic recession and the growing numbers of elderly Scandinavians in need of costly medical treatment, not to mention long-term care and accommodation, has overstretched the system. Gradually health care services have begun to suffer, encouraging the development of a fledgling private health care service for those with sufficient private funds or corporate benefits. To what degree these changes will limit the care, treatment and prevention of illness of the less affluent remains to be seen.

Famines, too, have ceased to plague the Nordic region. While the summers of the late 1770s, early 1780s and around 1800 were hot, the winters of 1880s and 1890s cold, and the summers of the 1810s, 1880s and 1910s cool and wet, such vagaries of climate gradually ceased to be occasions of crop failure and famine, so that, by the end of the last century, an era of sufficiency had arrived.[6] Today, Norden is one of the best-fed regions in the world, though this is not only a blessing, as the extremely high rates of heart disease indicate, though in the last few years even they may be on the decline.

Crime still remains a problem. Growing industrialization and the movement of population from country to town has continued throughout the period, and the typical dislocation of urban life has left a rising crime rate in its wake. The current murder rate in Helsinki at 12.5 per 100,000 people, is almost three-quarters that in New York City with 16.8. This compares very unfavourably with rates in most of southern Europe, where in Rome the murder rate is only 1.7 and in Athens 1.4. There are, however, certain anomalies in such a comparison: while Lisbon in the south has the unusually high rate of 9.7, in Stockholm in the north it is relatively low at 3, only slightly greater than that in England.[7] These statistics are difficult to compare in other ways, for, unlike the situation in New York, hardly any murders are committed through mugging. Rather, most are the result of domestic quarrels or violence amongst friends and acquaintances, exacerbated by drink. Perhaps, such crime as this can be said to be related to the so-called 'knive junkers' phenomenon in the west of Finland, where pockets of violent criminality have persisted when such characteristics as stubbornness and aggressiveness, virtues in a frontier society, become anti-social vices in a stable one, in which peacefulness and accommodation are more valued as manly virtues. Thus, the good face of 'sisu', that courageous stubbornness so prized still among men in Finnish society, has been shown to have a shadow side as well, not only evident in the occasional violent crime but in very high suicide rates among men, as well as social alienation. It may also have encouraged a growing dependency upon drug addiction, as elsewhere in the western world, a phenomenon which has increased dramatically recently in Scandinavia, despite police measures to contain drugs in special urban areas like Christiania in Copenhagen.

Other social problems typical of the modern western world have also made their appearance. For example, work careers, as in many other developed countries, can often no longer be seen as the life-long occupations they previously were. This is particularly true in Finland, and to a lesser extent in Sweden and Denmark, where a shrinking of the economy at least as far back as the 1980s and growing unemployment have also taken their toll. It is doubtful whether the welfare net which has insulated Scandinavians from harsh economic realities in the post-war years can be maintained in view of the increasing longevity of the general population. Indeed, only Norway, rich in oil, has succeeded in keeping aloof from the economic ills which plague its Nordic neighbours, but there the dangers of over-dependence on one economic resource continue to lurk.

In domestic terms, considerable changes have also occurred, but there is not so much a destruction, through egalitarianism, of the family group *per se*, as a reformulation of what constitutes the family, extrapolated from the past. The formal institution of marriage has long been weak in the Nordic nations, where common law marriage traditionally played such a major role. Thus, informal peasant marriages have given way not only to boyfriends and girlfriends setting themselves up in quasi-married states, but homosexuals and lesbians doing so too. For many young people, living together with a partner, unmarried but frequently with children, has become the normal social unit. And yet, with the long-term continued prevalence of the nuclear family unit in the Nordic region, there has also been a strong emphasis on the family as a source of good, a bulwark against the onslaughts of nature. This has gone hand in hand with a powerful nostalgia for a rural past, one in which a vivid memory of poverty, disease and ignorance has been largely repressed and replaced by an idealized picture of nature unaffected by man.

With respect to the old Nordic tropical colonies and outposts, whether in the Caribbean, Africa or Asia, little remains in the public consciousness. Indeed, a general amnesia about Nordic involvement in the trans-Atlantic slave trade can be said to have taken place, with few outside academic circles aware of Denmark's not insignificant role. Nor are many aware in Sweden that their King Oscar I was the last of the northern European monarchs to be in legal possession of black slaves in the middle of the nineteenth century, albeit in the far-off colony of St Barthelemy. The celebration in Ghana by Queen Margarethe of Denmark of 300 years of close relations with the dominant Aqwamu tribe in 1971 failed to explain to a wider public the mutually lucrative basis of the long-term relationship – slavery.

The peoples of the Nordic region have not generally been deeply preoccupied with race. In Finland, the only Nordic nation on the side of the Axis powers, no racial laws were ever introduced and many Jewish men volunteered to defend their homeland (sometimes in aeroplanes sporting swastikas, ancient emblems of Finland, but inverse in their form to those of the Nazis) against the Russians. Norway and Denmark, directly occupied as they were by German troops, were less fortunate, but many Jews escaped, especially to Sweden, aided by many of their countrymen. It was thus left to neutral Sweden to provide a safe haven for Jews, not only from the rest of Norden, but from Germany and other war-torn countries as well.

On other levels, too, the Nordic world has been a beacon for those of other countries. Architects like the Finn Alvar Aalto (1898–1976) and the Dane Arne Jacobsen (1902–1971), for example, came to achieve an international renown of immense proportions in the post-war years. Aalto's Säynätsalo town hall complex (1950–52) combines functionalist and indigenous Finnish elements, whilst Jacobsen's SAS building in Copenhagen (1959) – including the design of its interior decoration, the city's first skyscraper – have been extremely admired internationally and commissions from abroad have often followed for both Nordic architects. Aalto produced, for example, a post and telegraph office in Baghdad (1958) and the Institute of International Education, New York City (1964–5). Jacobsen went on to carry out work at St Catherine's College, Oxford, in 1964, where he sought to include an innovative if austere campanile, a good attempt at demonstrating the veracity of his adage that 'economy plus function equals style'.

Both also devoted considerable time and energy to the details of interior decoration and furniture design. Aalto's company Artek came to be noted throughout the world for the production of laminated ribbon-like furniture, while Jacobsen's three-legged stacking chair (1952) and so-called 'egg' chair (1959), the back and seat of which were made of cloth covered in plastic, were very influential in the realm of industrial design. Other architects of note include the couple Kaija and Heikki Sirén who built the innovative Forest Church of Otaniemi (1956–7), as well as Aarne Ervi, Jorma Järvi and Viljo Revell, all three of whom worked on various projects at Tapiola, a daring new suburb of Helsinki. In painting, artists like Ola Billgren (1940–), Olle Kåks (1941–) and J. Franzén (1942–) rejected the classical tradition of Nordic art only themselves to become the established figures of the art scene of today. In music, too, the works of Nordic composers like Edvard Grieg, Carl Nielsen and Jean Sibelius are to be heard throughout the world, at concerts, on radio and compact disc players; superstars who have entered the pantheon of international culture available to virtually everyone.

Yet, it is in precisely the success of such leading cultural figures that a certain danger lurks. For if each becomes an international commodity, more and more cut off from its cultural background and roots, it is in danger of losing the individuality of its essence and expression, the texture and tone of its unique identity and the ability to express the nuances and ephemeral beauties of the human condition. That is one reason why an awareness of the uniqueness of Nordic social and cultural history, for all its communion with the rest of Europe and the world at large, is so necessary.

Chronology of Political Events

1513–23
Christian II, King of Denmark.

1520
Massacre of Swedish Notables at Stockholm by allies of Christian II; revolt against the Danes by Swedes under Gustaf Vasa.

1523–60
Gustaf Vasa, King of Sweden.

1523–33
Frederik I, King of Denmark.

1527
Secularisation of many church estates, and bishops made subject to the king in Sweden.

1534–58,
Christian III, King of Denmark.

1544
Convocation of Reformed clergy at Västerås prohibits the saying of requiem masses, the adoration of saints and the use of incense in the Swedish Church.

1560–68
Erik IV, King of Sweden.

1568–92
Johan II, King of Sweden.

1588–1648
Christian IV, King of Denmark and Norway.

1592–1604
Sigismund III, King of Sweden.

1593
Council at Uppsala establishes the Lutheran Church in Sweden.

1604–11
Karl IX, King of Sweden.

1611–32
Gustaf II Adolf, King of Sweden.

1618–48
The Thirty Years War in which the Protestant powers and France fought the Catholic German kingdoms and principalities.

1624
Christiania (now Oslo) founded by Christian IV.

1630
Sweden enters the Thirty Years War.

1632
Death of Gustaf II Adolf at the Battle of Lützen in Germany.

1632–54
Christina, Queen of Sweden.

1638
The American colony of New Sweden established on the Delaware.

1648
The Treaties of Westphalia conclude the Thirty Years War. Sweden receives Further Pomerania and Wismar as an imperial fief.

1648–70
Frederik, King of Denmark and Norway.

1654–60
Karl X, King of Sweden.

1655
New Sweden taken by the Dutch under Peter Stuyvesant.

1655–60
First Northern War against Poland, with Russia and Denmark allied against Sweden and Brandenburg in 1656.

1657
Sweden driven out of Poland.

1658

Scania, Blekinge and Halland lost in war by Denmark to Sweden.

1660

Treaty of Copenhagen: Denmark formally surrenders Scania to Sweden; Polish King Jan Casimir Vasa relinquishes his claim to the throne of Sweden.

1660–97

Karl XI, King of Sweden.

1670–99

Christian V, King of Denmark.

1697–1718

Karl XII, King of Sweden.

1699–1730

Frederik IV, King of Denmark.

1700–21

Great Northern War in which Sweden confronts Denmark, Russia and Poland.

1709

Battle of Poltava: Russian army defeats Swedish forces; Karl XII takes refuge in Turkey.

1714

Karl XII returns to Sweden.

1718

Fatal shooting of Karl XII near Friedrichshall during a military campaign.

1718–20

Ulrika Eleonora, Queen of Sweden.

1720–51

Fredrik, King of Sweden.

1721

Treaty of Nystad between Sweden and Russia. Sweden cedes Livonia, Estonia, Ingermanland and parts of Karelia to Russia; Norwegian missionary Hans Egede establishes the first Danish colony in Greenland since the Norse period.

1730–46

Christian VI, King of Denmark.

1733

Serfdom re-established in Denmark.

1741–3

Renewed war between Sweden and Russia.

1746–66

Frederik V, King of Denmark.

1751–71

Adolf Fredrik, King of Sweden.

1766–1808

Christian VII, King of Denmark.

1770–71

Ascendency to power of Struensee in Denmark.

1772

Struensee executed.

1771–92

Gustaf III, King of Sweden.

1772

Gustaf III's coup d'état restores absolute monarchy.

1785

The French Caribbean island of St Barthelemy is ceded to Sweden in return for a mercantile entrepôt near Gothenburg, in Sweden.

1786

Reykjavik, in Iceland, granted the status of a city by the Danish government.

1787–8

Count A. P. Bernstorff abolishes serfdom in Denmark.

1788–90

Renewed war between Sweden and Russia.

1792

Assassination of Gustaf III at the Opera House in Stockholm.

1792–1809

Gustaf IV Adolf, King of Sweden.

1807

Debilitating continental blockade is introduced by Britain, causing great hardship in Norway.

1809

The sovereignty of the grand-duchy of Finland is transferred to Russia's Tsar Alexander I; Gustav IV Adolf deposed.

1809–18

Karl XIII, King of Sweden; Swedish constitution accepted.

1810

Karl Johan Bernadotte adopted as Crown Prince of Sweden; Sweden at war with France.

1811–12

Parts of Karelia, including Viipuri, are reunited to Finland; Helsinki is made the new capital.

1812
Sweden allies with Russia against France.
1814
Union of Norway to the Danish crown dissolved; Norway is ceded to Sweden and a Norwegian constitution is adopted providing for a unicameral national assembly; Norway, attempts to elect Prince Christian Frederik of Denmark as king, but Bernadotte invades Norway, enforcing the claims of the King of Sweden to the Norwegian throne.
1815
Act of Union binds Norway and Sweden.
1818–44
Karl Johan Bernadotte, King of Sweden.
1806–39
Frederik VI, King of Denmark.
1821–34
Establishment of four provincial representative advisory diets (assemblies) in Denmark (Sjæland with Fyn, Jutland, Schleswig and Holstein).
1839–48
Christian VIII, King of Denmark.
1844–59
Oskar I, King of Sweden.
1848–63
Frederik VII, King of Denmark.
1848–50
Denmark and Prussia at war over Schleswig-Holstein.
1849
Promulgation of constitution making Denmark a limited monarchy with a bicameral national assembly.
1857
Abolition of Denmark's rights to tolls on shipping in the Øresund.
1859
Complete religious toleration granted in Sweden.
1859–72
Karl XV, King of Sweden.
1864
Austro-Prussian War against Denmark, whose defeat leads to the ceding of Schleswig-Holstein and Lauenburg to the victorious powers; new constitu-

tion promulgated in Sweden, with the four estates abolished in favour of a bicameral legislature.
1866
Revision of the Danish constitution curtails the powers of the upper chamber of the national assembly.
1872–1907
Oskar II, King of Sweden.
1878
Sweden cedes her Caribbean colony of St Barthelemy to France.
1891–2
Introduction of laws in Denmark providing pensions for the elderly and health insurance.
1898
Universal male suffrage in Norway.
1899
Tsar Nicholas II promulgates the February Manifesto, which seeks to fully integrate Finland into the Russian Empire.
1905
Union of Norway and Sweden unilaterally dissolved by Norway; war between Sweden and Norway looms, but the Swedish parliament accepts dissolution of the union and Oskar II abdicates as King of Norway; Prince Carl of Denmark becomes Haakon VII, King of Norway (1905–57).
1906–12
Frederik VIII, King of Denmark.
1907
Universal female suffrage granted in Norway; parliamentary government established in Sweden with almost universal suffrage.
1907–50
Gustaf V, King of Sweden.
1912– 47
Christian X, King of Denmark.
1914–15
Virtual universal suffrage granted in Denmark; establishment of full parliamentary government.
1915
Iceland introduces prohibition; it is partially repealed in 1922 and completely repealed in 1934.

1917

Finland declares its unilateral independence from Russia and is eventually recognised by the Russian Provisional Government; P.E. Svinhufvud becomes the first head of state; Danish Virgin Islands ceded to the United States; Åland Islands vote to join Sweden, but an international settlement gives them to Finland as a demilitarised territory.

1918

Civil War in Finland in which conservative White forces are victorious, assisted by German forces under General von der Goltz; Prince Friedrich Karl of Hesse elected King of Finland; he renounces the crown and General Baron Karl Gustaf Mannerheim becomes head of state; Iceland recognised as a sovereign state under the Danish crown; universal suffrage introduced in Denmark.

1919

Finnish war with Russia; Karl J. Stahlberg elected President of Finland; Allied Supreme Council awards Norway sovereignty over Spitsbergen.

1919

Universal female suffrage introduced in Sweden.

1920

Sweden, Norway, Denmark and Finland join the League of Nations; Treaty of Dorpat (Tartu) concludes conflict with Russia; Finland given Petsamo on the Arctic coast, with a land corridor connecting to Finland; North Schleswig reunited with Denmark after a plebiscite; Hjalmar Branting (Socialist) elected Prime Minister of Sweden; re-elected in 1921.

1920–27

Prohibition of alcohol in Norway.

1921

The Åland Islands assigned by the League of Nations (under British pressure) to Finland, on condition that they are demilitarised.

1924

Hjalmar Branting (Socialist) re-elected prime minister of Sweden; Theodor Stauning (Socialist) elected Prime Minister of Denmark.

1925

Lauri Relander elected President of Finland.

1926

Danish parliament votes for virtually complete disarmament; T. Madsen-Mygdal (Liberal) elected Prime Minister of Denmark.

1927

Christopher Hornsrud (Labour) elected Prime Minister of Norway.

1928

J.L. Mowinckel (Liberal) elected Prime Minister of Norway; annexation by Norway of Bouvet Island in the South Atlantic; Arvid Lindman (Conservative) elected Prime Minister of Sweden.

1929

Annexation by Norway of Peter Island, in the South Atlantic and Jan Mayen in the Arctic; Theodor Stauning (Socialist) re-elected Prime Minister of Denmark.

1930

Right-wing Lapua Movement in Finland, under Kurt Wallenius, fails in an attempted coup to seize control of the government, Carl Ekman (Liberal) elected Prime Minister of Sweden.

1931

Pehr Svinhufvud elected President of Finland; dispute between Norway and Denmark over sovereignty in East Greenland; permanent Court of International Justice awards Denmark sovereignty; P. Kolstad (Farmers) elected Prime Minister of Norway.

1932

J. Hundseid (Farmers) succeeds as Prime Minister of Norway on the death of Kolstad; Per A. Hansson (Socialist) elected Prime Minister of Sweden and soon encourages a policy of rearmament.

1933

J.L. Mowinckel (Liberal) re-elected Prime Minister of Norway.

1934

Sweden passes eugenic law providing for compulsory sterilisation of those deemed unsuitable for procreating.

1935

Johan Nygaarsvold (Labour) elected Prime Minister of Norway.

1936

Axel Pehrsson (Agrarian) elected Prime Minister of Sweden in June, followed by Per A. Hansson (Socialist) in September.

1937

Kyosti Kallio elected President of Finland; Workers' Security Law and Seamen's Security Law enacted in Norway.

1939

Norway lays claim to one-fifth of Antarctica from Coats Land to Enderby Land.

1940

German troops invade Denmark, but the government is left intact and the Danish King retains titular command; German forces occupy Norway, but a Norwegian government-in-exile is established under the King who flees to London.

1942

Vilhelm Buhl is appointed Danish Prime Minister.

1943

German administration of Denmark introduced; deportation of Danish Jews decreed but most escape to Sweden.

1944

Iceland declares its independence from Denmark.

1944–6

Marshal Mannerheim, President of Finland.

1945

With the defeat of Nazi Germany, the Norwegian government-in-exile returns; a Labour government is elected and Norway becomes a founding member of the United Nations; a Liberation government is formed in Denmark under the Prime Minister Vilhelm Buhl; Denmark joins the UN.

1946

Sweden joins the UN.

1946

J. K. Paasikivi, President of Finland and a right-wing government comes to power.

1947

Denmark decides to join NATO.

1947–72

Frederik IX, King of Denmark.

1948

Finland signs a Treaty of Friendship and Mutual Assistance with the Soviet Union.

1949

Sweden joins the Council of Europe.

1950–73

Gustaf VI Adolf, King of Sweden.

1950–53

Urho Kaleva Kekkonen (1900–86) becomes Prime Minister of Finland.

1951

Nordic nations establish the Nordic Council, which encourages economic and cultural co-operation among Nordic nations.

1954–6

Urho Kaleva Kekkonen is re-elected Prime Minister of Finland.

1955

Finland joins the Nordic Council and the UN.

1956

Soviet naval base at Porkkala is returned to Finnish sovereignty.

1956–81

Urho Kaleva Kekkonen becomes President of Finland.

1957–91

Olav V, King of Norway.

1958

Nordic passport and customs union formed.

1960

Norway and Sweden join the European Free Trade Association.

1965

Coalition of right-wing parties wins the general election in Norway.

1970

Finland and the Soviet Union renew their Treaty of Friendship and Mutual Assistance for another twenty years.

1972 to the present

Margrethe, Queen of Denmark.

1972

Denmark joins the European Community.

1973 to the present

Carl Gustaf, King of Sweden; Norway, Sweden and Finland enter a free trade agreement with the European Community.

1974

Norwegian exploitation of oil and natural gas begins in the North Sea.

1975

Helsinki Conference on Security and Co-operation in Europe; Swedish monarchy limited to a symbolic role by constitutional amendments enacted two years previously.

1977

Norwegian pipeline laid from the Ekofisk oilfield, near Stavanger, to Emden in Germany; Labour Party wins 76 seats in Norwegian general election; Swedish royal succession opened to the eldest child irrespective of sex.

1979

Thorbjörn Fälldin, leader of the Centre Party, becomes Swedish Prime Minister.

1981

Social Democrat leader Gro Harlem Brundtland, Norway's first woman prime minister, succeeds Odvar Nordli; Conservative Kaare Willoch wins the general election later in the year; he is re-elected in 1985; Mauno Koivisto becomes President of Finland.

1982

Coalition of Social Democrats and Communists under Olof Palme wins the general election in Sweden; Palme is re-elected in 1985; Social Democrat Kalevi Sorsa leads a coalition government in Finland.

1985

Olof Palme is re-elected Swedish Prime Minister; Poul Schlüter becomes Denmark's first Conservative Prime Minister this century in coalition with other parties of the moderate right.

1986

Olof Palme is assassinated and Social Democrat Ingvar Carlsson takes over as Prime Minister.

1986,

Gro Harlem Brundtland elected Prime Minister of Norway.

1987

Social Democrat Harri Holkeri leads a coalition government in Finland.

1989

Right-wing coalition, under Conservative Jan P. Syse, wins the general election in Norway; Finland joins the Council of Europe; Finland's status as a neutral nation is recognised by the Soviet Union.

1990

Ingvar Carlsson re-elected Swedish Prime Minister; Gro Harlem Brundtland in Norway forms another government.

1991 to the present

Harald V (1937–), King of Norway; Conservative Carl Bildt becomes Prime Minister of Sweden; Esko Aho of the Centre Party becomes Prime Minister of Finland.

1992

Finland and the Soviet Union sign a new Treaty of Friendship in which the necessity for consultation and mutual assistance is omitted; referendum in Denmark rejects the government-supported initiative to join the European Union.

1993

Danish Social Democrat Poul Nyrup Rasmussen becomes Prime Minister through a centre-left coalition; a second referendum in Denmark supports the initiative to join the European Union; Gro Harlem Brundtland is re-elected Prime Minister of Norway.

1994

Referendum in Norway rejects membership of the European Union; Social Democrats under Ingvar Carlsson win the general election in Sweden; Social Democrat Martti Ahtisaari becomes Prime Minister of Finland.

1995

Sweden and Finland join the European Union; Social Democrat Paavo Lipponen becomes Prime Minister of Finland.

Chronology of Cultural and Scientific Events

1514

Danish humanist Christiern Pedersen (c. 1480–1554) publishes his *History of the Danes*.

1540

Oddur Gottskálksson translates the New Testament into Icelandic.

1548

Finnish priest Mikael Agricola (c. 1510–1557) completes his translation of the New Testament into Finnish.

1550

Beheading of Jón Arason (1484–1550), Bishop of Hólar in Iceland; Johannes Bugenhagen's translation of the Bible into Danish published.

1584

Lutheran bishop Gudbrandur Thorláksson publishes the Bible in Icelandic.

1572

Tycho Brahe (1546–1601), Danish astronomer, discovers a new star in the constellation of Cassiopeia, undermining the Aristotelian theory of the universe.

1606–1634

Christian IV has Rosenborg Castle built in Copenhagen.

1609

Icelandic scholar Arngrímur Jónsson (1568–1648) publishes his work *Crymogaea*, dealing with Iceland's cultural and historical past.

1624

Silver mine established at Kongsberg in Norway.

1644

Copper mine established at Røros in Norway.

1646

Swede Nicodemus Tessin the Elder (1615–1681) is appointed Court Architect in Stockholm.

1649

French philosopher René Descartes (1596–1650) arrives in Sweden at the invitation of Queen Christina, where he proceeds to write the statues for the newly founded Swedish Academy of Arts and Sciences, shortly before contracting pneumonia.

1658

Swedish poet Georg Stiernhielm (1598–1672) publishes his great political and social allegory *Hercules*.

1666

Icelandic priest and poet Hallgrímur Pétursson (1614–1674) publishes his popular spiritual work *Hymns on the Passion*.

1672

German historian and jurist Samuel (later Freiherr von) Pufendorf (1632–1694) publishes his work *Of the law and nature of nations*, whilst a Professor of Natural Law at the University of Lund in Sweden, emphasizing man's nature as a social being.

1674

Danish poet Thomas Kingo, Bishop of Fyn (1634–1703) publishes the first volume of his religious poetical work *Spiritual Chorus*, followed by a second volume in 1681 and his popular hymnbook in 1699.

1676

Olaus Rømer (1644–1710), Danish astronomer, discovers the speed of light.

1677

Danish natural scientist Nicolaus Steno (1638–1686), who explored the functions of the heart, is made Bishop and Apostolic Vicar in northern Germany.

1679

Swedish naturalist Olof Rudbeck the Younger (1660–1740) expounds in his book *Atlantica*

(1679–1702) that Sweden is the lost continent of Atlantis and the cradle of European civilization.

1688

German statesman and chancellor of the University of Halle, Veit von Seckendorff (1626–1692), publishes his *History of Lutheranism*, which helps to spread Pietistic values in Scandinavia.

1689

Swedish architect Erik Dahlbergh (1625–1703) builds his Lejonet fortification at Gothenburg.

1697

The Royal Palace of Stockholm burns down and Nicodemus Tessin the Younger (1654–1728) is put in charge of the rebuilding in the Baroque style; Swedish poet Gunno Eurelius (Gunno Dahlstierna) composes his majestic epic *Hymn to the King* for the funeral of Karl XI.

1699

Christopher Polhem (1661–1751), Swedish inventor, establishes the Stjärnsunds Works in Dalecarlia, run to a considerable degree by automatic water-powered machines.

1718–20

Icelandic Bishop Jón Thorkelsson Vídalín (1666–1720), a grandson of Arngrímur Jónsson, publishes his *Sermons for the Home*.

1721

Danish-Norwegian missionary Hans Egede arrives at Godthåb Fjord in Greenland.

1728

Danish explorer Vitus Bering (1681–1741) sails into the Arctic through the Bering Strait; Swedish courtier and art collector Carl-Gustaf Tessin (1695–1770) placed in charge of the rebuilding of the Royal Palace of Stockholm; he later wrote his didactic fairy tales for the moral edification of Gustaf III of Sweden, while tutor to him as crown prince during the 1750s.

1735

Swedish architect Carl Hårleman (1700–1753) begins work on Svartsjö Palace, the first building in Sweden constructed in the Rococo style.

1735–53

Carl von Linné (1707–1778), Swedish botanist and explorer, publishes his principles for catagorizing the genera and species of organisms.

1737

Danish theologian Erik Pontoppidan (1698–1764) expounds the catechism of Luther in a Pietistic and legalistic framework in *Truth which is unto Godliness*.

1742

Anders Celsius (1701–1744), Swedish Professor of Astronomy at Uppsala University, describes his centigrade thermometer to the Swedish Academy of Science.

1744

The Danish playwright Ludvig Holberg (1684–1754) gives out his philosophical work, *Moral Thoughts*.

1749–56

Emanuel Swedenborg (1688–1772) publishes his theological work *Heavenly Arcana*, followed in 1758 by *On Heaven and Its Wonders and on Hell* in which scientific and mystical elements are integrated together.

1765

Carl Michael Bellman (1740–1795), Swedish musician, begins to compose his irreverent cycle of 82 songs, *The Epistles of Fredman*, finally published in 1790.

1766–7

Danish artist Jens Juel (1745–1802) paints his portrait *A Holstein Girl*.

1769

Swedish architect Carl Fredrik Adelcrantz (1716–1796) completes the Rococo-influenced Chinese Palace at Drottningholm.

1772

Carl Wilhelm Scheele (1742–1786), Swedish chemist, discovers oxygen two years before Priestley, and later also discovers chlorine.

1774

Swedish neo-classical sculptor Johan Tobias Sergel (1740–1814) produces his *Faun*.

1775

Torbjörn Olof Bergman (1735–1784), Swedish chemist, publishes his tables listing the elements in order of their ability to react and displace other elements in a compound.

1782–3

King Gustaf III of Sweden travels through Italy, which exerts a profound influence on his architectural and artistic vision for Sweden.

1817–19

Danish neo-classical sculptor Bertel Thorvaldsen (c. 1768–1844), long resident in Rome, produces *The Three Graces*.

1818

German architect Carl Ludwig Engel (1778–1840) commences work on Senate Square in Helsinki; Jacob Berzelius (1779–1848), Swedish inventor of the system of chemical symbols and forerunner of atomic physics, publishes almost 2000 atomic formulae.

1818–19

German Romantic artist Caspar David Friedrich (1774–1840), from Swedish Pomerania, paints *Chalk Cliffs on Rügen*.

1820–40

Swedish composer Franz Adolf Berwald (1796–1868) produces his Romantic six symphonies.

1820

Danish physicist and chemist Hans Christian Ørsted (1777–1851) uncovers the relationship between electricity and magnetism.

1821

Swedish poet and author Erik-Johan Stagnelius (1793–1823) publishes his poems *Lilies in Saron*; Norwegian mathematician Niels Henrik Abel (1802–29) discovers elliptical functions.

1825

Swedish bishop and poet Esaias Tegnér (1782–1846) publishes *Frithiof's Saga*, a work inspired by Icelandic sagas.

1828

The 'Father of Danish painting' Christoffer Wilhelm Eckersberg (1783-1853) paints his great marine work *The Russian Ship 'Assow'*.

1832

Opening of the Göta Canal in Sweden, linking the North Sea and Baltic coasts.

1835

Elias Lönnrot (1802–1884) publishes his first version of the Finnish epic *Kalevala*, followed by a longer one in 1849, in which Karelian epic tales are reworked to form a unified literary whole expressive of Finnish ethnic and cultural values.

1835

Danish author Hans Christian Andersen publishes his first collection of fairy stories, *Tales Told for Children*.

1836

Danish artist Christen Købke (1810–1848) paints his luminous and picturesque work *Frederiksborg Castle in the Light of Evening Seen from Jægerbakken*.

1839

Swedish author Carl Jonas Almqvist (1793–1866) publishes his Romantic novel *Amorina*; Swedish chemist Carl Gustaf Mosander (1797–1858) discovers the element lanthanum.

1840

Swedish diva Jenny Lind (1820–1887) becomes Court Opera Singer in Stockholm, later achieving international renown as the 'Swedish nightingale' in such roles as Pamina in Mozart's *The Magic Flute*.

1841

Danish playwright, poet and critic Johan Ludvig Heiberg (1791–1860) publishes his play *A Soul after Death*.

1842

School Statute provides every parish in Sweden and Norway with its own publicly maintained primary school; Finnish-Swedish philosopher, literary figure and politician Johan Vilhelm Snellman (1806–1881) writes his Hegelian nationalistic work *Political Science*; August Bournonville (1805–1879), ballet-master of the Danish Royal Ballet, first stages his *Napoli*.

1848 and 1860

Finnish-Swede Johan Ludvig Runeberg (1804–1877) publishes, in two series, his *Tales of Ensign Stål* about the Russian-Finnish War of 1808–9.

1849

Norwegian landscape painter Johan Christian Dahl (1788–1857) paints his wild and Romantic *Birch Tree in a Storm*.

1850

Jón Thordarson Thoroddsen (1818–1868) publishes the first Icelandic novel *Lad and Lass*, which shows the influence of the writings of Sir Walter Scott.

1852

Norwegian historian Peter Andreas Munch (1810–1863) begins to publish his *History of the Norwegian Nation*, completed in 1863, which helped to foster a sense of Norwegian national identity.

1853

Norwegian linguist Ivar Aasen (1813–1896) publishes his work on Norwegian Landsmål, a new language which he has devised drawn from a variety of Norwegian dialects.

1859

Establishment of complete religious freedom in Sweden and Norway; Swedish author Viktor Rydberg (1828–1895) publishes *The Last Athenian*, focusing on the confrontation of Christianity and paganism in ancient Greece but with relevance to contemporary Sweden.

1862

American iron-clad warship *Monitor*, designed by Swedish inventor John Ericsson (1803–1889), is victorious against the Confederate warship *Merrimac* off Hampton Roads, Virginia.

1863

Finnish made an official language of Finland, along with Swedish, previously the sole official language of the grand-duchy.

1864

Norwegian composer Rikard Nordraak (1842–1866) composes *Yes, We Love This Land*, which became the Norwegian national anthem and was inspired by Norwegian folk music.

1867

Patent granted for the invention of dynamite by the Swede Alfred Bernhard Nobel (1833–1896), a descendant of the Swedish seventeenth-century naturalist Olof Rudbeck.

1870–1914

About 1.5 million Swedes (as well as many thousands of Norwegians, Danes, Finns and Icelanders) emigrate to the United States.

1870

Finnish author Aleksis Kivi (1834–1872), publishes *Seven Brothers*, the first novel written in Finnish, which helps to establish Finnish as an important modern literary language.

1872

Finnish-Swedish author Zacharias Topelius (1818–1898) publishes his historical novel *The King's Ring and the Surgeon's Stories*.

1876

Norwegian composer Edvard Grieg (1843–1907) composes his musical suite *Peer Gynt*, drawing considerable inspiration from Norwegian folk music.

1877

Swedish mathematician Magnus Gösta Mittag-Leffler (1846–1927) explains the relationship of the meromorphic function, that is, one restricted to polar singularities, in terms of partial fractions.

1878

Swedish-Finn Baron Adolf Erik Nordenskiold (1832–1901) accomplishes a north-eastern passage around Siberia to the Bering Strait with his ship *Vega*.

1879

Norwegian playwright Henrik Ibsen (1828–1906) publishes *A Doll's House*, a work realistic in its imagery and psychological insight as well as deeply moralistic.

1880

Norwegian author Alexander Kielland (1849–1906) publishes his witty but socially critical novel *Garman and Worse*; the consumptive Danish author Jens Peter Jacobsen (1847–1885) publishes *Niels Lyhne*, a naturalistic novel in which the principal character vainly strives to find meaning in his life.

1883

Norwegian author Jonas Lie (1833–1908) publishes *The Family at Gilje*, a naturalistic novel which deals with the role of women in society and the family; Swedish artist Carl Larsson (1853–1919) paints his naturalistic masterpiece *Old Man and New Planting*.

1884

Finnish author and member of 'Young Finland' Juhani Aho (1876–1921) publishes his novel *The Railway*, both realistic and humoristic in its focus upon an old couple in rural Finland.

1885

Finnish playwright and author Minna Canth (1844–1897) publishes her play *The Labourer's Wife*, a realistic work which looks at the role of women in Finnish society.

1888

Swedish playwright, author and artist August Strindberg (1849–1912) publishes the play *Miss Julie*, in which psychological insight and Naturalistic descriptions are use to great expressive effect.

1892–4

Akseli Gallen-Kallela (1865–1931), Finnish-Swedish artist, paints *Waterfall at Mäntykoski*, a Symbolist work glorifying Finnish nature; 1892, Swedish mathematician Edvard Phragmén (1863–1937) renowned for his work in analytical functions, becomes Professor of Mathematics at Stockholm's High School.

1892–1905

Danish architect Martin Nyrop (1849–1921) builds Copenhagen Town Hall.

1893

Jean Sibelius (1865–1957), Finnish-Swedish composer, publishes his tone poem *The Swan of Tuonela*, based upon a Finnish theme from the Kalevala; Norwegian explorer Fridtjof Nansen (1861–1930) sets sail with the *Fram* to prove that the Arctic ice off Siberia drifted towards Spitzbergen; Swedish composer Wilhelm Stenhammar (1871–1927) achieves international fame with his Piano Concerto in B minor; Norwegian Expressionist artist Edvard Munch (1863–1944) paints *The Scream*.

1895

Eric Axel Karlfeldt (1864–1931), Swedish poet, publishes *Songs of Wilderness and of Love*, which glorifies Swedish nature and rural life.

1896

Swedish poet Gustaf Fröding (1860–1911) publishes his erotic poem *Splashes and Spray*; Danish microbiologist Emil Christian Hansen (1842–1909) publishes his research on fermentation.

1897

First attempt to fly to the North Pole from Spitzbergen by the Swede Salomon August Andrée, who died in the failed attempt; Swedish artist Anders Zorn (1860–1920) paints *Midsummer Dance*, evoking the delights of a Nordic summer night.

1899

Danish artist Peder Severin Krøyer (1851-1909) paints his lyrical *Summer Evening at the Beach at Skagen*.

1901

Nobel Prizes first given out along the principles laid down by their benefactor, Alfred Bernhard Nobel, the Swedish inventor of dynamite. They were given for achievements in physics, chemistry, physiology or medicine, peace and literature.

1902

Danish composer Carl Nielsen (1865–1931) produces his symphony *The Four Temperaments*, characterized by sharply distinguished tonal progressions.

1902–7

Finnish architect Lars Sonck (1870–1956) works in an Arts and Crafts Gothic style at Tampere Cathedral.

1903

Norwegian Bjørnstjerne Bjørnson (1832–1910), author of the play *Over Aevne*, wins the Nobel Prize for Literature, with his vision expressing a need for social change and amelioration; Swedish composer and conductor Hugo Alfvén (1872–1960) creates his National Romantic instrumental work *An Archipelago Legend*; 1903, Swede Svante Arrhenius (1859–1927), famous for his 'panspermia' theory that life came to the earth by means of spores carried from outer space, wins the Nobel Prize for Chemistry for his work on electrolysis and electrolytic dissociation; Danish-Faeroese Niels Ryberg Finsen (1860–1904) wins the Nobel Prize of Medicine for his successful application of light to treat diseases; Dane Valdemar Poulsen (1869–1942) invents a device for the generation of radio waves.

1904–14

Finnish architect Eliel Saarinen (1873–1950) builds Helsinki Railway Station.

1905

Icelandic artist Thórarinn B. Thorláksson (1867–1924) paints *Sunset by the Lake*, a Symbolist silhouette of Reykjavik, the Icelandic capital, against the evening sky; Swedish architect Ferdinand Boberg (1860–1946) designs the Thielska Gallery in Stockholm.

1906

Dane Ludwig Mylius-Erichsen (1872–1907) sets off as leader of an expedition to explore the geographic extent of north-east Greenland, on which he dies.

1907

Swede Sven Wingquist (1876–1953) establishes the factory where he invents ball bearings.

1909–12

Dane Ejnar Mikkelsen (1880–1971), expedition leader in Greenland; he found the remains of Mylius-Erichsen and the records from his fatal journey of exploration.

1909

Swede Selma Lagerlöf (1848–1940), author of *Gösta Berlings Saga* (1891), a lyrical historical tale about a renegade priest in her native Värmland, wins the Nobel Prize for Literature; Danish chemist Søren Peter Lauritz Sørensen (1868–1939) introduces the concept of pH as a tool of measurement.

1910

Danish silversmith Georg Jensen (1866–1935) wins the Gold Medal at Brussels for his craftsmanship, going on to achieve great commercial success.

1911

Norwegian Roald Amundsen (1872–1928) becomes the first explorer to reach the South Pole; Swede Alvar Gullstrand (1862–1930) wins the Nobel Prize for Medicine for his work in ophthalmology; 1911, Finnish botanist Aimo Kaarlo Cajander (1879–1943) becomes Professor of Forestry at Helsinki University.

1912

Danish-Greenlandic explorer and ethnologist Knud Rasmussen (1879–1933) makes two crossings of the interior of Greenland from coast to coast; Gustaf Dalén (1869–1937) wins the Nobel Prize for Physics

for his invention of the AGA automatic lighting system for lighthouses.

1916

Swede Verner von Heidenstam (1859–1940), author-poet of *Hans Alienus*, many of whose works are infused with National Romantic themes, wins the Nobel Prize for Literature; Finnish poet Edith Södergran (1892–1923) publishes her Expressionist free verse collection *Poems*.

1917

Danes Karl Gjellerup (1857–1919), author of *The Pilgrim Kamanita*, and Henrik Pontoppidan (1857–1944), who wrote the novel *Lykke-Per*, win the Nobel Prize for Literature. The former deals with an Indian theme, featuring the Buddhist belief in reincarnation, while the latter is a loosely autobiographical novel which explores the central character's attempt to break away from his puritanical background by moving to Copenhagen, where he becomes an engineer and romantic adventures await him.

1919

Swedish composer Wilhelm Peterson-Berger (1867–1942) presents his comic opera *The Doomsday Prophets*, inspired by the music of Wagner and the philosophy of Nietzsche.

1920

Norwegian Knut Hamsun (1859–1952), the author of *Growth of the Soul*, wins the Nobel Prize for Literature; this and other works by him possess a Neo-Romantic focus on Nature as a means of spiritual revival; Danish explorer Lauge Koch sets forth on an expedition to survey Peary Land; Danish zoologist August Krogh (1874–1949) wins the Nobel Prize for Medicine for his work on the function of capillaries in relationship to muscles.

1922

Dane Niels Bohr (1885–1962) wins the Nobel Prize for Physics for his research into the atom; Fridtjof Nansen is awarded the Nobel Prize for Peace for his relief work after World War One.

1923

Stockholm Town Hall is completed by Swedish National Romantic architect Ragnar Östberg (1866–1945).

1924

Swede Manne Siegbahn (1886–1978) wins the Nobel Prize for Physics for work on X-ray spectroscopy; Finnish mathematician Rolf Nevanlinna (1895–1980), with his brother Frithiof, develops a complex theory in regard to the distribution of values in the meromorphic function.

1924–7

Swedish architect Gunnar Asplund designs and builds his classically inspired Stockholm City Library.

1926

The Swede The Svedberg (1884–1971) wins the Nobel Prize for Chemistry for his work on ultra-centrifugation of molecular compounds, enabling a determination of the molecular weight of many substances based on proteins.

1928

Norwegian Sigrid Undset (1882–1949), author of the trilogy *Kristin Lavransdatter*, in which religion and the role of woman are given a medieval historical setting, wins the Nobel Prize for Literature.

1929

Swede Hans von Euler-Chelpin (1873–1964) wins the Nobel Prize for Chemistry for work on the fermentation of sugar and enzymes.

1929–30

Antarctic explorations of the Norwegian Commander H. Riiser-Larsen in pursuit of new whaling grounds.

1929–33

Finnish architect Alvar Aalto (1898–1976) builds his radically designed tuberculosis sanitorium at Pemar.

1930

Danish author and poet Tom Kristensen (1893–1974) publishes *Havoc*, a soul-searching novel about the inter-war years; Swedish opera singer Jussi Björling (1911–1960) makes his debut at the Opera House in Stockholm in the role of Don Ottavio, in Mozart's *Don Juan*; German-Danish artist Emil Nolde (1867–1956) paints his Expressionist watercolour *Friesland Farm under Red Clouds*.

1932

Swedish composer Hilding Rosenberg (1892–1985) provides music for the opera *Journey to America*.

1934

Clarence Crafoord (1899–1983) wins the Nobel Prize for Medicine for his research on pulmonary embolism.

1937

Danish author Karen Blixen (pseudonym: Isak Dinesen) (1885–1962) publishes her autobiographical novel *Out of Africa* which deals with the joy's and tribulations of her life as a farmer in colonial Kenya; Swedish actress and singer Zarah Leander (1907–1981) joins UFA in Berlin, going on to achieve great popularity in Nazi Germany in films such as *It was an Enchanting Ball* (1939), about the composer Tchaikovsky.

1939

Finn F. E. Sillanpää (1888–1964), author of *Weak Heritage*, a novel which focuses upon Finland's troubled period of civil conflict after independence, wins the Nobel Prize for Literature.

1945

Swedish children's author Astrid Lindgren (1907–) publishes *Pippi Långstrump*, the first in a series of books based around the character in which the child's autonomy is stressed, rather than the moral authority of the parents.

1948

Swede Arne Tiselius (1902–1971) wins the Nobel Prize for Chemistry for his discovery of the electrophoresis of proteins.

1949

Danish author Hans Christian Branner (1903–1966) publishes his novel *The Riding Master*, a work rich in psychoanalytical insights; Swedish novelist Vilhelm Moberg (1898–1973) publishes *The Emigrants* about Swedes seeking a new life in America in the nineteenth century.

1950

Faeroese author William Heinesen publishes his novel *The Lost Musicians*, with its fine focus on life in the Faeroes; Alvar Aalto builds his Säynätsalo town hall complex (1950–52).

1951

Swede Pär Lagerkvist (1891–1974), author of the novel *Barabbas*, in which a Biblical subject is given a modern reference, wins the Nobel Prize for Literature.

1954

Swedish opera singer Birgit Nilsson (1918–) achieves international acclaim for her role as Elsa, in Wagner's *Lohengrin* at the Bayreuth Festival.

1955

Icelander Halldór Laxness (1902–1998), author of the novel *Salka Valka*, which focuses upon the arduous life of a working-class woman, wins the Nobel Prize for Literature; Swede Hugo Theorell (1903–1982) wins the Nobel Prize for Medicine for work in physiology.

1957

Swedish film director Ingmar Bergman (1918–1998) releases *Wild Strawberries*, a lyrical work dealing with the problems of growing old.

1958

Danish author and poet Klaus Rifbjerg (1931–) publishes his novel *The Chronic Innocence*, dealing with the difficulties of a youth entering manhood.

1959

Arne Jacobsen (1902–1971), Danish architect and designer, builds the SAS building in Copenhagen.

1968

Nobel Price for Economics established by the Bank of Sweden; it is awarded to the Norwegian economist Ragnar Frisch (Norway) and the Dutch Jan Tinbergen for work in econometrics.

1970

Swede Hannes Alfvén (1908–) wins the Nobel Prize for Physics for his work in magnetohydrodynamics; Dane Aage Bohr (1922–), son of Niels Bohr, wins the Nobel Prize for Physics for his work on atomic physics.

1974

Swedes Eyvind Johnson (1900–1976), the working-class author of *The Days of his Grace*, and Harry Martinson (1904–1978), who wrote the epic poem about travel in space, *A Review of Man in Time and Space*, win the Nobel Prize for Literature.

References

Introduction

1 The Danish historian Kristian Hvidt has maintained that the loose term Scandinavia can be used to refer not only to Denmark, Sweden and Norway, but even to Finland, Iceland, the Faeroes and Greenland. See Uffe Østergard, 'National identiteter. Tyskland, Norden, Skandinavien', in *Scandinavien och Tyskland. 1800–1914*, ed. Bernd Henningsen et al. (Berlin, 1997), p. 29.
2 During the late eighteenth century in Norway, for example, 25.1 per 1000 died in an average year, compared to 31.2 in Europe in general some 50 years later. Even the higher rate of 31.6 per 1000 in Iceland, in the late eighteenth century, compares quite favourably to the rest of Europe at this time. Richard F. Tomasson, *Iceland. The First Society* (Minneapolis, 1980), p. 70.
3 Birgit Grimm, 'Wilhelm och Norge', in *Skandinavien och Tyskland*, p. 101.

Christianity, Spirituality and the Church

1 Ole Grell, 'Scandinavia', in *The Reformation in National Context*, eds Bob Scribner, Roy Porter and Mikulá Teich (Cambridge, 1994), p. 113.
2 Grell, 'Scandinavia', in *The Reformation in National Context*, p. 119.
3 E. I. Kouri, 'The Early Reformation in Sweden and Finland, c. 1520–1560', in *The Scandinavian Reformation. From Evangelical Movement to Institutionalisation of Reform*, ed. Ole Grell (Cambridge, 1995), p. 69.
4 Sergiusz Michalski, *The Reformation and the Visual Arts* (London, 1993), p. 27.
5 *Ibid.*, p. 7.
6 *Ibid.*, p. 132.
7 Martin Schwartz Lausten, 'The Early Reformation in Denmark and Norway 1520–1559', in Grell, ed., *Scandinavian Reformation*, p. 24.
8 Ole Peter Grell, 'Scandinavia', in *The Early Reformation in Europe*, ed. Andrew Pettegrew (Cambridge, 1992), p. 109.
9 Ole Peter Grell, 'The Catholic Church and its Leadership', in Grell, ed., *Scandinavian Reformation*, p. 78.
10 Grell, 'Scandinavia', in *The Reformation in National Context*, p. 117.
11 Thorkild Lyby and Ole Peter Grell, 'The Consolidation of Lutheranism in Denmark and Norway', in Grell, ed., *Scandinavian Reformation*, pp. 123–5.
12 Schwarz Lausten, 'Early Reformation', pp. 28–9.
13 Jóhannes Nordal and Valdimar Kristinsson, eds, *Iceland 1986* (Reykjavik, 1987), p. 94.
14 Grell, 'Scandinavia', in *Early Reformation in Europe*, p. 98.
15 J. Rosén, *Svensk Historia*, 1 (Stockholm, 1969), p. 314.
16 Ungun Montgomery, 'The Institutionalisation of Lutheranism in Sweden and Finland', in Grell, ed., *Scandinavian Reformation*, p. 144.
17 Grell, 'Scandinavia', in *The Reformation in National Context*, p. 118.
18 Michalski, *Reformation and Visual Arts*, p. 135.
19 Montgomery, 'Institutionalisation of Lutheranism', pp. 172–6.
20 Ole Peter Grell, 'Exile and Tolerance', in *Tolerance and Intolerance in the European Reforation*, eds Ole Peter Grell and Bob Scribner (Cambridge, 1996), pp. 166–7.
21 Lyby and Grell, 'Consolidation of Lutheranism', pp. 118–23.
22 *Ibid.*, p. 135.
23 *Ibid.*, pp. 138–9.
24 *Ibid.*, p. 168.
25 Hanns Gross, *Rome in the Age of Enlightenment. The Post-Tridentine Syndrome and the Ancien Régime* (London, 1990), p. 21.
26 *Ibid.*, p. 30.
27 *Ibid.*, p. 9.
28 Lyby and Grell, 'Consolidation of Lutheranism', p. 143.
29 Brian P. Levack, *The Witch-hunt in Early Modern Europe*, 2nd edn (London and New York, 1995), p. 10.
30 *Ibid.*, p. 168.
31 Jens C. V. Johansen, 'Faith, Superstition and Witchcraft in Reformation Scandinavia', in Grell, ed., *Scandinavian Reformation*, pp. 200–01.
32 Levack, *Witch-hunt*, p. 207.
33 Bent Rying, *Danish in the North and South* (Copenhagen, 1988), vol. 2 , p. 149.
34 Levack, *Witch-hunt*, pp. 207–8.
35 Richard F. Tomasson, *Iceland. The First New Society* (Minneapolis, 1980), p. 110.
36 Johansen, 'Faith, Superstition and Witchcraft', p. 202.
37 John Milton, *Milton's Poetical Works: Paradise Lost*, Book II (1667), (London, 1966), p. 247.
38 Israel Ruong, *The Lapps in Sweden* (Stockholm, 1967), p. 18.
39 Levack, *Witch-hunt*, p. 211.
40 *Ibid.*

41 Johansen, 'Faith, Superstition and Witchcraft', pp. 203–9.

42 Levant, *Witch-hunt*, pp. 213–14.

43 Lyby and Grell, 'Consolidation of Lutheranism', p. 131.

44 Matti Klinge, *The Baltic World* (Helsinki, 1994), p. 84.

45 Ibid., p. 86.

46 Isidor Paiewonsky, *Eyewitness Accounts of Slavery in the Danish West Indies. Also Graphic Tales of Other Slave Happenings on Ships and Plantations* (New York, 1989), pp. 105, 111.

47 Per Eilstrup and Nils Eric Boesgaard, *Fjernt fra Danmark, Billeder fra vore Tropekolonier, Slavehandel oq Kinafart* (Copenhagen, 1974), p. 110.

48 Ibid., pp. 110–12.

49 Ibid., p. 111.

50 Ibid., p. 80.

51 Joseph Leo Koerner, *Caspar David Friedrich and the Subject of Landscape* (London, 1990), p. 50.

52 Eilstrup and Boesgaard, *Fjernt fra Danmark*, p. 43.

53 Anders Åman, *Om den Offentliga Vården. Byggnader och verksamheter vid svenska vårdsinstitutioner under 1800- och 1900-talen. En arkitekturhistorisk undersning* (Uppsala, 1976), p. 75.

54 Harry G. Carlson, *Out of Inferno. Strindberg's Reawakening as an Artist* (Seattle, Washington, 1996), p. 215.

55 Ibid., p. 217.

56 Nicholas Hope, *German and Scandinavian Protestantism 1700–1918* (Oxford, 1995), pp. 194–5.

57 Rying, *South and North*, pp. 197–8.

58 Anders Åman, 'Övre Norrlands Kyrkor – deras konsthistoria och geografi', p. 194. *Bebyggelsehistorisk tidskrift. Övre Norrlands kyrkor*, 22 (Stockholm, 1991),

59 Birgitta Ericsson, 'Panorama över svenska riket och dess förbindelser med Frankrike. Statskick och befolkning', in *Solen och Nordstjärnan. Frankrike och Sverige på 1700-talet*, ed. Pontus Grate (Högnäs, 1993), p. 146.

60 Amandus Johnson, *The Swedish Settlements on the Delaware 1638–1664*, 2 vols (New York, 1911), vol. 2, p. 546.

61 Ibid., vol. 1, pp. 200–05.

62 Ibid., vol. 1, p. 379.

63 Ibid., vol. 1, p. 658.

64 Gösta Franzén, *Svenskstad i Västindien. Gustafia på Saint Barthélemy i språk- och kulturhistorisk belysning* (Stockholm, 1974), pp. 39–44.

65 Ibid., pp. 45–7.

66 Edward Crain, *Historic Architecture in the Caribbean Islands* (Gainsville, FL, 1994), pp. 213–17.

67 Sten Carlsson, 'Upplyst despotism (1772–86)', *Svensk Historia. 2. Tiden efter 1718* (Lund, 1980), p. 168.

68 Rabbi Bradd H. Boxman, *A Short History of the Hebrew Congregation of St Thomas* (St Thomas, 1983), pp. 3–29.

69 Nordal and Kristinsson, *Iceland 1986*, p. 94.

70 Ibid.

71 Alf Henrikson, *Isländsk Historia* (Stockholm, 1981), p. 173.

72 Tomasson, *Iceland*, p. 104.

73 Ruong, *Lapps in Sweden*, p. 75.

74 Peter Sköld, 'The Saami Experience of Smallpox in Eighteenth-Century Sweden' (unpublished, 1995), pp. 2–5.

75 Ian Whitaker, 'Settler and Nomad in Northern Torne-Lappmark Polar Record', XXI (Cambridge, 1983), p. 337

76 Olv Isaksson and Folke Isaksson, *Gammelstad Kyrkby vid Lule Älv* (Stockholm, 1991), pp. 121–31.

77 Ibid., pp. 104–5.

78 Ibid., pp. 121–31.

79 Åman, 'Övre Norrlands kyrkor', p. 204.

80 Sten Åke Nilsson, *Konsten i Sverige. 1700-talet efter den karolinska tiden* (Stockholm, 1974), p. 174.

81 Åman, 'Övre Norrlands kyrkor', pp. 197–200.

82 Andreas Lindblom, 'Karolinskt Kyrkobygge' in *Sveriges Konsthistoria från Forntid till Nudid. Andra Delen: Från Gustaf Vasa till Gustaf III* (Stockholm, 1944), p. 473.

83 Andreas Lindblom, 'Gustafiadens och Karl johanstidens Kyrkor' in *Sveriges Konsthistoria*, p. 716.

84 Åman, 'Övre Norrlands kyrkor', p. 242.

85 Anders Åman, 'Kykornas norrländska landskap', *Provins. Norrländskt Magasin*, IV (1990), p. 28.

86 Ibid., p. 27.

87 Asbjørn Nesheim, *Samene. Historie og kultur* (Oslo, 1966), p. 38.

88 Sten Carlsson, 'Konservativ reformpolitik. 1810–40', *Svensk Historia*, p. 291.

89 In 1720, each priest had served some 1,300 parishioners, but by 1800 each one served some 1,884, and only 30 years later it was not unusual for a priest to have as many as 3,164 souls under his spiritual authority.

90 Michael Drake, *Population and Society in Norway. 1735–1865* (Cambridge, 1969), pp. 13–23.

91 Ibid., p. 10.

92 Vagn Poulsen, 'Guldalderen' *Dansk Kunst Historie. Billedkunst og Skulptur. Akademie og København. 1750–1850* (Copenhagen, 1972), III p. 272.

93 Koerner, *Caspar David Friedrich*, p. 23.

94 Ibid., p. 50.

95 Ibid., pp. 74, 76.

96 Flemming Lundgreen-Nielsen, 'Grundtvig og danskhed', *Dansk Identitetshistorie* (Copenhagen, 1992), vol. 3, pp. 88–9.

97 Ibid., p. 114.

98 Rying, *South and North*, p. 309.

99 Hakon Stangerup and F. J. Billeskov Jansen, *Dansk Litteratur Historie* (Copenhagen, 1967) vol. 3, p. 33.

100 J. P. Jacobsen, *Niels Lyhne* (Copenhagen, 1880), p. 117.

101 Adolf Törneros, *Bref och dagboks-anteckningar* (posthumously published, 1840), pp. 339–40.

102 Åman, 'Kykornas norrländska landskap', p. 28.

103 Ibid., pp. 27–8.

104 Michalski, *Reformation and Visual Arts*, p. 166.

105 Carlsson, 'De stora folkrörelserna', *Svensk Historia*, p. 393.

106 Nelson Annandale, *The Faeroes and Iceland: Studies in Island Life* (Oxford, 1905), p. 29.

107 Ibid., p. 155.

108 Bodil Kaalund, The Art of Greenland. Sculpture, Crafts, Painting (Copenhagen, 1979), pp.186–7.

109 Søren Vadstrup, 'Det syd- og vestgrønlandske stenbyggeri i årene 1830–1940', Forskning i Grønland. tussat 1/88 (Copenhagen, 1987), pp. 17–21.

The Family and Sexuality

1 Jonas Frykman and Orvar Löfgren, Den kultiverade människan (Lund, 1979), p. 155.

2 Eino Jutikkala, Bonden i Finland genom Tiderna (Helsingfors, 1963), pp. 62–3.

3 Nesheim, Samene, p. 33.

4 Jutikkala, Bonden i Finland, p. 64.

5 Eilert Sundt, Om bygnings-skikken på landet i Norge (Oslo, 1976), p. 77.

6 Bo Malmberg, 'Vräkningar från fattigbebyggelse. En mörk episod vid inrättandet av knonoparker i Vilhelmina socken under 1900-talets olika nordiska miljöer under de senaste tvåhundra åren', Den utsatta familjen. Liv, arbete och mamlevnad i olika nordisk miljöer under de senaste tvåhundra åren, ed. Hans Norman (Stockholm, 1983), p. 193.

7 Jan Hendrich, '1. Arkitektur 1536–1814', Norges kunsthistorie Bind 3. Nedangstid og ny reisning (Oslo, 1981), p. 105.

8 This was especially the case in Norway, where a considerable increase of population from the seventeenth to the eighteenth centuries occurred. With approximately 440,000 inhabitants in 1665, its population had risen to 616,000 by 1735. During the following century, despite the fact that marriage and reproductive patterns had remained fairly constant, the population increased dramatically (Drake, Population and Society, p. 95). The population in 1815 was 885,431, virtually doubling to 1,600,551 by 1865. Other Scandinavian countries showed similar, if less startling, rates of growth: the population of Sweden grew from 2,465,066 inhabitants in 1815 to 4,114,141 by 1865, while Denmark's population increased from 1,018,180 to 1,600,551 over the same period (ibid, pp. 41–2). Finland also showed a major increase over that confirmed in its first census of 1749, when there were 409,000 inhabitants in the province (Jutikkala, Bonden i Finland, p. 255.

9 Drake, Population and Society, p. 8.

10 Frykman and Löfgren, Kultiverade människan, p. 76.

11 Lena Rydin, Den Lustfyllda Vardagen. Hos Larsson i Sundborn (Stockholm, 1993), p. 53.

12 Anneli Ilmonen, 'Sauna in Pictorial Art' in Sauna Studies, eds Collan and Pirkko Valtakari (Helsinki, 1976), p. 29.

13 L. M. Edelsward, Sauna as Symbol. Society and Culture in Finland (New York, 1991), p. 185.

14 Eric Johannesson, 'Den heliga familjen. Om borgerlig familjekult under 1800-talet' in Den utsatta familjen, ed. Hans Norman, pp. 31–2.

15 Ibid., pp. 33-5.

16 Frykman and Löfgren, Kultiverade människan, p. 119.

17 Ibid., p. 38.

18 Kai Häggman, Perheen vuosisata. Perheen ihana ja sivistyneistön elämäntapa 1800-luvun Suomessa (Helsinki, 1994), p. 249.

19 Sixteen per cent reached adulthood in two-parent families in late eighteenth-century Finland, compared to 47 per cent in the late nineteenth: Häggman, Perheen vuosisata, p. 249.

20 Ibid., pp. 247–8.

21 Ronald Hyam, Empire and Sexuality. The British Experience (Manchester, 1990), p. 56.

22 Josef Ruff, Illustreradt Helsovårds-Lexicon. En populär handbok för alla (Stockholm, 1888), pp. 553–5.

23 Ibid., p. 553–5.

24 Oliver Rackham, The Illustrated History of the Countryside (place and date), p. 143.

25 Frykman and Löfgren, Kultiverade människan, p. 179.

26 Ulf Hamran, 'Det nye Norge bygger. Norsk Arkitektur 1814–1870', Norges kunsthistorie Bind 4. Det unge Norge (Oslo, 1981), p. 68.

27 Ibid., p. 67.

28 Stephan Tschudi-Madsen, 'Veien hjem. Norsk arkitektur 1870–1914', Norges kunsthistorie. Bind 5. Nasjonal vekst (Oslo, 1981), p. 55.

29 Lawrence Stone, The Family, Sex and Marriage in England 1500–1800 (London, 1977), p. 324.

30 Rying, North and South, vol. 2, p. 148.

31 Göran Rydén, 'Iron Production and the Household as a Production Unit in a Nineteenth Century Sweden', Continuity and Change. A Journal of Social Structure, Law and Demography in Past Societies (Cambridge, 1995), pp. 85–91.

32 Ståle Dyrvik, 'Farmers at Sea: A Study of Fishermen in North Norway, 1801–1920', Journal of Family History, XVIII/4 (1993), p. 355.

33 Kirsten Elisabeth Caning, 'Om den grønlandske befolknings historie', Forskning i Grønland. tusaat 1/82 (Copenhagen, 1982), p. 2.

34 Elsa Lunander, 'Bland handlare och hantverkare i en svensk landsortsstad under 1800-talet. Om hushålls- och familjestruktur i Örebro' in Den utsatta familjen, ed. Hans Norman, pp. 148–9.

35 Eilert Sundt, 'Om giftermall i Norge: bidrag til kundskab om folkets kaar og sædeligheds-tilstanden i Norge', in Drake, Population and Society, p. 27.

36 Ibid., p. 44.

37 Hans. Chr. Johansen, Per Madsen and Ole Degn, 'Fishing Families in Three Danish Coastal Communities', Journal of Family History, XVIII/4 (1993), p. 367.

38 Gísli Ágúst Gunnlaugsson and Ólöf Garsðarsdóttir, 'Availability of Offspring and the Household Position of Elderly Women: Iceland, 1901', Journal of Family History, XX/2 (1993), pp. 160–4.

39 Jutikkala, Bonden i Finland, pp. 58–9.

40 Beatrice Moring, 'Household and Family in Finnish Coastal Societies, 1635–1895', *Journal of Family History*, XVIII/4 (1993), p. 398.
41 *Ibid.*, p. 407.
42 *Ibid.*, p. 408.
43 Sundt, *Om giftermall i Norge*, pp. 62–3.
44 Christer Lundh, 'Households and Families in Pre-Industrial Sweden', in *Continuity and Change*, p. 37.
45 Stone, *Family, Sex and Marriage*, p. 642.
46 Eilstrup and Boesgaard, *Fjernt fra Danmark*, p. 111.
47 Vivi Horn, *Den sturske Mongomery* (Stockholm, 1938), p. 309.
48 E. O. E. Högström, *S. Barthelemy under svenskt välde* (Uppsala, 1888), p. 69.
49 Eilstrup and Boesgaard, *Fjernt fra Danmark*, p. 144.
50 Nilsson, *Konsten i Sverige*, p. 144.
51 Anna Maria Lenngren, 'Miss Juliana', (Fröken Juliana).
52 Gunilla Edström and Gunilla Gustafsson, '"Kontrollerat kvinnokött till salu!" Prostituerade i Uppsala år 1860–1900', *Den utsatta familjen*, ed. Hans Norman, p. 223.
53 In 1815 1,044,000 people were living in the countryside; by 1900 there were some 2,373,000. Jutikkala, *Bonden i Finland*, p. 370.
54 Sten Carlsson, 'Kvinnoöden i 1800-talets Sverige' in *Den utsatta familjen*, ed. Hans Norman, p. 53.
55 Gunnlaugsson and Garsðarsdóttir, 'Availability of Offspring', pp. 159 65.
56 Carlsson, 'Kvinnoöden i 1800-talets Sverige', pp. 43–6.
57 Tomasson, *Iceland*, pp. 104–5.
58 *Ibid.*, pp. 90–93.
59 Edström and Gustafsson, '"Kontrollerat kvinnokött till salu!"', p. 215.
60 *Ibid.*, pp. 217–18.
61 *Ibid.*, p. 225.
62 Stanislaw Przybyszewski, ed., *Das Werk des Edvard Munch. Vier Beiträge von Stanislaw Przybyszewski, Dr Franz Servaes, Willy Pastor, Julius Meier Graefe* (Berlin, 1894), p. 19.
63 Levack, *Witch-hunt*, p. 112.
64 Jan Löfström, 'A Premodern Legacy: The "East" Criminalization of Homosexual Acts Between Women in the Finnish Penal Code of 1889', *Journal of Homosexuality*, XXXV/3–4, part II, p. 55.
65 Löfström, 'A Premodern Legacy', p. 73.
66 Magnus Hirschfeld, *Die Homosexualität des Mannes und des Weibes* (Berlin, 1920), p. 539.
67 *Ibid.*, p. 536.
68 *Ibid.*, p. 539.
69 *Ibid.*
70 Löfström, 'A Premodern Legacy', p. 69.

Health, Hygiene and Disease

1 William James Burroughs, *Does the Weather Really Matter? The Social Implications of Climate Change* (Cambridge, 1997), p. 35.
2 Carlsson, 'Kvinnoöden i 1800-talets Sverige', p. 49.
3 Thorkild Kjaergaard, *The Danish Revolution. 1500–1800* (Cambridge, 1994), p. 13.
4 1779, in particular, was a bad year for the disease when seven out of every 1000 people in Sweden died of the disease; in a normal year the rate was about five in 1000. Most of these victims were children, smallpox mainly being a disease of childhood, though this was not the case everywhere. In Sweden alone, between 1750 and 1800, almost 300,000 people succumbed to it, out of a population of about 2,000,000. Peter Sköld, 'The Saami Experience of Smallpox in Eighteenth-Century Sweden' (unpublished, 1995), p. 3.
5 The Royal Society in London had published Emanuel Timoni's account of inoculation in the Ottoman Empire in 1714 and Karl XII, in exile in Adrianople, had a copy sent to Stockholm.
6 Åman, *Om den Offentliga Vården*, p. 13.
7 Sköld, 'Saami Experience of Smallpox', p. 6.
8 *Ibid.*, pp. 20–21.
9 *Ibid.*, pp. 3, 7.
10 William R. Mead, *An Experience of Finland* (London, 1993), pp. 100, 104.
11 Only 16 per cent of the Norwegian infants had been vaccinated at the start of this period, but by 1852 the number had increased to over 82 per cent, leading to a radical reduction in the incidence of smallpox. Drake, *Population and Society*, p. 13.
12 *Ibid.*, pp. 51–3.
13 *Ibid.*, p. 7.
14 Terry G. Lacy, *Ring of Seasons. Iceland – Its Culture and History* (Ann Arbor, Michigan, 1998), pp. 215, 227.
15 Caning, 'Grønlandske befolknings historie', p. 4.
16 Alf Henrikson, *Isländsk Historia*, (Stockholm, 1981), p. 173.
17 E. I. Kouri, 'Health Care and Poor Relief in Sweden and Finland c. 1500–1700', in *Health Care and Poor Relief in Protestant Europe 1500–1700*, eds Ole Peter Grell and Andrew Cunningham (London and New York, 1997), p. 169.
18 William R. Mead, *An Experience of Finland* (London, 1993), p. 100.
19 Edv. Bull and Einar Jansen, eds, 'Hansen, Gerhard Henrik Armauer', in *Norsk Biografisk Leksikon* (Oslo, 1931), vol. 5, p. 375.
20 Anders Åman, *Om den Offentliga Vården. Byggnader och verksamheter vid svenska vårdsinstitutioner under 1800- och 1900-talen. En arkitekturhistorisk undersökning* (Uppsala, 1976), pp. 217–19.
21 *Ibid.*, pp. 49–52.
22 *Ibid.*, p. 80.
23 *Ibid.*, pp. 28–31.
24 *Ibid.*, pp. 165–80.

25 Ibid., p. 312.

26 There had been 4,602 inmates at mental hospitals in 1900, but by 1940 there were 26,105.

27 Ibid., pp. 305-7.

28 Carlsson, 'Kvinnöden i 1800-talets Sverige', p. 44.

29 G. Utterström, 'Befolkningsutveckling och näringsliv efter mitten av 1700-talet', in En bok om Mälärlandskapen (Stockholm, 1953), p. 276.

30 Will Durant and Ariel Durant, The Story of Civilisation: Part IX. The Age of Voltaire. A History of Civilization in Western Europe from 1715 to 1756, with Special Emphasis on the Conflict between Religion and Philosophy (New York, 1965), p. 590.

31 Burroughs, Does the Weather Really Matter?, p. 35.

32 Jutikkala, Bonden i Finland, pp. 208-9.

33 Drake, Population and Society, pp. 54-9.

34 Jutikkala, Bonden i Finland, p. 340.

35 Henrikson, Isländsk Historia, pp. 173-4.

36 Steve Jones, The Language of Genes. Biology, History and the Evolutionary Future (London, 1994), p. 210.

37 Tomasson, Iceland, p. 57.

38 Ibid., p. 74.

39 Ibid., p. 64.

40 Gunnlaugsson and Garsðarsdóttir, 'Availability of Offspring', p. 161.

41 Tomasson, Iceland, p. 65.

42 Terry Lacy, Ring of Seasons, p. 118.

43 Drake, Population and Society, pp. 66, 72.

44 Franzén, Svensksstad i Västindien, p. 80.

45 Högström, S. Barthelemy, p. 80.

46 Engström, Christer (editor-in-chief), 'Malaria', in Nationalenchklopedin (Stockholm, 1993), vol. 12, p. 640,

47 Kjaergaard, Danish Revolution, p. 184.

48 Åman, Om den Offentliga Vården, pp. 211.

49 Richard J. Evans, 'Cholera in Nineteenth-Century Europe', in Epidemics and Ideas. Essays on the Historical Perception of Pestilence, eds Terence Ranger and Paul Slack (Cambridge, 1992), pp. 149-73.

50 Tomasson, Iceland, p. 64.

51 Åman, Om den Offentliga Vården, pp. 213-14.

52 Ibid., p. 294.

53 Ibid., p. 300.

54 Lacy, Ring of Seasons, p. 219.

55 Ole Peter Grell, 'The Protestant Imperative of Christian Care and Neighbourly Love', in Grell and Cunningham, eds, Health Care and Poor Relief, p. 59.

56 Åman, Om den Offentliga Vården, p. 80.

57 Ibid.

58 Heikki Ylikangas, Knivjunkarna. Väldskriminaliteten i Sydösterbotten. 1790-1825 (Borgå, 1985), p. 205.

59 Åman, Om den Offentliga Vården, p. 241.

60 Drake, Population and Society, p. 70.

61 Peter Baldwin, Contagion and the State in Europe 1830-1930 (Cambridge, 1999), p. 414.

62 Eström and Gustafsson, 'Kontrollerat kvinnokött till salu!', Den utsatta familjen, pp. 213-20.

63 Baldwin p. 408.

64 Ibid., pp. 223-5.

65 Åman, Om den Offentliga Vården, p. 362-3.

66 Ibid., p. 254.

67 Ibid., p. 70.

68 Ibid., pp. 254-66.

69 Ryding, South and North, vol. 2, p. 139.

70 Åman, Om den Offentliga Vården, pp. 71-7.

71 Ibid., p. 206.

72 Frykman and Löfgren, Kultiverade människan, p. 134.

73 Ibid., p. 167.

74 Annandale, Faeroes and Iceland, p. 39.

75 Paiewonsky, Accounts of Slavery, p. 28.

76 Ibid., pp. 48, 53.

77 Ibid., p. 46.

78 Eilstrup and Boesgaard, Fjernt fra Danmark, p. 83.

79 Lucinda Lambton, Temples of Convenience (London, 1978), pp. 5-12.

80 Frykman and Löfgren, Kultiverade människan, p. 168.

81 Ibid., p. 162.

82 Johnson, Swedish Settlements on the Delaware, vol. 1, p. 358.

83 Edelsward, Sauna as Symbol, p. 83.

Nordic Life in the Town and Country

1 Jutikkala, Bonden i Finland, pp. 206-7.

2 Kjaergaard, Danish Revolution, p. 9.

3 Ibid., p. 18.

4 Jutikkala, Bonden i Finland, pp. 149-51.

5 Ibid., p. 137.

6 Ibid., p. 207.

7 In 1685, some 125,000 barrels of tar were exported abroad, transported through Stockholm, in the west, or Viipuri (Viborg), in Karelia, in the east. Klinge, Baltic World, p. 79.

8 There were still some 1,800 abandoned farmsteads in 1731. Jutikkala, Bonden i Finland, pp. 210-20.

9 Ibid., p. 417.

10 Sverker Sörlin, 'Fransmans resor idet exotiska Lappland', in Solen och nordstjärnan. Frankrihe och sverige vå 1700-talet, (Stockholm, 1993) ed. Pontus Grate. p. 214.

11 Ian Whitaker, 'Settler and Nomad in Northern Torne-Lappmark', Polar Record, XXI, p. 336.

12 Ibid., pp. 329-44.

13 Ruong, Lapps in Sweden, p. 17.

14 Asbjørn Nesheim, Samene, p. 34.

15 Jutikkala, Bonden i Finland, p. 334.

16 Whitaker, 'Settler and Nomad', p. 335.

17 Out of the 7,453 inhabitants of Neder Luleå there were 16 people from the aristocracy, 23 were clergymen and 131 burghers, along with 4,959 soldiers, craftsmen, peasant farmers and farm labourers, Isaksson and Isaksson, Gammestad Kyrkby, p. 162.

18 Ibid., p. 107.

19 Jean François Battail, 'Relationerna mellan Frankrike och Sverige på 1700-talet', in Grate, ed., Solen och Nordstjärnan, p. 15.

20 Kjaergaard, Danish Revolution, p. 62.

21 Isaksson and Isaksson, Gammestad Kyrkby, p. 67.

22 By the 1770s, the population of Stockholm had grown modestly, to 75,000, but the country as a whole had increased significantly to over 2,000,000, 90 per cent of them living in the countryside.

23 Isaksson and Isaksson, Gammestad Kyrkby, pp. 11, 15.

24 Of 600,000 inhabitants, some 95.5 per cent of the entire population lived in the countryside. Birgitta Ericsson, 'Panorama över svenska', pp. 144, 179.

25 Ibid., p. 145.

26 Jutikkala, Bonden i Finland, p. 247.

27 Ibid., pp. 262–75.

28 Ibid., pp. 320, 375.

29 Carlsson, 'Kvinnoöden i 1800-talets Sverige', p. 42.

30 Klinge, The Baltic World, p. 125.

31 Kjaergaard, Danish Revolution, p. 63.

32 Isaksson and Isaksson, Gammestad Kyrkby, p. 160.

33 Anna-Maria Åström 'Herrgårdens Gårdsplan och Buggnader. Tolkning av en utveckling i Savolax 1780–1980', in Fynd och Forskning, ed. Ivar Nordlund (Helsingfors, 1981), p. 219.

34 Anna-Maria Åström, '"Herrskapsfolk och underlydande" Kansa Kuvastimessa', in Etnisyys ja identiteetti, eds Topps Korhonen and Matti Räsänen (Helsinki, 1989), p. 168.

35 Ibid., p. 185.

36 Kjaergaard, Danish Revolution, p. 148.

37 Ole Feldbæk, 'Slkole og identitet 1789–1848', in Dansk Identitetshistorie, ed. Ole Feldbæk, 4 vols (Copenhagen, 1992), vol. 2, p. 319.

38 Lorenz Rerup, 'Folkestyre og danskhed. Massenationalisme og politik 1848–1866', in Dansk Identitetshistorie, vol. 3, p. 348.

39 Ibid., p. 353.

40 Drake, Population and Society, p. 99.

41 Ibid., p. 59.

42 Ståle Dyrvik, 'Farmers at Sea: A Study of Fishermen in North Norway, 180-111920', Journal of Family History, XVIII/4, p. 345.

43 Drake, Population and Society, p. 80.

44 Dag Celsin, 'På tröskeln till industrialismen', in Karl Johan. Konst, iredningar och teknik i empirens Sverige, ed. Barbro Hovstadius (Stockholm, 1991) pp. 19–20.

45 Fyrkman and Löfgren, Kultiverade människan, p. 152.

46 Jutikkala, Bonden i Finland, p. 377.

47 For example, 14 per cent of the rural population were crofters in Finland in 1805 and 13 per cent in 1910; and 26 per cent of those living in rural areas had no land of their own in 1805 and also in 1910, ibid., p. 418.

48 Ibid., p. 470.

49 Ruong, Lapps in Sweden, p. 17.

50 Ericsson, 'Panorama över svenska', p. 150.

51 For example, some 10,000 tons had been exported in the early seventeenth century, the amount increasing to 40,000 tons by the third quarter of the eighteenth century, Rydén, 'Iron Production', p. 78.

52 Ericsson, 'Panorama över svenska', pp. 150–51.

53 Rydén, 'Iron Production', p. 78.

54 Ibid., p. 80.

55 Ibid., pp. 89–91, 97.

56 Ibid., pp. 93–5.

57 Celsin, 'På tröskeln till industrialismen', p. 80.

58 Drake, Population and Society, p. 80.

59 Celsin, 'På tröskeln till industrialismen', pp. 14–19.

60 Ibid., p. 25.

61 Jutikkala, Bonden i Finland, p. 341.

62 Georg Schreiber, Deutschland und die Kultur der Ostsee. Errinerungen an die Deutschen Hochschulwochen in Helsingfors und Riga 1926 (Münster, 1927), pp 24–5.

63 Rerup, 'Folkestyre og danskhed', p. 340.

64 Eilstrup and Boesgaard, Fjernt fra Danmark, p. 234.

65 In 1865, Christiania (Oslo), the capital, had a mere 57,382 inhabitants, while the second city Bergen had only 27,703 inhabitants: Drake, Population and Society, p. 9.

66 Tomasson, Iceland, p. 35.

67 Celsin, 'På tröskeln till industrialismen', pp. 28–31.

68 Eilstrup and Boesgaard, Fjernt fra Danmark, p. 72.

69 Ericsson, 'Panorama över svenska', p. 171.

70 Jutikkala, Bonden i Finland, p. 390.

71 Moring, 'Household and Family', p. 410.

72 Ericsson, 'Panorama över svenska', p. 166.

73 11,279 men were employed on Norwegian vessels in 1835 and the number more than trebled to 38,066 by 1865: Drake, Population and Society, p. 82.

74 Gísli Ágúst Gunnlaugsson and Loftur Guttormsson, 'Household Structure and Urbanisation in three Icelandic Fishing Districts, 1880–1930', Journal of Family History, XVIII/4 (1993), p. 316.

75 Dyrvik, 'Farmers at Sea', pp. 341–2.

76 Mara-Helen Wood, 'People and Surrounds in Kragerø around 1910', in Munch and the Workers (Newcastle, 1984), p. 39.

77 Johansen et al., 'Fishing Families', p. 360.

78 Kjaergaard, Danish Revolution, p. 11.

79 Rying, South and North, pp. 176–7.

80 Ruong, Lapps in Sweden, p. 77.

81 Feldæk, 'Slkole og identitet', p. 258.

82 Ericsson, 'Panorama över svenska', p. 207.

83 Whitaker, 'Settler and Nomad', p. 337.

84 Jutikkala, Bonden i Finland, p. 432.

85 Tomasson, Iceland, p. 17.

86 Gísli Ágúst Gunnlaugsson, '"Everyone's Been Good to Me, Especially the Dog": Foster Children and Young Paupers in Nineteenth-Century Southern Iceland', Journal of Social History, XVII/2 (Winter 1993), p. 343.

87 Tomasson, *Iceland*, pp. 118–24.

88 Annandale, *Faeroes and Iceland*, p. 154.

89 Tomasson, *Iceland*, p. 17.

90 Vadstrup, 'Det syd- og vestgrønlandske', p. 17.

91 Annandale, *Faeroes and Iceland*, p. 1.

92 Eilstrup and Boesgaard, *Fjernt fra Danmark*, p. 104.

93 Ibid., pp. 172–3.

94 Ibid., p. 214.

95 Högström, *S. Barthelemy*, p. 70.

96 Franzén, *Svenskstad i Västindien*, pp. 55–62.

97 Tuula Haavisto, '200 Years of Public Libraries in Finland', in *Life and Education in Finland* (Helsinki, 1994), p. 69.

98 Ole Peter Grell and Andrew Cunningham, 'The Reformation and Changes in Welfare Provision in Early Modern Northern Europe', in Grell and Cunningham, eds, *Health Care and Poor Relief*, p. 22.

99 In 1798 there were 199 inmates, though if foster homes be taken into account, more than 2,487 children were under its jurisdiction: Åman, *Om den Offentliga Vården*, p. 42. In Iceland, by contrast, where orphanages as such did not exist, the proportion of foster children in any given parish varied from 2.5 to 18.3 per cent between 1801 and 1816: Gunnlaugsson, '"Everyone's Been Good to Me"', p. 341.

100 Åman, *Om den Offentliga Vården*, pp. 154–62.

101 Ibid., p. 245.

102 Ibid., pp. 58–61.

103 Ibid., pp. 61–8, 95.

104 The numbers of the rural poor were by no means negligible. In Sweden alone, in 1910, some 24,000 inmates were accommodated in 450 agricultural poor houses all over the country. A further 28,000 were accommodated in ordinary poor houses, usually situated on the edges of towns and villages, with another 9,000 in poor cottages in the countryside. Together, this meant that one per cent of the country's entire population lived in poor houses, unable to maintain themselves without institutional intervention.

105 Each inmate was allotted 3.8 metres per man, sleeping in treble bunk beds distributed amongst five large rooms: Åman, *Om den Offentliga Vården*, pp. 128–36, 351–61.

106 Lundh, 'Households and Families', pp. 37–8.

107 Rydén, 'Iron Production', p. 93.

108 Åman, *Om den Offentliga Vården*, p. 142.

109 Drake, *Population and Society*, p. 72.

110 Moring, 'Household and Family', p. 398.

111 Lunander, 'Bland handlare', p. 151.

112 Edström and Gustafsson, '"Kontrollerat kvinnokött till salu!"', p. 223.

113 David Gaunt and Orvar Löfgren, *Myter om svensken* (Stockholm, 1984), p. 29.

114 Gunnlaugsson and Garsðarsdóttir, 'Availability of Offspring', p. 160.

115 Gunnlaugsson and Guttormsson, 'Household Structure', p. 323.

116 Drake, *Population and Society*, pp. 23–4.

117 According to the census of 1901, in the north-eastern coastal town of Seyðisfjörður, for example, there were some 1,000 females for 786 males in the local sedentary population.

118 Gunnlaugsson and Guttormsson, 'Household Structure', p. 323.

119 Rying, *South and North*, p. 182.

120 Jutikkala, *Bonden i Finland*, p. 172.

121 Johnson, *Swedish Settlements on the Delaware*, vol. 1, p. 461.

122 Gaunt and Löfgren, *Myter om svensken*, p. 32.

123 Åman, *Om den Offentliga Vården*, pp. 14–15, 46.

124 Ibid., pp. 84, 87.

125 Ibid., p. 87.

126 Ibid., pp. 104–5.

127 Ibid., pp. 105–16.

128 Ibid., pp. 90–91.

129 In 1800, out of a population of some 80,000 people, about 2,000 men, usually young, died a violent death, an enormously high figure, especially for the Nordic region: Ylikangas, *Knivjunkarna*, p. 263.

130 Ibid., pp. 9–46, 106–7.

131 Otto Risanger, *Russerna på Svalbard. Hvem er de? Hva gjør de?* (Langyearbyen/Oslo, 1978), pp. 35–6.

132 Franzén, *Svenskstad i Västindien*, p. 65.

133 Ibid., p. 72.

134 Högström, *S. Barthelemy*, p. 54.

135 B. Arvidsson, 'En helig källas teologi före och efter reformationen. Helene kilde i Tisvild och Erich Hansens "Fontinalia Sacra" 1650', *Kirkehistoriske Samlinger* (Copenhagen, 1991), p. 98.

136 Esko Häkli, ed., *Gelehrte Kontakte zwischen Finnland und Göttingen zur Zeit der Aufklärung. Austellung aus Anlass des 500 jähringen Jubiläums des finnischen Buches* (Göttingen, 1988), pp. 13–28.

137 Schreiber, *Deutschland und die Kultur der Ostsee*, p. 21.

138 Edelsward, *Sauna as Symbol*, p. 76.

139 Gustaf Näsström, *Dalarna som svenskt ideal* (Stockholm, 1937), p. 76.

140 Mats Wigardt, 'Träslotten i Skyttomon', *Provins. Norrländskt Magasin*, IV (1990), p. 3.

141 Tor Hedberg, *På Torpa Gård* (Stockholm, 1888), p. 4.

142 Przybyszewski, ed., *Das Werk des Edvard Munch*, p. 14.

Germans, Xenophobia and the Growth of National Identities

1 Schreiber, *Deutschland und die Kultur der Ostsee*, pp. 53–5.

2 Ibid., p. 62.

3 Klinge, *The Baltic World*, p. 54.

4 Pauli, *Det Svenska Tyskland. Sveriges tyska besittningar. 1648–1815*, (Stockholm, 1989), p. 18.

5 Ibid., p. 78.

6 Ibid., p. 102.

7 Ibid., p. 18.

8 Ibid., p. 82.

9 Nina Witoszek, 'Fugitives from Utopia', in *The Cultural Construction of Norden*, eds Øystein Sørensen and Bo Stråth (Oslo, 1997), p. 75.

10 Ole Feldbæk, 'Fædreland og Indfødsret. 1700-talets danske identitet', in *Dansk Identitetshistorie*, vol. 1, p. 122.

11 Karin Kryger, 'Dansk identitet i ny klassicistisk kunst', in *Dansk Identitetshistorie*, vol. 1, p. 252.

12 Ibid., p. 268.

13 Ole Feldbæk and Vibeke Winge, 'Tyskerfejden 1789–1790', in *Dansk Identitetshistorie*, vol. 2, p. 38.

14 Rying, *South and North*, p. 227.

15 Pauli, *Det Svenska Tyskland*, p. 37.

16 Koerner, *Caspar David Friedrich*, p. 50.

17 Ibid., p. 50.

18 Out of a total population at the time of 2,900, 846 were Russian, 412 Swedes and 362 Germans, with the remainder principally Finnish in ethnic and linguistic identity: Schreiber, *Deutschland und die Kultur der Ostsee*, p. 27.

19 Conrad Flemming, 'Konkurrencen om en Dansk Nationalsang', in *Dansk Identitetshistorie*, vol. 2, p. 239.

20 Isaiah Berlin, 'Nationalism', *Against the Current. Essays in the History of Ideas* (Oxford, 1981), p. 351.

21 Lorenz Rerup, 'Fra litterær til politisk nationalisme. Udvikling og udbredelse fra 1808 til 1845', in *Dansk Identitetshistorie*, vol. 2, pp. 454–55.

22 The title refers to the ancient fortified wall which historically separated the Danes from the Germans.

23 Lundgreen-Nielsen, 'Grundtvig og danskhed', in *Dansk Identitetshistorie*, vol. 3, p. 112.

24 Ibid., p. 113.

25 Ibid., p. 127.

26 Rying, *South and North*, p. 274.

27 Ibid., p. 288.

28 Danish territory dwindled from 58,000 to 39,000 square kilometres, while its population fell from 2,500,000 to 1,700,000: ibid., p. 294.

29 Lundgreen-Nielsen, 'Grundtvig og danskhed', in *Dansk Identitetshistorie*, vol. 3, p. 145.

30 Povl Bagge, 'Nationisme, antinationalisme og nationalfølelse i Danmark omkring 1900', in *Dansk Identitetshistorie*, p. 445.

Regal and Imperial Visions

1 Isaiah Berlin, 'The Originality of Machiavelli', in *Against the Current*, p. 67.

2 Neil Kent, 'Royal Treasure House. Christian IV's Rosenborg Castle in Copenhagen', *Antique Collector* (London, November 1992), pp. 86–8.

3 Bent, *South and North*, p. 154.

4 Johannes Jørgensen, 'Un re danese in Toscana', *L'Ambra. Rivista di cultura scandinava* (Florence, December 1994), pp. 45–8.

5 Ibid., pp. 48–50.

6 Kjaergaard, *The Danish Revolution*, p. 13.

7 Battail, 'Relationerna mellan Frankrike och Sverige' in Grate, ed., *Solen och Nordstjärnan*, p. 27.

8 Marie-Christine Skuncke, 'Teater, riddarspel, dans och musik', in Grate, ed., *Solen och Nordstjärnan*, p. 360.

9 Göran Alm, 'Louis Masreliez', in Grate, ed., *Solen och Nordstjärnan*, p. 354.

10 Ericsson, 'Panorama över svenska', p. 198.

11 Gunnar von Proschwitz, 'Den gustavianska tridens Fransk-svenska kultur förbinde', in Grate, ed., *Solen och Nordstjärnan*, p. 298.

12 Georg Göthe, *Johan Tobias Sergel. Hans Lefnad och Verksambet* (Stockholm, 1898), p. 145.

13 Ibid., p. 140.

14 Andrew Wallace-Hadrill, *Houses and Society in Pompeii and Herculaneum* (Princeton, 1994), p. 25.

15 Ulf Cederlöf, Ragnar von Holten, Nils-Göran Hökby and Magnus Olausson, eds, *Louis Jean Desprez. Tecknare, Teaterkonstnär, Arkiteck. En utställning ingående i Nationalmuseums 200-årsjubileum* (Stockholm, 1992), pp. 101–6.

16 Ibid., pp. 34–5.

17 Gunnar von Proschwitz, 'Den Gustafianska tidens fransk-svenska kulturförbinelser', in Grate, ed., *Solen och Nordstjärnan*, p. 308.

18 Wallace-Hadrill, *Pompeii and Herculaneum*, p. 23.

19 Henrik Lilius, 'Arkitekturikonografiska problem i finsk nyklassicism', in *Konsthistoriska Studier. Taidehistoriallisia tutkimuksua 7* (Helsinki, 1984), pp. 40–43.

20 Kasper Monrad Hverdagsbilleder, *Dansk Guldalder – kunstnerne og deres vilkår* (Copenhagen 1989), p. 18.

21 Bo Lindwall, 'Empire, Karl Johan och hans konstnäre', in *Karl Johan, inredningar och teknik i empirens Sverige*, ed. Barbro Hovstadius (Stockholm, 1991), pp. 41–9.

22 Ibid., pp. 45–6.

23 Ibid., p. 47.

24 Barbro Hovstadius, 'Empire, Jarl Johan och Biedermeier som stilbegrepp', in *Karl Johan*, pp. 1–13.

25 Bo Vahlne, 'Natur och nationalitet i nära inredningar på Rosendals slott', in *Karl Johan*, pp. 106–8.

26 Lindwall, 'Empire, Karl Johan och hans konstnäre', p. 64.

27 Ibid., pp. 67–8.

28 Margareta Mutreich, 'Helsingin asemakaava vuosina 1812–17', *Entisaikain Helsinki VIII* (Helsinki, 1970), pp. 175–7.

29 Victor Hugo, *Notre-Dame of Paris* (London, 1978), p. 191.

30 Lilius, 'Arkitekturikonografiska problem i finsk nyklassicism', p. 46.

31 Kalevi Pöykkö, *C. L. Engel. Huvudstadens arkitekt* (Helsingfors, 1990), pp. 91–4.

32 Ibid., p. 27.

33 Ibid., pp. 29–30.

34 Lilius, 'Arkitekturikonografiska problem i finsk nyklassicism', pp. 46–7.

35 Ibid., p. 47.

36 Ibid., pp. 56–7.
37 Pöykkö, Engel, pp. 109–12.
38 Ibid., pp. 125–34.
39 Ibid., p. 142.
40 Ibid., p. 130.

European Arctic Hegemony: Scandinavian Overseas Colonies in the Far North

1   Susan Barr, Jan Mayen. Norges utpost I vest Øyas historie gjennom 1500 år (Oslo, 1991), p. 9.
2   Nordal and Kristinsson, Iceland 1986, p. 88.
3   Tomasson, Iceland, p. 4.
4   Ibid., p. 57.
5   Rying, South and North, p. 118.
6   Tomasson, Iceland, p. 57.
7   Rying, South and North, p. 118.
8   Barr, Jan Mayen, p. 7.
9   Thor B. Arlov, A Short History of Svalbard (Oslo, 1989), p. 36.
10 Ibid., p. 16.
11 Ibid., p. 25.
12 This was a mere fraction of the 120,000 inhabitants of which Iceland could previously boast and its population would remain at this figure well into the late 1820s. Tomasson, Iceland, p. 68.
13 Nordal and Kristinsson, Iceland 1986, p. 89.
14 Rying, South and North, p. 139.
15 Tomasson, Iceland, p. 71–9.
16 Henrikson, Isländsk Historia, p. 173.
17 Rying, South and North, p. 191.
18 Vadstrup, 'Det syd- og vestgrønlandske', p. 16.
19 Rying, South and North, p. 192.
20 Ole Marquardt, '"Jeg bested det menneskegjorte fjeld"', Forskning i Grønland, tusaat 11/92 (Copenhagen, 1992), pp. 20–21.
21 Nordal and Kristinsson, Iceland 1986, p. 91.
22 Henrikson, Isländsk Historia, p. 173.
23 Three-quarters of the island's livestock and one-fifth of Iceland's population died in the ensuing famine.
24 Henrikson, Isländsk Historia, pp. 173–4.
25 Ibid., p. 172.
26 Gunnalugsson and Guttormsson, 'Household Structure', p. 316.
27 Tomasson, Iceland, p. 54.
28 Ole Marquardt, 'Grønland og den globale kolonisation', Forskning i Grønland. tusaat 2/92 (Copenhagen, 1992), p. 10.
29 Søren Vadstrup, 'Nedrivningstruede ældre stenbygninger i Sydgrønland', Forskning i Grønland. tusaat 1/883 (Copenhagen, 1988), p. 28.
30 Marquardt, 'Grønland og den globale kolonisation', p. 10.
31 Vadstrup, 'Det syd- og vestgrønlandske', p. 14.
32 Ibid., p. 14.
33 Arlov, Svalbard, p. 36.
34 Ibid., pp. 44–6.

35 Risanger, Russerne på Svalbard, pp. 23–9.
36 Henrikson, Isländsk Historia, p. 175.
37 Ibid.
38 Ibid., p. 179.
39 Gunnalugsson and Guttormsson, 'Household Structure', p. 320.
40 Marquadt, 'Grønland og den globale kolonisation', p. 15.
41 According to the first reliable census of 1834, Europeans had fallen in number to a total of 196, only 2.6 per cent of the total population, while native Greenlanders and those of mixed race (an increasingly large proportion) had grown to 7,356. Ibid., p. 10.
42 Vadstrup, 'Det syd- og vestgrønlandske', pp. 15–16.
43 Gunnalugsson and Guttormsson, 'Household Structure', p. 320.
44 Ibid., p. 316.
45 By 1890, 12 per cent of the population lived in urban areas, though of these only 15 per cent lived in towns or villages with more than 300 inhabitants, and some 10 per cent were now engaged in fishing: Tomasson, Iceland, p. 54.
46 Some areas had just a few, like Frederikshåb (Paamiut), with only eight, while Godthåb was quite a centre of European settlement. Altogether, Europeans in the middle of the nineteenth century made up only 2 per cent of the entire population. Even by 1901, Europeans still composed just under 2.33 per cent of the population, while native Greenlanders of Inuit background had risen in number to 11,190.
47 Marquadt, 'Grønland og den globale kolonisation', p. 10.
48 Vadstrup, 'Nedrivningstruede ældre stenbygninger i Sydgrønland', p. 30.
49 Whereas in 1876 the Icelandic fishing fleet consisted of 38 vessels with decks, there were, in 1904, 160 vessels with decks. The number of open rowboats remained at about 3000: Tomasson, Iceland, p. 35.
50 Gunnlaugsson, '"Everyone's Been Good to Me"', pp. 343–5.
51 Annandale, Faeroes and Iceland, p. 137.
52 Ibid.
53 Nordal and Kristinsson, Iceland 1986, p. 94.
54 Ibid.
55 Annandale, Faeroes and Iceland, p. 1.
56 Ibid., p. 39.
57 Ibid., p. 40.
58 Ibid., p. 42.
59 Barr, Jan Mayen, pp. 52–67.
60 Arlov, Svalbard, p. 51.
61 Torbjørn Torkildsen, ed., Svalbard. Vårt nordligste Norge (Drammen, 1991), pp. 39–49.
62 Ibid., pp. 48–9.
63 Ibid., p. 49.
64 Arlov, Svalbard, p. 39.
65 Ibid., p. 52.

66 Ibid., p. 58.
67 Ibid., p. 62.
68 Gunnalugsson and Guttormsson, 'Household Structure', p. 325.
69 Nordal and Kristinsson, Iceland 1986, p. 97.
70 Gunnalugsson and Guttormsson, 'Household Structure', p. 321.
71 From 1906 to 1915, net immigration there totalled about 48–9 per 1000 population, not counting up to 2000 summer immigrants: ibid., p. 325.
72 Vadstrup, 'Nedrivningstruede ældre stenbygninger i Sydgrønland', p. 30.
73 Jens Rosing, 'Hovedjæger i Ammassalik', Forskning i Grønland. tusaat 2/96 (Copenhagen, 1996), p. 20.
74 More than 300,000 tonnes were exported between 1925 and 1929, some 90 per cent from the Norwegian-owned mines. Productivity varied seasonally, with just over 900 miners at work in the summer, as opposed to about 600 in the winter. Still, by the end of the 1930s, production had more than doubled to 784,000 tonnes and the number of miners had grown accordingly, with over 1800 men at work throughout the year: Arlov, Svalbard, p. 71.

A Peculiar Institution: Slavery, the Tropics and Scandinavian Colonial Expansion

1 Johnson, Swedish Settlements on the Delaware, vol. 1, pp. 150–58, 193.
2 Ibid., p. 204.
3 Ibid., p. 345.
4 Israel Acrelius, Beskrifning Om De Swenska Församlingars Forna och Närvarande Tilstånd, Uti Det så kallade Nya Swerige, Men nu för tiden, Pansylvanien, samt naestliggande Orter mid Ulfwen De la Ware, Naest Yersey och NewCastle County uti Norra America (Stockholm, 1759), p. 85.
5 Johnson, Swedish Settlements on the Delaware, vol. 2, pp. 537–54.
6 Acrelius, Beskrifning Om De Swenska Församlingars Forna, p. 85.
7 Johnson, Swedish Settlements on the Delaware, vol. 2, p. 655.
8 Nathaniel Weyl and William Marina, American Statesmen on Slavery and the Negro (New York, 1971), p. 412.
9 Paiewonsky, Accounts of Slavery, p. 1.
10 Eilstrup and Boesgaard, Fjernt fra Danmark, p. 54.
11 By the eighteenth century, partially as a result of the migrations propelled by the upheavals of the War of the Spanish Succession (1701–13), the white population had grown to 524. Especially striking, however, was the increase in the number of slaves, of which 4,500 were black or mulatto. There were 167 plantations, 77 of which produced sugar cane. In many ways self-maintaining, 28 of these plantations had their own sugar mills and eleven their own rum distilleries: ibid., p. 54.
12 The French colony of Saint Domingue, on the western half of the island of Hispaniola, for example, had only 35,000 whites, but a total of 500,000 or more slaves, whilst French Guyana, with 500 whites, had 50,000 slaves: Robert Debs Heinl, Nancy Gordon Heinl and Michael Heinl, Written in Blood. The Story of the Haitian People, 1492–1995 (Lanham, Maryland and London, 1996), p. 33.
13 Wilhelm Bosman's letter in Fjernt fra Danmark. Billeder fra vore Tropekolonier, Slavehandel og Kinafart, ed. Per Eilstrup and Nils Eric Boesgaard (Copenhagen, 1974), p.50.
14 Beskvrinvning av St Barth. (1788). In Svenska Läkarsällskapets arkiv, Chr. Carlanders samling, Hanlingar.
15 C. B. Wadström, An Essay on Colonization particularly applied to the Western Coast of Africa with some free thoughts on Cultivation and Commerce: also Brief Descriptions of the Colonies Already Formed, or Attempted, in Africa, Including Those of Sierra Leone and Bulama (London, 1794), p. 193.
16 L. F. Rømer, Tilforladelig Efterretning om Kysten Guinea (Copenhagen, 1760).
17 Eilstrup and Boesgaard, Fjernt fra Danmark, p. 117.
18 Ibid.
19 Rømer, Tilgorladelig Efterretning.
20 Eilstrup and Boesgaard, Fjernt fra Danmark, p. 92.
21 Ibid., p. 83.
22 Ibid.
23 Of the approximately 200 crew members employed in the Danish-Norwegian slave trade from 1777 to 1790, for example, almost 70 died during the voyage, or more than one-third: ibid., p. 86.
24 Ibid., p. 89.
25 Rømer, Tilgorladelig Efterretning.
26 Eilstrup and Boesgaard, Fjernt fra Danmark, p. 90.
27 Ibid., pp. 94–7.
28 Boxman, Hebrew Congregation of St Thomas, p. 6.
29 Karen Zukowski, 'The Pissarro–Melbye Church Connection', in Camille Pissaro in the Caribbean, 1850–1855: Drawings from the Collection at Olana, eds Richard R. Brettell and Karen Zukowski (St Thomas, 1983), p. 18.
30 Boxman, Hebrew Congregation of St Thomas, pp. 22–7.
31 Ibid., p. 5.
32 Richard R. Brettell, 'Camille Pissaro and St Thomas: The Story of an Exhibition', in Pissarro in the Caribbean, pp. 6–11.
33 Zukowski, 'Pissarro-Melby Church Connection', p. 18.
34 Arni Magnusson, Optegnelser (Copenhagen, 1918).
35 Eilstrup and Boesgaard, Fjernt fra Danmark, p. 161.
36 Ibid., p. 10.
37 Rying, South and North, p. 202.
38 Ericsson, 'Panorama över svenska', pp. 172–3.
39 Ibid., p. 175.
40 Eilstrup and Boesgaard, Fjernt fra Danmark, p. 161.
41 J. L. Carstens, En almindelig Beskrivelse om alle de danske, amerikanske eller vest indiske Eij-Lande (Copenhagen).
42 Paiewonsky, Accounts of Slavery, pp. 150–51.
43 Ibid., p. 36.
44 Wadström, An Essay on Colonization, pp. 175–7.

45 While this was a population increase of over 25 per cent over the beginning of the year, the increase of slaves was considerable, with their numbers almost doubling to 408: Högström, *S. Barthelemy*, p. 2.

46 Franzén, *Svenskstad i Västindien*, p. 15.

47 Ibid., p. 15.

48 Wadström, *An Essay on Colonization*, p. 179–82.

49 Ibid., p. 187.

50 Ibid., p. 189.

51 Högström, *S. Barthelemy*, pp. 10–14.

52 Franzén, *Svenskstad i Västindien*, p. 22.

53 Ibid., p. 75.

54 Ibid., p. 27.

55 Ibid., p. 25.

56 Ibid., p. 17.

57 Eilstrup and Boesgaard, *Fjernt fra Danmark*, p. 212.

58 Franzén, *Svenskstad i Västindien*, p. 14.

59 Ibid., p. 17.

60 Högström, *S. Barthelemy*, p. 48.

61 Ibid., p. 74.

62 Eilstrup and Boesgaard, *Fjernt fra Danmark*, p. 206.

63 Ibid., p. 188.

64 John Iliffe, *Africans. The History of a Continent* (Cambridge, 1995), pp. 143–9.

65 Eilstrup and Boesgaard, *Fjernt fra Danmark*, p. 214.

66 Ibid., p. 177.

67 Iliffe, *Africans*, pp. 132 and 151.

68 There were, in 1860, only 1,819 inhabitants left, the vast majority women for whom emigration to the other islands of the Caribbean was difficult. Of the 983 citizens of Gustafia, in that year, 643 were women, the overwhelming majority of black or mixed race. In the countryside, though, the balance was more even, 855 men to 964 women: *Census St Barts*.

69 Franzén, *Svenskstad i Västindien*, p. 91.

Some Conclusions

1 Between 1900 and 1920 up to 12.5 per cent of parliamentary members were women: Löfström, 'A Pre-modern Legacy', pp. 64–5.

2 Birgit Stolt, 'Nordisk Värdegemenskap? – Den Splittrade Lutherska Traditionen', in *Värdetraditioner I nordiskt perspektiv. Rapport från ett symposium I Helsingfors*, eds Göran Bexell and Henrik Stenius (Lund, 1997), p. 66.

3 Henrik Stenius, 'Konformitetsideal blev Universalitetsprincip', in *Värdetraditioner I nordiskt perspektiv*, p. 77.

4 Ibid., p. 85.

5 Bernd Benningsen, 'The Swedish Construction of Nordic Identity', in *The Cultural Construction of Norden*, p. 117.

6 Burroughs, *Does the Weather Really Matter?*, p. 111.

7 Crime statistics as presented by the Home Office in the *Guardian*, 19 August 1998, p. 7.

Bibliography

Acrelius, Israel, *Beskrifning Om De Swenska Församlingars Forna och Närvarande Tilstånd, Uti Det så kallade Nya Swerige, Men nu för tiden, Pensylvanien, samt naestliggande Orter mid Ulfwen De la Ware, Naest Yersey och New-Castle County uti Norra America* (Stockholm, 1759)

Åman, Anders, 'Kyrkobyggandet i det långa perspektivet', *Bebyggelsehistorisk tidskrift. Övre Norrlands kyrkor*, 22 (Stockholm, 1991), pp. 9–18

—, 'Kyrkornas norrländska landskap', *Provins. Norrländskt Magasin*, 4 (Piteå, 1990), pp. 26–30

—, *Om den Offentliga Vården. Byggnader och verksamheter vid svenska vårdsinstitutioner under 1800- och 1900-talen. En arkitekturhistorisk undersökning* (Uppsala, 1976)

—, 'Övre Norrlands kyrkor – deras konsthistoria och geografi', *Bebyggelsehistorisk tidskrift. Övre Norrlands kyrkor*, 22 (Stockholm, 1991), pp. 189–253

Annandale, Nelson, *The Faroes and Iceland: Studies in Island Life* (Oxford, 1905)

Arlov, Thor B., *A Short History of Svalbard* (Oslo, 1989)

Arneborg, Jette, Hans Chr. Gulløv and Jens P. Hart Hansen, 'Menneske og miljø i fortidens Grønland', *Forskning i Grønland. tusaat* 1/88 (Copenhagen, 1988), pp. 39–47

Arvidsson, B., 'En helig källas teologi före och efter reformationen. Helene kilde i Tisvild och Erich Hansens "Fontinalia Sacra" 1650', *Kirkehistoriske Samlinger* (Copenhagen, 1991)

Åström, Anna-Maria, 'Herrgårdens Gårdsplan och Byggnader. Tokning av en utveckling i Savolax 1780–1980', *Fynd och Forskning*, ed. Ivar Nordlund (Svenska Litteratursällskapet i Finland, Nr 496) Meddelanden från Folkkultursarkivet, 7 (Helsingfors, 1981), pp. 215–48

—, 'Herrskapsfolk och underlydande', *Kansa Kuvastimessa. Etnisyys ja identiteetti*, eds. Teppo Korhonen and Matti Räsänen (tietolipas, 114) (Helsinki, 1989), pp. 162–98

Baldwin, Peter, *Contagion and the State in Europe 1830–1930* (Cambridge, 1999).

Barr, Susan, *Jan Mayen. Norges utpost I vest øyas historie gjennom 1500 år* (Oslo, 1991)

Bexell, Göran and Henrik Stenius, eds, *Värdetraditioner I nordiskt perspektiv. Rapport från ett symposium I Helsingfors* (Lund, 1997)

Bull, Edv. and Einar Jansen, eds, 'Hansen, Gerhard Henrik Armauer', *Norsk Biografisk Leksikon*, (Oslo, 1931), vol. 5, pp. 371–6

Burckhardt, Jakob, *The Civilization of the Renaissance in Italy* (1860) (London, 1995)

Boxman, Rabbi Bradd H., *A Short History of the Hebrew Congregation of St Thomas* (St Thomas, US Virgin Islands, 1983)

Brettell, Richard R. and Karen Zukowski, *Camille Pissarro in the Caribbean, 1850–1855: Drawings from the Collection at Olana St Thomas* (US Virgin Islands, 1997)

Briggs Jr., J. Morton, 'Aurora and Enlightenment. Eighteenth-Century Explanations of the Aurorea Borealis', *ISIS, LVIII* (1967), pp. 491–503

Burroughs, William James, *Does the Weather Really Matter? The Social Implications of Climate Change* (Cambridge, 1997)

Caning, Kirsten Elisabeth, 'Om den grønlandske befolknings historie', *Forskning i Grønland. tusaat* 1/82 (Copenhagen, 1982), pp. 2–11

Carey, John, *The Intellectuals and the Masses. Pride and Prejudice among the Literary Intelligentsia, 1880–1939* (London, 1992)

Carlson, Harry G., *Out of Inferno. Strindberg's Reawakening as an Artist* Seattle (Washington, 1996)

Carlsson, Sten, 'Kvinnoöden i 1800-talets Sverige', *Den utsatta familjen. Liv, arbete och samlevnad i olika nordiska miljöer under de senaste tvåhundra åren*, ed. Hans Norman (Stockholm, 1983), pp. 39–54

Carlsson, Sten *Svensk Historia. 2. Tiden efter 1718* (Lund, 1980)

Cederlöf, Ulf, Ragnar von Holten, Nils-Göran Hökby and Magnus Olausson, eds, *Louis Jean Desprez. Tecknare, Teaterkonstnär, Arkitekt. En utställning ingående i Nationalmuseums 200-årsjubileum* (Stockholm, 1992)

Carstens, J. L., *En almindelig Beskrivelse om alle de danske, amerikanske eller vest indiske Eij-Lande* (Copenhagen)

Crain, Edward E., *Historic Architecture in the Caribbean Islands* (Gainsville, FL, 1994)

Crow, Thomas E., *Painters and Public Life in Eighteenth-Century Paris* (New Haven and London, 1985)

Drake, Michael, *Population and Society in Norway. 1735–1865* (Cambridge, 1969)

Durant, Will and Ariel Durant, *The Story of Civilisation: Part IX. The Age of Voltaire. A History of Civilization in Western Europe from 1715 to 1756, with Special Emphasis on the Conflict between Religion and Philosophy* (New York, 1965)

Dyrvik, Ståle, 'Farmers at Sea: A Study of Fishermen in North Norway, 1801–1920', *Journal of Family History*, XVIII/4 (1993), pp. 341–56

Edelsward, L. M., *Sauna as Symbol. Society and Culture in Finland* (New York, 1991)

Edström, Gunilla and Gunilla Gustavsson, '"Kontrollerat kvin-nokött till salu!" Prostituerade i Uppsala år 1860–1900', Den utsatta familjen. Liv, arbete och samlevnad i olika nordiska miljöer under de senaste tvåhundra åren (En antologi från Familjehistoriska projektet vid Historiska institutionen, Uppsala Universitet), ed. Hans Norman (Stockholm, 1983), pp. 213–25

Eggum, Arne, Edvard Munch. Malerier-Skisser og Studier (Oslo, 1983)

Eilstrup, Per and Nils Eric Boesgaard, Fjernt fra Danmark. Billeder fra vore Tropekolonier, Slavehandel og Kinafart (Copenhagen, 1974)

Engström, Christer (editor-in-chief), 'Malaria', Nationalencyklopedin, vol. 12 (Stockholm, 1993), p. 640

Evans, Richard, 'Cholera in nineteenth-century Europe', in Epidemics and Ideas. Essays on the Historical Perception of Pestilence, eds Terence Ranger and Paul Slack (Cambridge, 1992), pp. 149–73

Feldbæk, Ole, ed., Dansk Identitetshistorie, 4 vols (Copenhagen, 1992)

Franzén, Gösta, Svenskstad i Västindien. Gustavia på Saint Barthélemy i språk- och kulturhistorisk belysning, Acta Academiæ Regiæ Scientiarum Upsaliensis. Kungl. Vetenskapssamhällets i Uppsala Handlingar, 16 (Stockholm, 1974)

Frykman, Jonas and Löfgren, Orvar, Den kultiverade människan (Lund, 1979)

Gaunt, David and Löfgren, Orvar, Myter om svensken (Stockholm, 1984)

Göthe, Georg, Johan Tobias Sergel. Hans Lefnad och Verksamhet (Stockholm, 1898)

Grate, Pontus, ed., Solen och Nordstjärnan. Frankrike och Sverige vå 1700-talet, Generalkommissarie, Nationalmusei utställningskatalog, 568 (Högnäs, 1993)

Grell, Ole Peter, ed., The Scandinavian Reformation. From Evangelical Movement to Institutionalisation of Reform (Cambridge, 1995)

—, 'Scandinavia', in The Early Reformation in Europe, ed. Andrew Pettegree (Cambridge, 1992), pp. 94–119 [Author: spelled Pettegrew in note: which is correct?]

—, 'Scandinavia', in The Reformation in National Context, eds Bod Scribner, Roy Porter and Mikulá Teich (Cambridge, 1994) pp. 111–27

Grell, Ole Peter and Andrew Cunningham, eds, Health Care and Poor Relief in Protestant Europe (London and New York, 1997)

Gross, Hanns, Rome in the Age of Enlightenment. The Post-Tridentine Syndrome and the Ancien Régime (London, 1990)

Gunnlaugsson, Gísli Ágúst, '"Everyone's Been Good to Me, Especially the Dog": Foster Children and Young paupers in Nineteenth-Century Southern Iceland', Journal of Social History, XVII/2 (Winter, 1993), pp. 341–58

Gunnlaugsson, Gísli Ágúst and Garsðarsdóttir, Olöf, 'Availability of Offspring and the Household Position of Elderly Women: Iceland, 1901', Journal of Family History, XX/2 (1993)

Gunnlaugsson, Gísli Ágúst and Loftur Guttormsson, 'Household Structure and Urbanization in three Icelandic Fishing Districts, 1880–1930', Journal of Family History, XVIII/4 (1993), pp. 315–40

Haavisto, Tuula, '200 Years of Public Libraries in Finland', LEIF. Life and Education in Finland (Helsinki, 1994), pp. 69–70

Häggman, Kai, Perheen vuosisata. Perheen ihanne ja sivistyneistön elämänta-pa 1800-luvun Suommessa, Historiallisia Tutkimuksia, 179 (Helsinki, 1994)

Häkli, Esko, ed., Gelehrte Kontakte zwischen Finnland und Göttingen zur Zeit der Aufkärung. Austellung aus Anlass des 500 jährigen Jubiläums des finnischen Buches (Göttingen, 1988)

Hamran, Ulf, 'Det nye Norge bygger. Norsk Arkitektur 1814–1870', Norges kunsthistorie Bind 4. Det Unge Norge (Oslo, 1981), pp. 7–125

Hedberg, Tor, På Torpa Gård (Stockholm, 1888)

Heinl, Robert Debs, Nancy Gordon Heinl and Michael Heinl, Written in Blood. The Story of the Haitian People, 1492–1995 (Lanham, Maryland and London, 1996)

Henningsen, Bernd, Janine Klein, Helmut Müssener and Solfrid Söderlund, eds, Skandinavien och Tyskland. 1800–1914. Möten och vänskapsband (Berlin, 1997)

Henrikson, Alf, Isländsk Historia (Stockholm, 1981)

Hirschfeld, Magnus, Die Homosexualität des Mannes und des Weibes (Berlin, 1920)

Högström, E. O. E., S. Barthelemy under svenskt välde (Uppsala, 1888)

Hope, Nicholas, German and Scandinavian Protestantism. 1700–1918 (Oxford, 1995)

Horn, Vivi, Den sturske Montgomery (Stockholm, 1938)

Hovstadius, Barbro, ed., Karl Johan. Konst, inredningar och teknik i empirens Sverige, Årsbok för Statens Konstmuseer, 37 (Stockholm, 1991)

Hugo, Victor, Notre-Dame of Paris (London, 1978)

Hyan, Ronald, Empire and Sexuality. The British Experience (Manchester, 1990)

Iliffe, John, Africans. The History of a Continent (Cambridge, 1995)

Ilmoinen, Anneli, 'Sauna in Pictorial Art', in Sauna Studies, eds Collan and Pirkko Valtakari (Helsinki, 1976)

Isaksson, Olov and Folke Isaksson, Gammestad Kyrkby vid Lule Älv (Stockholm, 1991)

Jacobsen, Jens Peter, Niels Lyhne (Copenhagen, 1880)

Johannesson, Eric, 'Den heliga familjen. Om borgerlig famil-jekult under 1800-talet', Den utsatta familjen. Liv, arbete och samlev-nad i olika nordiska miljöer under de senaste tvåhundra åren, En antologi från Familjehistoriska projektet vid Historiska institutionen, Uppsala universitet, ed. Hans Norman (Stockholm, 1983), pp. 30–38

Johansen, Hans Chr., Per Madsen and Ole Degn, 'Fishing Families in Three Danish Coastal Communities', Journal of Family History, XVIII/4 (1993), pp. 357–68

Johnson, Amandus, The Swedish Settlements on the Delaware 1638–1664, vols 1 and 2 (New York, 1911)

Jones, Steve, The Language of the Genes. Biology, History and the Evolutionary Future (London, 1994)

Jutikkala, Eino, Suomen Talonpojan historia, trans. Göran Seleén as Bonden i Finland genom Tiderna (Helsingfors, 1963)

Jørgensen, Johannes, 'Un Re danese in Toscana', L'Ambra. Rivista di cultura scandinava, Anno II, n. 2 (Florence, December, 1994), pp. 45–52

Kaalund, Bodil, The Art of Greenland. Sculpture. Crafts. Painting

(Copenhagen, 1979)

Kent, Neil, 'Royal Treasure House. Christian IV's Rosenborg Castle in Copenhagen', *Antique Collector* (London, November, 1992), pp. 86–8

Kjaergaard, Thorkild, *The Danish Revolution. 1500–1800* (Cambridge, 1994)

Klinge, Matti, *The Baltic World* (Helsinki, 1994)

Koerner, Joseph Leo, *Caspar David Friedrich and the Subject of Landscape* (London, 1990)

Lacy, Terry G., *Ring of Seasons. Iceland – Its Culture and History* (Ann Arbor, Michigan, 1998)

Lambton, Lucinda, *Temples of Convenience* (London, 1978)

Lenngren, Anna Maria, *Miss Juliana (Fröken Juliana)* (Stockholm, 1789)

Levack, Brian P., *The Witch-hunt in Early Modern Europe*, 2nd edn (London and New York, 1995)

Lexow, Jan Hendrich, '1. Arkitektur 1536–1814', *Norges hunsthistorie Bind 3. Negangstid og ny reisning* (Oslo, 1981)

Lilus, Henrik, 'Arkitekturikonografiska problem i finsk nyklassicism', *Konsthistoriska Studier. Taidehistoriallisia tutkimuksua, 7* (Helsingin yliopiston taidehistorian laitos) (Helsinki, 1984), pp. 33–61

Lindblom, Andreas, 'Karolinskt Kyrkobugge', *Sveriges Konsthistoria från Forntid till Ntudid. Andra Delen: Från Gustav Vasa till Gustav III* (Stockholm, 1944), pp. 465–75

Lunander, Elsa, 'Bland handlare och hantverkare i en svensk landsortsstad under 1800-talet. OM hushålls- och familjestruktur i Örebro', *Den utsatta familjen. Liv, arbete och samlevnad i olika nordiska miljöer under de senaste tvåhundra åren, En antologi från Familjehistoriska projektet vid Historiska institutionen, Uppsala universitet*, ed. Hans Norman (Stockholm, 1983), pp. 147–58

Lundh, Christer, 'Households and Families in Pre-industrial Sweden', *Continuity and Change. A Journal of Social Structure, Law and Demography in Past Societies*, x/1 (1995), pp. 33–68

Löfström, Jan, 'A Premodern Legacy: The "Easy" Criminalization of Homosexual Acts Between Women in the Finnish Penal Code of 1889', *Journal of Homosexuality* xxxv/3–4: Scandinavian Homosexualities, Part II (New York, 1998), pp. 53–79

Magnusson, Arni, *Optegnelser* (Copenhagen, 1918)

Malmberg, Bo, 'Vräkningar från fattigbebyggelse. En mörk episod vid inrättandet av kronoparker i Vilhelmina socken under 1900-talets första år', *Den utsatta familjen. Liv, arbete och samlevnad i olika nordiska miljöer under de senaste tvåhundra åren, En antologi från Familjehistoriska projektet vid Historiska institutionen, Uppsala Universitet*, ed. Hans Norman (Stockholm, 1983), pp. 187–212

Marquardt, Ole, 'Grønland og den globale kolonisation', *Forskning i Grønland. tusaat 2/92* (Copenhagen, 1992), pp. 8–19

—, 'Jeg besteg det menneskegjorte fjeld', *Forskning i Grønland. tusaat 2/92* (Copenhagen, 1992), pp. 20–21

Mead, W. R., *An Experience of Finland* (London, 1993)

Michalski, Sergiusz, *The Reformation and the Visual Arts. The Protestant Image Question in Western and Eastern Europe* (London, 1993)

Moring, Beatrice, 'Household and Family in Finnish Coastal Societies. 1635–1895', *Journal of Family History*, xviii/4 (1993), pp. 395–414

Mutreich, Margareta, 'Helsingin asemakaava vuosina 1812–17', *Entisaikain Helsinki*, viii (Helsinki, 1970), pp. 175–7

Nesheim, Asbjørn, *Samene. Historie og kultur* (Oslo, 1966)

Nilsson, Sten Åke, *Konsten i Sverige. 1700-talet efter den karolinska tiden* (Stockholm, 1974)

Nordal, Jóhannes and Valdimar Kristinsson, eds, *Iceland 1986* (Reykjavik, 1987)

Näsström, Gustaf, *Dalarna som svenskt ideal* (Stockholm, 1937)

Paiewonsky, Isidor, *Eyewitness Accounts of Slavery in the Danish West Indies. also Graphic Tales of Other Slave Happenings on Ships and Plantations* (New York, 1989)

Przybyszewski, Stanislaw, ed., *Das Werk des Edvard Munch. Vier Beiträge von Stanislaw Przybyszewski, Dr. Franz Servaes, Willy Pastor, Julius Meier-Graefe* (Berlin, 1894)

Pöykkö, Kalevi, *C. L. Engel. Huvudstadens arkitekt*, Memoria, 6 (Helsingfors, 1990)

Risanger, Otto, *Russerne på Svalbard. Hvem er de? Hva gjør de?* (Langyearbyen/Oslo, 1978)

Rømer, L. F., *Tilgorladelig Ffterretning on Kysten Guinea* (Copenhagen, 1760)

Rosén, J., *Svensk Historia*, I, 3rd edn (Stockholm, 1969)

Rosing, Jens, 'Hovedjæger i Ammassalik', *Forskning i Grønland. tusaat 2/96* (Copenhagen, 1996), pp. 20–23

Ruff, Dr Josef, *Illustreradt Helsovårds-Lexikon. En populär handbok för alla* (Stockholm, 1888)

Ruong, Israel, *The Lapps in Sweden* (Stockholm, 1967)

Rydén, Göran, 'Iron Production and the Household as a Production Unit in a Nineteenth-century Sweden', *Continuity and Change. A Journal of Social Structure, Law and Demography in Past Societies*, x/1 (1995), pp. 69–104

Rydin, Lena, *Den Lustfyllda Vardagen. Hos Larssons i Sundborn* (Stockholm, 1993)

Rying, Bent, *Danish in the South and North*, vol. 2 (Copenhagen, 1988)

Schreiber, Georg, ed., *Deutschland und die Kultur der Ostsee. Errinerungen an die Deutschen Hochschulwochen in Helsingfors und Riga 1926* (Münster, 1927)

Sköld, Peter, 'The Saami Experience of Smallpox in Eighteenth-Century Sweden' (unpublished, 1995)

Stangerup, Hakon and F.J. Billeskov Jansen, *Dansk Litteratur Historie*, vol. 3

Stone, Lawrence, *The Family, Sex and Marriage in England 1500–1800* (London, 1977)

Sundt, Eilert, *Om bygnings-skikken på landet i Norge* (Oslo, 1976)

Sundt, Eilert, *Om giftermall i Norge: bidrag til kundskab om folkets kaar og sæder* (Christiania, 1855)

Sørensen, Øystein and Bo Stråth (eds.), *The Cultural Construction of Norden* (Oslo, 1997)

Tomasson, Richard F., *Iceland. The First New Society* (Minneapolis, 1980)

Torkildsen, Torbjørn, ed., *Svalbard. Vårt nordligste Norge* (Drammen, 1991)

Tschudi-Madsen, Stephan, 'Veien hjem. Norsk arkitektur 1870–1914', *Norges kunsthistorie. Bind 5. Nasjonal vekst* (Oslo, 1981), pp. 7–108

Törneros, Adolf, *Bref och dagboks-anteckningar* (posthumously published, 1840)

Utterström, G., 'Befolkningsutveckling och näringsliv efter mitten av 1700-talet', *En bok om Mälärlandskapen* (Stockholm, 1953)

Vadstrup, Søren, 'Det syd- og vestgrønlandske stenbyggeri i årene 1830–1940', *Forskning i Grønland. tusaat 2/87* (Copenhagen, 1987), pp. 14–27

—, 'Nedrivningstruede ældre stenbygninger i Sydgrønland', *Forskning i Grønland. tusaat 1/88*, (Copenhagen, 1988), pp. 28–38

Wadström, C. B., *An Essay on Colonization particularly applied to the Western Coast of Africa with some free thoughts on Cultivation and Commerce; also Brief Descriptions of the Colonies Already Formed, or Attempted, in Africa, Including Those of Sierra Leona and Bulama, Part Second* (London, 1794)

Wallace-Hadrill, Andrew, *Houses and Society in Pompeii and Herculaneum* (Princeton, 1994)

Weyl, Nathaniel and William Marina, *American Statesmen on Slavery and the Negro* (New York, 1971)

Whitaker, Ian, 'Settler and Nomad in Northern Torne-Lappmark', *Polar Record*, vol. XXI

Wigardt, Mats, 'Träslotten i Skyttmon', *Provins. Norrländskt Magasin*, 4 (Piteå, 1990), pp. 3–6

Witoszek, Nina, 'Fugitives from Utopia' in Sørensen, Øystein and Stråth, Bo (eds), *The Cultural Construction of Norden* (Oslo, 1997)

Wood, Mara-Helen, ed., *Munch and the Workers* (Newcastle, 1984)

Ylikangas, Heikki, *Knivjunkarna. Våldskriminaliteten i Sydösterbotten. 1790–1825*, trans. Eva Stenius (Borgå, 1985)

Photographic Acknowledgements

Below are listed the locations of buildings, sculptures and other artworks, together with owning bodies and other individuals and institutions who have supplied their own or other picture material and/or permission to reproduce it, and to whom the author and publishers express their thanks:

Hannu Aaltonen: 127, 223; Åbo Turun taidemuseo, Turku: 83, 130; Jörg P. Anders: 24; Århus Kunstmuseum: 7, 131; Ateneum, Helsinki: 55, 57, 113, 127, 145, 223; Sophus Bengtsson: 138, 180; Bergen Billedgalleri, Bergen: 88; Per Bergström: 69; Bildarkivet, Stockholms Stadmuseum: 87, 139, 141, 149; A. Brandt: 152, 171, 175; Bridgeman Art Library: 103; British Library, London: 110, 268; Ebbe Carlsson: 112, 134; Central Art Archives, Helsinki: 55, 57, 113, 127, 145, 223; Christiansborg Palace, Copenhagen: 204; Copenhagen City Museum: 121; Erik Cornelius. 132; De Danske Kongers Kronologiske Samling (Rosenborg Slot): 185, 202, 211; C. L. Davids Samling: 111; DOWIC Fotografi: 205; Drottningholm Slott (Slottsarkivet): 189, 194; Fåborg Museum for Fynsk MalerKunst: 77; Faroese Museum of Art, Tórshavn: 246; Göteborgs Historiska Museum: 89; Göteborgs Konstmuseum: 51, 76, 112, 122, 134; Gripsholms Slott: 47, 70; Hallwylska Museet, Stockholm: 128; Handels- og Søfartsmuseet på Kronborg, Helsingør: 256, 263–4, 267, 269–71; Ole Haupt: 208, 254; Helsingin kaupunginmuseo (and the kaupunginmuseo's kuva-arkisto): 222; Helsingin yliopiston kirjasto: 225; Den Hirschsprungske Samling, Copenhagen: 15, 63, 73; Holckenhavn: 106; Kirsten A. Jappe: 270; Geir S. Johannessen: 88; Kansallisarkisto, Helsinki: 224, 227; Kendall Whaling Museum, Sharon, MA: 229; Kiruna-Bild/ B. Rönnberg: 31; Mogens Koch: 247; Det Kongelige Bibliotek, Copenhagen: 27, 155–8, 169, 182, 231–2, 242, 257; Det Kongelige Danske Kunstakademi, Copenhagen: 161, 164; Konstakademien, Stockholm: 43; Kungliga Akademien för de Fria Konsterna, Stockholm: 197; Kunstakademiets Bibliotek, Copenhagen: 164; Lennart Larsen: 19, 40, 172, 178, 203, 244; Kari Lehtinen: 83, 130; Linnémuseet, Uppsala: 107; Listasafn Íslands, Reykjavík: 239–40, 247; LSH Fotoavdelningen: 218; Åsa Lundén: 214; Karin März: 23; Moderna Museet, Stockholm: 30; Munch-museet, Oslo (photos, © Munch-museet [Svein Andersen/Sidsel de Jong] 1999; copyright © Munch-museet [Munch-Ellinsen Group] 1999): 56, 61, 79, 117–19, 124–6; Musée du Louvre, Paris: 193; Museum der bildenden Künste, Leipzig/Gerstenberger: 168; Nasjonalgalleriet, Oslo (photos, J. Lathion, © Nasjonalgalleriet 1999): 17, 28, 36, 58, 75, 82, 93–4, 102, 150; National Maritime Museum, London: 255; National Museum of Denmark, Copenhagen: 243–4; National Museum of Finland, Helsinki: 199, 221, 228; Nationalmuseum, Stockholm: 9, 16, 35, 46, 52–4, 80, 115, 120, 132, 136, 140, 190–92, 195–6, 213–15, 217, 219–20; Det Nationalhistoriske Museum på Frederiksborg, Hillerød: 19, 38, 39, 40, 138, 147, 152, 159, 171, 172, 175, 178, 180, 203, 212, 254, 258; Nationalgalerie, Berlin: 24; Nationalmuseet, Copenhagen: 67, 234; New York State Office of Parks, Recreation & Historic Preservation: 261; Nordiska Museet, Stockholm: 65, 104, 114; Nordiska Museets Picture Agency: 65, 104, 114; Norsk Folkemuseum – Bygdøy: 37; Ny Carlsberg Glyptotek, Copenhagen, gift of Ny Carlsberg Foundation: 208; Office of the Commissioner of Social Services, Copenhagen: 91, 143; Olana State Historic Site, Hudson, NY: 261; Ordrupgaard: 105; Orlogsmuseet, Copenhagen: 272; Thomas Pedersen: 7, 131; Hans Petersen: 1–2, 15, 18, 26, 39, 41–2, 44, 50, 63, 66, 68, 73–4, 90, 92, 111, 123, 148, 160, 163, 165, 166, 170, 201, 206, 210, 212; Postmuseum, Stockholm: 154; Prins Eugens Waldemarsudde, Stockholm: 209; private collections: 29, 49, 60, 64, 78, 101, 109, 116,133, 184, 245, 249, 250–51, 253; Qaqortoq Katersugaasivia, Greenland: 248; Randers Kunstmuseum: 71; Rigsarkivet, Copenhagen: 137, 259, 266; Riksantikvaren, Oslo: 135, 216; Riksarkivet, Stockholm: 188–9, 194; RMN, Paris: 193; Birger Roos/STORA: 129; Rosenborg Slot, Copenhagen: 181, 185, 202, 211; St Peter's, Rome: 4; Sixter Sandell: 122; Allan Scharff: 20, 21; Schloss Charlottenburg, Berlin: 23; Skoklosters Slott: 218; Staatliche Kunstsammlung, Weimar: 25; Staatliche Kunstsammlungen, Dresden: 22, 167; Staatliches Museen zu Berlin – Preußischer Kulturbesitz: 23–4; Stadtarchiv, Stralsund: 153; Statens konst-museer: 9, 16, 35, 46, 47, 52–4, 70, 80, 115, 132, 136, 140, 190, 191–2, 195–6, 213–15, 217, 219; Statens Museum for Kunst, Copenhagen: 1, 2, 18, 26, 42, 44, 50, 66, 68, 74, 90, 92, 108, 111, 123, 148, 160, 163, 165–6, 170, 200–201, 205–6, 210; Statens sjöhistoriska museet, Stockholm: 241; Stockholm University Collection of Paintings: 69; Stora Kopparbergs Bergslags AB, Falun: 129; Swedish Linnæan Society: 107; Thielska Galleriet, Stockholm: 81; Uppsala University: 3; Uppsala University Library: 8; Vestsjællands Kunstmuseum, Sorø: 41; Vigeland-Museet (Oslo Kommunes Kunstsamlinger): 59; Vigelandsparken, Oslo: 59; Kit Weiss: 38, 159, 243; Henrik Wichmann: 243; Wilberforce House Museum, Hull: 103; Ole Woldbye: 105.

Index

Note: page numbers in **bold** refer to illustrations.